TQM

PLANNING, DESIGN & IMPLEMENTATION

TQM

PLANNING, DESIGN & IMPLEMENTATION

V.K. Khanna
B.Sc., M.E., PGDBM, Ph.D.
Director
Galgotia Business School
Greater Noida, U.P.

Prem Vrat
Ph.D., FNAE, FIIE, FNASc., FWA, FISTE
Vice Chancellar
U.P. Technical University
Lucknow, U.P.

B.S. Sahay
M.Tech., Ph.D.
Director
Institute of Management Technology
Ghaziabad, U.P.

Ravi Shankar
Associate Professor
Department of Management
Indian Institute of Technology
Delhi

PUBLISHING FOR ONE WORLD

NEW AGE INTERNATIONAL (P) LIMITED, PUBLISHERS
New Delhi • Bangalore • Chennai • Cochin • Guwahati • Hyderabad
Jalandhar • Kolkata • Lucknow • Mumbai • Ranchi

Visit us at **www.newagepublishers.com**

Published by New Age International (P) Ltd., Publishers
First Edition: 2008
Reprint: 2009

Branches:

- 36, Malikarjuna Temple Street, Opp. ICWA, Basavanagudi, **Bangalore**. © (080) 26677815
- 26, Damodaran Street, T. Nagar, **Chennai**. © (044) 24353401
- Hemsen Complex, Mohd. Shah Road, Paltan Bazar, Near Starline Hotel, **Guwahati**. © (0361) 2543669
- No. 105, 1st Floor, Madhiray Kaveri Tower, 3-2-19, Azam Jahi Road, Nimboliadda, **Hyderabad**. © (040) 24652456
- RDB Chambers (Formerly Lotus Cinema) 106A, Ist Floor, S.N. Banerjee Road, **Kolkata**. © (033) 22275247
- 16-A, Jopling Road, **Lucknow**. © (0522) 2209578
- 142C, Victor House, Ground Floor, N.M. Joshi Marg, Lower Parel, **Mumbai**. © (022) 24927869
- 22, Golden House, Daryaganj, **New Delhi**. © (011) 23262370, 23262368

ISBN(10): 81-224-2233-0
ISBN(13): 978-81-224-2233-7

Rs. 295.00

C-09-05-3680

Printed in India at Nisha Enterprises, Delhi.

PUBLISHING FOR ONE WORLD
NEW AGE INTERNATIONAL (P) LIMITED, PUBLISHERS
4835/24, Ansari Road, Daryaganj, New Delhi-110002
Visit us at **www.newagepublishers.com**

Dedicated
to
Our parents

Preface

In the present competitive environment, survival of the organizations depends on their ability to continuously improve the expectations of the customers. Quality is critical in achieving competitiveness in domestic and global market, as quality is a prerequisite to have satisfied customers. Customer expectations for quality products and services have prompted organizations to adopt the principles of total quality management (TQM).

With liberalization, the Indian automobile sector feels the necessity of improving quality for its survival and growth. This sector has tremendous potential for economic growth provided it addresses to some of the key issues that form the core of TQM philosophy. Award models are helpful in this regard as these are generally based on the synthetic framework involving enablers, results and processes. Most of the authors have treated TQM and award models as a system, yet the dynamics of interactions among their subsystems have not received due attention in literature. TQM initiatives often fail due to the lack of understanding of the interactions among TQM variables.

The motivation of this research is to model some of the complexities in the dynamic interaction of the variables that play an important role in the survival and growth of the Indian automobile sector. The objectives of this book are:

- to assess the current state-of-art for TQM practices being followed in the Indian automobile sector and getting insight into major strengths and weaknesses of this sector
- to understand the complex interactions and the dynamics of factors affecting TQM on a long-term basis
- to understand the different transition phases that are possible during a TQM journey
- to understand the system behavior of organizations under different market scenarios

- to understand the contribution of different enablers on performance measures related to TQM.

Major research contribution of the present research is real life modeling of TQM variables for the Indian automobile sector. The model attempts to analyze four categories of organizations under different market scenarios. Significant research contributions of the study are summarized as follows:

- A review and categorization of literature on TQM have been undertaken to establish the trend and current state of art in this area.
- A questionnaire-based survey related to TQM issues has been conducted for Indian automobile manufacturers, suppliers and sub-contractors to understand the TQM practices.
- A system dynamics model has been developed by integrating all important enabler and result variables. TQM index (TQM) has been proposed, which provides a synthetic score for the enablers and results of the business processes.
- A simulation-based model has been developed in this research, which is useful to the organizations in devising policies for effective deployment of enablers to improve results and ultimately enhance the TQM index. This is also helpful in providing insight to the management for devising strategies under different scenarios.

The integrated models show the impact of four different types of market scenarios, which emerges when external enablers are (i) strong, (ii) moderate, (iii) weak, and (iv) crash. This approach would help the organization in choosing the path for growth under different market scenarios.

V.K. Khanna
Prem Vrat
B.S. Sahay
Ravi Shankar

Acknowledgment

The authors would like to express their sincere thanks and gratitude to the following for their help and support during various stages of preparation and publication of this book:

- to all those organisations and individuals with whom the authors have interacted and benefited in order to use their experiences in writing this book.
- to our colleagues, research scholars and managers who have willingly shared their experiences and opinions which has helped in shaping our ideas and perceptions.
- The study would not have been possible without the active participation of the Indian automobile organizations that formed a part of the study. We are grateful to all the respondents who spared their valuable time in providing the useful data and information required for writing this book.

Lastly, we would like to express our gratitude to our families who have been the source of encouragement and inspiration and have provided support at various stages of writing this book.

V.K. Khanna
Prem Vrat
B.S. Sahay
Ravi Shankar

Contents

List of Tables

List of Figures

List of Abbreviations

ABSR	Actual Business Results
ACM	Adoptive Control Methodology
ACMA	Automotive Components Manufacturers Association
ACUS	Actual Customer Satisfaction
AHRS	Actual Human Resource Satisfaction
AIOS	Actual Impact on Society
APQP	Advanced Product Quality Planning
AQA	Australian Quality Award
ASQC	American Society for Quality Control
ASUS	Actual Supplier Satisfaction
BEM	Business Excellence Model
BPI	Business Process Improvement
BPR	Business Process Re-engineering
BSF	Balanced Scorecard Framework
BSR	Company Specific Business Results
CFT	Cross Functional Team
CII	Confederation of Indian Industry
CMF	Customer and Market Focus
CO_2	Carbon dioxide
CPM	Critical Path Method
CQI	Continuous Quality Improvement
CSF	Critical Success Factor
CUS	Customer Satisfaction
CWQC	Company Wide Quality Control
DBSR	Desired Business Results
DCUS	Desired Customer Satisfaction
DF	Decision Fraction
DHRS	Desired Human Resource Satisfaction
DIOS	Desired Impact on Society
DOE	Design of Experiment

DSUS	Desired Supplier Satisfaction
EEC	External Enabler Crash
EEM	External Enabler Moderate
EES	External Enabler Strong
EEW	External Enabler Weak
EFQM	European Foundation for Quality Management
ENB	Enabler
EQA	European Quality Award
ER	Evidential Reasoning
ERP	Enterprise Resource Planning
FEAST	Feedback, Evaluation and Software Technology
FMEA	Failure Mode and Effect Analysis
FMS	Flexible Manufacturing Systems
FREAK	Foreign Trade Effect Assessment Kit
GBSR	Gap in Business Results
GCUS	Gap in Customer Satisfaction
GOP	Gross Domestic Product
GHRS	Gap in Human Resource Satisfaction
GIOS	Gap in Impact on Society
GMCDA	A Group Multicriteria Decision Aid
GOI	Government of India
GPNQA	Golden Peacock National Quality Award
GSUS	Gap in Supplier Satisfaction
HRF	Human Resource Focus
HRS	Human Resource Satisfaction
IDS	Intelligent Decision System
IMC	Indian Merchants Chamber
INM	Information Management
lOS	Impact on Society
ISO	International Organizations for Standardization
IT	Information Technology
JIT	Just-In-Time
JUSE	Union of Japanese Scientists and Engineers
LDS	Leadership
MADM	Multiple Attribute Decision Making
MAIT	Manufacturer's Association for Information Technology
MBNQA	A Malcolm Baldrige National Quality Award
NC	Numerically Controlled
NIST	National Institute of Standards and Technology
NQA	National Quality Award
OHSAS	Occupational Health and Safety Assessment Series
PDCA	Plan-Do-Check-Act

PERT	Programme Evaluation Review Technique
PID	Proportional-Integral-Derivative
PIP	Productivity Improvement Programme
ppm	parts per million
PRM	Process Management
PST	Physical System Theory
QA	Quality Assurance
QC	Quality Control
QFD	Quality Function Deployment
QMSA	Quality Management Self Assessment
QS	Quality System
QWL	Quality of Work Life
RABSR	Actual Company Specific Business Results Rate
RABSRF	Actual Company Specific Business Results Rate Fraction
RACUS	Actual Customer Satisfaction Rate
RACUSF	Actual Customer Satisfaction Rate Fraction
RAHRS	Actual Human Resource Satisfaction Rate
RAHRSF	Actual Human Resource Satisfaction Rate Fraction
RAIOS	Actual Impact on Society Rate
RAIOSF	Actual Impact on Society Rate Fraction
RASUS	Actual Supplier Satisfaction Rate
RASUSF	Actual Supplier Satisfaction Rate Fraction
RCMF	Customer and Market Focus Rate
RCMFF	Customer and Market Focus Rate Fraction
RGNQA	Rajiv Gandhi National Quality Award
RHRF	Human Resource Focus Rate
RHRFF	Human Resource Focus Rate Fraction
RINM	Information Management Rate
RINMF	Information Management Rate Fraction
RLDS	Leadership Rate
RLDSF	Leadership Rate Fraction
RPRM	Process Management Rate
RPRMF	Process Management Rate Fraction
RST	Result
RSTP	Strategic Planning Rate
RSTPF	Strategic Planning Rate Fraction
RSUF	Supplier Focus Rate
RSUFF	Supplier Focus Rate Fraction
SCORE	Supply Cost Reduction
SD	System Dynamics
SME	Small and Medium Sized Enterprise
SPC	Statistical Process Control

SQC	Statistical Quality Control
SQM	Strategic Quality Management
S-T-E-P	Social-Technological-Economic and Political
STP	Strategic Planning
SUF	Supplier Focus
SUS	Supplier Satisfaction
SWOT	Strength, Weakness, Opportunity and Threat
TBEM	Tata Business Excellence Model
TC	Technical Committee
TPM	Total Productive Maintenance
TQ	Total Quality
TQC	Total Quality Control
TQM	Total Quality Management
TQMI	Total Quality Management Index
TS	Technical Specification
TSM	Transportation System Management
UTP	Urban Transportation Planning

1

Chapter

Introduction: TQM Basics and Beyond

1.1 TQM: INTRODUCTION

In the present competitive environment, survival of the organizations depends on their ability to continuously improve as per the expectations of the customers. Quality is critical in achieving competitiveness in domestic and global market, as quality is a prerequisite to have satisfied customers (Sun, 2000). Garvin (1988) describes quality by identifying eight dimensions across which product quality can be viewed. These dimensions are performance, features, reliability, conformance, durability, serviceability, aesthetics and perceived quality. Gitlow and Gitlow (1987) define quality as surpassing customer needs and expectations throughout the life of a product. Quality has been defined as conformance to requirements (Crosby, 1992), fitness for use (Juran, 1988a), meeting and/or exceeding customers' expectations (Parasuraman *et al.*, 1985), defect avoidance (Crosby, 1984) etc. Though there are wide variety of concepts surrounding the term "quality", all writers agree that quality is one of the important "critical success factors" to achieve competitiveness in organizations. Quality has expanded beyond the concept of "customer satisfaction with products and services" to the concept of "creation of worth for all stakeholders" (Karapetrovic and Willborn, 2002). In this context, overall business excellence is replacing the narrow objective of meeting customer specifications to improving the performance of the whole system. This includes array of issues, including environment, occupational health and safety, and social responsibility.

Customer expectations for quality products and services have prompted organizations to adopt the principles of total quality management (TQM). Proponents of total quality management claim that TQM can be implemented in any organization and it can result into improved products and services, reduced costs, more satisfied customers and employees, and improved financial performance (Easton and Jarrell, 1998). Empirical studies show that TQM improves organizational performance (Powell, 1995). As a result of this correlation, numerous companies have embraced total quality management and there has been a flurry of interest in TQM-related practices. In fact, TQM has been adopted in a wide variety of sectors including manufacturing, service, healthcare, governments and general administration. The success of TQM mainly depends on the achievement of internal as well as external customer satisfaction. Internal customer satisfaction is a prerequisite to achieve external customer satisfaction (Oakland, 1989). TQM therefore, can be simply defined as "managing the entire organization so that it excels on all the dimensions of products and services that are important to the customer" (Sharma, 1997). It can be stated that TQM is a structured, systematic process for creating organization-wide participation in planning and implementing continuous improvement in quality (Shortell *et al.,* 1995). Manufacturing organizations are more likely to achieve better performance in employee relations, customer satisfaction, operational performance and business excellence with TQM (Terziovski and Samson, 1999). In a large number of the Indian organizations, quality has emerged as a key strategic issue due to the challenges posed by globalization and liberalization. Many Indian organizations have taken the route of TQM to face these challenges. Many organizations have gone for ISO 9000 and QS 9000 certification to improve the quality of their products or services. These certifications and TQM implementation have coalesced into a major management movement. With the process of liberalization, India has initiated a comprehensive range of policy initiatives to provide a favorable environment for industrial investments and growth.

With liberalization, the Indian automobile sector feels the necessity of improving quality for its survival and growth and therefore, has started taking TQM initiatives. Though there has been a steady growth in the automobile sector, contribution of India in the world auto market production is negligible (Indiainfoline, 2002). This sector has a tremendous potential for economic growth provided it addresses to some of the key issues that form the core of TQM philosophy (Rao *et al.*, 1997).

1.2 BASIC CONCEPTS

1.2.1 Evolution and Significance

Garvin (1988) has classified evolution of TQM as the outcome of four major areas of development describing it to be (i) strategic in nature (ii) with continuous improvement as the driving force and achieved through (iii) quality planning and (iv) employee involvement. TQM as a strategic component affects the levels of profitability by reducing the costs and increasing the market share. This evolutionary pattern is presented in Table 1.1.

Table 1.1: Evolutionary pattern of quality movement

Identifying characteristics	***Phase of quality movement***			
	Inspection →	*S.Q.C. →*	*Q. A. →*	*TQM*
Primary concern	Detection	Control	Coordination	Strategic view
Emphasis	Product uniformity	Product uniformity with reduced inspection	Entire production chain	Market and customer needs
Methods	Gauging and measuring	Statistical tools and techniques	Programmes and systems	Strategic planning and goal setting
Role of quality professionals	Inspection, acceptance sampling	Trouble shooting and the application of statistical methods	Quality measurement, planning and programme design	Goal setting, education, training and consultation
Who has the responsibility for quality?	Inspection department	Manufacturing and engineering departments	All departments	Everyone in the organization
Orientation and approach	Inspects in in quality	Controls in quality	Builds in quality	Manages in quality

1.2.2 Dimensions of Quality

Quality is a journey starting from design, to conformance, and ends at better performance. This process considers quality as a 'never ending' improvement (Gitlow, 1989).

Quality of design → conformance → performance

a. Quality of design: This is the degree of achievement of purpose by the design itself. It starts with market research, sales feedback analysis and continues the development of a product/service that would satisfy the customer.
b. Quality of conformance: It is the extent to which a firm, its processes and its suppliers are able to surpass the design specifications required to serve the needs of the customer.
c. Quality of performance: This identifies the extent to which customer needs are satisfied by performance of a product/service over a period of time.

Researchers have suggested that 'eight dimensions' of quality levels heavily influence customers (Garvin, 1988).

a. Performance: It refers to the primary operating characteristics of a product.
b. Features: The secondary characteristics that supplement the product's basic functioning.
c. Reliability: The probability of a product's failing within a specified period of time.
d. Conformance: The degree to which a product's design and operating characteristics match with pre-established standards.
e. Durability: It is a measure of product life, having both economic and technical dimensions.
f. Serviceability: It refers to speed, courtesy and competence of repair.
g. Aesthetics: It refers to as to how a product looks, feels, sounds etc.
h. Perceived quality: It refers to assessment of standards relying on indirect measures when comparing product brands.

Based on Table 1.1, evolutionary pattern of TQM emerges in the form of two extremes as follows:

(i) from *control driven* to *culturally driven* quality, and
(ii) from *controlling-in* to *managing-in* quality.

The tangible and intangible benefits of TQM are well acknowledged and these are summarized in Table 1.2.

Table 1.2: Benefits of TQM

Benefits	***Authors***
• Better quality	Deming (1986); Juran (1974)
• Promoting continuous improvement	Spencer (1994); Reed *et al.* (1996)
• Increasing flexibility	Oakland (1989); James (1996)
• Enhancing profitability/productivity	Lemak *et al.* (1997); Samson and Terziovski (1999)
• Faster organizational learning	Oakland (1989); Ross (1993); James (1996)
• Safe and healthy communities	Oakland (1989); Crosby (1979)
• Better customer service/greater loyalty and customer satisfaction	Terziovski and Samson (1999); Sun (2000)
• Strong organizational economy	Juran (1974); Spencer (1994); Reed *et al.* (1996)
• Improvement in market share	Mohanty and Lakhe (1998), Buzzel and Gale (1987)
• Better organizational management	Oakland (1989); Terziovski and Samson (1999)
• Better performance in employee relations	Terziovski and Samson (1999); Anderson *et al.* (1994)
• Competitive advantage	Curkovic and Pagell (1999); Seawright and Young (1996)

Various TQM models can help the Indian automobile sector in the effective implementation of the TQM philosophy.

1.3 TQM MODELS

The conceptual framework provided by various TQM experts are at variance on some account, but all agree that TQM covers all the aspects of organization's systems, procedures and processes. Some popular models of TQM have been compiled is shown in Table 1.3.

Various quality award models have been used for self-assessment and benchmarking. These models are for business excellence and are the manifestations of various definitions of TQM (Spitzer, 1995).

Table 1.3: Focus of various TQM models

TQM Model	***Focus***
Crosby (1979, 1992)	• Conformance to requirements • Zero defects • Quality is free • Cost of quality concept

Contd...

TQM Model	*Focus*
	• Quality maturity grid involving five stages of maturity as uncertainty, awakening, enlightenment, wisdom and certainty·
Deming (1990)	• Quality through constancy of purpose • Leadership • Reduce variations • Use of statistical methods • Continuous improvement of cost • Deming cycle (Plan-Do-Check-Act)
Feigenbaum (1961, 1982)	• Total quality control • Concept of quality cost • Hidden plant for waste • Quality is affected by 9M's such as Markets, Money, Management, Men, Motivation, Materials, Machines and mechanization, Modern information methods, and Mounting product requirements
Juran (1988b)	• Quality is fitness for use • Statistical tools • Planning for quality (quality planning, quality control and quality improvement) • Human aspects in quality management
Ishikawa (1984)	• Company-wide Quality Control (CWQC) and participation by all • Education and training • Use of quality circles • Quality audits by the president and senior executive twice a year • Use of statistical methods and a focus on problem prevention • Welcoming complaints
Imai (1986)	• Kaizen (Continuing improvement involving everyone – managers and workers) • The Kaizen strategy begins and ends with people· Sustained continuous improvement culture· Small improvements involving everybody
Oakland (1989)	• Management commitment • Customer-supplier chains • Systems approach of documented sets of procedures and standards Statistical Process Control (SPC) • Team work and continuous improvement
Sohal *et al.* (1989)	• Customer (internal and external) focus· • Management commitment

Contd...

	• Total participation; total employees involvement • Statistical Quality Control (SQC) • Systematic problem solving process [Plan-Do-Check-Act (PDCA)] Cycle
ISO 9000:2000	*Eight management principles* • Customer focus • Leadership • Involvement of people • Process approach • System approach to management • Continual improvement • Mutually beneficial supplier relationships • Factual approach to decision making
QS 9000: 1998/TS 16949: 2002	• Development of fundamental of quality systems that provide for continuous improvement • Emphasizing defect prevention and the reduction of variation and waste in the supply chain • Emphasize on advanced product quality planning and control plan • Failure mode and effect analysis • Measurement systems and analysis • Fundamental SPC • Quality system assessment

1.4 NATIONAL QUALITY AWARD MODELS

National Quality Awards (NQA), like Deming Prize, Malcolm Baldrige National Quality Award (MBNQA), Australian Quality Award (AQA) and European Quality Award (EQA) model have contributed a lot for business excellence in countries like Japan, the USA, Australia and European nations (Bester, 2000). In a broad sense these models are based on TQM philosophy. These models consider the whole organization and its associated activities. The criteria in the award models are well defined and can be used for a self-assessment during TQM journey. There are many definitions of self-assessment and therefore, several approaches are deployed to use of the award models (Hillman, 1994). Self-assessment is a cyclic, comprehensive, systematic and regular review of an organization's activities and results against a TQM model and culminates into planned improvement actions (EFQM, 1995). Self-assessment must be considered from a holistic perspective to yield maximum results (Samuelsson and Nilsson, 2002).

The MBNQA criteria, its framework and the weightages structure have been continuously evolving. The main objectives of a NQA model are perceived as:

- to help stimulate organizations to improve quality of their products/services

- to recognize the achievement of organizations, which attain commanding heights for their quality, and are source of inspiration for others
- to act as a motivator for organizational learning and to provide guidelines for initiating quality improvement
- to act as a driving force for a national movement on quality improvement for a turnaround.

Bohris (1995) made a competitive assessment of some major quality award models, as presented in Table 1.4. Various award models appear to be different, however, a closer examination reveals a number of common areas.

Table 1.4: Deming, Australian, Baldrige and European Quality Awards criteria

Factors	***Deming Prize (1951)***	***Baldrige Award (1987)***	***Australian Award (1988)***	***European Quality Award (1991)***
Leadership	Organization and its management	Leadership	Leadership	Leadership
Strategic quality planning	Company policy and planning	Strategic planning	Policy and planning	Policy and strategy
Information and analysis	Collection, transmission and management	Information and analysis	Information and analysis	Resources
Human resource management and development	Quality control education and dissemination	Human resource development	Human resource development	People management
Managing process quality	Analysis and quality assurance	Process management	Processes, products	Processes
Standardization	Standardization	—	—	—
Customer focus and satisfaction	Control	Customer focus and satisfaction	Customer focus	People satisfaction
Quality and operational results	Effects	Business results	Business results	Business results
Impact on society	Future plans	—	—	Impact on society

1.4.1 National Quality Award Models in Indian Context

In Indian organizations a number of quality award models are in operation, but none of these has so far succeeded in generating the national awareness about quality. Some of the important Indian Quality Award models have been compiled in Table 1.5. While the first five award models presented in this table are being practiced, the last one is due to a research outcome and not being practiced as yet.

Table 1.5: National Quality Award models in Indian context

S. No.	*Award model*	*Initiated/proposed by*	*Development based on*
1.	Golden Peacock National Quality Award (GPNQA) 1991	Institute of Directors	MBNQA
2.	Rajiv Gandhi National Quality Award Model (RGNQA) 1992	Bureau of Indian Standards	Various core values and other NQA award criteria
3.	CII-EXIM Award for Business Excellence (1994)	Confederation of Indian Industry (CII)	European Quality Awárd Model
4.	MAIT Quality Recognition Programme (1995)	Manufacturer's Association for Information Technology (MAIT)	European Quality Award Model
5.	Tata Business Excellence Model (1994)	Tata	Leadership, strategic planning, customer and market focus, human resource focus, process management, information and analysis, and business result
6.	Agrawal's Business Excellence Model (1999)	Agrawal (Proprized)	Positive attributes of various award models considering Indian socio-cultural value system.

Award models are generally based on the synthetic framework involving enablers, results and processes. This is based on a system approach. Most of the authors have treated TQM and the award models as a system, yet the dynamic interaction among their subsystems has not received due attention in literature (Leonard *et al.,* 2002). TQM initiatives often fail due to a lack of essential quality measures to monitor important factors such as customer satisfaction, supplier satisfaction, management leadership, product quality and employee morale. It is, therefore, imperative for the Indian automobile sector to understand and analyze the complex interactions and the dynamics of factors affecting TQM, and factors, which are the outcome of TQM over a longer time horizon. The use of dynamic models for TQM in organizations is essential for an appreciation of a complex, dynamic system, which enables management to manage in a comprehensive way and to decide and act for long-lasting success (Bauer *et al.*, 2001).

System dynamics (SD) has served as an important tool, which can capture the interactions among a range of system variables and predict the implication of each over a period of time (Forrester, 1969).

1.5 ISSUES IN TQM IMPLEMENTATION

TQM initiatives often fail due to the lack of clear understanding of the complex interactions among different TQM variables. It is therefore, imperative to understand and analyze the complex interactions and the dynamics of factors affecting TQM over a longer time horizon so as to evolve a plan that can integrate all the dominant factors. System dynamics can serve as an important tool, as it has the ability to capture the interactions among system variables. It can also predict the implications of each interaction over a period of time.

Case Study

American Electric Power (AEP)

American Electric Power (AEP) received Ohio's governor's award for excellence in quality in 2001. The AEP Plant achieved the performance excellence with a lot of efforts involving development of quality measurement system. It shifted from an old culture representing conservative top down leadership style, non-interacting functional groups, hostile unions and lack of commitment and strategic planning to ingrate to a fast track quality driven work culture. The first few ingredients, which the top management brought into forefront is committed leadership, strategic planning, involvement of all customer focus and use of quality tools. Employee development programmes were involved to shift towards empowerment and learning, concept of internal customer and supplier, system thinking, improved communication, use of problem solving tools and leadership teams involving union representatives. Balance score card and process focused management approach was used to develop a new performance management programme.

The plant achieved more than 100% increase in employee's productivity, 45% reduction in operations and maintenance cost along with saving of $ 5 million due to process improvement. The achievements of AEP bring out the importance of leadership and strategic planning as key issue to start TQM journey.

Source: Ohio Award for Excellence governors award winners presentation.

Case Study

Maruti: Case of Challenge 50

Maruti Udyog Ltd. (MUL) was established in February 1981 to meet the growing demand of a personal mode of transport caused by the lack of efficient public transport system. Maruti launched a programme titled 'Challenge 50' in May 2002 for vendor upgradation and implementing Toyota Production System (TPS). The purpose of 'challenge 50' was to increase productivity by 50% and slash cost by almost a third. Accordingly Maruti had kept the target to increase the productivity by 50%, rise in first check OK by 15%, reduction in cost per vehicle by 30% and cut in-house warranty cost by 36%. The year-by-year targets set by Maruti are shown in Figure 1.1 to benchmark Kosai Plant. Under this programme Maruti has been able to reduce number of steps a worker has to walk to fetch parts and tools from their racks from 10-15 earlier to five. By introducing "Synchro-trolleys" that move along the conveyor lines, and relocating racks closer to the line operator. With about 200 workers manning one assembly line, the savings have led not just to increase in productivity but safety as well. Maruti has been working to reduce its set up time by implementing single-minute exchange of dies (SMED) techniques. Apart from these efforts, Maruti has been instrumental in implementing TPS in some of its key vendors as a part of cluster group.

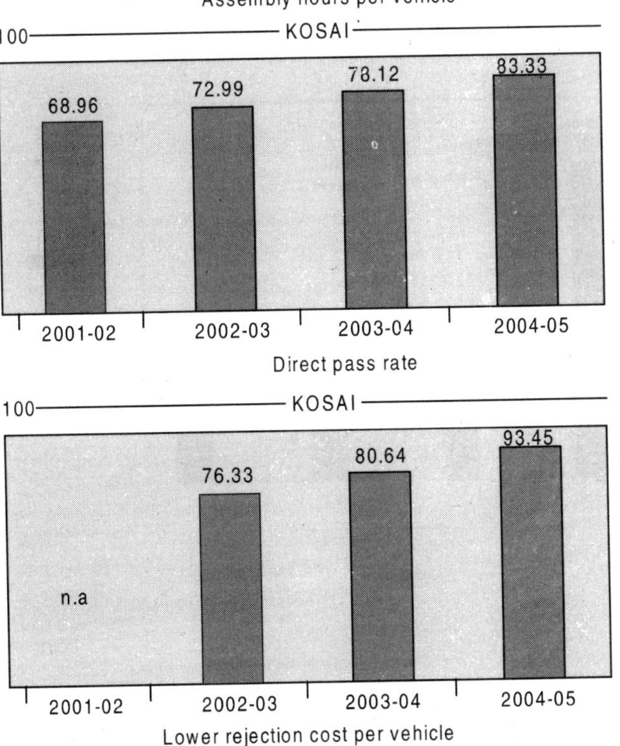

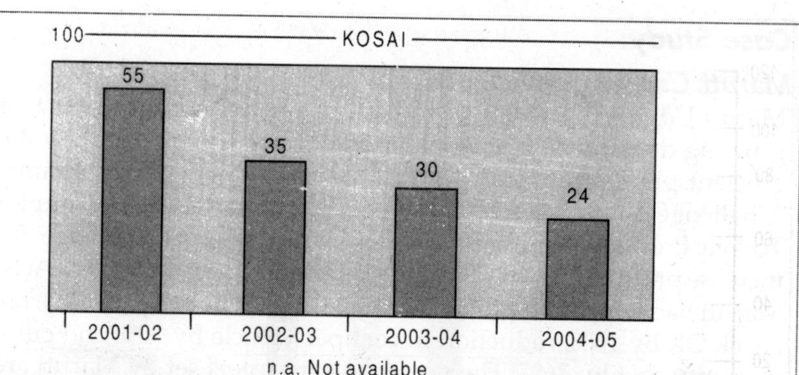

Fig. 1.1: KOSAI: Benchmark as 100 per cent & figures in percentage

Various activities have been undertaken for implementing TPS in various vendor base such as: awareness programme, launch of project, finalization of targets in measurable units, make action plan to reduce waste, compilation of cycle time vis-à-vis takt time, layout change, implementation of various kaizen and balancing of the lines. With the initiatives of Maruti under programme 'challenge 50' in Maruti's plant and in various vendor base following results have been achieved as shown in Figure 1.2.

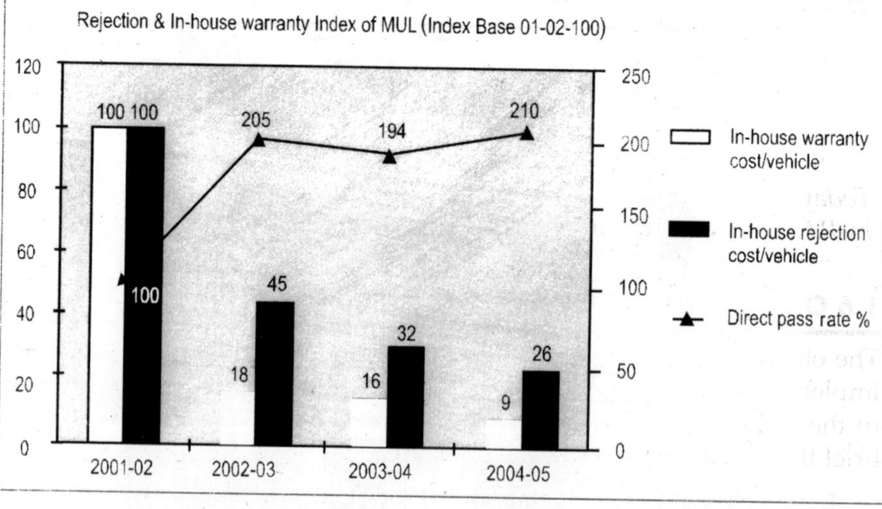

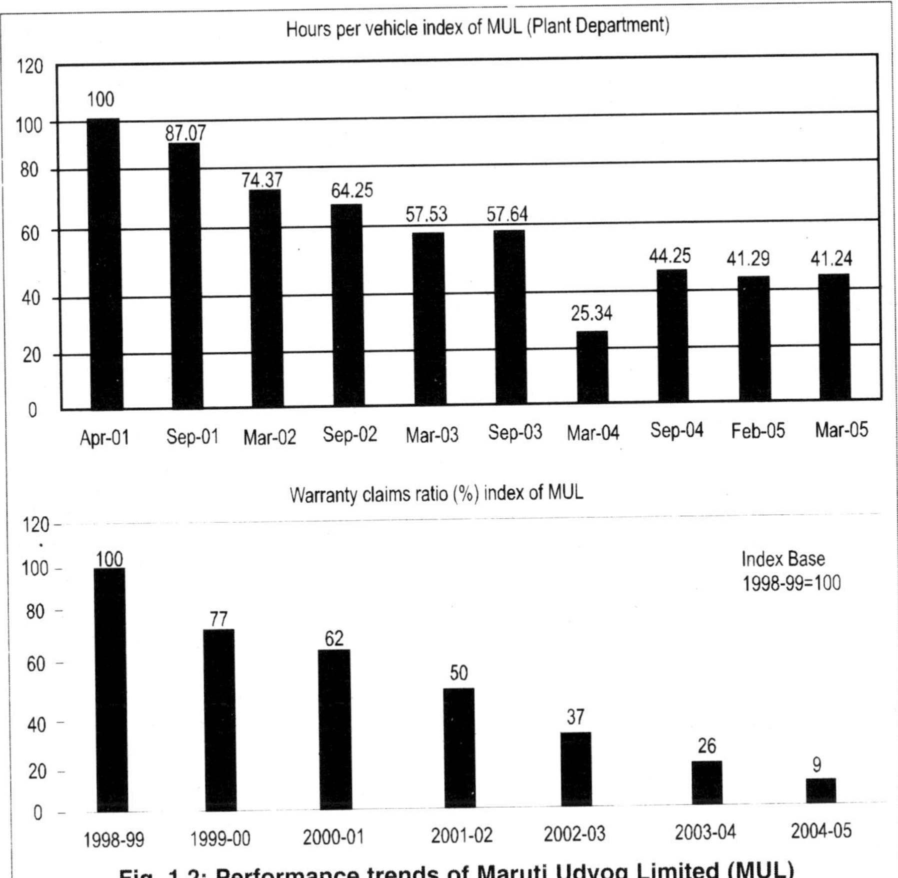

Fig. 1.2: Performance trends of Maruti Udyog Limited (MUL)

Source: Sinha, S. K., 2003, Maruti Udyog Destination Kosai, in Business Today, March 2, pp. 108-112& letter no. MUL/MISC/2005 Dated 26th, Sep 2005 by R.Nagaraju DPM(Corporate Planning)

1.6 OBJECTIVES OF THIS BOOK

The objective of this book is to discuss in detail planning, designing and implementation of TQM in an organization. The book also discusses some of the complexities and problems associated with its implementation. In brief the broad objectives of the book are:

1. to assess the current state-of-art for TQM practices with reference to the Indian automobile sector.
2. to understand the complex interactions and the dynamics of factors affecting TQM.
3. to develop TQM model which can be used by any organization.
4. to build different scenario for TQM policy experimentation.
5. to develop TQM implementation strategies.

1.7 ORGANIZATION OF THIS BOOK

The book has been organized in seven chapters as shown in Figure 1.3.

A brief outline of different chapters is given as follows:

Chapter 1 deals with the introduction of the study, identification of the problem, objectives of the book, brief outline of the methodology and organization of this book.

Chapter 2 reviews the TQM basic concepts relevant to this book. Literature review covers general concepts of TQM and system dynamics model. The literature is classified into the following categories: basic concept of quality and TQM, evaluation of TQM and its concepts, general TQM principles, TQM models, National Quality Award models, studies on quality practices in India, quality practices in other countries.

Chapter 3 presents the findings of a survey related to the TQM practices in the automobile sector. It covers methodology adopted for conducting survey, structuring of survey questionnaire, analysis of feedback and identification and validation of weightages of TQM variables for effective implementation of TQM in the automobile sector. Responses from various categories in this sector have been analyzed and the application of different quality tools in the Indian automobile sector has been discussed.

Chapter 4 deals with the development of TQM model which can be used by any organization. In order to develop the models certain variables are to be identified under two categories, one as variables of TQM and another results of TQM which can be quantified and measured.

In this chapter, base model for TQM has been developed and flow diagram equations for TQM variables have been discussed. This chapter deals with a case study to validate the proposed system dynamics model. The model has the capability to project the future scenarios.

Chapter 5 includes the findings of scenario building and policy experimentation under four different market scenarios. These are "external enabler strong", "external enabler moderate", "external enabler weak" and "external enabler crash". The organizations have been categorized in four types depending on the status of their performance. These categories are *'quitter', 'slipper', 'disillusioned'* and *'climber'*. In this chapter, a total of 145 policy experimentations have been attempted to understand the model behavior and mapping of real life situations. Framework for experimentations has been developed under different scenarios such as pessimistic scenario, most likely scenario and optimistic scenario.

Chapter 6, deals with major TQM implementation strategies.

1.8 CONCLUSION

In this chapter, an overview of context related to the book has been presented. The objectives of this book, problem statement, book methodology and outline of the book are also presented. The general statement of the problem and book methodology outlined in this chapter would be elaborated in the subsequent chapters after critically reviewing the literature on this subject. This would be followed by the development of models, policy experimentation and scenario building.

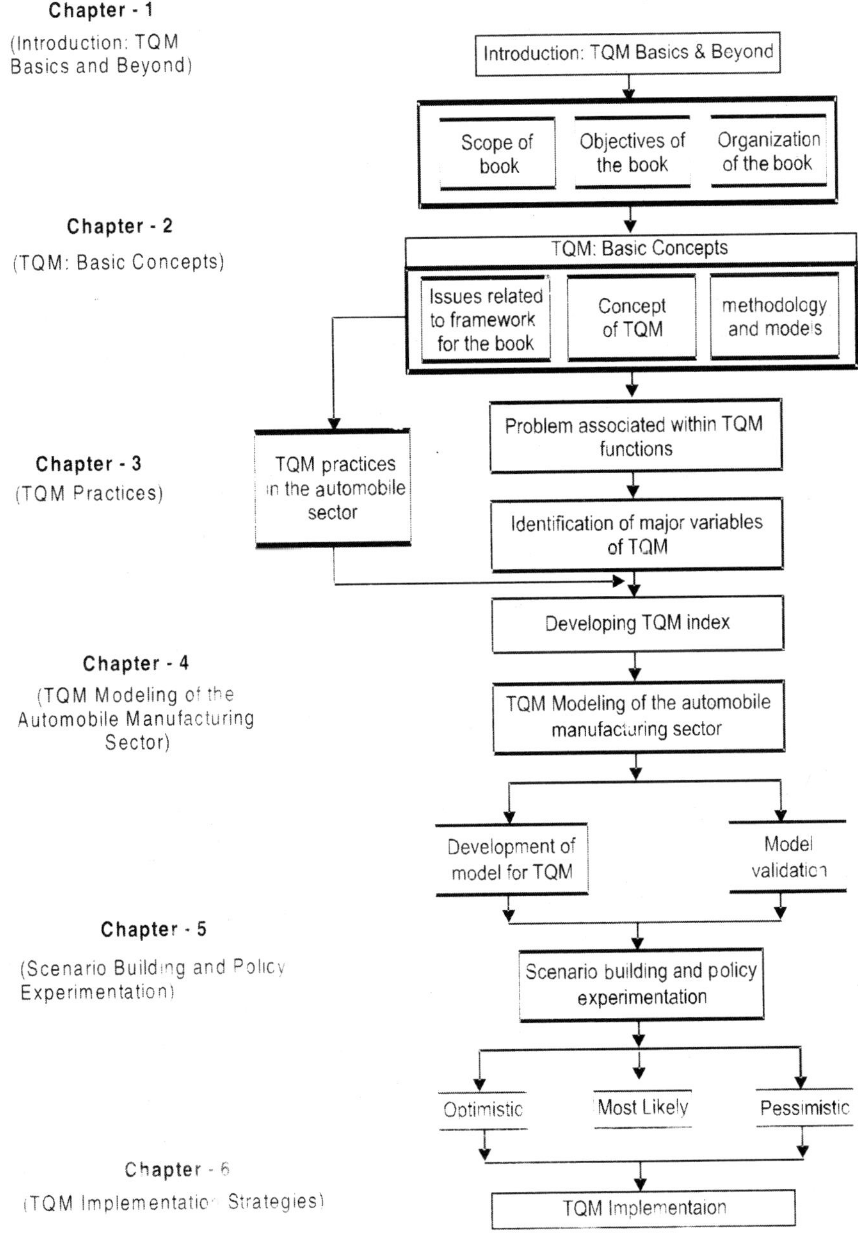

Fig. 1.3: Flow diagram of the book

2

Chapter

TQM: Basic Concepts

2.1 INTRODUCTION

It has been more than a decade now since the 'quality movement gained significant momentum' (Dooley and Mahmoodi, 1996). Many authors justify the development of total quality management (TQM) based on the performance of Japanese companies in the world market during last three decades. This has often been enhanced by the acknowledged influence of quality practitioners such as Deming, Juran, Ishikawa and Imai (Ishikawa, 1976; Imai, 1986). In 1987, the United States constituted the Malcclm Baldridge National Quality Award (MBNQA) and it became a *de facto* definition of TQM. Other nations followed with similar awards and criteria. In India also awards like Rajiv Gandhi National Quality Award (RGNQA), Golden Peacock National Quality Award (GPNQA) and CII-EXIM Business Excellence Award model have been instituted to give momentum to quality movement. The success stories of organizations on TQM path are well known. Japan's automobile industry started out several decades behind the USA's but in 1980 it overtook the USA's and became the biggest in world using this philosophy (Ulrich *et al.*, 2000). In the developed countries the quality movement is underway for quite some time. On the other hand, in most of the developing countries like India, this is a more recent phenomenon (Rao *et al.*, 1997).

The policy of economic liberalization initiated by Government of India (GOI) in the year 1991, had given an impetus to the growth of the Indian automobile sector. Major car manufacturers such as General Motors, Hyundai, Fiat and Honda had set up their manufacturing bases in India. With liberalization, this sector is realizing the competition ahead and feels the necessity of improving quality for the survival and growth. Since TQM philosophy is based on the principles of continuous improvement, teamwork, cultural change and customer satisfaction, TQM implementation assumes a vital role for the survival and growth of this sector. Though there has been a steady growth in the Indian automobile sector, its full potential in the global market is still untapped (Indiainfoline, 2002). As per World Competitiveness Yearbook Report 2001 (IMD, 2002), the competitiveness of India has been ranked very low (41 out of 49 countries). Though there are some signs of improvement as per Global Competitiveness Report 2002-03 released by the World Economic Forum (The Economic Times, 2002), yet there is a need to hasten this process. Since growth of automobile in any country is an indication of overall economy, a lot needs to be done by the Indian automobile sector in implementing TQM. In view of the growing realization of vital significance of TQM in the actual business world, academia has brought out a vast literature on the subject. It is considered worthwhile to carry out a literature review to establish the current state of the art, in terms of the policy issues and the methodological approaches used for TQM modeling.

2.2 LITERATURE REVIEW AT A GLANCE

The purpose of selective literature review presented in this chapter, is to identify the key issues related to concept and approach of TQM and methodological aspects of its modeling. An extensive literature review has been carried out to gain understanding in the area of quality, various aspects of TQM, and National Quality Award (NQA) models, accordingly, the literature has been broadly classified in five categories namely, (a) a review of TQM, (b) National Quality Award models, (c) Quality award models in India (d) studies on quality practices in India and (e) quality practices in other countries. Review of literature has been broadly classified according to the structure shown in Figure 2.1.

While reviewing the literature, limitations of the present approaches and the potential areas of further research are also reported in this chapter.

2.3 BASIC CONCEPTS OF QUALITY AND TQM

2.3.1 Development of Quality

Quality is critical in achieving competitiveness in domestic and global market, as quality is a prerequisite to have satisfied customers (Voss and Johnson, 1995; Voss *et al.,* 1997; Sun, 2000). Hardie and Walsh (1994) observed that different definitions of quality led to confusion in the field of quality. Table 2.1 compiles different quality function from literature.

2.3.1.1 Eight Dimensions of Quality

Researchers have suggested that 'eight dimensions' of quality levels heavily influence customers.

a. Performance: It refers to the primary operating characteristics of a product. For example acceleration, brake horse power, fuel consumption of a car may be clubbed under performance dimension of quality.
b. Features: The secondary characteristics that supplement the product's basic functioning. For example an air conditioner, CD player, adjustable seat etc. of a car may be clubbed under dimensions of quality.
c. Reliability: The probability of a product's failing within a specified period of time. For example the start of a car in all seasons may be treated as reliability feature of quality.
d. Conformance: The degree to which a product's design and operating characteristics match with pre-established standards. The adherence to the specification such as fit and finish, dimensional accuracy, smooth start etc. may be treated as conformance characteristic of a quality.
e. Durability: It is a measure of product life, having both economic and technical dimensions. For example the corrosion resistance and life of an engine of a car may be clubbed under durability characteristic of a quality.
f. Serviceability: It refers to speed, courtesy and competence of repair. Availability of spare parts, service stations and prompt response and repair of a car at low cost may fall under this category.
g. Aesthetics: It refers to as to how a product looks, feels, sounds etc. Good look, colour and finish are some of the aesthetic features a car.
h. Perceived quality: It refers to assessment of standards relying on indirect measures when comparing product brands. For example a vintage car whose perceived value is quite high due to its antique nature falls under this category. An other example could be high brand like Mercedes car, rolex watch etc.

2.3.1.2 The Three Dimensions of Quality

Quality of design → conformance → performance: This process considers quality as a 'never ending' improvement (Gitlow, 1989).

a. Quality of design: This is the degree of achievement of purpose by the design itself. It starts with market research, sales feedback analysis and continues the development of a product/ service that would satisfy the customer.

   Take the example of a car, the manufacturer can design it with a life of 5 to 10 years, or one with a life of 10 to 20 years. Generally, if one wishes to raise quality of design the cost also rises.

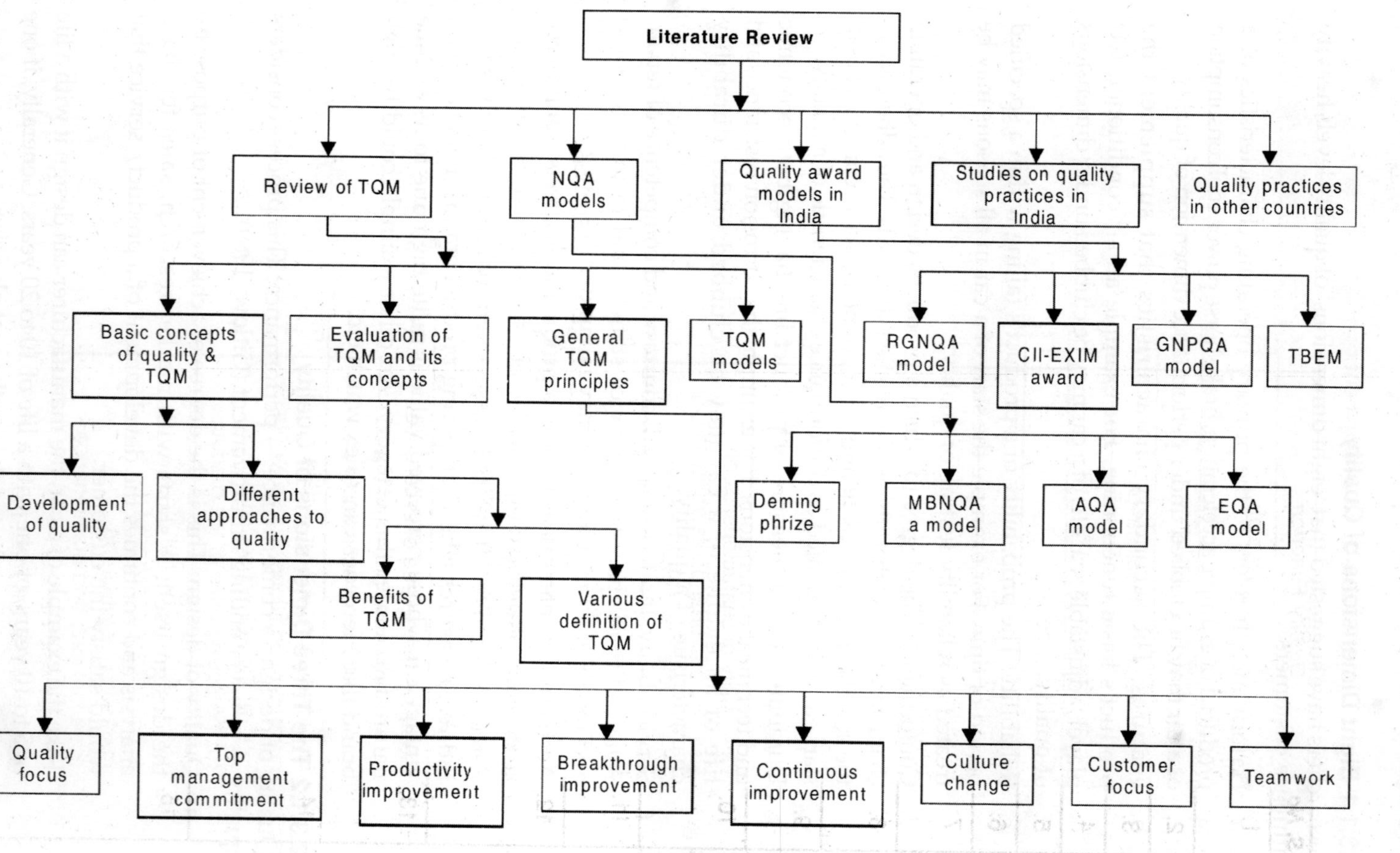

Fig. 2.1: Classification of literature

Table 2.1: Development of quality

S. No.	Quality Function	References
1.	Quality in the Language of Statisticians	Shewhart (1990)
2.	Quality defined as value	Feigenbaum (1951)
3.	Conformance to specifications	Gilmore (1974)
4.	Conformance to requirements	Crosby (1979, 1984, 1992)
5.	Quality as Excellence	Peters and Waterman (1982)
6.	Fitness for use	Juran (1974, 1982, 1985)
7	Product conformance which results in customer satisfaction	Juran (1988a, 1989, 1995)
8.	Quality as the loss imparted to society once a product is delivered	Taguchi (1986)
9.	Meeting and or exceeding customers expectations	Deming (1982) Parasuraman *et al.* (1985)
10.	The totality of characteristics of an entity that bear on its ability to satisfy stated or implied needs	ISO 8402 (1994)
11.	Degree to which a set of inherent characteristics fulfills requirements	ISO 9000 (2000)
12.	Total quality is performance leadership in meeting customers' requirements by doing the right things right the first time	Westinghouse (1999)
13.	Quality is the degree of excellence at an acceptable price and the control of variability at an acceptable cost	Broh (1982)
14.	Quality means best for certain customer conditions. These conditions are (a) the actual used and (b) the selling price of the product	Feigenbaum (1983, 1990)
15.	The total composite product, service characteristics of marketing, engineering, manufacturing and maintenance through which product and service in use will meet the expectations of the customer	Feigenbaum (1991)

Contd....

16. *Transcendent definition*: Quality is neither mind nor matter, but a third entity independent of the other two—even though, quality cannot be defined, you know what it is	Garvin (1987)
17. *Product-based definition*: Differences in quality amount to differences in the quantity of some desired ingredient or attribute	Garvin (1987)
18. *User-based definition*: Quality consists of the capacity to satisfy norms	Garvin (1987)
19. *Manufacturing-based definition*: Quality means conformance to requirements	Garvin (1987)
20. *Value-based definition*: Quality is the degree of excellence at an acceptable price and the control of variability at an acceptable cost	Garvin (1987)
21. A condition of excellence implying fine quality as distinct from poor quality. Quality is achieving the highest standard as against being satisfied with the sloppy or fraudulent	Tuchman (1980)
22. Minimizing dissatisfaction to customers	Singh (1997)
23. Delighting the customer by continuously meeting and improving upon agreed requirements	Macdonald and Piggot (1992)
24. Most economical, most useful and always satisfactory to consumer	Ishikawa (1985)
25. The degree of conformance of all the relevant features and characteristics of the product to all the aspects of a customers' need, limited by the price and delivery he or she will accept	Groocock (1986)
26. Reduction to variability	Deming (1990)

Contd...

27. Anything that can be improved	Imai (1986)
28. The extent to which the customers or users believe the product or service surpasses their needs and expectations	Gitlow *et al.* (1989)
29. Meeting, exceeding, and delighting customers' needs and expectations	Downey *et al.* (1994)
30. Set of characteristics of a system that makes it able to satisfy the needs of the customer, of the user and of the society	Galetto (1999)
31. Quality assurance, contract conformance and customer driven	Murgatroyd and Morgan (1993)
32. A property which can be assessed either against the accepted standards of merit or against the interests of the relevant stakeholders	Smith (1993)

b. Quality of conformance: It is the extent to which a firm, its processes and its suppliers are able to surpass the design specifications required to serve the needs of the customer. If there is a discrepency between quality of design and quality of conformance, it means that there are defects or rework. When quality of conformance goes up, cost comes down.

c. Quality of performance: This identifies the extent to which customer needs are satisfied by performance of a product/service over a period of time. As quality of conformance improves, incidences of defects, reworks, and adjustments decline, resulting in cost reduction and productivity gain.

   Japanese cars have become highly competitive in the world market. This success has been the result of the qualities of design, conformance and performance.

2.3.2 Different Approaches to Quality

Different authors with varying perspectives and orientations have defined the term 'quality' in different manner. The different approaches to the understanding of quality have been compiled in Table 2.2.

Table 2.2: The different approaches to quality

Approach	*Basic tenets*	*Proponents*	*Comments*
Product-based	Quality is attribute dependent, the precise, measurable and part of the	Crosby (1979); Ishikawa (1985); Garvin (1988)	Approach relies on quantification; but it is not easy to clearly

Contd...

	characteristics of the product.		identify and quantify attributes of services.
User-based	Quality is meeting the needs and wants of the user, fitness for purpose.	Deming (1986); Juran (1989); Feigenbaum (1983); Ishikawa (1985); Garvin (1984); Juran and Gryna (1995); Gitlow and Hertz (1983)	Approach relies on the organization's ability to determine the customer requirements and then meet them. Products may conform to specifications, be fit for use and be available at an economic cost but still may not satisfy the customer.
Manufacturing-based/Process and supply led	Quality is conformance to requirements; conformance to specification.	Crosby (1979); Taguchi (1986); Garvin (1983); Imai (1986); Price (1989)	Approach pre-supposes that the specifications are understood and accepted by everyone. This may not always hold good. In this approach, quality focus is internal rather than external.
Value-based	Quality is value of money; it is cost to the producer and price to the customer.	Groocock (1986); Ishikawa (1985); Garvin (1983); Broh (1982); Feigenbaum (1983); Dale and Plunkett (1991)	Focus is external; this approach implies a trade-off between quality, price and availability.
Transcendence	Quality is innate excellence.	Garvin (1988)	Prior identification of determinants of quality is often not possible in the service sector.

Contd...

Transformation	Quality is a qualitative change for enhancing and empowering participants.	Garvin (1988)	Focus on organization-wide transformation.

Amidst a wide gamut of such definitions, there seems to be no consensus definition. From the perspective of the consumers or users, the product or service-based definition is more useful. From the perspective of the organization providing goods/services, a process-perspective is more useful. In order to manage quality, organizations need to have system in place to establish customer requirements and to confirm that their expectations have been met.

2.4 EVALUATION OF TOTAL QUALITY MANAGEMENT AND ITS CONCEPT

The genesis of TQM started with the development of work-study before the First World War and the credit for this goes to the work of three Americans, Federick W. Taylor, Frank B. Gilbreth and Charles E. Bedaux (Tapiero, 1996; Youssef *et al.,* 1996).

The most crucial breakthrough in the modern quality movement came in 1931 with the publication of Shewhart's article on "Economic control of quality of manufactured product". Shewhart became the first "to recognize that variability was a fact of industrial life and that it could be understood and managed using the principles of probability and statistics" (Ishikawa, 1985). However, business interest in quality did not fully materialize until World War II in the U. S. and post World War II in Japan. In the early days of World War II, the department of defense used quality-sampling procedures to accept or reject munitions, thus causing defense suppliers to be more concerned with quality assurance (Garvin, 1988). But the modern roots of what we now call TQM originated around 1949 in Japan with the adoption, by a committee of the Union of Japanese Scientists and Engineers, of many of the statistical methods of Deming (Walton, 1986). Deming, a recognized scholar in the field of sampling, is the one who introduced quality control to Japan through his visits in 1950, 1951 and 1952. Juran is credited to introduce TQM in Japan through his visit in 1954 (Gehani, 1993). Juran's visit marked a transition in Japan's quality control activities from the dealing primarily with technology based in factories to an overall concern for the entire management. The Juran visit created an atmosphere in which quality control (QC) was to be regarded as a tool of management, thus creating an opening for the establishment of total quality control (TQC) (Ishikawa, 1985).

Feigenbaum defined TQC through an article in Industrial Quality Control in May 1957. According to him, TQC requires participation of all divisions in an organization. But he felt that quality, which is everybody's job in an organization, could become nobody's job. He suggested that essentially quality control specialists should manage the quality function. But TQC advocated by Feigenbaum did not find wide application and hence did not become popular (Ganapathy *et al.*, 1994). The Japanese accepted the basic concept of Feigenbaum's theory of TQC, however, the Japanese did not agree to this view that quality function may be managed by quality control specialists. The success of Japanese manufacturers during the 1960's and the 1970's, changed the emphasis from a quality control approach to a quality assurance approach leading to a greater number of business functions being involved in the management of quality. Success stories in Japan and its capturing of a larger share of world markets, paved a way for acceptance of quality in the United States and in Europe. Quality and its control became TQC as Feigenbaum called it in the 1960's; and its management became TQM by the 1980's and 1990's.

Dale and Plunkett (1991) presented a hierarchy of quality management starting from inspection to quality control to quality assurance to total quality management. Zaire (1991) also identified the evolution of two extremes, one from control driven to culturally driven, and two, from controlling-in to managing-in quality. Miller (1993) however, mapped the evolution into four phases – quality control, quality assurance, total quality management and quantum quality. Sallis (1996) depicted the evolution in terms of a sequential movement from inspection to TQM, through quality control and quality assurance. Kehoe (1996) identified three phases: (i) 1940's and 1950's – quality control phase; (ii) 1960's and 1970's – quality assurance phase; and (iii) 1980's and 1990's – total quality phase. Hermel (1997) remarked that the search for quality has been present in organizations for a long time and along the way, it has taken different forms varying with an evolving paradigm and conceptualization. He distinguished four great eras/periods, from the beginning of the century to the 1980's. He identified them as: (i) beginning of the century – inspection era; (ii) 1930's to 1950 – quality control era; (iii) 1950's to 1970 – quality assurance era; (iv) 1970's and onwards – total quality management era. This philosophy of TQM underlines the Malcolm Baldrige National Quality Award in the United States, the European Quality Award, the Australian Quality Award, and the Japanese Deming Prize. Proponents of total quality management claim that TQM can be implemented in any organization and it can result into improved products and services, reduced costs, more satisfied customers and employees, and improved financial performance (Easton and Jarrell, 1998; Hendricks and

Singhal, 1997). TQM has been accepted by both service and manufacturing organizations globally, as a systematic management approach to meet the competitive and technological challenges. It redefines the quality with emphasis on top management commitment and customer satisfaction.

2.4.1 Benefits of TQM

The tangible and intangible benefits of TQM are well acknowledged and are summarized in Table 2.3.

Boaden (1997) pointed out that it is important to consider the definition of TQM for a number of reasons, viz., TQM is increasingly taught as an academic subject; there is a broad-based developing body of research on TQM; TQM and quality management are often confused; and evidence regarding the 'success' of TQM is mixed. Dale and Plunkett (1990) also emphasized the importance of the issue of definition for better understanding and communication. However, they admitted that there are difficulties in finding generic definition to describe specific tasks or activities.

Oakland (1989) defined TQM as an approach to improve the effectiveness and flexibility of business as a whole. The essential part of this is to involve the total organization. Witcher (1990) defined the term by breaking the phrase into three terms whereby, 'total', implies every person is involved (including customers and suppliers); 'quality', implies customer requirements are met exactly; and 'management', implies senior executives are committed. Jablonski (1992) defined TQM as a co-operative form of doing business that relies on the talents and capabilities of both labour and management to continuously improve quality and productivity using teams. This definition emphasizes three essential ingredients necessary for the successful implementation of TQM: participative management, continuous process improvement and the use of teams. However, Youssef *et al.* (1996) remarked that the definition does not explicitly mention the role that the suppliers and customers play in the success of TQM.

Lawler (1994) observed that there is no single theoretical formulation of TQM approach or any definitive shortlist of practices that are associated with it. Many individuals have shaped the philosophies underlying TQM. Constructing a universal definition of TQM may sound difficult, since a particular managerial situation or problem may bias the interpretation. As an illustration, July 1995 special issue of Quality Progress presented 13 articles on TQM and 12 of these have given different definitions of TQM. There seems to be no consensus on a single definition for TQM (Reed *et al.*, 1996). One of the most striking features of TQM literature is the absence of any uniform definition of TQM.

Table 2.3: A select list of benefits of TQM as reported in literature

Benefits	***Authors***
• Better Quality·	Deming (1986); Juran (1974); Holloway *al.* (1995); Oakland (1989); James (1996); Mohanty and Lakhe (1998); Reed *et al.* (1996)
• Promoting continuous improvement	Spencer (1994); Reed *et al.* (1996); Waldman (1994); James (1996); Ross (1993); Bounds *et al.* (1994)
• Increasing flexibility	Reed *et al.* (1996); Oakland (1989); James (1996); Ross (1993); Bounds *et al.* (1994)
• Enhancing firm's profitability/ productivity	James (1996); Ahire and Kiran (1995); Banerjee and Ramesh (1993); Waldman (1994); Oakland (1989); Ross (1993); Mohanty and Lakhe (1998); Sun (2000); Easton and Jarrel (1998); Hendricks and Singhal (1997); Lemak *et al.* (1997); Samson and Terziovski (1999); Shetty (1993); Wisner and Eakins (1994); Anderson *et al.* (1995); Pfau (1989); Buzzel and Gale (1987)
• Faster organizational learning	Oakland (1989); Ross (1993); James (1996)
• Safe and healthy communities	Oakland (1989); Crosby (1979)
• Better customer service/ Greater loyalty and customer satisfaction	Reed *et al.* (1996); James (1996); Ahire and Kiran (1995); Terziovski and Samson (1999); Sun (2000); Sakofsky (1996); Anderson *et al.* (1994); Anderson *et al.* (1995)
• Strong organizational economy	Juran (1974); Spencer (1994); Reed *et al.* (1996)
• Improvement in market share	Ross (1993); Reed *et al.* (1996); Mohanty and Lakhe (1998); Buzzel and Gale (1987)
• Better organizational management	Oakland (1989); Ross (1993); Terziovski and Samson (1999); Gehani (1993)
• Better performance in employee relations	Terziovski and Samson (1999); Anderson *et al.* (1995)
• Competitive advantage	Curkovic and Pagell (1999); Feigenbaum (1990, 1992); Hewitt (1994); Noori (1991);

Contd...

	Reich (1994); Seawright and Young (1996); Tobin (1990); Powell (1995); Reed *et al.* (1996); Pfau (1989)

2.4.2 Definitions of TQM

Table 2.4 compiles different definitions of TQM.

Table 2.4: Various definitions of TQM as reported in literature

Author	*Definition*	*Remark*
Feigenbaum (1983)	An effective system for integrating the quality development, quality maintenance and quality improvement efforts of various groups in an organization so as to enable production and service at the most economical level which allows for full customer satisfaction.	This definition includes development, maintenance and improvement of quality.
Pike and Barnes (1988)	A process of individual and organizational development, the purpose of which is to increase the level of satisfaction of all those concerned with the organization: customers, suppliers, stakeholders and employees.	This definition emphasizes on the process of individual and organizational development to increase the level of satisfaction of all those concerned with the organization.
Oakland (1989)	An approach to improve the effectiveness and flexibility of business completely. It is an essential way of organizing and involving the whole organization, every department, every activity and every single person at every level.	This definition explains the term "total" from functional and organizational hierarchy perspectives.
Tobin (1990)	The totally integrated effort for gaining competitive advantage by continuously improving every facet of the organizational culture.	This definition places emphasis on organizational culture to gain competitive advantage.
Horowitz (1990)	A total process in which one recognizes that everyone in the organization contributes in some form or the other to the end product	This definition places emphasis on the involvement of each individual in the

Contd...

	or service to the customer. Everyone means that every function and every level in the organization is involved.	organization.
British Standard BS 4778: Part 2 (1991)	A management philosophy embracing all activities through which the needs and expectations of the customers and the community, and the objectives of the organization, are satisfied in the most efficient and cost effective way by maximizing the potential of all employees in a continuing drive for improvement.	This definition gives emphasis on the maximization of the potential of all employees.
Wilkinson and Witcher (1991)	TQM means: "Total": Every person in the firm is involved; "Quality": Customer requirements are met exactly; "Management": Senior executives are fully committed.	This definition is most acceptable for the success of TQM.
Sink (1991a)	TQM efforts can be successful only if the operational definition for the organizational system is evolved by the leadership of the organization and is crystallized and communicated with conviction and clarity.	This definition places emphasis on the role of the leadership in the success of any TQM program, and its commitment.
Bemowski (1991)	TQM should pursue and achieve continuous improvement in every process of an organization's environmental compliance program through the integrated efforts of all members of the program to lead to a reduction in the total environmental cost.	This definition shows concern for environmental quality management.
Zairi and Simintiras (1991)	The combination of socio-technical process control towards doing the right things (externally), every thing right (internally), first time and all the time, with economic viability considered at each stage of each process.	This definition considers the main elements of TQM, that is, satisfaction at internal and external customers level.
Jablonski (1991)	A co-operative form of doing business that relies on the talents and capabilities of both labour and	This definition emphasizes three pillars for successful

Contd...

	management to continually improve quality and productivity using teams.	implementation of TQM: participative management, continuous process improvement and the use of teams. However, the definition does not explicitly mention the role that suppliers and customers play in the success of TQM.
Zairi (1991, 1993); Zairi *et al.* (1994)	A positive attempt by the organization concerned to improve structural, attitudinal, behavioural and methodological ways of delivering the product to the end customer, with emphasis on consistency, improvements in quality, competitive enhancements, all with the aim of satisfying or delighting the end customer.	This definition is most acceptable for the success of TQM according to the Malcolm Baldridge Award.
Chase and Aquilano (1992)	Total quality management may be defined as managing the entire organization so that it excels in all dimensions of products and services that are important to the customer.	This definition gives emphasis on the involvement of total organization.
British Standard 5750: Part 1: Section 3.1 (1992)	A management philosophy and company practices that aim to harness the human and material resources of an organization in the most effective way to achieve the objectives of the organization.	This definition gives emphasis on the optimum utilization of human force and material resources.
ISO 9004 (1993)	A managerial philosophy and company practices which aim to harness the human and material resources of an organization in the most effective way to achieve the objectives of the organization.	This definition gives emphasis on the optimum utilization of human force and material resources.
Kanji and Asher (1993)	Continuous performance improvement of individuals, groups and organization.	This definition shows that to improve performance, people need to know what to do, how to do it and have the right tools to do it, to be able to measure performance and to

Contd...

		receive feedback on current level of achievement.
Ross (1993, 1995)	The integration of all functions and processes within an organization in order to achieve continuous improvement of the quality of goods and services. The goal is customer satisfaction. The system is the inter-related set of quality policies, processes, technology and personnel needed to achieve the quality transformation.	This definition gives emphasis on integration of various functions and processes for customer satisfaction.
ISO 8402 (1994)	A management approach of the organization, centered on quality, based on the participation of all its members and aiming at long term success through customer satisfaction and benefits to the members of the organization and to the society.	This definition gives emphasis on the participation of all employees to achieve customer satisfaction.
Lewis and Smith (1994)	Total quality is "total" in three senses – it covers every process, every job and every person.	This definition explains the term "total" from functional and organizational hierarchy perspectives.
Youssef and Zairi (1995)	A total philosophy whose objective is to meet or exceed the needs of internal and external customers by creating an organizational culture in which every one at every stage of creating the product and every level of management is committed to quality and clearly understands its strategic importance.	This definition gives emphasis on the commitment of each and every level of management to meet or exceed the needs of internal and external customers.
Dahlgaard *et al.* (1998)	A management process which any organization can implement through long term planning, by using continuous quality management plans which lead the organization towards the fulfillment of its vision.	This definition gives emphasis on long-term planning to fulfill organization vision.

Contd...

Shortell *et al.* (1995)	Total quality management is a structured, systematic process for creating organization-wide participation in planning and implementing continuous improvement in quality.	This definition gives emphasis on organization-wide participation in planning and implementing continuous improvement in quality.
Miller (1996)	An ongoing process whereby top management takes whatever steps necessary to enable everyone in the organization in the course of performing all duties to meet or exceed the needs and expectations of their customers, both external and internal.	This definition gives emphasis on top management commitment.
Tapiero (1996)	TQM is viewed as a total (societal, organizational and operational) commitment to manage a firm's resources to achieve the highest levels of performance in everything in which the firm is involved.	This definition gives emphasis on total commitment to achieve the highest levels of performance.
Mohanty and Lakhe (1998)	A pragmatic long-term systems approach initiated and driven by the top management to bring about a total culture change to meet the dynamic needs of the customer and create a loyal but at the same time a diversified customer base.	This definition has 'the entire features of TQM from long-term systems approach to its strategic direction, driven by top management support to total change in the culture'.
Evans and Lindsay (1999)	A total, company wide effort-through full involvement of the entire work-force and a focus on continuous improvement - that companies use to achieve customer satisfaction.	This definition gives emphasis on company wide effort to focus on continuous improvement.
Kanji and Tambi (1999)	A process of continuously satisfying customer requirements at the lowest possible cost by harnessing the capabilities of everyone.	This definition highlights the importance of harnessing the capabilities of everyone.
McAdam and Mc-Keown (1999)	A process of individual and organizational development and change, the purpose of which is to increase the level of satisfaction of all organizational stakeholders.	This definition gives emphasis to increase the level of satisfaction of all organizational shareholders.

Contd...

Zhu and Scheuermann (1999)	TQM stresses the involvement of everyone inside an organization and related persons outside the organizations, such as, customers and suppliers.	This definition gives emphasis on the integration of customers and suppliers.
ISO 9000 (2000)	What the organization does to ens-ure that its product conform to the customers' requirements.	This definition highlights the importance of meeting customers' requirements.
Saferpak (2003)	TQM is a set of systematic activities carried out by the entire organization to effectively and efficiently achieve company objectives so as to provide products and services with a level of quality that satisfies customers, at the appropriate time and price.	This definition highlights the importance of "systematic activities". It means organized activities to achieve the company's mission (objectives) that are led by strong management leadership and guided by established clear mid- and long-term vision and strategies.

2.5 GENERAL TQM PRINCIPLES

In this review, TQM principles are classified in eight categories as shown in Figure 2.2. However, it may be noted that these principles are mutually reinforcing. Continuous improvement means search for better methods, which is most effective when driven by customer needs. To achieve continuous improvement, teamwork is essential. Customer focus is expressed by the organization's attempt to design and deliver products and services that fulfill customers' stated and implied needs. Quality and productivity improvement can be achieved only through the top management commitment. These principles are reviewed in the following sections.

2.5.1 Quality Focus

Reddy (1980) has taken into consideration the concept of quality and cost as competitive strategies. He has described five systems for quality assurance (QA) and has explained how to integrate quality strategy with corporate strategy to improve quality along with productivity. Similarly, Mathew and Madrecha (1994) discussed the issues of quality planning, quality measurement, quality control (QC), quality improvement and use

Fig. 2.2: General TQM principles

of the quality management strategy for improving customer satisfaction. Samuels (1994) emphasized quality management and has suggested that the knowledge about the "true" results of a quality management system is important when new quality programs are being implemented.

As per Singh (1993) and Bounds (1994), quality has become the yardstick of conducting trade and business and is no more an option but an urgent need for the survival and growth in the competitive environment. Tersine and Hummingbird (1995) in their conceptual article discussed about TQM, JIT, lead-time, competitive advantage and their important role in quality and productivity improvement programmes. Crosby (1991) has brought clarity to "quality management" by emphasizing on issues like quality, quality management, learning and quality system in developing nations.

Singh (1991) described in a survey article the concept of TQM and its practices in India. He has taken into consideration the important issues like quality, quality system, and quality circles. Raman (1985) opined that quality and productivity play a crucial role in economic development of any country. It is, therefore, necessary for every country to evolve its own quality strategy taking local factors into consideration.

2.5.2 Top Management Commitment

Deming (1986, 1993) has emphasized the need for managers to develop leadership to usher the transformation process. Feigenbaum (1961) viewed senior executives' commitment as the means for promoting organizational commitment. Kano (1993) discussed about senior executives' commitment as the most important factor of TQM. Crosby (1979) placed management commitment on the top of the essentials of TQM implementation. Juran (1993) attributed the quality excellence of Japanese companies to senior managers' commitment to quality. Atkinson (1992) stated that the lack of management commitment is the main reason for 80 percent of TQM failures. Zairi and Youssef (1995) and Porter and Parker (1993) have also made similar observations.

Most TQM failures can be attributed to lack of consistency of purpose and inadequate leadership, and failure of pilot improvement teams (Bemowski, 1995). Dale and Lightburn (1992), Doyle (1992), Fenwick (1991), Sashkin and Kiser (1993), Gilbert (1990) and Gibson (1990) stressed that an active commitment from top management is essential for the success of TQM and blamed many of its failures on the absence of that leadership.

2.5.3 Productivity Improvement

Productivity is the key in enhancing the quality of life and economic well being of people. According to Mohanty (1992), productivity management is, in most organizations, a top down approach imposed on the rest of the organization. The design of an effective productivity management process requires involvement of all concerned (Rahman, 1990). Snowdon (1986) and Takeuchi (1981) in their conceptual paper based on the Japanese approach have highlighted the issues of quality, productivity, TQC and quality circles.

Chen and Adam (1991) observed that the impact of flexible manufacturing systems (FMS) on productivity and quality has long-term advantages. Mohanty and Lakhe (1994) in a qualitative and conceptual paper towards understanding TQM have considered the issue of quality and productivity improvement. Gondhalekar *et al.* (1991) have discussed productivity improvement in a conceptual way using a case study of Godrej Soaps Limited in India. Kaizen concept has been used in the organization as a means for improvement in the productivity as an ongoing basis. They reported an interesting aspect of the Kaizen system that it demands very little investment and is very effective. Stonebraker and Leong (1994) have discussed productivity, customer expectations and quality, and focused on productivity and people.

In a conceptual article, Wildemann (1993) has discussed productivity and market success. In a rapidly changing business environment, productivity is not merely a ratio of output to input. He recommended that various other performance indicators should be integrated into the productivity analysis and suggested that administrative processes should also receive more attention. Gitlow and Hertz (1983) have focused on productivity and product defects in a conceptual and survey-based article, using a case study approach. Quality-productivity relationships as per various authors have been compiled and are shown in Table 2.5.

Table 2.5: Quality-productivity relationships as per various authors

Authors	*Relationship*
Deming (1982)	Quality means improved productivity
Crosby (1979)	Quality means improved operating measures
	Quality means prevention
	Prevention implies improved productivity
Juran (1988b)	Analytical tools improve quality
	Improved quality means improved productivity
Garvin (1983)	Quality and productivity have similar roots: Both rely on reduction of disruptions and rework, improvement to work processes, and well-trained workforce. Quality and productivity reflect how workers feel about their jobs Productivity and quality are positively related.

2.5.4 Breakthrough Improvement

Today the organizations face both domestic and international market in which even the leaders are competing with fast-growing followers. In order to succeed in such a dynamically changing business environment, an organization needs breakthrough improvement. This requires creative use of human potential and synergy. Worldwide, organizations are using Business Process Re-engineering (BPR) as an innovative tool for dramatic improvement (Hammer and Champy, 1993).

Martin and Florida (1993) have given details of innovation-mediated production system based on concepts of multi-skilled workers and self-organizing work teams. They also recommended cross-functional team working to maximize improvements. Stephan and Arnold (1994) presented a management model that covers business systems as a whole and explained methodology to focus on processes and people to meet growing customer requirements and improving operating performance. Their model emphasized on reward and recognition as an important aspect for breakthrough improvement.

2.5.5 Continuous Improvement

Continuous improvement means a constant examination and improvement of all processes on a continuing basis. Harrington (1987) has observed that the complexity of present business environment has made it necessary for organizations to evaluate all the alternatives before committing resources to an improvement process. He proposed the use of quality cost concepts to avoid ambiguity and improve understanding of quality improvement. Hitoshi (1987), Eugene and Richard (1988), Forrest (1992) and Michael *et al.* (1992) have also demonstrated usefulness of SQC tools to improve product quality and reduce costs. Slater (1991) offered a dynamic process management model derived from the experience of successful corporations.

Corsten and Will (1995) have discussed the concepts of integrated production, quality, cost reduction, cost leadership and the amount of attention which must be paid to these factors as key elements in quality and profitability improvement. Pursglove and Dale (1995) discussed essential features involved in developing a quality costing system. Predpall (1994) discussed issues like quality improvement, customer focus, leadership, training, employee involvement, personal effectiveness, and the importance of these factors in improving quality and customer satisfaction, which ultimately improve the business prospects and profitability.

Hauser and Clausing (1988) have observed in their study the issues of quality and customer attributes as the most important factors to be taken care of in any quality improvement programmes. Harrington (1987) combined total business management, total cost management, total productivity management, total quality management and total technology management into a methodology called Business Process Improvement (BPI).

The rationale behind this is to eliminate errors, minimize delays, maximize use of assets, and promote understanding, to gain competitive advantage. Harrington identified five phases for BPI and inter linked them, as given in Figure 2.3.

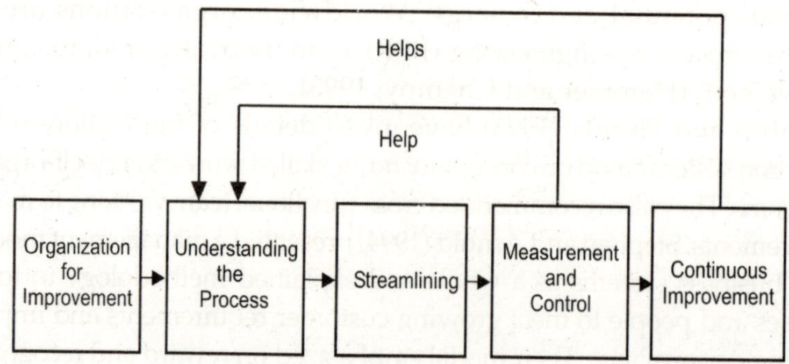

Fig. 2.3: Five phases of business process improvement

Cary (1995) emphasized that for a Kaizen (continuous improvement) strategy, the most important concern should be the quality of people. Table 2.6 shows different approaches suggested in the literature for continuous improvement.

Table 2.6: Approaches for continuous improvement

Reference	*Approach*
Hitoshi (1987); Eugene and Richard (1988); Frank *et al.* (1993); Forrest (1992); Michael *et al.* (1992); Wickman and Doyle (1993)	SQC tools
Slater (1991)	Process management mode
Miller and Krumm (1992)	Human resource, Team approach
Tedaldi *et al.* (1992)	Production planning
Norothey and Southway (1993)	Cycle time management
Nakamura (1993)	Standardization methods
Boznak and Decker (1993)	Product development

2.5.6 Culture Change

TQM requires management to create a new, more flexible environment and culture that will encourage and accept change. Organizations without well-developed ethical work cultures do not have the power to implement total quality. The work of Kohlberg (1981) and Gilligan (1982) on individual moral development can be extended to organizational moral development to provide a six-stage road map of ethical work cultures and the work environments. They called these stages of development as: (i) social darwinism, (ii) machiavellianism, (iii) popular conformity, (iv) allegiance to authority, (v) participative management, and (vi) collaborate management.

Hirotaka and Quelch (1983) extended the concepts of quality from product and process to the work culture and employee's attitude. Aubrey and Felkins (1988) provided an effective approach to meeting challenges of declining productivity, increasing competition, and low employee motivation based on employee and management surveys. Griffiths (1990) observed that to install quality, it is to be developed as a process in the organization, not as a programme or project. Lawler and Mohraman (1985) described the concept of quality circles as an effective and risk-free way out to involve employees and inculcate participative culture in the organization.

Rao and Raghunathan (1994) in an empirical study discussed about TQM, work culture and customer satisfaction. Edgar and Hodgson (1991) argued that success in business depends on an individual's ability to quickly and effectively change. Singh (1994) elaborated the role of ISO 9000 certification in shaping the work culture. According to him, strategic thinking, strategic attitude, teamwork and commitment are the essential ingredients for developing a positive work culture. Ahluwalia (1993) felt that the concept of total quality, provides an opportunity to people to rethink about their value systems and beliefs. TQM calls for a change in mindset as depicted in Figure 2.4.

Jain and Bagchi (1998) have found that to change focus towards customers, attitudinal change of senior management is a must. Melis *et al.* (1998) has cautioned in selecting and implementing motivational techniques so as to involve and engage everyone.

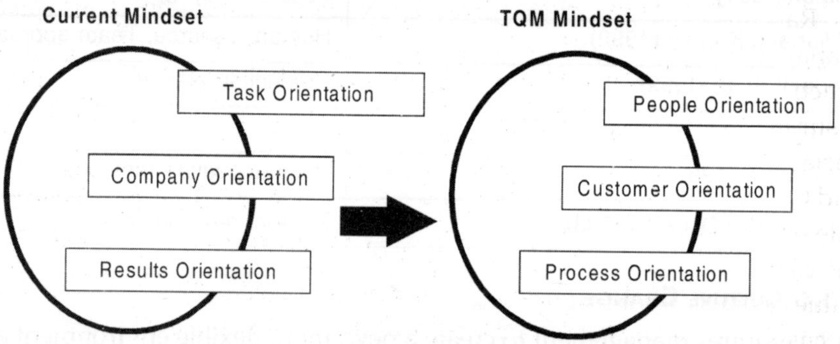

Fig. 2.4: Change in mindset for TQM

Sinclair and Collins (1994) regarded culture as a tool in determining organizational performance. McLaurin and Bell (1991) pointed out that implementation of TQM is sometimes distressing and difficult, as the behaviour change required by it does not come easily and naturally. They suggested that by opening communication lines, before implementation of TQM, cultural and behavioural changes need to be obtained. According to Strolle (1991), creating a TQM culture is not restricted to the individual or group, but is the responsibility of everyone in the organization.

Kimmerling (1993) found during his survey that high-performing organizations spend 3.3% of payroll costs on training against a recommended industry norm of only 1.5% to create conducive work culture. Ishikawa (1985) stated that organizational cultural change is needed to achieve a significant breakthrough in TQM. Rodrigues (1994) stated that the effectiveness of TQM implementation depends on the appropriateness of corporate culture. Sinclair and Collins (1994) regarded culture as a tool in determining organizational performance.

2.5.7 Customer Focus

Customer focus is another important TQM principle. Buzzel and Gale (1987) found strong evidence that quality pays in terms of profit, market share and productivity. Successful organizations give high priority in understanding and responding to current and future customer needs. Bossert (1990) opined that quality function deployment (QFD) helps focusing on customer requirements, teamwork and communication, thereby improving product quality. Cohen (1995) stated the ultimate benefits of QFD are to increase market share and profitability. Burchill and Shen (1995) and Shiba *et al.* (1993) stated that the goal of QFD is to move from the invisible or vague feelings of the customers to clear, grounded customer requirements that serve real customer needs. Hauser and Clausing (1988) have found that customer satisfaction is fundamental to TQM and is an important requirement for long-term organizational success.

Rao and Raghunathan (1994) have presented a model on quality management practices. The model contends that quality management practices depicted by strategic quality planning, work culture, quality assurance and supplier relationship will have an effect on the outcome variable, namely, customer satisfaction. In a qualitative article, Takeuchi and Quelch (1983) discussed the issues of quality, customers' values, after-sale service, and customer service programme. Burt (1989) has brought out the clarity on product quality, competitive quality, and focus on customer values as important factors. Chatterjee (1993) illustrated the need to invest in customer satisfaction vis-à-vis TQM taking into consideration quality, TQM, quality excellence, and productivity improvement. Conduit and Mavondo (2001) study found evidence for the critical role of internal customer orientation for achieving effective market orientation. They stressed that only through satisfying the requirements of employees can superior value be provided at each stage of the value chain, and the end user receive optimal service.

2.5.8 Team Work

Teamwork as collaboration between managers and subordinates, between functions, and between customers and suppliers, is another TQM principle. Employees can make important contributions when they have the power and necessary preparation. Kepner and Tregoe (1981) provided insight into the art of managing people, information and capital resources. Scholtes and Hacquebord (1988) provided details on how to work with project teams to implement quality improvement principles. Harrington (1987) presented a comparison of American and Japanese business practices and listed benefits of teamwork. Shores (1990) provided a framework that incorporates and interrelates participative management, quality function deployment (QFD), statistical quality control and management commitment. Seng (1989) described the importance of understanding philosophies, methods and techniques in holistic sense for effective implementation of improvement plans in complex environment. Kenneth and Gary (1991) demonstrated based on example how training improves productivity, product quality and competitive position. Karl and Motiska (1962) emphasized that quality improvement requires team effort and in excellent organizations teams are an integral part of an organization's decision-making process. Ryan and Oestreich (1991) have found that fear could limit and corrupt employee-performance and observe that to succeed, organizations must drive fear out of the workplace.

Kinlaw (1992) explained a team-based approach to improve the quality at every level. Anderson (1993) emphasized that the key to success of an organization is the strength of its work force and presented a strategy that links an employee's skills to education, the job and improved productivity. Oakland (1993) has found that the complexity of most of the processes that are operated in industry, commerce and the services places them beyond the control of any one individual. The only different way to tackle process improvement is through teamwork. Kamran (1991, 1993) discussed the issues like quality, TQM, Malcolm Baldrige Process, and the importance of teamwork in his conceptual article. Eisenhardt (1989) research has shown that cross-functional teams can help reduce product development times to a greater extent. Roberts (1997) argued that teams are the vehicles for carrying out training, and a 1997 survey of American organizations found that 75% of organizations used training for team building and leadership development and 63% for quality improvement.

2.6 TQM MODELS

Different TQM frameworks have been promoted by different authors (Deming, 1986; Juran, 1986; Crosby, 1979; Saraph *et al.*, 1989; Flynn *et al.*, 1994; Black and Porter, 1993, 1995, 1996). Saraph *et al.* (1989) identified eight factors of quality management in a business unit. Flynn *et al.* (1994) identified seven dimensions of quality management from which they developed a set of 14 perceptual scales. Black and Porter (1993, 1995, 1996) identified ten factors of quality management and developed a reliable and validated instrument for the measurement of a TQM Programme.

TQM has been represented in a variety of models as a philosophy reflecting modern competitiveness. Some of the following models are a clear illustration of TQM as an organizational dynamic system. Oakland model (1989) defined TQM as a pyramid representing five basic elements of TQM, and Sohal *et al.* (1989) and Zaire (1991) presented a building block model of TQM. An overwhelming proportion of TQM literature has been primarily focused on techniques, prescriptions and procedures. In order to develop an insightful understanding of existing TQM concepts, the work of various quality leaders is examined in this section. The focus of various quality models has been compiled and is given in Table 2.7.

Table 2.7: Focus of various TQM models

TQM Model	*Focus*
Crosby (1979, 1992)	Conformance to requirements. Zero defects. Quality is free. Cost of quality concept. Quality maturity grid (uncertainty, awakening, enlightenment, wisdom and certainty). Three principles of completeness as: cause employees to be successful; cause supplier to be successful and cause customers to be successful
Deming (1990)	Quality through constancy of purpose. Leadership. Reduce variations. Continuous improvement of cost. Deming cycle (Plan-Do-Standardize-Act cycle)
Feigenbaum (1961, 1982)	Total quality control. Concept of quality cost. Hidden plant for waste. 9M's affecting quality are: Markets, Money, Management, Men, Motivation, Materials, Machines and mechanization, Modern information methods, and Mounting product requirements
Juran (1988a)	Quality is fitness for use. Statistical tools. Planning for quality (Quality planning, quality control and quality improvement). Human aspects in quality management
Ishikawa (1984)	Company-wide Quality Control (CWQC) and participation by all. Education and training. Use of quality circles. Quality audits by the president and senior executive twice a year. Use of statistical methods and a focus on problem prevention. Welcoming complaints
Imai (1986)	Kaizen (Continuing improvement involving everyone – managers and workers). The Kaizen strategy begins and ends with people. Sustained continuous improvement culture. Small improvements involving everybody
Oakland (1989)	Management commitment. Customer-supplier chains. Systems approach of documented sets of procedures and standards. Statistical Process Control. Team work and continuous improvement
Sohal *et al.* (1989)	Customer (internal and external) focus. Management commitment. Total participation; Total Employees Involvement. Statistical Quality Control. Systematic problem solving process [Plan-Do-Check-Act (PDCA)] Cycle

Contd...

Anderson (Khanna and Roy 1995)	Eliminate non-value-adding activities. Continuous improvement. Empower people. Customer alignment. Technology. Organize around outcomes. Time compression
ISO 9000:2000	Eight Management Principles. Customer focus. Leadership. Involvement of people. Process approach. System approach to management. Continual improvement. Factual approach to decision making. Mutually beneficial supplier relationships
QS 9000: 1998/TS 16949: 2002	Development of fundamental of quality systems that provide for continuous improvement, emphasizing defect prevention and the reduction of variation and waste in the supply chain. Emphasize on advanced product quality planning and control plan. Failure mode and effect analysis. Measurement systems and analysis. Fundamental SPC. Quality System Assessment
McKinsey (Graham, 1992)	Design process. Process quality. Company quality. Elements of process quality have been defined as: product quality, process capability, service quality and logistics quality
Agrawal *et al.* (1996); Van der Wiele (1996b) *et al.*	Quality management self assessment (QMSA) Self-assessment by organizations. Self-assessment by quality specialists
Schonberger (1982, 1987, 1994)	Perfection Improvement as a habitProcess control. Empowerment of operators to stop the line in case of quality problem. Project by project improvement. Housekeeping. Foolproof devices. QC circles
Taguchi (1986)	Non-quality is the loss imparted to the society. Variation in a product performance characteristic about its target value incurs a loss to the user
Dooley and Flor (1998)	Gap between perceived and expected results. Effectiveness of TQM implementation is judged by the realization of the perceived results. Attitudes towards TQM
Gatewood and Riordan (1997)	Organizational practices. Quality principles. Employee fulfillment. Customer satisfaction
Stone and Eddy (1996)	Individual factors such as: values, goals, abilities and needs. Organizational factors such as: continuous improvement of process, learning and customer focus. Organizational mechanisms

Contd...

	such as: team based structure, design of jobs, organizational policies and practices and human resource systems
Hoffman and Mehra (1999)	Top management leader ship. Reward system. Performance measurement system. Empowerment. Education and training. Total employee involvement. Successfully/productivity improvement programme
Pun *et al.* (2000)	Market-driven. Customer focus. Competitor performance. Business strategies. Quality cost reduction. Market leadership. Profitability. Survival
Yusof and Aspinwal (2001)	Quality initiatives such as: SPC, quality assurance system, benchmarking, employee recognition, pay and reward system, human resource policy, cost of quality, quality circles, quality teams, supplier quality assurance, customer surveys, quality measurement, communication, employee perceptions, Kaizen, TPM, Muri, Muda, Mura, 5S, advance quality planning and self-assessment. General methodology such as: planning, education/training, trials, review, improve and standardize
Leonard and McAdam (2001)	Five model TQM framework. TQM points of application model. TQM strategic drivers model. TQM profiles model. TQM environment model. TQM lifecycle model

The conceptual framework of various TQM experts may be at variance, but all agree that TQM covers all aspects of an organization's systems, procedures, and processes. Therefore, TQM tools should be capable of capturing philosophical underpinnings of quality. In order to understand the conceptual philosophy of TQM models, the following are included in this review:

a. Anderson Consulting TQM Model
b. Crosby's TQM Concept
c. Deming's System of Profound Knowledge
d. Feigenbaum's TQC Model
e. Ishikawa's Quality Model
f. ISO 9000 Quality System
g. Juran's TQM Concepts

h. Quality Management Self-assessment
i. McKinsey TQM Model
j. Schonberger Quality Concepts
k. Taguchi Quality Loss Concept
l. Dooley and Flor Model of Attitudes Towards TQM
m. Gatewood and Riordan Process Model of Quality Management
n. Stone and Eddy Model of Individual and Organizational Factors Affecting Quality Related Outcomes
o. Hoffman and Mehra Model for Successful Productivity Improvement Programme
p. Pun et al. Synergy framework model among ISO 9000, CQI and TQM
q. Yusof and Aspinwal TQM Conceptual Framework Model
r. Leonard and McAdam five model TQM framework

Each of these concepts is briefly outlined in the following sub-sections.

2.6.1 Anderson Consulting TQM Model

Anderson Consulting developed a TQM model based on the study of a large number of excellent organizations (Khanna and Roy, 1995). This model shows inter-relationship among various elements as given in Figure 2.5. Salient features of this model are: eliminate non-value added activity, continuous improvement, empower people, customer alignment, time compression, organize around outcomes and use of technology. The model is in practice by a number of organizations to make employees understand the importance of inter-relationship among various elements of TQM.

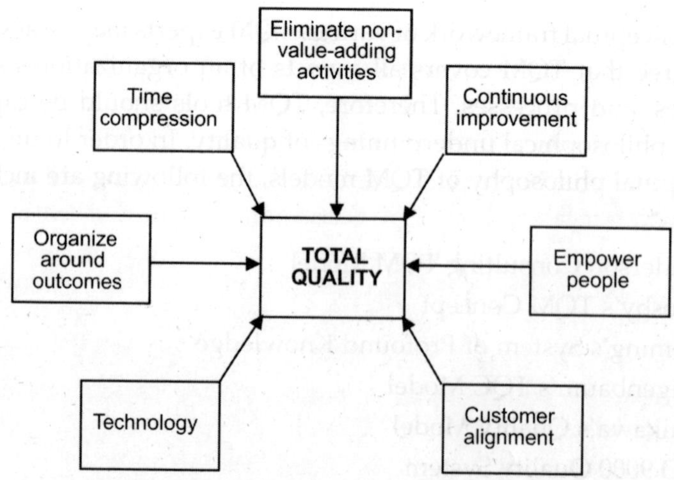

Fig. 2.5: Anderson consulting model for total quality

2.6.2 Crosby's TQM Concept

Crosby (1979, 1981) first introduced cost of quality concept and gave his popular slogans: quality is free, do it right the first time and zero defects. He introduced four 'absolutes' of quality management.

- The definition of quality is *conformance to requirements.*
- The system of quality is *prevention of problems.*
- The performance standard of quality is *zero defects.*
- The measurement of quality is *cost of non-conformance* (Cost of Quality).

Crosby proposed a 14 step programme to quality improvement and also introduced quality maturity grid concept. The five maturity phases are uncertainty, awakening, enlightenment, wisdom and certainty. These stages provide good insights and help self-assessment. The shortcomings of Crosby's concepts are:

- It lacks customer focus
- It lacks emphasis on software part of quality (shared vision, craftsmanship etc.)
- It lacks emphasis on teamwork and role of quality in business strategy
- It lacks emphasis on management of process quality
- It also ignores time as a dimension of quality

Crosby (1992) proposed the role model concept to develop the future managers. He described three principles of completeness as: cause employees to be successful; cause suppliers to be successful and cause customers to be successful.

2.6.3 Deming's System of Profound Knowledge

Deming's system of profound knowledge provides the foundations behind his 14 points of management. He addresses four issues: (i) appreciation for systems approach, (ii) understanding variation, (iii) theory of knowledge, and (iv) use of psychology. Deming's quality philosophy is based on statistical methods, but it also addresses the management system as well as social system and culture of the organization. Walton (1986) and Scherkenbach (1986) explained Deming's management techniques including his 14 points for management, seven deadly diseases, and other obstacles. Deming (1990) emphasized that transformation is the key to optimization. Optimizing the system leads the total organization toward continuous growth, stronger market position, and more jobs. Delavigne and Robertson (1994) compared Deming's philosophy and systems with typical management practices in today's world. Salient features of Deming's philosophy are summarized below:

- Emphasized the systemic nature of organizations
- Leadership is important
- Emphasized the need to reduce variations in organizational processes
- Emphasized on-the-job training
- Deming Cycle (PDCA Cycle)

The shortcomings of Deming's philosophy are as follows:

- Lacks customer focus and satisfaction
- Lacks emphasis on software part of quality (Shared vision, craftsmanship etc.)
- Less emphasis on teamwork, and role of quality in business strategy
- Ignores time as a dimension of quality

2.6.4 Feigenbaum's TQC Model

Feigenbaum (1961, 1982) has propagated the idea of quantifying various parameters of quality management in terms of various types of quality costs. He coined the term total quality control (TQC). Salient features of Feigenbaum's TQC model are enumerated below:

- Total quality is a continuous work process, starting with customer requirements and ending with customer satisfaction.
- Documentation allows visualization and communication of work assignments.
- Quality system provides for greater flexibility because of greater use of alternatives.
- Systematic reengineering of major quality activities leads to greater levels of continuous improvement.
- Nuts and bolts approach to quality.
- Concept of Hidden plant (Waste and rework account 15 to 40%). Similar to the concept of cost of quality proposed by Crosby.
- 9M's affecting quality are: markets, money, management, men, motivation, materials, machines and mechanization, modern information methods, and mounting product requirements.

2.6.5 Ishikawa's Quality Model

Ishikawa (1984) introduced the use of quality control circle for improving quality and performance. Ishikawa identified seven critical success factors as essential for quality improvement. They are:

- Company-wide Quality Control (CWQC) and participation by all.
- Education and training in all aspects of total quality.
- Use of quality circles to update standards and regulations.

- Quality audits by the president and senior executives twice a year.
- Widespread use of statistical methods and a focus on problem prevention.
- Nation-wide quality promotion, with the national imperative of keeping Japanese quality number one in the world.
- Improved mental attitude on part of both management and workers toward one another and towards the customer, including welcoming complaints.

2.6.6 ISO-9000:2000 Quality System

ISO:9000 series of quality standards are widely accepted quality system and are based on the philosophy that only an integrated, systematic and planned approach can ensure quality. These were developed by amalgamating quality system standards of various countries. The standard provides generic requirements and guidance to quality.

Lamprecht (1992) provided information on how to organize, document, and implement a quality system along with comprehensive reviews of the five ISO standards. Hutchins (1992) in his work focused on techniques of quality auditing. Quality audit by ISO 9000 (2000) has been defined as systematic, independent and documented process for obtaining audit evidence and evaluating it objectively to determine which agreed criteria are fulfilled. A widespread criticism of the ISO 9000 programme is that it is not connected directly enough to product quality (Stavros, 1997).

2.6.7 Juran's TQM Concepts

Juran (1988a) developed the trilogy concept (quality planning, quality control, and quality improvement) for organization's transformation. He described a perpetual spiral of progress for continuously striving toward quality. Steps on this spiral in ascending order are customers, product development, operations, marketing, and then back to customers and product development. Juran (1988a, 1992) also described the human aspects of quality management in great details. He believed that only better people, better management and better organizational communication could achieve TQM. Juran and Gryna (1995) detailed out quality planning analysis in their work. Juran's philosophy lacks customer focus and satisfaction, role of quality in business strategy and it ignores 'time' as a dimension of quality.

2.6.8 Quality Management Self-Assessment

Agrawal *et al.* (1996) defined quality management self-assessment (QMSA) as a periodic, comprehensive, systematic and regular review of an organization's systems, procedures and results against a recognized TQM model culminating in planned improvement actions. Large numbers of quality professionals are advocating the use of self-assessment with the ultimate objective of sustained quality improvement as its benefits (Zink and Schmidt, 1998; Kristensen and Juhl, 1999; Kristensen *et al.*, 2000; Jordan, 1994; Knutton, 1994; Zaremba and Crew, 1995; Brereton, 1996; Wu *et al.*, 1997; Fountain, 1998).

Van der Wiele *et al.* (1996b) defined QMSA as a management approach based on a mission to achieve business excellence. They concluded that QMSA should be done in stages. First, an organization has to be fairly advanced to be able to start self-assessment. Second, the assessment is to be done by quality specialists as assessors. The result of these two stages should be confidential to the unit concerned. In more advance stage, the organization can use line managers as assessors and share the results across units.

2.6.9 McKinsey TQM Model

Graham (1992) described McKinsey TQM model. This model is based on design process, process quality and company quality. Elements of process quality have been further elaborated as product quality, process capability, service quality and logistic quality as shown in Figure 2.6.

2.6.10 Taguchi's Quality Loss Concept

The heart to Taguchi's (1986) method is his definition of the term quality. According to him, 'non-quality is the loss imparted to the society' from the time a product is shipped.

The essence of Taguchi's definition of quality is that the societal loss generated by a product from the time a product is shipped to the users determines its desirability. Any variation in a product performance characteristic about its target value incurs a loss to the user. Taguchi argued that a product does not start causing losses until it is out of specification but more importantly when there is deviation from the target value. The more the deviation from the targets, the greater is the losses. He found that loss increases exponentially as the parameter value moves away from the target, and is at a minimum when the product or service is at the target value as shown in Figure 2.7. Foster (1993) and Roy (1990) revealed through their study that the Taguchi method has been adopted by many firms to improve process design by developing robust processes.

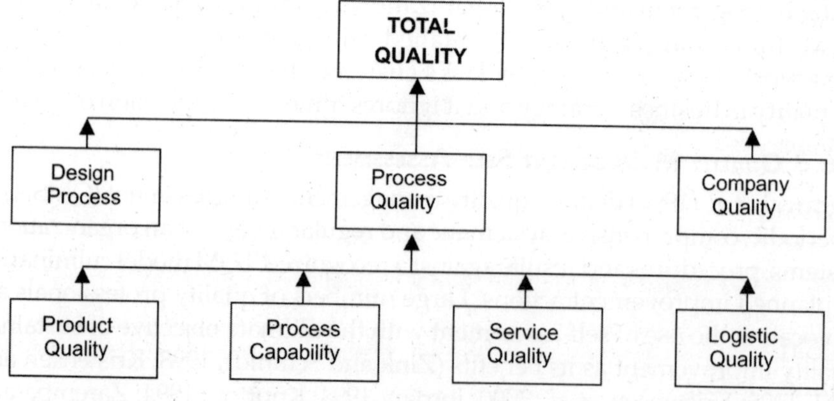

Fig. 2.6: McKinsey TQM model

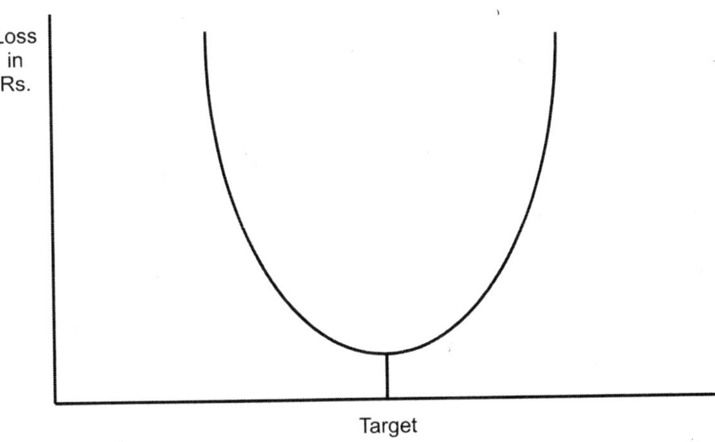

Fig. 2.7: Taguchi's quadratic loss function

2.6.11 Gatewood and Riordan Process Model of Quality Management

Gatewood and Riordan (1997) proposed a "Process Model of Quality Management" as shown in Figure 2.8. They provided in this model a framework for conceptualizing and studying the relationships among variables, which are necessary in implementing a total quality (TQ). Reeves and Bednar (1994) defined total quality as conformance to specifications, conformance to requirements, fitness for use, loss avoidance and meeting or exceeding customers' expectations. The model developed by Gatewood and Riordan (1997) has been based on the literature, which suggests that both individual and organizational factors affect quality-related outcomes (Riordan and Gatewood, 1996).

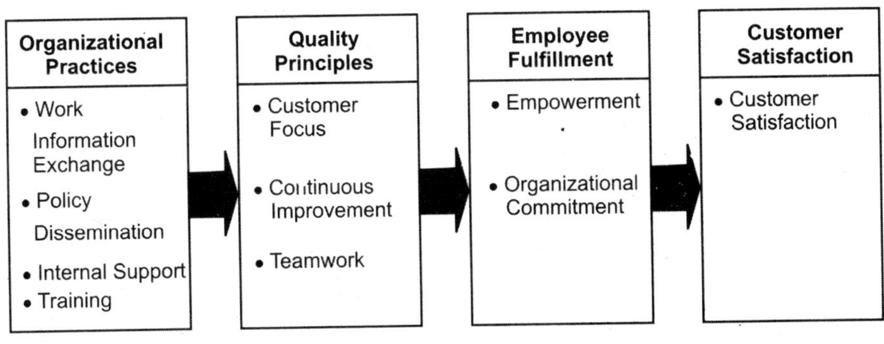

Fig. 2.8: A process model of quality management

Salient features of Gatewood and Riordan (1997) model are enumerated below:

- Customer focus:
  a. The primary goal of the organization is to deliver goods and/or services to the satisfaction of the customer
  b. Employees should anticipate customers' expectations
  c. Customer is the key factor in determining standards and measuring performance
- Continuous improvement:
  a. Constant review of administrative and technical processes to identify better ways of delivering goods and/or services
  b. Emphasis on statistical techniques
  c. Training
  d. Improved customer satisfaction
- Teamwork
  a. Focus of all employees activities on a common goal of quality
  b. Sharing of information
  c. Collaborative decision making
  d. Agreement on performance measures
  e. Suppliers and customers as part of team

2.6.12 Dooley and Flor Model of Attitudes Towards TQM

Dooley and Flor (1998) developed a model of attitudes towards TQM. Their model explains the reasons for the success or failure of TQM initiatives. The model revolves around the gap between perceived and expected results. The more that perceived results match or exceed expectations, the more positive perceptions become towards TQM implementation. Perceived results are related to the effectiveness of TQM implementation, modified by observer bias due to limited rationality. Expected results are related to how TQM is "framed" and to the perceived success that other firms have had in implementing TQM. The model is shown in Figure 2.9.

This model highlights the four most important factors affecting TQM implementation successes, which are:

- Top management's attitude
- Trade union support
- Employees' attitudes towards change
- Middle management's attitudes towards change

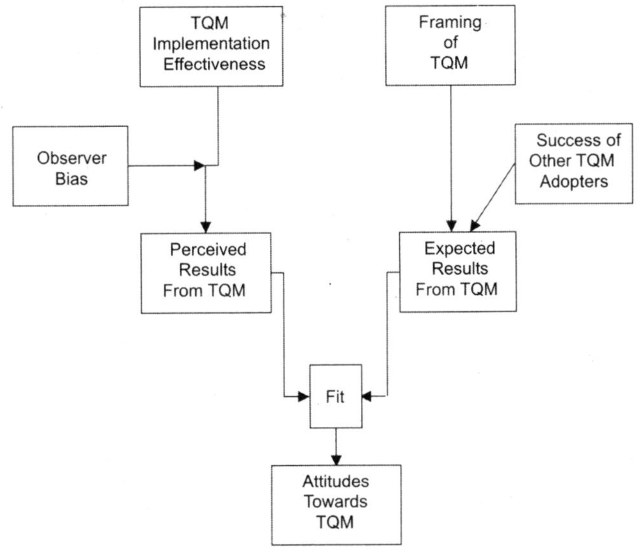

Fig. 2.9: A model of attitudes towards TQM

2.6.13 Schonberger's Quality Concepts

Schonberger (1982, 1987) was the first to demystify and explain what the Japanese were really doing. He believed that the statistical tools are not quite so important in the spectrum of concepts that constitute Japanese total quality control. He attempted to group a large number of TQC factors into categories is shown in Table 2.8. In reality these findings provide a series of practical steps.

Table 2.8: TQC concepts and categories as per Schonberger

TQC Concepts	*TQC Category*
Organization	Production responsibility
Goals	Habit of improvement Perfection
Basic principles	Process control Easy to see quality Insistence on compliance Line stop Correcting one's own errors 100 percent check Project by project improvement
Facilitating concepts	QC as facilitator Small lot size Housekeeping Less than full capacity scheduling Daily machine checking

Contd...

Techniques and aids	Exposure of problems Foolproof devices N = 2 (Inspection of first and last item) Analysis tools QC Circles

2.6.14 Thin Stone and Eddy Model of Individual and Organizational Factors Affecting Quality-Related Outcomes

Stone and Eddy (1996) developed a model based on individual and organizational factors affecting quality. The model suggests that both organizational and individual factors affect the achievement of quality-oriented outcomes as shown in Figure 2.10.

Their model suggests four internal mechanisms for achieving quality goals. These are (i) the team-based structure of the organization, (ii) the design of jobs, (iii) organizational policies and practices, and (iv) human relations systems. Customer satisfaction and the production of quality products and services have been referred as quality-related outcomes in this model. This model also takes into account the number of individual factors such as values, abilities, and needs affecting the achievement of quality outcomes. A critical aspect of this model is the concept of congruence or fit between individuals and organizations.

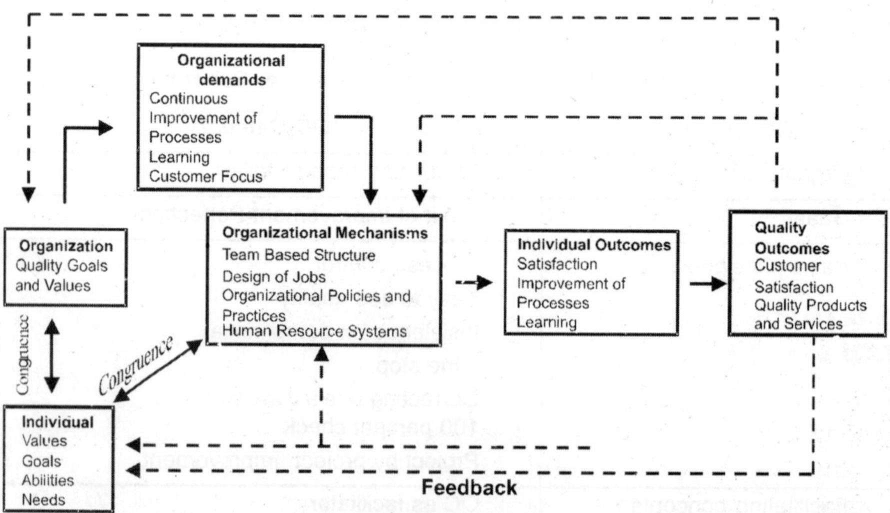

Fig. 2.10: Model of individual and organizational factors affecting quality-related outcomes

2.6.15 Hoffman and Mehra Model for Successful Productivity Improvement Programme

Hoffman and Mehra (1999) proposed a performance/reward-based model to enhance productivity improvement programme (PIP).

This model highlights the importance of top management support for effective implementation of TQM programme. The lack of top management leadership causes improvement programmes like TQM to fail (Connors, 1997). The model is shown in Figure 2.11.

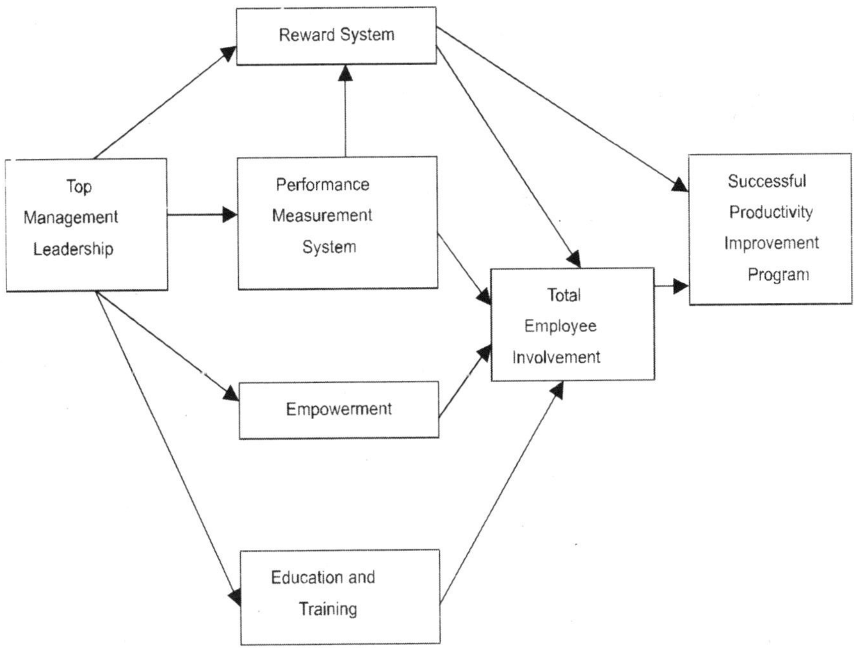

Fig. 2.11: Conceptual model for successful productivity improvement programmes

2.6.16 Pun *et al.* (2000) Synergy Framework Model Among ISO 90[illegible] CQI and TQM

Pun *et al.* (2000) advocated a synergy framework to explain the [illegible] among ISO 9000, continuous quality improvement (CQI) [illegible] quality transformation process. As per their model, th[illegible] competitor performance, internal business strat[illegible] quality costs are often the main CQI forces d[illegible] model has been instrumental for majo[illegible] management efforts in China (Chin *et al.*, 2[illegible] in Figure 2.12.

2.6.17 Yusof and Aspinwal TQM Conceptual Framework Model

Yusof and Aspinwal (2001) proposed TQM implementation framework model as shown in Figure 2.13. This model comprises of three boxes as shown in Figure in 2.13.

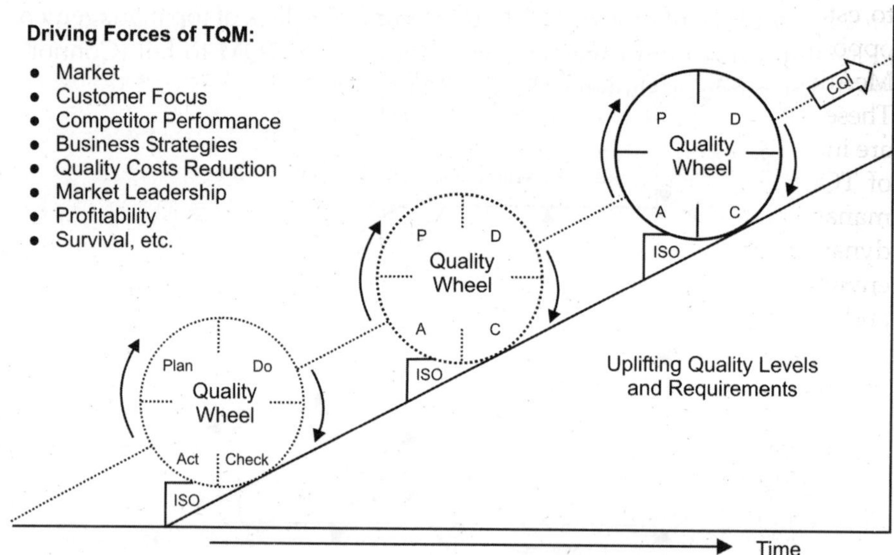

Fig. 2.12: Quality transformation process model

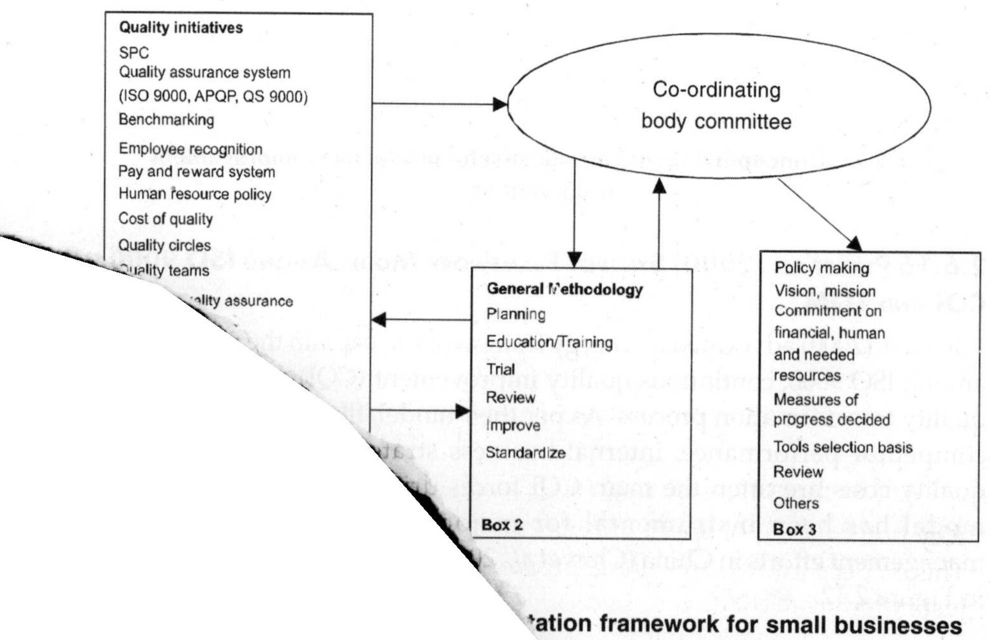

…tation framework for small businesses

2.6.18 Leonard and McAdam (2001) Model

Leonard and McAdam (2001) model has been developed based on the dynamics of TQM development within organizations. This model move beyond the auditing and operational roles of TQM evaluative models, such as business excellence model (BEM), Baldrige and Deming. The objective of this model is to establish the dynamics of TQM development within organizations, as opposed to a static audit at a given point in time (Leonard, 2000). Leonard and McAdam developed a five-model TQM framework as shown in Figure 2.14. These models provide a rich and complex representation of TQM. The models are inter-related. Each model in its own right helps to articulate the dynamics of TQM. The framework is called the strategic dynamics of total quality management framework. This framework provides an overview of TQM dynamics in regard to quality awards, corporate strategy and the wider business environment, including detailed considerations of the selection of quality tools and techniques and the measurement of improvement activities.

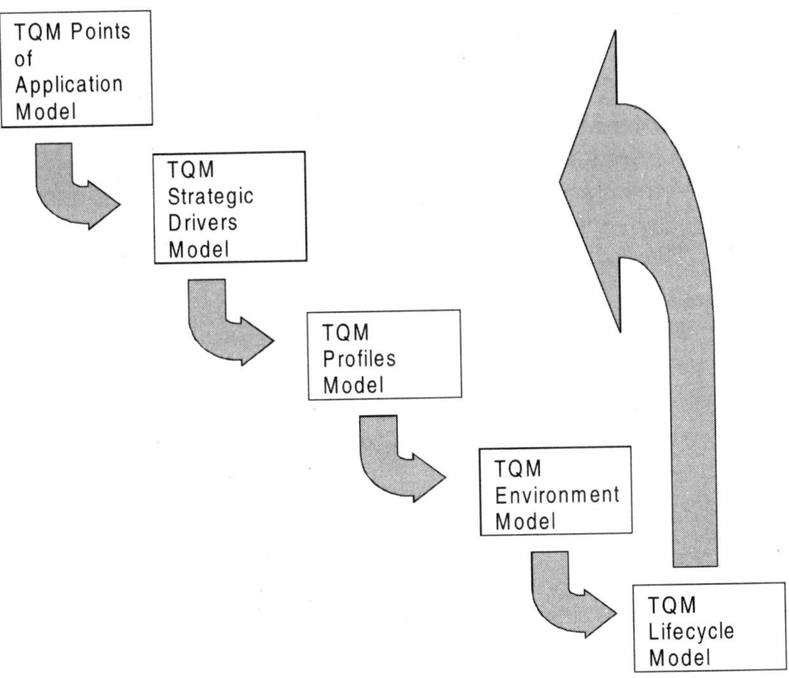

Fig. 2.14: The strategic dynamics of TQM framework

A brief description of each model is given as follows:

Key points of TQM application model

This model shows the resulting implications of the organizations that have just introduced TQM.

Strategic drivers model

The strategic drivers model shows the current positioning and drivers of TQM within the organization. At the strategic level, the strategic drivers are the predominant factors that motivate and influence corporate decision-making.

TQM profiles model

This model is composed of four distinct profiles or scenarios. These are as stated below:

1. In this scenario TQM is not considered a strategic issue, is delegated to middle management at the tactical level and has its greatest application and impact at the operational level.
2. In this case senior managers are aware of TQM's strategic impact potential but these have not been fully implemented.
3. Senior management and staff are committed to TQM and have benefited from its impact but difficulties at the tactical level exist due to communication problems and middle management's negative reaction to change.
4. Represents motivated middle management hampered in their efforts to create impacts from TQM by non committed senior managers, which ultimately limits operational and strategic impacts.

TQM environment model

The TQM environment model shows four key TQM elements involved in relating TQM to an organizational setting. These are: (i) TQM philosophy and culture, (ii) strategy and drivers, (iii) tools and techniques, and (iv) business excellence model and other award models.

TQM lifecycle model

TQM lifecycle shows, a number of tools and techniques or initiatives will always be operating in different stages of achievement or maturity. The TQM lifecycle model is shown in Figure 2.15.

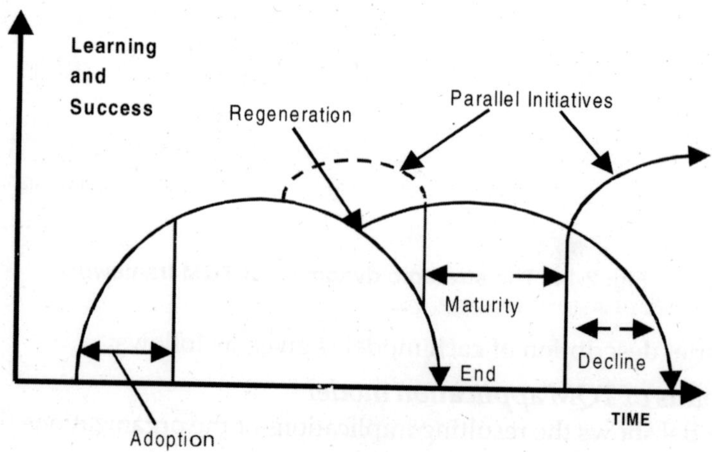

Fig. 2.15: The TQM lifecycle model

The need for the regeneration (updating and continuing) or the ending of these initiatives or techniques is directly and constantly related to the degree to which the corporate strategy is being attained and the degree to which the tools or philosophies are influencing the formation of these strategies. These models provide an accurate picture of the dynamics of TQM as reflected by the practitioner (Buckley and Chapman, 1997).

2.7 INTERNATIONAL QUALITY AWARD MODELS

National Quality Award (NQA) models provide a systematic framework for understanding and implementing TQM. These models have contributed a lot for business excellence in countries like Japan, the USA, Australia and European nations (Mody, 1996; McAdam and O'Neill, 1999; Bester, 2000). These models consider the whole organization and the associated activities. The criteria in the award models are well defined and can be used for self-assessment during TQM journey. There are many definitions of self-assessment and several approaches are deployed to make use of the award models (Conti, 1993; Hillman, 1994). Self-assessment is a cyclic, comprehensive, systematic and regular review of an organization's activities and results against a TQM model and culminates into planned improvement actions (EFQM, 1995).

The Deming Prize, Malcolm Baldrige National Quality Award, Australian Quality Award and European Quality Award represent some major quality award models. In India few NQA Award models are in operation and these award models are also briefly discussed in the next section. The MBNQA criteria, its framework and the weightage structure have been continuously evolving. The main objectives of NQA model as perceived are given below (Van der Wiele *et al.,* 1996a):

- To help stimulate organizations to improve quality of their products/ services.
- To recognize the achievement of organizations which attain commanding heights for their product quality, and are a source of inspiration to others.
- To act as a motivator for organizational learning and to provide guidelines for initiating quality improvement.
- To act as a driving force for a national movement of quality improvement for turnaround.
- To create a focus on the TQM model portrayed by the award criteria.

Van der Wiele *et al.*(1996a) identified five most important steps for the successful implementation of self-assessment process. These steps have been identified as:

1. Business unit should develop an improvement plan.
2. Outcomes of the self-assessment should be linked to the business planning process.
3. Assessors should present their written findings to the management team of the business unit.
4. Senior management should monitor improvement targets.
5. Management team of the business unit should present its improvement plans to senior management.

Pannirselvam and Ferguson (2001) stated that a number of common measures exist between the MBNQA model and the other models; however, substantial differences exist between these models. They further stated that the MBNQA model is more comprehensive and less prescriptive than the other models. In most of the existing award models, companies are assessed on their approaches, the depth of deployment in their approaches, and performance results associated with operations, quality, and customer satisfaction (EFQM, 1999a; NIST, 1999). Samuelsson and Nilsson (2002) claimed that self-assessment must in itself be considered from a holistic perspective to yield maximum results. Few important award models are briefly reviewed in the following sub sections.

2.7.1 Deming Prize Model

The Deming Prize was established in 1951 by the Union of Japanese Scientists and Engineers (JUSE) to commemorate Deming's contribution to Japanese industry and to promote further the development of quality revolution in Japan. The Deming Prize model proved to be an effective tool for spreading quality awareness throughout Japan. Deming Prize model gives equal weightages to each factor and is not a competitive prize. The aim of the award is to find out how well a company implements total quality control (TQC) by assessing its quality assurance policies and activities, and the results achieved (quality improvement, productivity improvement, cost reduction, expanded sales, increased profits, etc.) through the application of statistical techniques and quality circles. Deming Prize criteria are: policies, organization and its operations, education and dissemination, information gathering, communications and utilization, analysis, standardization, control/management, quality assurance and effects and future plans.

2.7.2 Malcolm Baldrige National Quality Award (MBNQA)

MBNQA model was initiated in 1987 to promote TQM in the USA. The award recognizes small and large service and manufacturing organizations. The MBNQA award is given to those American organizations that demonstrate exemplary performance in both, the way they run their business and in the quality of their products and/or services. The criteria recognizes the crucial role of top management in creating goals, values and systems. The National Institute of Standards and Technology (NIST), a division of the Department of Commerce administers the award. However, volunteer examiners do all evaluations and determination of award. The core values are contained in the seven categories for the assessment. The points assigned to each category indicate priorities. These point values have been periodically revised, since the award was first established. The MBNQA criteria implicitly assume that higher customer satisfaction translates into improved market share and profitability hence provides more weightage to customer satisfaction. Pannirselvam and Ferguson (2001) stated that organizations that aim at being world-class must focus on instilling a few core values such as good leadership, customer focus, respect for employees, and continuous improvement. They recommended MBNQA model should be used to achieve the world-class status. Hill (1993) reported that there is much doubt about the effectiveness of these programmes. He drew this conclusion based on organizations where TQM seemed to have failed. The Wallace Company is one example, where winning the Baldridge Award was followed by near bankruptcy the next year. Xerox (1993) disclosed the application submitted for the MBNQA, which they won. It includes the lessons learned from the Xerox quality journey over 15 years.

Brown (1994, 1997) found that there is substantial evidence that following the award model makes a company successful in the long run. Steeples (1993) and Brown (1994) stated that the biggest benefit of the Baldridge model is that organizations have a common framework for understanding and implementing various TQM theories, tools, and approaches. Main (1990), Garvin (1991), Hart (1993) and Moore (1995) reported that the use of self-assessment technique against MBNQA criteria has become a powerful TQM tool in American organizations. Lee and Quazi, (2001) and Kanda *et al.* (2002) have provided Baldrige Award criteria framework with relative weights and dynamic relationships as shown in Figure 2.16. The percentage of weight to each aspect is also shown in this figure.

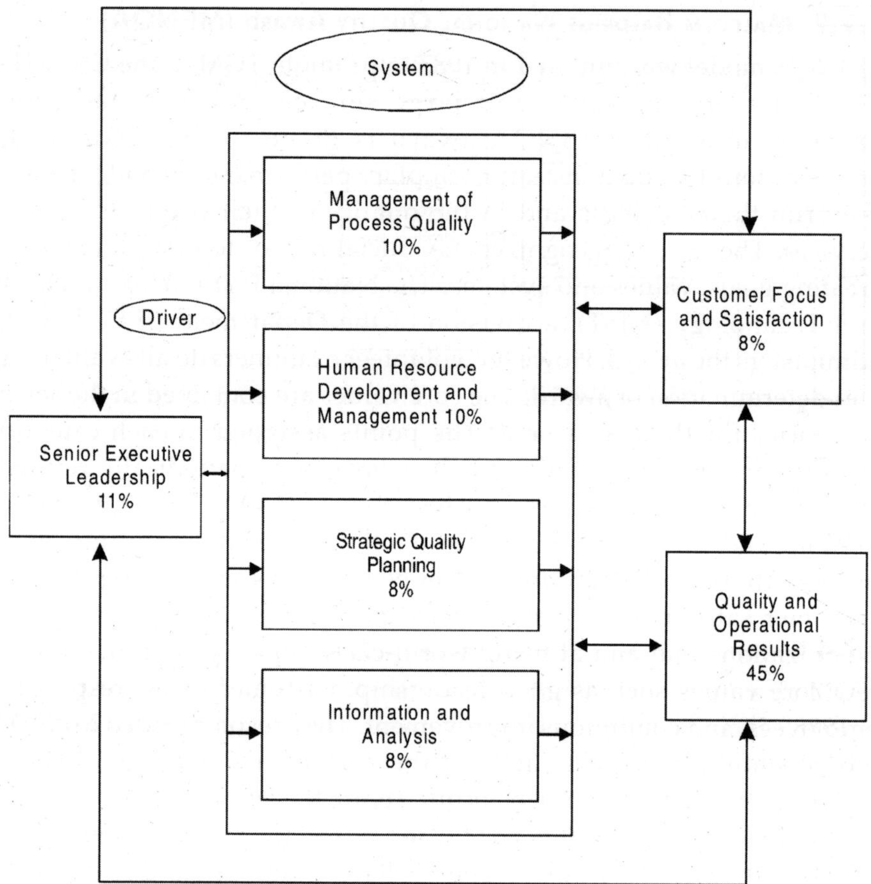

Fig. 2.16: Malcolm Baldrige Quality Award criteria framework

2.7.3 Australian Quality Award (AQA) Model

The Australian Quality Award (AQA) is given to encourage organizations to improve product quality, raise their performance to world-class level, and to provide a benchmark. AQA award is not a competitive award, as there are no restrictions on the number of prizes like Deming prize. The AQA model is based on a premise that quality improvement requires an enlightened and influential leadership which drives quality movement forward and nurtures an innovative and creative workforce capable of meeting customers' expectations (Abby and Hong, 1996). The award framework is shown in Figure 2.17. The respective weights of each criterion are also shown in this figure.

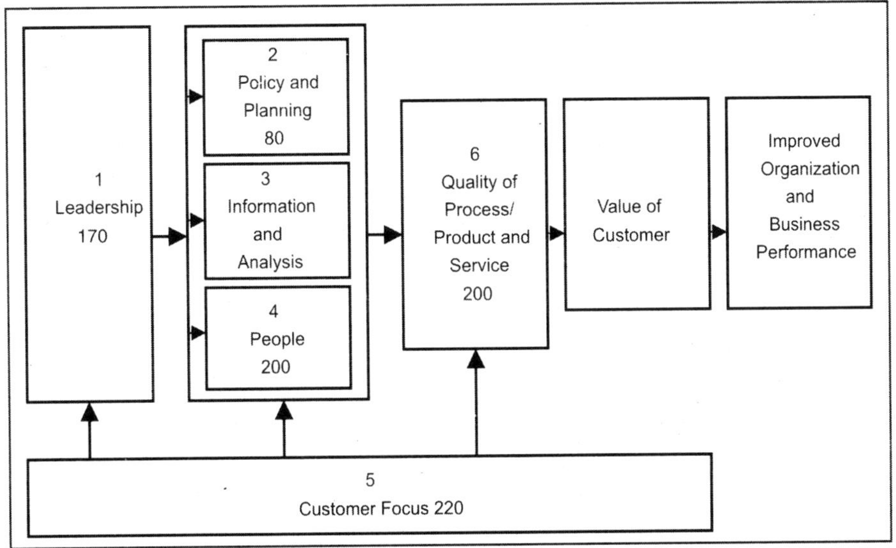

Fig. 2.17: Australian Quality Award framework

2.7.4 European Quality Award (EQA) Model

EFQM (European Foundation for Quality Management) was established in 1988 with the support of the European Commission to promote outstanding performance in European organizations. The EFQM excellence model is a non-prescriptive framework based on nine criteria. Five of these are 'enablers' and four are 'results'. The 'enablers' criteria cover what an organization does. The 'results' criteria cover what an organization achieves. 'Results' are caused by 'enablers'.

Since its launch, the business excellence model (BEM) has become increasingly well established amongst European organizations as a diagnostic tool, and many countries in Europe have based their national quality award on the BEM framework and criteria (Porter *et al.,* 1998). The award framework is shown in Figure 2.18. The percent of weight to each aspect is also shown in this figure.

2.7.5 Elcina Quality Awards

The Elcina Quality Award criteria has been revised to be in line with quality management process model contained in the proposed ISO 9000:2000 series of standards. The checklist largely includes the aspects outlined in the above standards, particularly ISO 9004:2000 (Draft) (Kanda *et al.,* 2002). The details are shown in Table 2.9.

To qualify for consideration for the Elcina quality awards, the organizations should be compulsory at the maturity level 3 tending towards 4, which is possible to be determined by the marking/weightage scheme proposed below in Table 2.10.

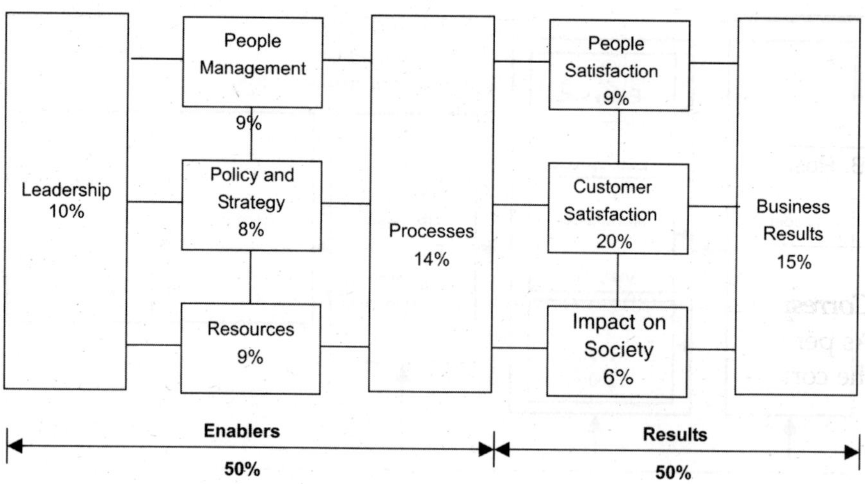

Fig. 2.18: The European Quality Award framework (Business Excellence Model)

Table 2.9: ISO 9004:2000 (Draft) used in the criteria

Maturity Level	*Performance Level*	*Guidance*
1	No formal approach	No systematic approach evident; no results or unpredictable results.
2	Reactive approach	Problem or prevention based systematic approach; minimum data on improvement result available.
3	Stable formal system approach	Systematic process-based approach and early stage of systematic improvements; data available on conformance to objectives and existence of improvement trends.
4	Continual improvement emphasized	Improvements process in use; good results and sustained improvement.
5	Best-in-class performance	Strongly integrated improvement process; best-in-class benchmarked results demonstrated.

Table 2.10: Marking/weightage scheme

Aspects	*Criteria*	*Weightage*
A. Enablers/ Mechanism	(01) Leadership & Management Commitment	20

Contd...

	(02) Resource management (03) Product realization (04) Measurement analysis and improvement	15 15 15
B. Results	(05) Product Quality (06) Customer/stakeholder satisfaction (07) Business results	10 10 15

Correspondence between maturity levels and making/weightage scheme

As per the characteristics/features identified for different maturity levels, the corresponding marking/weightage are as follows:

Maturity level	*Marking/weightage*
Level 1	25
Level 2	50
Level 3	70
Level 4	80
Level 5	80-100

An organization has to secure a minimum of 70 marks to be eligible for consideration of Elcina quality award.

2.8 QUALITY AWARD MODELS IN INDIA

2.8.1 Rajiv Gandhi National Quality Award (RGNQA)

Rajiv Gandhi National Quality Award (RGNQA) model has been instituted by the Bureau of Indian Standards in 1991, with a view to encourage Indian companies to strive for excellence and giving special recognition to those who are considered to be the leaders of quality movement in India. Rajiv Gandhi National Quality Award helps the Indian industry to improve quality by:

- Encouraging the Indian industry to make significant improvements in quality for maximizing consumer satisfaction and for successfully facing competition in the global market.
- Recognizing the achievements of those organizations, which have improved the quality of their products and services and thereby set an example for others.
- Establishing guidelines and criteria that can be used by industry in evaluating their own quality improvement efforts; and
- Providing specific guidance to other organizations that wish to learn how to achieve excellence in quality, by making available detailed information on the 'Quality Management Approach' adopted by award winning organizations to change their cultures and achieve eminence.

2.8.2 CII-EXIM Award for Business Excellence Model

CII-EXIM Award for Business Excellence was established in 1994 by the Confederation of Indian Industries (CII) to promote business excellence. This award is an effort of collaboration between EXIM bank and CII. The CII-EXIM model for business excellence is an accepted criterion for measuring the integration of TQM as a business strategy. In brief, a TQM practicing company must provide:

- World class products to satisfy its customers and users, which are competitive in price, quality and delivery performance
- A work culture which makes it the most loved organization amongst its people
- A high shareholder value
- New products are developed faster and cheaper than the competitors to improve the standard of living of people.

2.8.3 Golden Peacock National Quality Award (GPNQA) Model

The GPNQA was instituted by Institute of Directors in 1991. Awards are conferred annually to recognize Indian companies for excellence and to encourage total quality improvement. Both manufacturing and service sector organizations in India including public and private undertakings, all sectors of industry and commerce, government and semi-government departments, trade and professional associations and educational, service and research establishments are included. The GPNQA stimulates and helps organizations to rapidly accelerate the pace of a customer-oriented improvement processes.

2.8.4 IMC Ramakrishna Bajaj National Quality Award

The Indian Merchants Chamber (IMC) instituted "IMC Ramakrishna Bajaj National Quality Award" in 1995, with the aim to promote quality standards, both in processes and product, among Indian organizations, and to make them achieve global standards. The Malcolm Baldrige Award criteria have been customized to suit Indian conditions with special focus on exports, innovation, environment and safety. Award framework of IMC Ramakrishna Bajaj National Quality Award is provided in Figure 2.19 (Kanda *et al.*, 2002).

2.8.5 MAIT Quality Recognition Programme

The Manufacturers Association of Information Technologies (MAIT) quality recognition programme has been initiated with the aim to give an impetus to the quality movement in the Indian IT industry and to facilitate members to achieve significant progress in this area (MAIT Publication, 1998). The model is based on EQA award model.

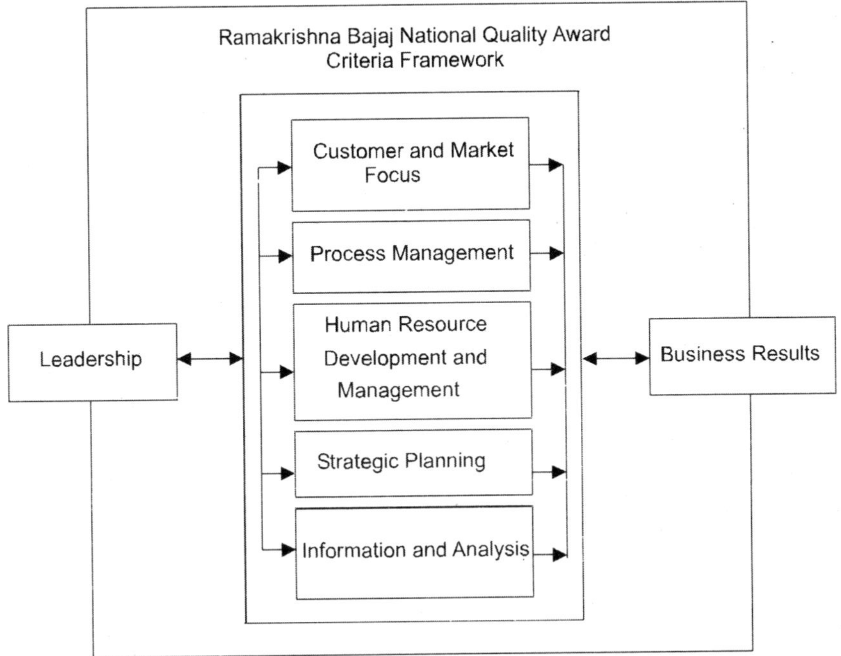

Fig. 2.19: IMC Ramakrishna Bajaj National Quality Award

2.8.6 Tata Business Excellence Model

The genesis of TBEM (Tata Business Excellence Model) started in 1994 with a need for making processes and practices customer-centric, focus on agility, performance standards. The award framework is shown in Figure 2.20.

2.8.7 Agrawal and Vrat Business Excellence Model

This model has been developed by Agrawal during his doctoral research under Prof. Vrat's supervision and is based on MBNQA in the year 1999 after considering Indian socio-cultural value system and work culture. This model is an outcome of research and not being practiced as yet. The model incorporates seven enablers of business performance and five result areas. The details of the model and weightages are shown in Figure 2.21.

2.9 STUDIES ON QUALITY PRACTICES IN INDIA

Sink (1991a) stated that TQM efforts can be successful only if the leadership of the organization evolves the operational definition for the organizational system and it is crystallized and communicated with conviction and clarity. The study carried out by Singh (1991) revealed that very few companies

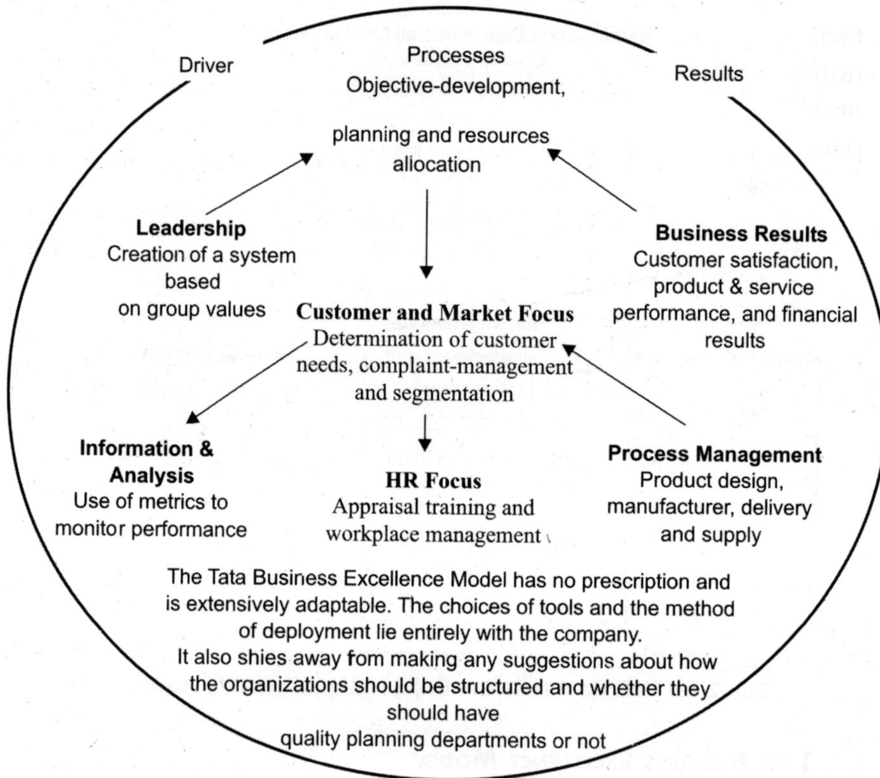

Fig. 2.20: Tata Business Excellence Model

were adopting TQM practices in India. Kasul and Motwani (1996) identified critical factors and supporting performance measurements of TQM in manufacturing environment.

Chakarvarty (1994) stated that one needs quality mindset to achieve total quality. His report disapproved the existing approaches of TQM practices in India. Business Today (1995) reported the survey conducted by CII. This survey indicated the present scenario of TQM in India. The survey provided information on some of the common problems to implement TQM. The reasons for these problems have been identified as: lack of commitment by top management, lack of TQM strategy, lack of training and TQM skills, lack of updated technology and lack of desired motivation level in employees. Mohanty (1995) presented a number of Indian examples, where TQM has been implemented. He has identified the reasons for the relative success/failure of many TQM programmes. Mohanty and Lakhe (1998) identified 18 critical success factors for TQM implementation based on survey of the Indian industry. These 18 critical factors are organized around four significant factors and incorporate holistic paradigm of TQM. These factors are (i) proactive business orientation, (ii) internal support, (iii) competitive assessment and (iv) participatory orientation.

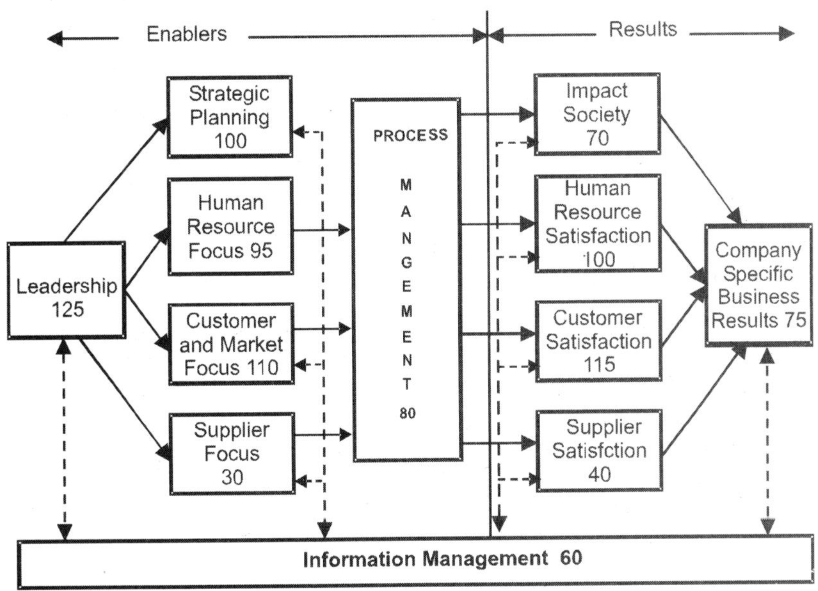

Fig. 2.21: Framework for Business Excellence Model suggested by Agrawal (1999)

Motwani *et al.* (1994) conducted a study to identify the degree to which quality management practices were present in the Indian manufacturing organizations. According to a survey conducted by CII among ISO 9000 certified companies, 54 percent of 330 respondents stated that there had been an improvement in their product and process quality after obtaining certification (Business Today, 1995). A study by Philipose and Venkateswarlu (1980) indicated that only 24 percent of the organizations use some type of sampling plans. Indian organizations appreciated the necessity of effective leadership, customer focus, fast-response, proactive organizational culture, and employee involvement and development to achieve excellence (Ahluwalia, 1993).

Maheshwari and Zhao (1994) also assessed the status of quality management practices in India. The results of their study showed that the majority of the Indian companies are well aware of the modern quality management concepts and philosophies. Sharma (1997) presented an overview of TQM implementation in the Indian engineering industry. Agrawal (1999) developed a business excellence model for the Indian organizations based on MBNQA. A pilot study has been carried out by Kumar *et al.* (1999) to study the status of TQM implementation in India.

Malliga and Jayabalan (1999) considered ISO 9000 as a marketing tool and key to the European market. Rao *et al.* (1997) conducted a study to identify the triggers for quality management programmes in the Indian industries. The study showed that the main triggers for initiation of quality management programmes are due to increased competition (52%), demanding customers (43%), the need to reduce costs (31%) and survival of the company (16%). Ahluwalia (1996) provided a compendium of papers by Indian experts during 6th World Congress on Total Quality. Gondhalekar *et al.* (1995) identified seven input variables, which are significant for steering TQM mission in the Indian organizations. They stated these as: (i) cadre of the individual (higher the better), (ii) age (between 30 and 50 is better than extreme age), (iii) recognition, (iv) type of work, (v) educational level (higher the better), (vi) communication ability (better communicators give more Kaizens), and (vii) reading habits (good readers give more Kaizens).

Shah (1999) described TQM as a modern management philosophy and a journey, not a destination, and implementation of TQM requires unwavering commitment of the organizational people, substantial time and effort and sweeping changes in organizational culture, attitudes and business practices. Ramamurthy (1999) suggested the following linking will help achieving the strategic quality management (SQM): regular exploitation of human knowledge, constant learning from failures, continuous customer feedback, monitoring of quality system, small group activity, quality circles, value engineering, industrial engineering and suggestion schemes. Arora (1999) and Khanna (1999) described the increased interdependence of buyers and suppliers have brought into focus the importance of quality. Lakhe and Mohanty (1994) based on their study identified four approaches for TQM implementation. These are: (i) development of a vision, (ii) policy promotion on quality, (iii) creating a total quality-oriented culture, and (iv) training and education.

Maheshwari and Zhao (1994) conducted a survey of 42 Indian company executives to examine quality-management practices in India. They found that the majority of the Indian companies are well aware of the modern quality management concepts and philosophies, and company executives believe that they are doing a good job of providing high-quality products or services to their customers. Sharma (1997) reported that many Indian organizations began to implement TQM programmes since 1991 onwards, but India still lacks effective TQM systems and application at the enterprise level. According to Malliga and Jayabalan (1999), 77% of the ISO 9000 surveyed organizations in India felt positive about quality awareness and TQM implementation. The country's product quality as a whole still needs improvement. Quality has been perceived as 6.2 on a scale of 0 to 10 in a recent survey carried out by Business Today-IMC survey of consumers in 5 select cities of India (Business Today, 2000).

According to Kumar and Garg (2002) study in the Indian organizations, 75% of the automobile, 83% of poly. prod., 78% electronics and 33% institutions are following TQM. During their study they considered six main factors, which have a vital role in TQM implementation. These six factors are: (i) top management leadership and commitment, (ii) continuous improvement (Kaizen), (iii) customer focus and satisfaction, (iv) education and training, (v) statistical process control, and (vi) quality awards. Aravindan *et al.* (1996) identified five phases for the implementation of strategic quality management (SQM). Joseph *et al.* (1999) identified nine critical success factors for TQM implementation in the Indian organizations as: (i) organizational commitment, (ii) human resources management, (iii) supplier integration, (iv) quality policy, (v) role of quality department, (vi) quality information systems, (vii) technology utilization, (viii) operating procedures, and (ix) training.

Lakhe and Tidke (1991) study indicated that most of the Indian organizations are handicapped in implementing TQM due to the following reasons:

- Lack of employee involvement and participation in quality improvement efforts.
- Lack of management commitment and motivation.
- Perception that quality is an optional extra and not a necessity for development.
- Traditional belief that "quality costs money".

Lakhe and Mohanty (1994) outlined the attributes and approaches of customers and business towards quality in different national settings. This is given in Table 2.11.

2.10 QUALITY PRACTICES IN OTHER COUNTRIES

Various authors have shared their experience in quality field to provide contemporary quality practices. These provide insights into quality problems and suggest solution followed by the authors or their peers in solving these problems.

Garvin (1986) conducted a systematic study on real-life quality improvement projects in the USA and Japan, and came out with a set of critical factors. Saraph *et al.* (1989) made an attempt to develop an instrument for measuring the critical success factors (CSFs) of quality management. Hunt (1990) introduced the principles and methods for implementing a TQM system in government. Dale *et al.* (1990) identified six different levels of TQM adoption in organizations, and termed them as (i) uncommitted, (ii) drifters, (iii) tool-pushers, (iv) improvers, (v) award winners, and (vi) world class.

Benson *et al.* (1991) proposed a systems model of quality management, and first used the organization theory to explain the fundamentals of quality management. Little *et al.* (1992) studied TQM programs in organizations and came to the conclusion that the best results could be reached with TQM programmes, which were focused on the key business processes, and not the programmes with broad training activities for all the employees. Choong (1991) discussed successful adoption of Japanese management techniques in Korean industries.

Katsuya (1992) summarized the basics for TQC implementation as: the quality attitude, point of view, and promotion. He further suggested five key words for the effective implementation of TQC as: (i) fact-based management, (ii) process control, (iii) QFD, (iv) cross-functional management, and (v) QC audit. Goldratt and Cox (1992) detailed out global principles of manufacturing. These can be used to understand the creation and acceptance of improvements—change for the better. Carr and Littman (1993) gave examples of how federal, state and local governments can use TQM methods for better service and enhanced performance levels. Srikanth and Cavallaro (1993) provided a hands-on-tool for implementing improvement processes. Greene (1993) showed how to co-ordinate and manage the implementation of several different quality systems simultaneously. He presented 20 successful global approaches for achieving total quality and to remain competitive. Collins (1994) provided insight on how American organizations became competitive, based on top management commitment to quality.

An Ugboro and Obeng (2000) empirical study revealed that there is a positive correlation between top management leadership, employee empowerment, job satisfaction, and customer satisfaction. Atkinson *et al.* (1994) laid out a road map to link quality initiatives with increased profitability and competitiveness. Flynn *et al.* (1994) opined that very little empirical research focuses specially on quality management practices, despite the prevalence of TQM in the literature. Lam (1996) conducted a research study in Hong Kong-based organizations. This research suggested that different organizations have adopted different objectives for TQM. Boland and Silbergh (1996) said that the quality management framework is incomplete without appropriate resource management process and administrative structure.

Table 2.11: Perception of customers and business approaches towards quality (Based on Lakhe and Mohanty, 1994)

Nation	***Consumer's view about quality***		***Approaches of business towards quality***	
	Quality determined by	Decision to buy product determined by	Quality promotion activity aims at	Emphasis for achieving quality
U.S.A.	Well known name Word of mouth Past experience	Price Quality Performance	Use of SQC Administration of QC system Selling Quality consciousness	Use of process simplification techniques Customer satisfaction in strategic planning Quality performance as criterion for compensating senior management
Japan	Well known name Performance Ease of use	Performance Price Ease of use	Motivating people Improving skills Providing better jobs	Incorporating customer expectations in design of products and services. Employee participation in regularly scheduled meeting about quality. Customer satisfaction in strategic planning Process simplification and cycle time reduction.
Europe	Price Well known name	Price Quality itself	Comprehensive quality Improvement Education Use of measurement systems	Incorporating customer expectations in design of new products and services. Past performance as criterion for compensating senior management
Developing nations like India	Price Well known name Appearance	Price Appearance World of mouth	Inspection and measurement Promoting brand name	Use of technologies to meet customer expectations Use of process simplification and cycle time reduction

Leonard *et al.* (2002) opined that existing quality models mainly emphasize the operational level improvements attributed to TQM. However, there is lack of representation of TQM at the strategic formulation level. Thus, the representation of TQM in these models is limited and will ultimately lead to limited organization applications and ultimately, business results. Terziovski and Samson (1999) conducted a research study in the manufacturing sector of Australia and New Zealand. Their findings are that organizations that are using TQM are more likely to achieve better performance in employee relations, customer satisfaction, operational performance and business performance. These conclusions are supported by Sun (2000) who found that "TQM criteria such as quality leadership, human resource development, quality information etc. contribute to the improvement of customer satisfaction and business performance".

In terms of the evaluation of TQM, Liburd and Zairi (2001) have suggested that over the last decade the focus of management has moved from an introspective emphasis that was product oriented, through service and then customer orientation to a market-oriented focus. Appleby and Mitchell (2000) while comparing organizations with good performance concluded that there are no shortcuts for the organizations to be successful on the long-term basis. Adam *et al.* (1997) reviewed Malcolm Baldrige Award winners (NIST, 1995) and emphasized the fact that different companies built outstanding quality improvement systems by utilizing different quality management approaches.

Powell (1995) conducted a research study in United States organizations to establish relationship between TQM and organization performance. His empirical results concluded that TQM could produce competitive advantage. Reed *et al.* (1996) emphasized that TQM philosophy generates a market advantage, enhancing product design efficiency, boosting product reliability, and increasing process efficiency. Puffer and McCarthy (1996) provided a framework for leadership in a TQM context.

Curkovic and Pagell (1999) cautioned that ISO 9000 registration could result in non-value-added costs if it is pursued only for its marketing appeal. Choi and Behling (1997) pointed out from the result of McKinsey and Company that TQM implementation had dropped from 86 percent to 63 percent. The study showed that this happened because reductions in defect rates were not realized. Lawler *et al.* (1992) reported their research findings that TQM had been adopted by as many as 77% of large U.S. organizations as a means of restoring their diminishing competitive advantages. 63% of the CEO's of the Fortune 1000 organizations believed that employee involvement in TQM is positively associated with worker satisfaction and quality of work life. Kassiciech and Yourstone (1998) reported that removing barriers to improvement is essential for TQM to work effectively in an organization. A significant barrier to improvement is a lack of communication throughout the organization.

Clinton *et al.* (1994) suggested three areas of training that are basic to TQM implementation: (i) instruction in the philosophy and principles of TQM, (ii) specific skills training such as in the use of statistical process control, and (iii) interpersonal skills training to improve team problem-solving abilities. On the basis of four years of experience as an examiner for the MBNQA, Easton (1993) reported that in the best quality companies, employees receive 40 to 80 hours of training per year with training expenditures around 3-5% of payroll. Ernst and Young and American Quality Foundation (1991) conducted a study in four developed nations i.e. the USA, Canada, Germany and Japan. During the study, it was found that strategic quality planning had significant effects on organizational performance measures.

Port *et al.* (1992) reported based on their study that the TQM practices have resulted in a 38% decrease in customer complaints at Xerox, an 80% reduction in defects at Motorola, decreased turnaround time for refunds in the State of Wisconsin, substantial cost savings at the University of Michigan hospital, and reduced purchasing costs in the U.S. Navy. Garvare and Wiklund (1997) reported that many small and medium sized enterprises (SME's) are still dealing with considerable costs due to poor quality.

Peters (1987) and Senge (1990) emphasized in their research work regarding the importance and need for setting a clear and realistic vision in the process of formulating certain strategy for an organization. Maslen (1996) also explained that the method for creating a manufacturing vision consisted of four main steps: (i) generate ideas, (ii) cluster ideas, (iii) refine vision, and (iv) prioritize vision. Ahmed *et al.* (1998) defined innovation as the process by which an organization builds insights about its major functions (customers, suppliers, employees and other stakeholders) and identifies potential opportunities in the market (local, national or global).

Ahmed (2002) proposed the framework, which consists of a number of critical and strategic functions for any organization. He identified these functions as: purpose, business values, mission statements, individuals' knowledge, the learning process, information system, innovation, resources utilization, reward schemes, benchmarking, stakeholders' relationships, leadership and performance measures. Golhar *et al.* (1996) investigated the differences in TQM practices and performance of TQM organizations versus non-TQM organizations in an empirical study. Zink and Schmidt (1998) stated that self-assessment has become an important management technique for continuously improving the overall business performance. Povey (1996) stated that an approach to self-assessment must consider the organization's maturity and culture, and must be correctly positioned as a part of an overall management process. He stressed the need to select the criteria of the framework relevant to the organization. By contrast, EFQM (1999b) claims that its model can be applied in all organizations.

When an approach has been designed and a plan has been established, it is crucial that there is strong commitment among middle and top management for the implementation of self-assessment (Thiagarajan and Zairi, 1998; Van der Wiele *et al.*, 1996a; Hillman, 1994). Training of key management and in-house facilitators should be one of the organization's first priorities when implementing self-assessment (Laszlo, 1999; Rao *et al.*, 1996; Van der Wiele and Brown, 1999). A critical phase of self-assessment is the establishment of an improvement plan that must be presented to higher management, linked to business planning, and then communicated to the whole organization (EFQM, 1999b; Van der Wiele and Brown, 1999; Reed and Shergold, 1996). Much too often, organizations fail to do this, and consequently, self-assessment activities do not lead to lasting improvements (Povey, 1996). It is also vital to ensure that monitoring and implementation of actions become a natural part of the business review process and not a separate activity (Zink and Schmidt 1998; Povey, 1996; Van der Wiele *et al.*, 1996a).

Kristensen and Juhl, (1999) and Kristensen *et al.* (2000) empirically verified that the application of holistic management models such as the EFQM excellence model has a positive effect on corporate performance. Eskildsen *et al.* (2001) conducted a research study in Danish companies regarding the weights structure of the EFQM excellence model. The findings of their research was that 70 percent should constitute enabler points and 30 percent should constitute result points for achieving better performance in Danish organizations. Van der Wiele *et al.* (2000) have found during their study that self-assessment generally lead to better agreement on the organization's strengths and improvement opportunities and better planning. Meyers and Heller (1995), Markels (1999) and Prybutok and Spink (1999) suggested that Baldrige award-based self-assessment leads to organizational change—stemming from managerial actions to improve management processes and practices.

Lascelles and Peacock (1996), Porter and Tanner (1998), and Van der Wiele *et al.* (1996a) reported based on their study that most of the organizations face problem of accuracy and consistency in scoring during self-assessment and same concern has been shown by the other researchers (Conti, 1994; Fuchs and Stuntebeck, 1994; Jernberg *et al.*, 1994; Martellani, 1994).

A majority of the academic literature on self-assessment has concentrated on the main quality/excellence award model and comparison of their criteria, and the relationship between award winners and business results (Cole, 1991; Nokhai and Newes, 1994; Wisner and Eakins, 1994; Easton and Jarrell, 1998; Schmidt and Zink, 1998). Other work has concentrated on the self-assessment process with respect to issues such as deciding the assessment approach, management of the process, resources required and selecting performance measures (e.g. Bemowski and Stratton, 1995; Coulambidou and Dale, 1995; Teo and Dale, 1997; Ritchie and Dale, 2000). In the Malcolm Baldrige conceptual framework, top management support is the driver of the quality management process in organizations (Steeples, 1993). Hendricks and Singhal (1997) and Wisner and Eakins (1994) examined the financial performance of Baldrige quality award winning companies and concluded that these companies are strongly correlated to high achievements in financial parameters.

Yang *et al.* (2001) and Ahmed *et al.* (2003) advocated the use of the evidential reasoning (ER) approach and multiple attribute decision making (MADM) in the self-assessment process against the criteria of the EFQM excellence model to help minimize the scoring variation amongst members of the team. They emphasized that a MADM model requires a generalized set of evaluation grades before an assessment can be undertaken. They established five evaluation grades as (i) world-class, (ii) award winners, (iii) improvers, (iv) drifters, and (v) uncommitted, based on the work of Dale and Lascelles (1997); Dale and Smith (1997). Yang and Xu (1999) developed a intelligent decision system (IDS) software on the basis of the ER approval to facilitate the calculations during self-assessment. This software can be used by an organization to keep track of its progress over a period of time. Conti (1997) stated that the organizations that are trying to stay in competitive world are focusing on enabler criteria to improve the performance rather then focusing on the result criteria.

Siow *et al.* (2001) provided the evaluation grade to judge the current performance of the organization to create a business improvement plan. The evaluation grades developed by them are (i) world-class, (ii) award winners, (iii) improvers, (iv) drifters, and (v) uncommitted. Chin and Pun (2002) provided self-assessment scoring scheme based on the work done by Chin *et al.* (2000). The evaluations grades developed by them are (i) achiever, (ii) improver, (iii) initiator, (iv) uncommitted, and (v) unaware.

During the period of 1992 to 1997, several authors presented the argument that the decline in applications for the MBNQA indicated a decline in interest in quality and in the award (Grossman, 1994; Marsh, 1994; Ettorre, 1996; Gradig and Harris, 1994). NIST (1999) argued that the number of applicants for the MBNQA is not an indicator of overall interest in quality or the award programme.

Flynn *et al.* (1995) conducted a comprehensive study on quality practices, quality management infrastructures, and performance based on a survey of US plants in the machinery, electronics and transportation industries. Their study indicates that top management support and supplier relationship had a direct effect on the performance of the product design process. Adam *et al.* (1997) conducted cross-cultural quality management research on the effect of quality practices on quality and financial performance. They grouped 52 quality practices into nine factors. Their research measured the relationships among each of these nine factors, and their effect on quality measures and financial measures. The results of this study indicate that although all nine factors affected the quality performance measures, the activities that most influenced the outcome were in the top management domain.

Dow *et al.* (1999) conducted a survey consisting of a large, random sample of manufacturing sites to identify the primary dimensions of quality management and investigate the relationship between quality practices and quality outcomes. The results indicate that the practices can be divided into nine dimensions. Of these dimensions, workforce commitment, shared vision and customer focus combine to yield a positive correlation with quality outcomes. The other dimensions of benchmarking, use of teams, personnel training, advanced manufacturing systems, just-in-time principles and co-operative supplier relations do not relate to quality outcomes.

Yong and Wilkinson (2001) reported the findings based on the survey of quality management practices in Singapore companies. They summarized their findings that it takes 15 years to change the company's culture from inspection-based to quality assurance-based, and it will probably be equally long for the company to evolve from a quality assurance orientation towards a holistic approach to quality management.

Ahmed (2002) provided a model depicting seven typical life-stages of a manufacturing business organization. He referred these as: (i) *an infant cluster*: this is usually a brand new start-up by an individual or a group of founder members with very limited business procedures and guidelines, (ii) *the pioneer cluster*: this is a typical small but fast-growing business dependent on the strength of the individual or group of managers driving it, (iii) *the rational cluster*: this is a business which has outgrown its initiators and become independent, bigger and more complex, (iv) *the established cluster*: this is a well-set-up business with standard and formal procedures being practised, (v) *the wilderness cluster*: this is an organization that has lost its way and become out of touch, (vi) *the dying cluster*: this is an organization that is failing and moving towards bankruptcy, and (vii) *the transforming cluster*: this is an organization that has decided that it need not die and has found a new purpose, new identify and new life.

Fenghueih (1998) proved that implementing ISO with the TQM spirit of continuous improvement and company-wide employee participation results in significant benefits for small and medium sized enterprises. Douglas *et al.* (1999) proved through a case study that ISO 9000 benefits could only be achieved if the motives for certification are true and internal and it is part of an overall quality strategy. Withers and Ebrahimpour (2000) proved that quality, as reflected by its eight dimensions, improves as a result of ISO 9000 implementation, but the degree to which it can be improved is influenced by the reasons for seeking implementation. Also Sun (1999), based on the results of an empirical survey in Norway, suggested that in the future, ISO 9000 standards should be part of a TQM programme.

Lu and Sohal (1993) discussed the factors, which contribute to the success in a TQM program and identified improvement opportunities in the approaches adopted by Australian organizations. Capon *et al.* (1996) provided empirical evidence in their research that measuring and displaying results increases the chance of success in a TQM program. Their work was carried out in one of the industries of UK by forming different teams and checking the effects of such monitors.

Shortcomings of TQM and the reasons for its failure can be attributed to implementation problems or a disregard for contextual factors (Sitkin *et al.*, 1994; Roger *et al.*, 1994). Reasons for failure to implement a quality program may include a mismatch of organizational culture (Kekale and Kekale, 1995), a lack of management leadership and inadequate training (Doyle, 1992). Sila and Ebrahimpour (2002) analyzed 347 survey articles on TQM published between 1989 and 2000. Their findings reveal that the most frequently covered TQM factors are customer focus and satisfaction, employee training, leadership and top management commitment, employee involvement, continuous improvement and innovation, and quality information and performance measurement.

The study by Saraph *et al.* (1989) has used data collected from 162 general managers and quality managers from 20 companies in the Minneapolis/St. Paul area of USA to identify the critical factors for quality management practice. They identified eight factors, which are: (i) role of management leadership and quality policy, (ii) role of quality department, (iii) training, (iv) product/service design, (v) supplier quality management, (vi) process management, (vii) quality data and reporting, and (viii) employee relations.

Black and Porter (1995, 1996), in their empirical study of UK organizations (both manufacturing and services), identified ten critical factors as: (i) strategic quality management, (ii) customer satisfaction, (iii) people and customer management, (iv) communication of information, (v) external interface management, (vi) improvement measurement systems, (vii) corporate quality culture, (viii) supplier partnerships, (ix) operational quality planning, and (x) teamwork structures for process improvement. Tamimi (1998) identified eight critical success factors for TQM implementation as: (i) top management commitment, (ii) supervisory leadership, (iii) education, (iv) cross functional communications to improve quality, (v) supplier management, (vi) quality training, (vii) product/service innovation, and (viii) providing assurance to employees. Sink (1991b) study showed that performance of an organization system is composed of seven interrelated criteria: (i) effectiveness, (ii) efficiency, (iii) total quality, (iv) productivity, (v) quality of work life, (vi) innovation, and (vii) financial performance.

Kuei *et al.* (2001), Tracey and Vonderembse (1998) and Wong *et al.* (1999) empirical study have confirmed the positive correlation between supplier performance and organizational performance. Genna (1997) suggested that steps to improve supplier product quality, such as defect-free and on-time shipments, often could carry through to help provide the same quality to end-users.

Lewis and Smith (1994) have suggested six common approaches that should be used to develop and/or implement TQM. These are: (i) *Guru approach* – Deming's 14 point model, Crosby's 14 steps, and Juran's trilogy, (ii) *Japanese model approach* – Ishikawa and educational guidelines (e.g. Kaizen, 5S, etc.) of the Union of Japanese Scientists and Engineers (JUSE), (iii) *Total quality element approach* – quality circles, statistical process control, and quality function deployment, (iv) *Hoshin planning approach* – focuses on successful planning, deployment and execution and diagnosis of quality practices and performance measurement, (v) *Quality awards business excellence criteria approach* – MBNQA, EQA, AQA, etc., and (vi) *Industrial company/leader model approach* – visiting and learning from the quality/excellence award winners. Lindsay and Petrick (1997) suggested that the most useful TQM implementation plan is an integrated blend of these approaches.

2.11 TQM LITERATURE AT A GLANCE

A comprehensive review of various approaches for TQM and system dynamics has been done in the previous sections. In this section, we summarize the reviewed literature to drive some general observations and concluding remarks. Table 2.12 shows the period-wise representation of all the researches reviewed in the earlier sections. For example, the second last column in this table covers the researches made during year 2001 to the first quarter of year 2003.

Table 2.12: Summary of the literature reviewed

		Approach \ Period	Till 1975	1976-80	1981-85	1986-90	1991-95	1996-2000	2001- first quarter of 03	**Sum**
Classification of Literature	Basic concept of quality and TQM		156, 205, 285	108, 576	110, 427, 286, 287, 128, 425, 66, 159, 267, 191, 207, 190	508, 289, 291, 558, 160, 193, 223, 130, 259, 209, 208, 194, 129, 444, 119, 593, 418, 602, 432, 76, 571, 435, 254	588, 589, 231, 112, 293, 271, 161, 365, 139, 408, 525, 284, 197, 188, 617, 386, 120, 275, 346, 250, 531, 591, 474, 59, 10, 36, 507, 601, 23, 22, 162, 242, 414, 460, 442, 64, 600, 519, 41, 616, 274, 618, 620, 82, 65, 269, 300, 475, 357, 613, 511	551, 268, 595, 518, 187, 562, 614, 485, 310, 241, 143, 239, 53, 458, 277, 393, 352, 487, 567, 484, 113, 499, 115, 387, 562, 155, 302, 378, 625	480	**121**
	General TQM Principles	Quality Focus		456	452		377, 488, 516, 58, 566, 111, 515			**9**
		Top Management Commitment	157	108		129, 203, 201	131, 304, 292, 29, 621, 439, 42, 118, 137, 165, 492, 623			**17**
		Productivity Improvement			207, 560, 128, 108, 190	450, 528, 290	394,85, 392, 213, 546, 599			**14**
		Breakthrough Improvement					228, 375, 544			**3**
		Continuous Improvement				232, 248, 154, 238	170, 384, 524, 102, 448, 443, 80, 184, 596, 385, 564, 415, 409, 60			**18**
		Culture Change			322, 204, 247, 345, 267	30, 222	453, 145, 517, 11, 514, 381, 548, 320, 471			**16**
		Customer focus				76, 57, 238, 72	93, 71, 509, 453, 559, 83		96	**11**
		Team Work	306		314	498, 232, 510, 500, 150	313, 477, 319, 21, 419, 297, 298			**14**
	TQM Models		157	108	158, 266, 495	129, 288, 491, 418, 529, 130, 289, 259, 496, 558, 593, 493	168, 49, 50, 617, 112, 316, 218, 497, 127, 340, 258, 294, 284, 281, 321, 623, 182	51, 268, 449, 7, 582, 135, 196, 545, 249, 447, 538, 626, 327, 326, 63, 608, 183, 583, 459, 465, 97, 87, 354, 70	575, 615, 353	**61**
	InternationalQuality Award Models					367	98, 245, 147, 244, 609, 67, 539, 195, 237, 398	389, 379, 47, 582, 148, 412, 68, 1, 438	424, 489, 348, 299	**24**
	Quality Award Models in India					299		370		**2**
	Studies on Quality Practices in India			433			519, 515, 81, 73, 395, 407, 11, 366, 212, 337, 338	308, 393, 5, 505, 330, 368, 455, 12, 503, 451, 27, 317, 75, 26, 282	333	**28**
	Quality Practices in Other Countries					192, 491, 256, 116, 189, 429, 501	44, 361, 90, 309, 210, 79, 535, 220, 95, 28, 168, 339, 337, 411, 442, 347, 92, 151, 437, 245, 383, 99, 186, 279, 373, 94, 413, 601, 43, 103, 539, 224, 372, 215, 169, 362, 522, 473, 311, 137, 50, 520, 357	578, 55, 567, 551, 25, 3, 458, 446, 113, 89, 307, 376, 14, 211, 626, 441, 149, 569, 582, 344, 454, 580, 457, 327, 326, 581, 371, 445, 343, 440, 143, 494, 565, 466, 239, 117, 121, 611, 100, 87, 153, 412, 138, 164, 136, 603, 550, 77, 51, 561, 574, 606, 198, 360	355, 358, 13, 152, 610, 15, 521, 88, 612, 513, 328	**115**
Sum			**6**	**6**	**27**	**64**	**196**	**132**	**22**	**453**

The numbers in this table (except those in last column and last row) indicate the corresponding serial number of reference provided at the end of this book. On the basis of the reviewed literature and the summary provided in Table 2.12, we present the following observations.

1. The research efforts in TQM have started building-up after 1970 and continued till 1985. It can be said to be in the rapid development phase since then.
2. A majority of the works in TQM pertains to the period 1991-1995. However, during 1991-95, the researches in TQM dominated on the development of quality award models. During this period quality award models approach also started getting momentum in India.
3. The empirical research supporting a direct relationship between the adoption of total quality management and improved organizational performance gained momentum during 1996-2000.
4. With the beginning 90's, the focus of the research has gradually shifted to practical considerations in TQM modeling and in the development of general TQM principles.
5. Dynamic interactions among TQM variables have not received due attention in literature. System dynamics has been used for modeling policy issues and operational problems in many areas but has not been extensively used to model TQM.

2.12 STRENGTHS OF THE EXISTING LITERATURE

Based on the literature review, the following strengths of research efforts can be outlined.

1. TQM has been extensively attempted in the literature. Despite most of the authors describing TQM as a system, so far dynamic interactions among the sub-systems of TQM have not received due attention. New researches in this area should address this aspect.
2. Many diverse approaches have already been proposed in the form of ISO 9000, TQM models and NQA models, which facilitate development and improvement of these methods in future works.

2.13 CRITICAL APPRAISAL

Reduction of cost and improvements in quality and productivity has proved to be essential for almost all the organizations. Indian automobile sector is no exception. The reviewed literature demonstrated that quality has emerged as the most crucial competitive weapon. Therefore, organizations are taking TQM route for managing the future. The literature also revealed that TQM is far wider in its application than assuring product or service quality – it is a way of managing business processes to ensure complete 'customer satisfaction' at every stage.

TQM literature is vague on the structure of TQM programs and methodology though a few NQA award models (Business Excellence) have been developed as working models of TQM. These Business Excellence models provide a framework and help in developing ownership for quality in top management, because it enables them to examine their own activity and develop their own plans for their own areas, in their own way.

A critical phase of self-assessment is the establishment of an improvement plan that must be presented to higher management, linked to business planning, and then communicated to the whole organization. Much too often, organizations fail to do this, and consequently, self-assessment activities do not lead to lasting improvements. It is also vital to ensure that monitoring and implementation of actions become a natural part of the business review process and not a separate activity. Few reports suggest that most of the organizations face problem of accuracy and consistency in scoring during self-assessment leading the organizations to draw wrong conclusions.

Few authors advocated the use of the evidential reasoning (ER) approach and multiple attribute decision making (MADM) in the self-assessment process against the criteria of the EFQM excellence model to help minimize the scoring variation amongst members of the team. They emphasized that a MADM model requires a generalized set of evaluation grades before an assessment can be undertaken and few other authors have provided the evaluation grades.

The key cultural assumptions of an organization are critical for the success of TQM implementation. An organization with a weak ethical work culture will not have the character for sustained implementation of total quality. The development of ethical work culture requires regular assessment and monitoring. Further, TQM requires unwavering top management commitment and a systematic, non-stop effort to eliminate tasks and processes that are non-value adding as far as the customer is concerned. Effective TQM implementation requires:

- Clarity of corporate mission and vision among all employees.
- Effective strategic planning and information management.
- Improve work culture and an open trustworthy environment.
- Problem-solving through synergetic teamwork.
- Accuracy and consistency in scoring during self-assessment.
- Regular assessment and monitoring.

- Understanding of complex interactions among different TQM variables.

Most of the authors describe TQM as a system but so far dynamic interactions between its subsystems have not received due attention in literature. System dynamics has been used for modeling policy issues and operational problems but has not been used extensively to model TQM. Vagueness of philosophies and intangible nature of TQM parameters has been considered as major problem area in modeling it. TQM initiatives often fail due to lack of essential quality measures to monitor customer satisfaction, supplier satisfaction, management leadership, product quality and employee morale. System dynamics model can help in understanding and removing these barriers. It can also help in understanding and analyzing the complex interactions and the dynamics of factors affecting TQM over a longer time horizon. This can equip the management to evolve a strategy for growth and success.

2.14 GAPS IDENTIFIED IN LITERATURE

Bauer *et al.* (2001) concluded that the use of dynamic models for TQM in organizations is essential for an appreciation of a complex, dynamic system, which enables managers in turbulent days to manage in a comprehensive way and to decide and act for long-lasting success.

A review of literature has led to the identification of following gaps in literature:

- A systematic study of the issues related to the implementation of TQM in automobile sector of India is not available in literature. The differences in the level of acceptability of TQM tools among manufacturers, suppliers and subcontractors in automobile sector are still unexplored.
- TQM tools are not sufficient for situations with circular causality (Kumar, 1995). All management control systems are feedback systems, in which results govern actions, which create further results. Graphical tools used in TQM show one-way causality, which are not sufficient to capture a circular causality. Due to this gap existing in literature, there is a need to model interactions among TQM variables.
- Present TQM tools can transform data but generally rely on intuition to draw conclusions. TQM tools are not sufficient when strategic issues related to top management are under focus. Many strategic decisions require policy experimentation. There is hardly any quality tool available with practitioners that can effectively model the policies and simulate the system performance over a long-term basis.
- Most of the authors describe TQM as a system. However, the

dynamic interactions among its subsystems have not received due attention to bridge some of the existing gaps identifies in the previous section. An attempt has been made to.

2.15 OBJECTIVE OF THIS BOOK

The motivation of this book is to bridge some of the existing gaps identified in the previous section. An attempt has been made to model some of the complexities in the dynamic interaction of the variables that are responsible for the survival and growth of the Indian automobile sector. The book aims to gain insight into TQM practices being followed in this sector. The focus is to model TQM practices using system dynamics approach for the Indian automobile sector with a view to carry out policy experimentations. The major objectives of this book are listed as follows:

- To assess the current state-of-art for TQM practices being followed in the Indian automobile sector and to get an insight into major strengths and weaknesses of this sector
- To understand the complex interactions and the dynamics of factors affecting TQM on a long-term basis
- To understand the different transition phases that are possible during a TQM journey
- To understand the system behavior of organizations under different market scenarios
- To understand the contribution of different enablers on the performance related to TQM.

2.16 CONCLUSIONS

In this chapter various issues on total quality management and related issues have been discussed. The literature has been classified into various classes such as basic concept of quality and TQM, general TQM principles, TQM models, National Quality Award models, Quality Award models in India, studies on quality practices in India, system dynamics modeling etc.

Literature survey has been supportive in identifying gaps in terms of integrated approach for total quality management in the Indian automobile sector. In the next chapter a survey of TQM practices will be carried out in the automobile sector to identify strengths and weaknesses of this sector.

3

Chapter

TQM Practices in the Automobile Sector - A Survey

3.1 INTRODUCTION

Total quality management (TQM) is a management philosophy that builds customer-driven learning organizations dedicated to total customer satisfaction with continuous improvement in the efficiency and effectiveness of the organization and its processes (Corrigan, 1995; Spitzer, 1995). TQM fortifies an organization's competitive stance while it also cuts product cost through reduced waste, enhanced productivity and elevated employee morale. The success stories of organizations on TQM path are well known. Japan's automobile industry started out several decades behind the USA's but in 1980, it overtook the USA's using this philosophy (Ulrich *et al.,* 2000). Japan is the first country to start a quality award as early as in 1950s. The institution of Deming Prize has helped in the rapid progress of Japanese auto sector (Itasaka, 1989; Mody, 1996). It was soon realized by Americans that superior quality of Japanese products, particularly the automobiles, was responsible for the change in the competitive position. As a consequence of this realization, MBNQA was established in the USA in 1987. The MBNQA is in itself an aggregation of elements involved in TQM. Impact of this award in the USA auto sector can be seen from the fact that USA is a leader with around 20.8% market share in total world market and every sixth worker is involved in the making of an automobile (Indiainfoline, 2001a). Though Indian automobile sector is also taking TQM route, its full potential in the global market is still untapped. India's car production in the year 1998 was 3,83,798 units as against world's total production of 40,345,198 units in the same year. This comes to around 0.9% of world market share. In contrast, the USA, Japan, Germany, France, Spain, Canada and U.K. have 20.8%, 19.7%, 13.1%, 6.4%, 5.6%, 5.2% and 4.3% market share in the world's production in the same year (Indiainfoline, 2001a). India's car production is only 6.25 per 1000 against 532, 514, 489 and 430 of Italy, the USA, Germany and France, respectively (Baig, 2001).

Many Indian automobile organizations are taking ISO 9000 and QS 9000 certification as a route to implement TQM philosophy. Many executives actually believe that the mere accreditation will bring about the overall improvement in the quality levels (Agrawal, 1993; Agrawal and Vrat, 1993; Das, 1996). This is a somewhat myopic view of reality.

At present automobiles are contributing a low share – nearly 5% of the country's industrial output compared to the 8-10% range in developing countries like Mexico and Brazil and a much higher 15-17% range in developed countries like the USA and Germany (Sharma, 2000). Indian automobile sector contributes 4.55% to the gross domestic product (GDP) of India (Autometet, 2002). The automotive industry has maintained a steady share in the total exports of the country. During 1999-2000 this share was 2.8%. The export of transport vehicles has grown by 54.8% i.e., \$443.2 million in 1998-99 to \$685.9 million in 1999-2000 (Automobileindia, 2002). In overall auto sector, exports grew by a healthy 60% in April-July 2002 compared to the same period last year. The importance of this sector in India is also due to 13% growth in the year 2001-02 over 2000-01 (Siamindia, 2002). The overall vehicle production in the financial year 2001-02 has been 5,579,994 units. The total export of auto components in the financial year 2001-02 was Rs. 27,750 million (One \$ = Rs. 46.54 as on 20th June 2003). This sector is also responsible for providing employment to more than 10 million people (ACMA, 2001-02). Despite these gains, Indian automobile sector has not been able to make use of its full potential. The competitiveness of India has been ranked 41 out of 49 countries as per World Competitiveness Yearbook Report 2001 (IMD, 2002). Thus TQM practice assumes a vital role for the survival and growth of any organization. For the survival and growth, the Indian automobile sector needs a quality revolution. There are some signs that a movement may be gathering momentum as per Global Competitiveness Report 2002-03 released by the World Economic Forum (Mohanty, 1996; The Economic Times, 2002). The literature survey discussed in Chapter – 2 reveals that the TQM philosophy is now established on a worldwide basis. While some sincere efforts have been made by the Indian automobile sector to nurture this philosophy, still efforts are not adequate. The present chapter makes an attempt to gain insight regarding the TQM practices being followed by the Indian automobile sector. The findings are likely to be useful in devising a suitable methodology for TQM implementation and modeling. Accordingly, a survey has been conducted in the automobile sector of the Indian organizations. The automobile sector has been divided into three categories i.e. automobile manufacturers, suppliers and sub-contractors. The 1st tier vendors have been termed as suppliers. In accordance with the nomenclature prevailing in ISO 9000:1994 and QS 9000:1998, we have considered sub-contractor as a term to identify supplier's supplier. This chapter presents the major findings of the survey.

3.2 SURVEY METHODOLOGY

It has been experienced that organizations are hard pressed for their valuable time to provide quantitative information in any type of survey questionnaire seeking statistical data. Moreover, some data are published in balance sheet and other documents of the organizations. The survey questionnaire was designed based on few previous survey questionnaires and an outcome of consultation with academicians, researchers and practitioners. However, the variables/elements of TQM and weightages have been taken on the basis of Agrawal business excellence model (Agrawal, 1999).

The survey questionnaire, so designed, was validated with a pilot survey. The modifications were made in order to get the required and necessary information from the different organizations under the purview of the survey. The survey questionnaire was also designed to survey the applicability of quality tools in the Indian automobile sector. The survey questionnaire also incorporated twenty-one keys TQM tools, which were selected based on literature review (Weaver, 1995; Caravatta, 1997; Sharma, 1997).

3.3 STRUCTURE OF SURVEY QUESTIONNAIRE

The detailed questionnaire has been divided into two sections. Section-I deals with general background of the organizations and is directed towards understanding the existing TQM practices, while section-II seeks self-assessment score in key issues pertaining to all twelve variables/elements of the TQM model to gain an insight of the organizations in terms of their major strength and weaknesses.

The respondents are specifically requested to ignore their personal feelings and use their best judgement on a five-point scale.

A five-point scale has been devised as under:

Score of 5 means outstanding (above 80% achievement)

Score of 4 means very good (60 to 80% achievement)
Score of 3 means good (50 to 60% achievement)
Score of 2 means below average (40 to 50% achievement)
Score of 1 means poor (below 40% achievement)
The survey questionnaire is enclosed as Annexure A1.

3.4 ANALYSIS OF FEEDBACK

The survey questionnaire was mailed to Chief Executives/Managing Directors of 350 organizations covering automobile manufacturers, suppliers and sub-contractors. The category-wise details of the mailed questionnaire and received responses are shown in Table 3.1

Table 3.1: Category-wise break up of response received

Automobile category	*Questionnaire mailed*	*Response received*	*% response*
Automobile manufacturers	66	12	18.18%
Suppliers	227	26	11.45%
Sub-contractors	57	10	17.54%
Total	**350**	**48**	**13.71%**

It is noted that the analysis and interpretation of findings is based on the 48 (13.71%) responses received out of 350 organizations. Statistically, it may appear to be inadequate. However, given the type of information (generally considered confidential by the organizations) needed, it was very difficult to seek responses from a sizable number of organizations. It may further be mentioned that these 48 responses have been collected after vigorous follow up. Series of detailed discussions were also held with TQM practitioners, chief executives and academicians to identify major variables/ elements, methods, practices being followed and difficulties encountered during TQM implementation. The responses are converted into a total model score using statistical method. Thus a self-assessment score against the business excellence model developed by Agrawal (Agrawal, 1999) is arrived at. These feedbacks were analyzed and findings from the survey are discussed in the subsequent sections.

3.4.1 Profile of the Respondent Organizations

(i) Feedbacks were received from 48 organizations. The response was markedly better from automobile manufacturer category with 18% response, as against 11% and 17% in case of suppliers and sub-contractors, respectively (Table 3.1).

(ii) All organizations except two have indicated TQM as a guiding philosophy in their organizations in automobile manufacturer category i.e., 83% of automobile manufacturers follow TQM as a guiding philosophy. In supplier category all organizations except 7 have indicated TQM as a guiding philosophy i.e. 73% of suppliers follow TQM as a guiding philosophy. In sub-contractor category, 3 out of 10 have indicated TQM as a guiding philosophy i.e. 30% of sub-contractor category follow TQM as a guiding philosophy. The data show that sub-contractor category is the weakest among the three categories in following the TQM as a guiding philosophy. It is evident from Figure 3.1 that most of the organizations are following TQM as a guiding philosophy in automobile manufacturer and supplier category but response from sub-contractor category is very poor. Unless sub-contractor category also gears up in following TQM as a guiding philosophy, gains of automobile manufacturer and supplier category cannot be sustained for a long run.

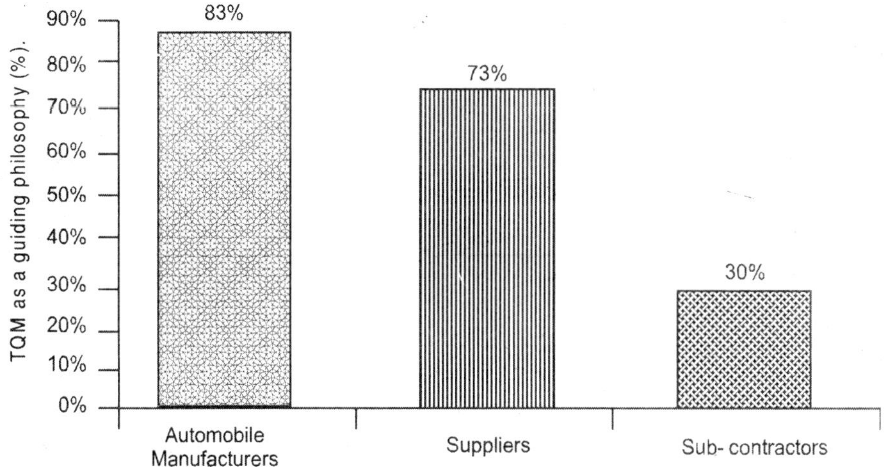

Fig. 3.1: TQM as a guiding philosophy (in percentage)

Bound (1994) findings have been that international competition and requirements for continuous improvement became an issue of importance in the 1980s in Western countries and in the 1990s in the Indian organizations. The policy of economic liberalization initiated by the Government of India in the year 1991, had given a further impetus to the growth of the auto industry. Soon after, the permit licence raj was dismantled and investment was invited in all sectors, including the automobile sector. Liberalization had resulted in an influx of foreign capital and technology into the Indian automobile sector with the minimum regulatory norms.

Major car manufacturers such as General Motors, Hyundai, Daewoo, Fiat, Honda etc. had set up their manufacturing bases in India. The Government of India had made it mandatory for the car-makers to indigenize the various components during a given span of time. This had given a major boost to the growth of the Indian auto ancillaries. This boost has resulted in making automobile sector very important from the view point of the Indian economy. At present also, this sector is contributing appreciably to national income and generating employment in the economy (Table 3.2.).

Table 3.2: The Indian automobile sector – A profile 2001-02

	Vehicle industry	*Auto component industry*	*Total*
Production			
Vehicle (in Nos.)			
1997-98	4,260,453	—	4,260,453
1998-99	4,476,531	—	4,476,531
1999-2000	5,114,626	—	5,114,626
2000-2001	5,005,375	—	5,005,375
2001-2002	5,579,994	—	5,579,994
Value in Rs. Million			
1997-98	365,411	120,318	485,729
1998-99	368,262	129,968	498,230
1999-2000	422,933	163,560	586,493
2000-2001	492,024	178,569	664,483
2001-2002	N.A	210,135	—
Exports (Rs. Million)			
1996-97	20,040	10,330	30,370
1997-98	17,928	12,273	32,273
1998-99	14,536	13,990	28,526
1999-2000	N.A	18,270	—
2000-2001	N.A	27,060	—
2001-2002	N.A	27,750	—
Employment (Nos.)			
Direct	200,000	250,000	450,000
Indirect	10,000,000	—	10,000,000

Source: Facts & Figures: 2001-02 Estimated by ACMA

There has been high degree of penetration of information and communication technologies and growing importance of services in the vehicle sector, and the automotive industry is closely linked to the dynamic development of the new economy (Indiainfoline, 2001b; Business Today, 1989-90, 1997).

Nearly 25% of the respondent organizations in automobile manufacturers have adopted TQM as a guiding philosophy prior to liberalization. Fifty eight percent of the respondent organizations adopted TQM as a guiding philosophy after liberalization and 17% of the balance respondent organizations have still not adopted TQM as a guiding philosophy.

Nearly 11% of the respondent organizations in supplier category have started TQM as a guiding philosophy prior to liberalization. Sixty two percent of the respondent organizations adopted TQM as a guiding philosophy after liberalization and 27% of the balance respondent organizations have not yet started TQM as a guiding philosophy.

Nearly 10% of the respondent organizations in sub-contractor category have started TQM as a guiding philosophy prior to liberalization. Twenty percent of the respondent organizations started TQM as a guiding philosophy after liberalization and 70% of the balance respondent organizations have not yet started TQM as a guiding philosophy. After liberalization, competition among different organizations is increasing. Therefore, for the survival and growth, organizations are following TQM as a guiding philosophy to nurture a culture of continuous improvement, which is evident from Figure 3.2.

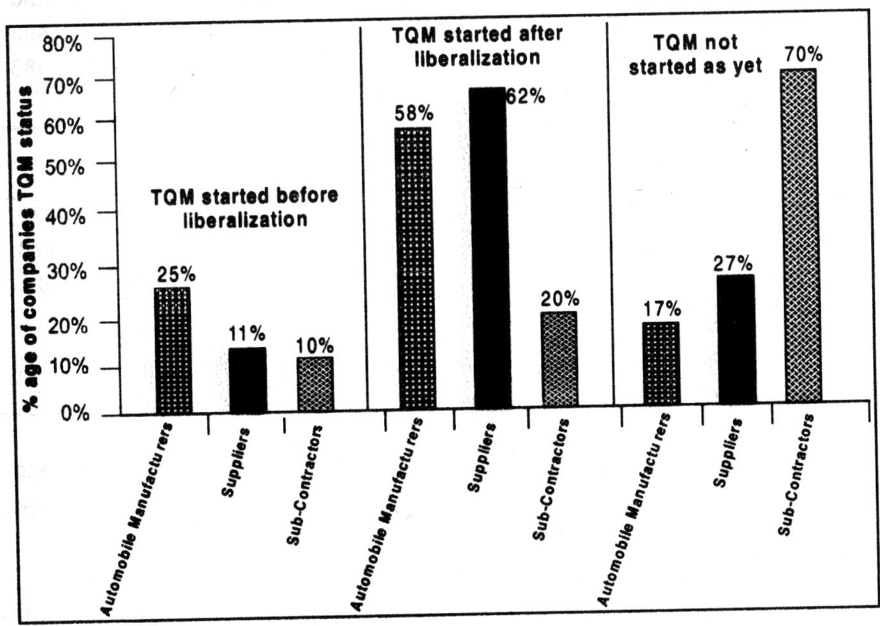

Fig. 3.2: Comparison of pre and post-liberalization era (TQM as a guiding philosophy)

(iii) Sixty seven percent of the surveyed organizations in automobile manufacturers have been reported to be ISO 9000 certified. Seventeen percent have been reported to be both QS 9000 and ISO 14001 certified. Eight percent have been reported to be ISO 14001 certified and balance eight percent has not achieved any certification. One organization is reported to have started ISO 14001 and one is in the final stages of QS 9000 certification. One organization has reported to achieve CII-EXIM Award.

Twenty seven percent of sample organizations in supplier category have been reported to be ISO 9000 certified. Sixty five percent have been reported to be QS 9000 certified, which includes 4% of the respondent organization to be certified for both QS 9000 and ISO 14001. Only one company could achieve ISO 14001 certification. Eight percent of the respondent organizations are reported to have not achieved any certification. One company reported to be in the progress for QS 9000 certification. One company is reported to be in progress for ISO 9000 certification, another company is reported to be working on Total Productive Maintenance (TPM) implementation.

Thirty percent of sample organizations in sub-contractor category reported to have been ISO 9000-certified. Thirty percent of respondent organizations are in progress of ISO 9000 certification and balance 40% of the respondent organizations have yet not started work on certification.

It is evident from Table 3.3 that 92% of the respondent organizations in the category of automobile manufacturers and suppliers have achieved either ISO 9000/QS 9000 or ISO 14001 certification and in sub-contractor category only 30% respondent organizations have achieved ISO 9000 certification. The above analysis establishes the fact that all out efforts are being made to nurture continuous improvement philosophy through these certifications. However, sub-contractor category efforts are at a slow pace.

Table 3.3: Category-wise ISO 9000/QS 9000/ISO 14001 certification achieved

Category	*ISO 9000/QS 9000/ ISO 14001*	*Not Started*	*Others*
Automobile manufacturers	92%	8%	CII-EXIM Award
Suppliers	92%	8%	
Sub-contractors	30%	70%	

(iv) Fifty nine percent of respondent organizations in automobile manufacturers category have been reported to achieve more than

95% on-time delivery. Thirty three percent have been reported to achieve on-time delivery between 85-95%. Balance 8% has been reported to achieve 75-85% on-time delivery.

Fifty eight percent of respondent organizations in supplier category have reported to achieve more than 95% on-time delivery. Twenty seven percent are reported to achieve 85-95% on-time delivery. Balance 15% is reported to have achieved 75-85% on-time delivery. Forty percent of respondent organizations in sub-contractor category have reported to achieve more than 95% on-time delivery. Forty percent have reported to achieve 85-95% on-time delivery and balance 20% have reported to achieve less than 75% on-time delivery. It is evident from this analysis that overall on-time delivery concept is on the increase.

(v) Sixteen percent of respondent organizations of automobile manufacturers are reported to have 75–100% self-certified components. Seventeen percent are reported to have self-certified components between 50-75%. Other 50% are reported to have self-certified components between 25-50%. Balance 17% of the manufacturers are reported to have less than 25% self-certified components.

Forty–two percent of respondent organizations of supplier category are reported to have self-certified components between 75-100%. Twelve percent of the sample suppliers are reported to have self-certified components between 50-75%, 15% of suppliers are reported to have self-certified components between 25-50%. Balance 31% of the suppliers have less than 25% of self-certified components. Twenty percent of respondent organizations of sub-contractor category are reported to have self-certified components between 50-75%, another 20% between 25-50%. Balance 60% of the sub-contractors are reported to have self-certified components less than 25%.

(vi) Hundred percent, 96% and 40% of respondent organizations in automobile manufacturers, suppliers and sub-contractors categories respectively reported to have undertaken cost reduction programmes. Post-liberalization era is an era of competition and thus for survival there is a need to continuously reduce the cost. Therefore, cost-cutting programmes should be initiated in the organization in a big way involving each and everyone in the organization. This phenomenon is evident through Figure 3.3. However, initiative from sub-contractor category is yet to pickup.

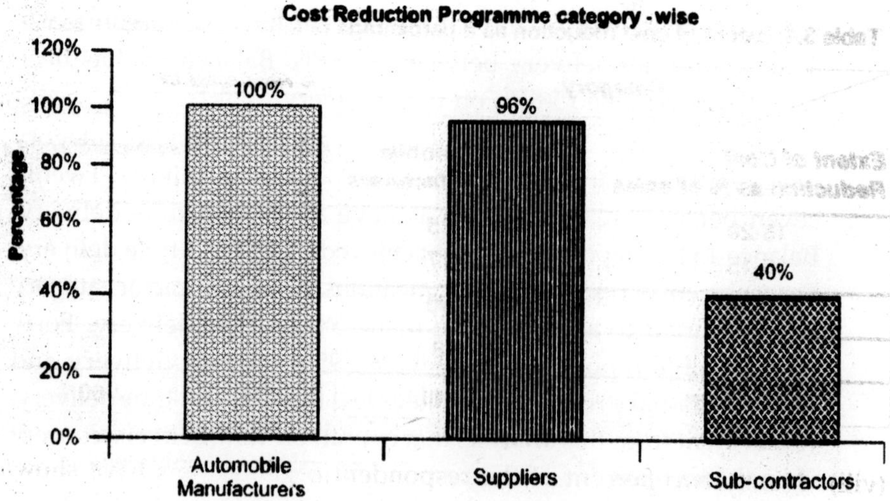

Fig. 3.3: Cost reduction programme

(vii) In automobile manufacturer category, 25% of the organizations are reported to have achieved cost reduction as per percentage of sales between 15-20%, 17% of the manufacturers are reported to have cost reduction achieved between 10-15% of sales, 50% of the manufacturers are reported to have achieved cost reduction between 5-10% of sales. Balance 8% of the organizations are reported to have achieved less than 5% cost reduction of sales.

In supplier category, none of the organizations is reported to have achieved cost reduction as per percentage of sales between 15-20%, 31% of the suppliers are reported to have achieved cost reduction between 10-15% of sales, 34% of supplier category are reported to have achieved cost reduction between 5-10% of sales. Thirty one percent of supplier category is reported to have achieved cost reduction less than 5% and balance 4% of supplier category has not taken up cost reduction as yet. Forty percent of the respondent sub-contractor category is reported to have achieved cost reduction less than 5% of sales. Balance 60% have yet not started cost reduction programme. The extent of cost reduction as percentage of sales undertaken by three categories is shown in Table 3.4.

Table 3.4: Extent of cost reduction as a percentage of sales in automobile sector

Category / Extent of Cost Reduction as % of sales	% Respond in		
	Automobile Manufacturers	***Suppliers***	***Sub-contractors***
15-20	25	—	—
10-15	17	31	—
5-10	50	34	—
<5	8	31	40
Not Started	Nil	4	60

(viii) Ninety-two percent of the respondent organizations have shown reduction in rejection percentage in the 1998-99 financial year compared to 1997-98. Balance 8% of the respondent organizations are reported to have increased rejection in the financial year 1998-99 over 1997-98. Twenty-two percent of respondent organizations have less than 1% rejection. Sixty percent of respondent organizations have rejection between 1% to 4% and balance 18% are reported to have rejections more than 4%.

In supplier category overall there has been reduction in rejection in the 1998-99 financial year over 1997-98. Fifty percent of the respondent supplier category is reported to have rejections less than 1%. Twenty-five percent of the respondent suppliers are reported to have rejections between 1 to 4% and balance 25% are reported to have rejections more than 4%, which is quite alarming.

In sub-contractor category overall there has not been appreciable reduction in rejection in the 1998-99 financial year over 1997-98. Ten percent of the respondent organizations in sub-contractor category are reported to have less than 1% rejection. Twenty percent of the respondent organizations are reported to have rejection between 1 to 4%. Balance 70% of the respondent organizations have rejection more than 4%.

World-class organizations are monitoring their rejections in ppm (parts per million) and their rejections are between two to three digits in ppm, whereas Indian automobile sector is monitoring rejection in percentage as it is evident in Figure 3.4. This shows that the Indian automobile sector has to go a long way in achieving that kind of performance.

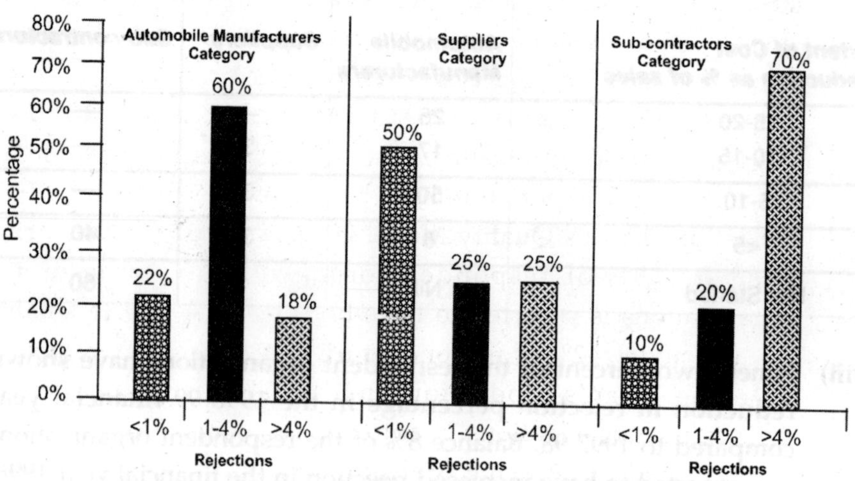

Fig. 3.4: Rejection percentage category-wise

(ix) Harrington (1987, 1991, 1994, 1997) observed that the complexity of today's business environment has made it necessary for the organizations to evaluate all the alternatives before committing resources to an improvement process. Use of quality cost concepts (cost of poor quality) is needed to avoid ambiguity and improve understanding related to quality improvement. Quality data and reporting are the most important determinants of success of any TQM programme. Very few organizations are using quality cost as a measure of their quality performance and thus they are losing the opportunity to identify critical areas for improvement (Table 3.5).

Table 3.5: Percentage of organizations using quality cost concept

Category / ***Quality cost status***	***% Respond in***		
	Automobile manufacturers	***Suppliers***	***Sub-contractors***
Using quality cost	20	15	Nil
Not using quality cost	80	85	100

(x) Seventeen percent of respondent organizations in automobile manufacturers category are reported to be using CII-Business Excellence Award Model. Crosby's approach to quality is being used by 25% of respondent organizations. Deming approach to quality is quite popular and is being used by 58% of respondent organizations. Deming Prize model is being used by 17% of respondent organizations. Only 8% of respondent organizations are using European Quality Award (EQA) model. None of the organizations is reported to have been using Feigenbaum's TQC model. Ishikawa's Quality Model is quite popular and is being used by 58% of respondent organizations. None of the organizations is reported to have been using JRD Tata Quality Award model, 42% of respondent organizations are reported to be using Juran's Model for Quality. Seventeen percent of respondent organizations in automobile manufacturer category are reported to be using Malcolm Baldrige National Quality Award (MBNQA) Model. Eight percent of respondent organizations are using Rajiv Gandhi National Quality Award (RGNQA) Model. Twenty five percent of respondent organizations are using Taguchi Model.

Twelve percent of respondent organizations in supplier category are reported to be using CII-Business Excellence Award Model. None of the organizations of respondent organizations is reported to be using Crosby's approach to Quality. Fifteen percent of respondent organizations are using Deming approach to Quality. None of the organizations is reported to be using Deming Prize Model. Four percent of respondent organizations are reported to be using EQA Model. Twelve percent of respondent organizations are reported to be using Feigenbaum's TQC Model, and 8% of respondent organizations are reported to be using Ishikawa Quality Model. None of the organization is reported to be using JRD Tata Quality Award Model. Eight percent of respondent organizations are using Juran's Model for Quality. Four percent of respondent organizations are using MBNQA Model. None of the organizations is using RGNQA Model and 4% of respondent organizations are using Taguchi Model.

None of the models except two is reported to be used by the sub-contractor category. Twenty percent of the respondent organizations

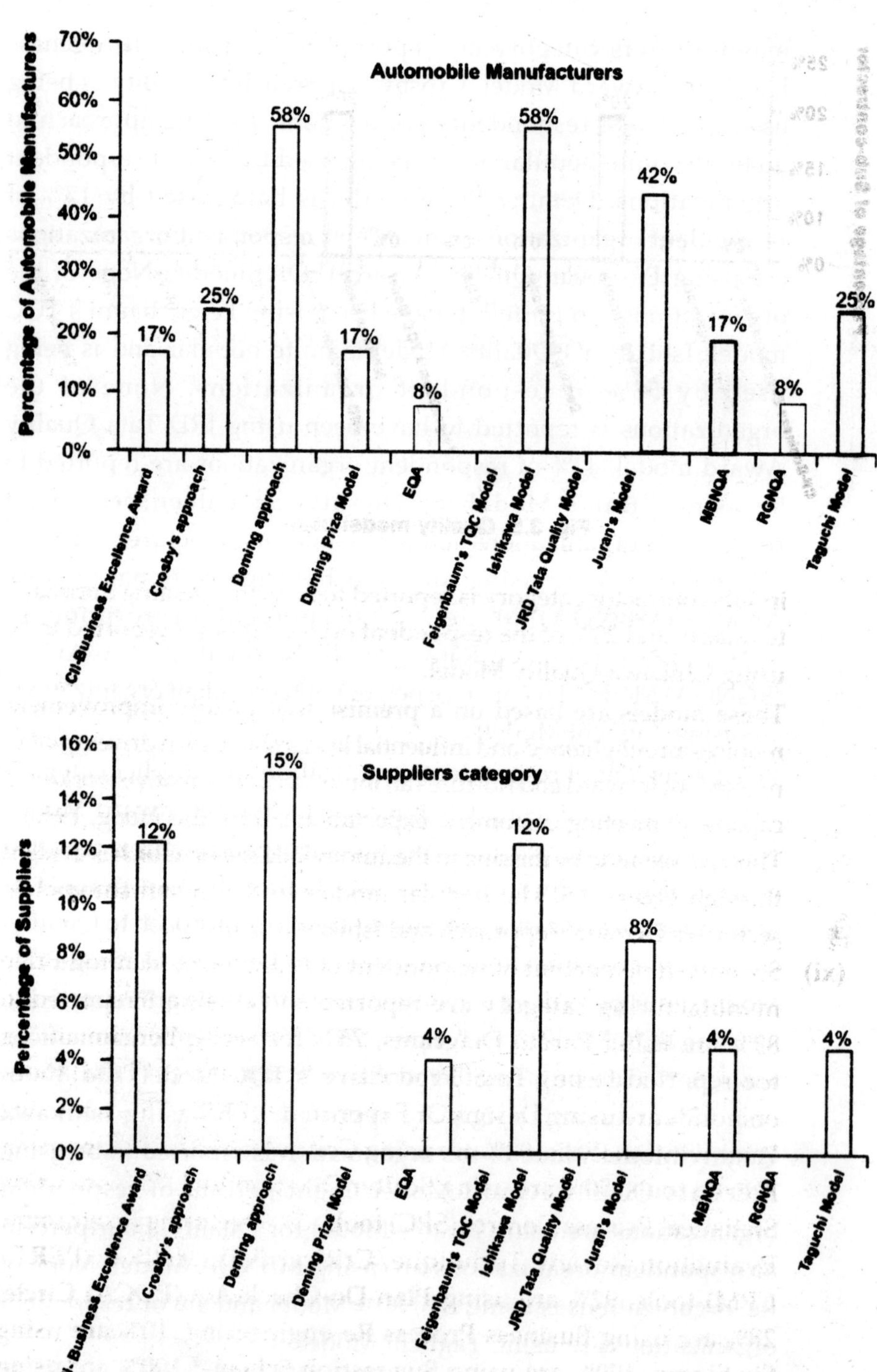
Automobile Manufacturers
Percentage of Automobile Manufacturers
70%
60%
50%
40%
30%
20%
10%
0%
17%
25%
58%
17%
8%
58%
42%
17%
8%
25%
CII-Business Excellence Award
Crosby's approach
Deming approach
Deming Prize Model
EQA
Feigenbaum's TQC Model
Ishikawa Model
JRD Tata Quality Model
Juran's Model
MBNQA
RGNQA
Taguchi Model
Suppliers category
Percentage of Suppliers
16%
14%
12%
10%
8%
6%
4%
2%
0%
12%
15%
4%
12%
8%
4%
4%
CII- Business Excellence Award
Crosby's approach
Deming approach
Deming Prize Model
EQA
Feigenbaum's TQC Model
Ishikawa Model
JRD Tata Quality Model
Juran's Model
MBNQA
RGNQA
Taguchi Model

Contd....

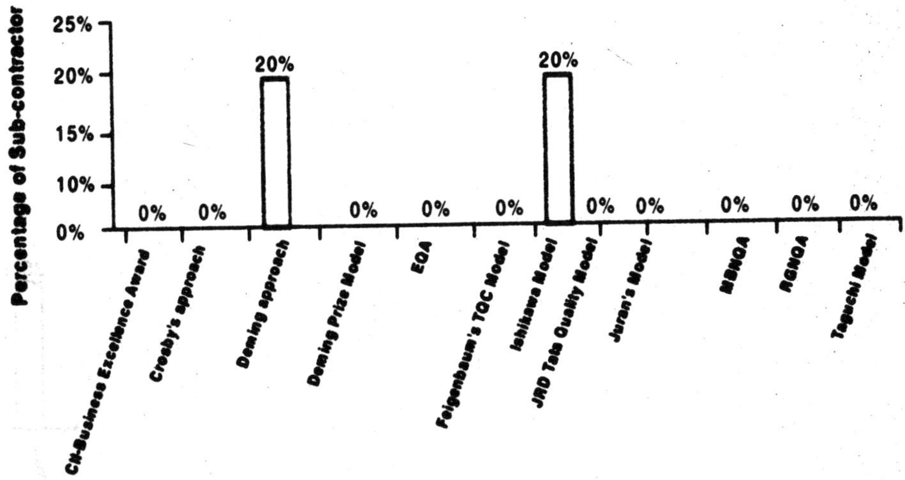

Fig. 3.5: Quality model used

in sub-contractor category is reported to be using Deming approach to quality and 20% of the respondent organizations is reported to be using Ishikawa Quality Model.

These models are based on a premise that quality improvement requires an enlightened and influential leadership which drives quality movement forward and nurtures an innovative and creative workforce capable of meeting customers' expectation (Abby and Hong, 1996). This zeal seems to be missing in the automobile sector, which is evident through Figure 3.5. The popular models in the Indian automobile sector are Deming's approach and Ishikawa model.

(xi) Seventy-nine percent of respondent organizations in automobile manufacturing category are reported to be using 5S activities, 83% are using Pareto Diagrams, 75% are using Benchmarking tools, 67% are using Total Productive Maintenance (TPM) tools, only 42% are using Design Of Experiment (DOE), 75% are using Why-why Analysis, 92% are using Control Charts, 70% are using Kaizen tools, 50% are using Scatter Diagram tool, 75% are using Statistical Process Control (SPC) tools, 33% are using Programme Evaluation Review Technique/Critical Path Method (PERT/CPM) tools, 92% are using Plan-Do-Check-Act (PDCA) Circle, 28% are using Business Process Re-engineering, 10% are using Six Sigma, 100% are using Suggestion Scheme, 100% are using Run Chart, 83% are using Brainstorming, 83% are using Fish

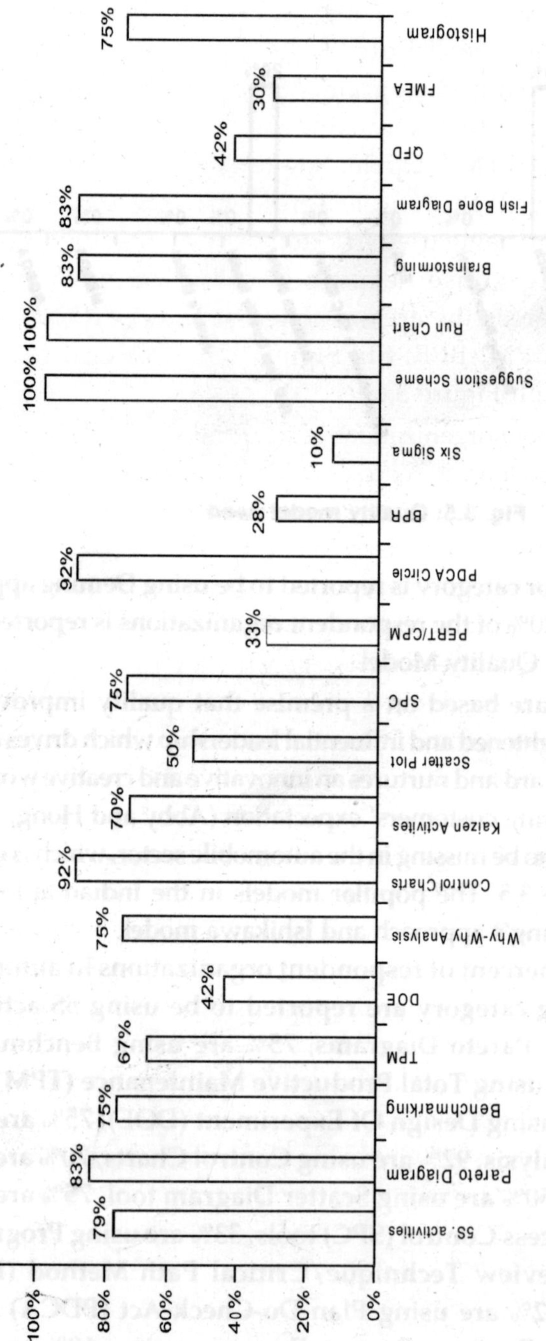

Fig. 3.6: Quality tools used in automobile manufacturers

Bone Diagram, 42% are using Quality Function Deployment (QFD), 30% are using Failure Mode and Effect Analysis (FMEA), and 75% are using Histogram. 5S activities, Pareto Diagram, Benchmarking, Why-Why Analysis, Control Charts, Kaizen activities, SPC, PDCA Circle, Suggestions Scheme, Run Chart, Brainstorming, Fish Bone Diagram and Histogram are very popular and are being used in automobile manufacturer category for improving house keeping and solving quality-related problems whereas the area of concerns are TPM, DOE, Scatter Plot, PERT/CPM, BPR, Six Sigma, QFD and FMEA. This is evident through Figure 3.6.

40% of respondent organizations in supplier category are reported to be using 5S activities, 85% are using Pareto Diagram, 30% are using Benchmarking tools, 20% are using TPM tools, only 19% are using DOE, 62% are using Why-Why Analysis tools, 77% are using Control Chart tool, 40% are using Kaizen tools, 35% are using Scatter Diagram tool, 74% are using SPC, only 23% are using PERT/CPM, 50% are using PDCA Circle, only 20% are using BPR tools, 5% are using Six Sigma, 69% are using Suggestion Scheme, 60% are using Run Chart, 63% are using Brainstorming tool, 63% are using Fish Bone Diagram, only 31% are using QFD, 25% are using FMEA and 59% are using Histogram tool. Pareto Diagram, Why-Why Analysis, Control Charts, SPC, Suggestion Scheme, Run Chart, Brainstorming, Fish Bone Diagram and Histogram are very popular among supplier category and are being used for improving house keeping and solving quality related problems. The area of concerns are 5S activities, Benchmarking, TPM, DOE, Kaizen activities, Scatter Plot, PERT/CPM, PDCA Circle, BPR, Six Sigma, QFD and FMEA. Same is evident through Figure 3.7.

Ten percent of respondent organizations in sub-contractor category are reported to be using 5S activities, 30% are using Pareto Diagram. None of the organization is using Benchmarking, TPM, DOE, Why-Why Analysis and Control Charts, 10% are using Kaizen tool, none is using Scatter Diagram tool, 10% are using SPC, none is using PERT/CPM, 20% are using PDCA Circle, none is reported to be using BPR, Six Sigma and Suggestion Scheme, 30% are using Run Chart, 30% are using Brainstorming tool, 30% are using Fish Bone Diagram, none is using QFD and FMEA, only 10% are using Histogram. Pareto Diagram, Run Chart, Brainstorming and Fish Bone Diagram are very popular among sub-contractor category where as other tools are not being extensively used for solving quality related problems. It is evident through Figure 3.8.

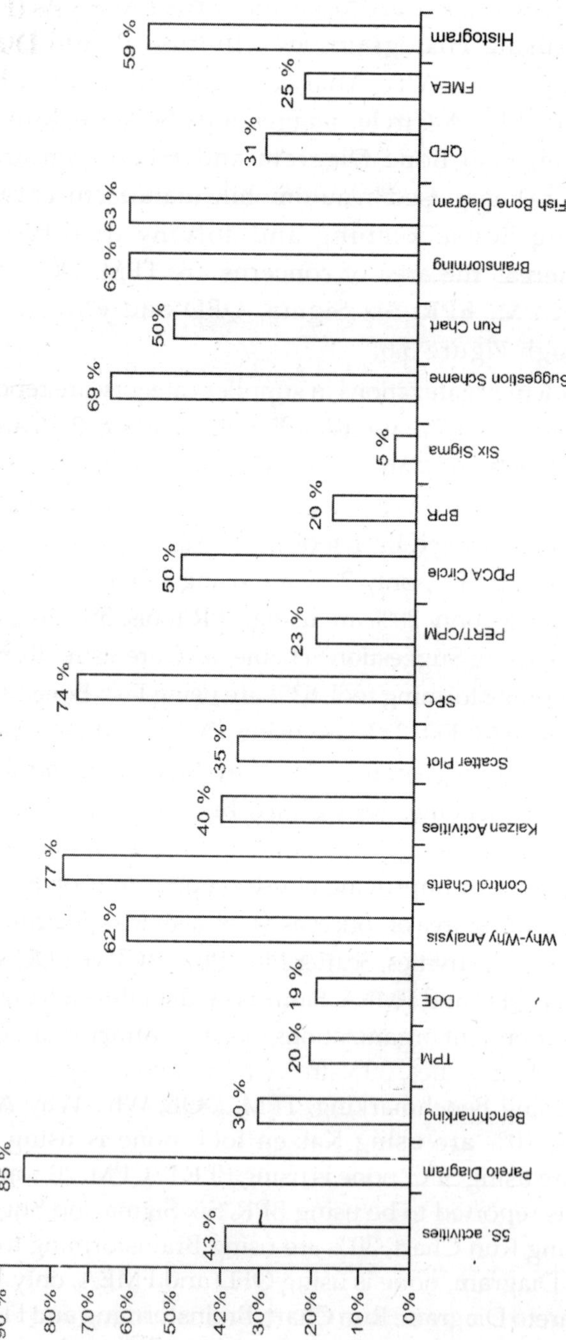

Fig. 3.7: Quality tools used in suppliers category

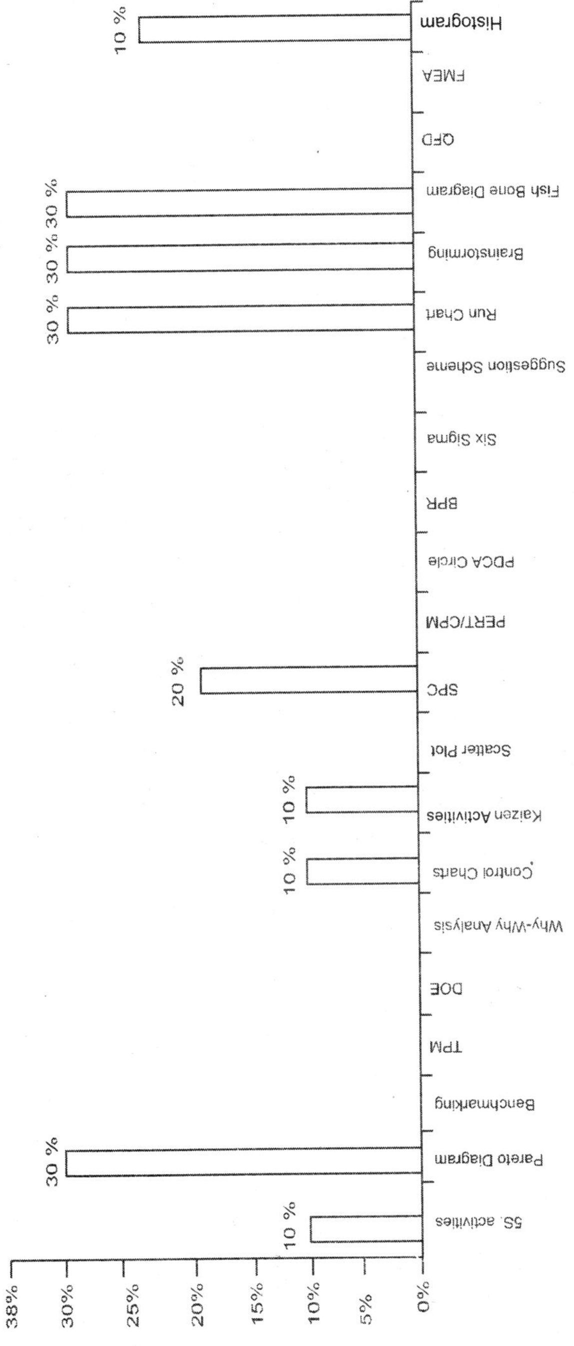

Fig. 3.8: Quality tools used in sub-contractors category

3.4.2 Usages of TQM Tools by Automobile Sector

In the automobile sector, Fish Bone Diagram, Brainstorming, Run Chart and Pareto Diagram are very popular and are being used for solving quality related problems whereas the TQM tools of lesser use are Histogram, FMEA, QFD, Suggestion Scheme, Six Sigma, BPR, PDCA, PERT/CPM, SPC, Scatter Plot, Kaizen activities, Control Chart, Why-Why Analysis, DOE, TPM, Benchmarking and 5S activities, which are also very essential for continuous improvement and better housekeeping. The overall usage of quality tools by the Indian automobile sector is shown in Figure 3.9.

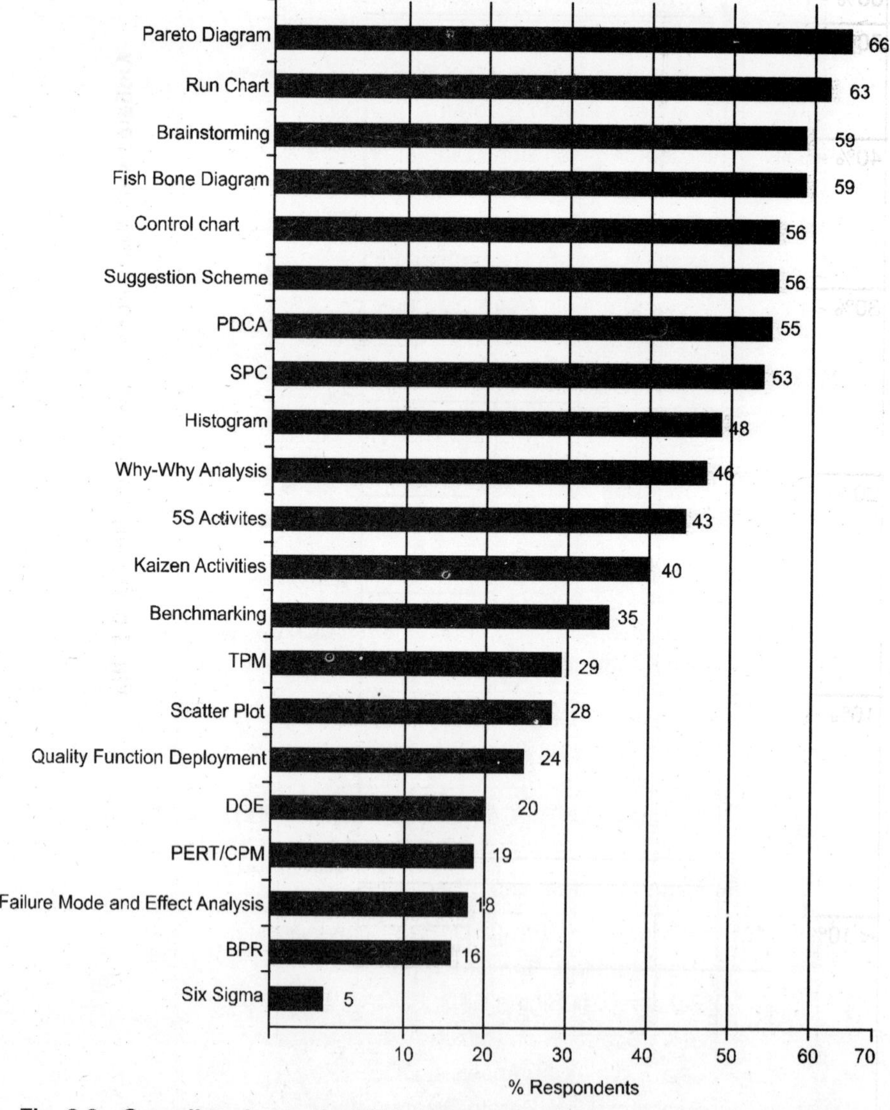

Fig. 3.9: Overall tools applicability by the respondent organizations of the Indian automobile sector

The overall applicability of various quality tools by the respondent organizations of the Indian automobile sector have been summarized in Table 3.6.

Table 3.6: Applicability of TQM tools in Indian automobile sector

Respondent organizations	*Applicability of quality tools*	*No. of quality tools used by respondent organizations*
60% - 70%	Run Chart and Pareto Diagram	2
50% - 60%	Fish Bone Diagram, Brainstorming, Run Chart, Suggestion Scheme, PDCA, SPC, Control Chart and Pareto Diagram	8
40% - 50%	Histogram, Fish Bone Diagram, Brainstorming, Run Chart, Suggestion Scheme, PDCA, SPC, Kaizen Activities, Control Chart, Why-Why Analysis, Pareto Diagram and 5S Activities	12
30% - 40%	Histogram, Fish Bone Diagram, Brainstorming, Run Chart, Suggestion Scheme, PDCA, SPC, Kaizen Activities, Control Chart, Why-Why Analysis, Bench-marking, Pareto Diagram and 5S activities	13
20% - 30%	Histogram, QFD, Fish Bone Diagram, Brainstorming, Run Chart, Suggestion Scheme, PDCA, SPC, Scatter Plot, Kaizen Activities, Control Chart, Why-Why Analysis, DOE, TPM, Benchmarking, Pareto Diagram and 5S activities	17
10% - 20%	Histogram, FMEA, QFD, Fish Bone Diagram, Brainstorming, Run Chart, Suggestion Scheme, BPR, PDCA, SPC, Scatter Plot, Kaizen Activities, Control Chart, Why-Why. Analysis, DOE, PERT/CPM, TPM, Benchmarking, Pareto Diagram and 5S activities	20
< 10%	Histogram, FMEA, QFD, Fish Bone Diagram, Brainstorming, Run Chart, Suggestion Scheme, Six Sigma BPR, PDCA, PERT/CPM, SPC, Scatter Plot, Kaizen Activities, Control Chart, Why-Why Analysis, DOE, TPM, Benchmarking, Pareto Diagram and 5S activities	21

It has been observed that the most popular quality tools among the Indian automobile sector are Run Chart and Pareto Diagram as 60-70% of the respondent organizations are using only these two tools to solve their quality related problems.

Further, 50–60%, 40-50%, 30-40%, 20-30%, 10-20%, and less than 10% of the respondent organizations are using 8, 12, 13, 17, 20 and 21 quality tools, respectively. However, the least understood tool is Six Sigma, which is being used in less than 10% of the organizations. This is a cause for real concern. Six Sigma quality represents a 2941-fold improvement in quality when compared to products built under the constraint of 99% capability. Using this vital tool the Japanese clearly outwitted, outsmarted and outsold the Americans in the car industry (Grant *et al.,*1995).

To be globally competitive it is very important that Indian automobile sector must vigorously focus for the implementation of six sigma tool along with other tools. The details about the applicability of each quality tools are given below:

Histogram

The success of any organization depends upon taking decisions that are based on facts and figures and not on the basis of intuition or gut feeling. Arranging the data in the form of Histogram can help in understanding the dispersion (extent of variation) and central tendency of the process. The extent of variation can be compared with tolerance to know the process conformance to specifications. A process is set to be operating in statistical control when the only sources of variation are from common causes. One function of a process control system, then, is to provide a statistical signal when special causes of variation are present, and to avoid giving false signals when they are not present. This allows appropriate action(s) to be taken upon those special causes (Kanji and Asher, 1996). For effective process control it is very important to use Histogram but only 48% of the responding Indian automobile organizations claim to be using Histogram as a quality tool (Figure 3.9). Overall, there is a need for improving process control for getting better results using this vital quality tool.

Failure Mode and Effect Analysis (FMEA)

To remain competitive it is very important not only to identify the present causes of failure but also to identify potential causes of failure during design and process stage itself. FMEA helps in building the prevention while planning through designing and process stage (Sharma, 1997). Only 18% of the Indian automobile sector is using FMEA as a tool for assessing potential failure for investigation (Figure 3.9), which is very low.

Quality Function Deployment (QFD)

For the success of any organization it is very important to understand the concept of internal and external customer. The desired results cannot be achieved unless internal and external customers are satisfied. Worldwide, organizations are using QFD tool for assuring that the 'voice of the customers' is not lost in the noise of product development (Bossert, 1990; Day, 1993; Akao,1990, 2002; Akao and Glenn, H, 2003). The usage of QFD in the Indian automobile sector is very low as only 24% of the organizations are focusing on QFD (Figure 3.9).

Fish Bone Diagram

Today, market needs are rapidly becoming more diversified and sophisticated, technical innovations are arriving on the scene at a bewildering pace, and competition is becoming more and more ferocious. To ride out these successive waves of change, every company now urgently requires people with a superior capacity for solving problems (Hosotani, 1992). Fish Bone Diagram, which was developed in 1943 by Ishikawa in Japan as a problem-solving technique is being used worldwide. About 59% of the Indian automobile organizations are using Fish Bone Diagram as a vital tool for solving quality related problems, which is still quite low.

Brainstorming

Brainstorming is an idea-generating technique pioneered by Alex Osborn. Worldwide organizations are using this tool to encourage team working and group discussion and progressively build on the collective wisdom in a non-threatening, non-criticizing atmosphere. Indian automobile sector has understood the vitality of this tool and 59% of the organizations are using this tool (Figure 3.9).

Run Chart

Run Chart displays the trend of changes of a characteristic over a period of time. It is a specialized graph, which uses connected lines instead of bars to illustrate data. Decision based on facts and figures is very important for effectiveness of any organization. In the surveyed organizations, about 63% of the organizations are using this chart to understand the trends and effects of various counter measures being implemented in the plant.

Suggestion Scheme

In order to improve the performance of the organization, the organization should consider employees as their most valuable assets. Globally there is a trend to improve the involvement of the employees through Suggestion Scheme. It has been an established fact that through involvement of people, an organization can get better results. Though 56% of organizations claim to have "suggestion scheme" in their organizations (Figure 3.9), still they have not been able to make full use of the potential of all employees. This is evident with the results of organizations having rejections more than 4% as discussed before.

Six Sigma

For the Indian automobile sector, "6-Sigma" implementation is not well-adapted as a tool for making continuous improvement. Only 5% of respondent organizations claim to follow "6-Sigma" tool. That is the reason why Indian automobile sector in general has not been able to achieve consistent level of quality based on ± 3 Sigma, which means that the parts falling outside the normal process range will be around 2700 parts-per-million (2700 ppm) whereas rejections in automobile sector is more than 4% (40,000 ppm). Motorola Corporation which received Malcolm Baldrige National Quality Award (MBNQA) in 1988 based its major efforts on "6-Sigma" (Pande *et al.*, 1997). A critical part of six sigma work is to define and measure variation with the intent of discovering its causes and to develop efficient operational means to control and reduce the variation. The expected outcomes of six sigma efforts are faster and more robust product development, more efficient and capable manufacturing processes, and more confident overall business performance (Sanders and Hild, 2000). In order to reduce the variation to a very low level, the first step is to "design for productivity". This means that designers configure a product in such a manner that its performance is "shielded" against variation. By doing this, the organization can be sure that its specified levels i.e. all of the product will be on target with minimum difference between units of product (Harry, 1988). When Indian automobile sector rejection is compared with sigma conversion table (Terziovski and Samson, 1999; Motorola, 2002), it provides lot of opportunities for the Indian automobile sector to make improvement to match with the performance of world-class organizations (Table 3.7).

Table 3.7: Sigma conversion table

Quality level (Yield)	*Defects per million opportunities (DPMO)*	*Sigma*	*Cost of poor quality (% of sales)*	*Types of companies*
30.9	690,000	1.0	>40	Non-competitive
69.2	308,000	2.0	30-40	Industry Average
93.3	66,800	3.0	20-30	
99.4	6,210	4.0	15-20	World Class
99.98	320	5.0	10-15	
99.9997	3.4	6.0	<10	

To be globally competitive, it is essential for the Indian automobile sector to follow "Six Sigma" as an effective continuous improvement tool to deploy TQM philosophy. The foremost reason for low implementation of Six Sigma tool in the Indian automobile sector has been identified as lack of top management commitment. Seventy percent of the top management team has not shown interest in implementation of this tool because of high cost involved in training the people for green belt, black and master black belt (Ingle and Roe, 2001). However, Blakeslee (1999) has articulated seven principles that need to be considered when implementing Six Sigma quality tools.

PDCA Circle

Worldwide organizations are using PDCA circle for problem solving. The PDCA circle was adopted and popularized by Deming and that is why this is also called Deming Circle as shown in Figure 3.10.

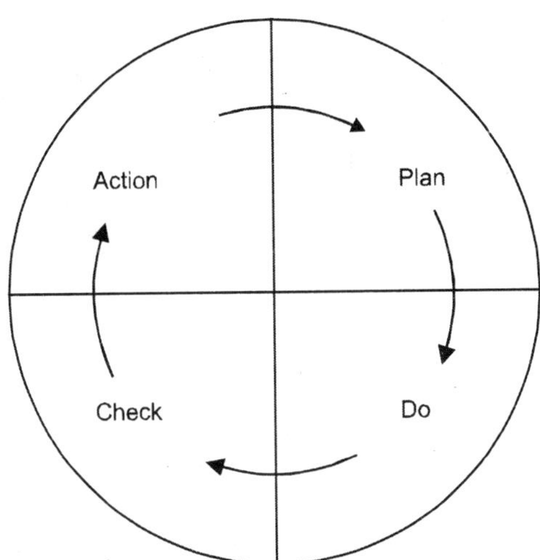

Fig. 3.10: PDCA circle

Though 55% of the Indian automobile sector claim to be following PDCA circle (Figure 3.9), the earlier result of higher rejection level and few organizations seriously focusing on cost reduction speaks to the contrary.

PERT/CPM

In the context of TQM, many global organizations are using PERT/CPM to achieve customer deadline and to complete a complex task with the best available approach (Anderson *et al.*, 1994). The result of the survey indicates that the Indian automobile sector has not effectively used the potential of this tool, which is reflected in the fact that only 19% of the organizations are using this tool (Figure 3.9). That is one of the reasons why most Indian projects undergo overruns.

Statistical Process Control (SPC)

SPC is used to separate out random variation (often called common cause or non-assignable variation) from the real variation caused by changes to the process. Control charts allow decisions to be made about processes on the basis of fact rather then gut feeling (Oakland and Followell, 1990; Ganpathy *et al.,* 1994). Though 53% of the Indian automobile organizations claim to be using SPC (Figure 3.9), the higher average rejection rate of 4% (40,000 ppm) does not corroborate the same.

Scatter Diagram

Scatter Diagram is one of the seven quality control tools for problem solving. It aims at establishing relationships between two variables. It is an investigative tool, which works backward by plotting the effect against experimentally controlled changes in the causes in the process. The strength of correlation is determined by correlation coefficient, which can be calculated by drawing a line of best fit after plotting the points, which represent independent variable (cause) on x-axis and dependent variable (effect) on y-axis (Besterfield and Dale, 1990). In our survey, only 28% of the organizations claim to be using Scatter Diagram (Figure 3.9).

Kaizen Activities

Kaizen is a Japanese term meaning 'Change for the Better'; the concept implies a continuous improvement in all company functions at all levels (Imai, 1986). Dahlgaard *et al.* (1990), surveyed companies in Japan and Korea and found that the number of companies engaged in Kaizen activities through quality circles are about 97% in Japan and Korea. Though 40% of the Indian automobile organizations claim to follow Kaizen activities (Figure 3.9), yet effective participation in quality circles is almost negligible considering the vast population of the country. Therefore, to be globally competitive it is essential for the Indian automobile sector to create conducive atmosphere where everyone is involved in Kaizen activities individually or through quality circles.

Control Chart

Control Charts are one of the seven quality control tools for continuous improvement. These are effective tools to understand process variation and help to achieve statistical control. The operator often maintains these charts at the job station. Control charts, by distinguishing special from common causes of variation, give a good indication of whether any problems are likely to be correctable locally or will require management action. Only 56% of the surveyed Indian automobile sector claim to follow control charts (Figure 3.9). The low percentage is mainly due to extremely poor use of this tool by sub-contractors of the automobile sector. The high rejection level of the organizations does not corroborate the effective use of this vital tool.

Why-Why Analysis

Why-Why Analysis helps in the identification of root causes of a problem for taking effective corrective and preventive action. The survey indicates that 46% of the Indian automobile sector claim to follow Why-Why Analysis (Figure 3.9). Majority of the organizations are working only on symptoms and that is the reason why problems keep on repeating. Overall there is a need for using this effective tool for getting better results.

Design Of Experiment (DOE)

Design Of Experiment (DOE) is a technique for the optimization of products or processes. Taguchi involves a two-stage experimental design that gives the benefits of robustness and efficiency with the minimum number of experiments. Experimental design usually involves attempt to optimize a process, which can involve several factors (e.g., temperature, time, chemical composition) at several levels (e.g., five possible temperatures, four possible times, six possible chemical compositions). World-class organizations are very effectively using this tool particularly when these organizations are working for Six Sigma. However, by and large the Indian automobile sector has not understood the utility of DOE and only 20% of the organizations have responded that they are using this tool (Figure 3.9).

Total Productive Maintenance (TPM)

Total Productive Maintenance (TPM) was introduced in Japan by Seiichi Nakazima. TPM first took root in the automobile industry and rapidly became a part of the corporate culture in companies such as Toyota, Nissan, and Mazda, and their suppliers and affiliates. Today, organizations are using TPM to achieve startling results, particularly in reducing equipment breakdowns, minimizing idling and minor stoppages, reducing quality defects and claims, boosting productivity, trimming labor and cost, shrinking inventory, cutting accidents and promoting employee involvement (Suzuki, 1994). Still, Indian automobile sector has not understood the utility of TPM and only 29% of the organizations claim to be using TPM (Figure 3.9). To achieve world-class results, the Indian automobile sector has to focus on TPM much more vigorously.

Benchmarking

The success of any organization depends upon taking decisions to fill the gaps in performance by putting in place best practices, thereby establishing superior performance. There are three distinct types of benchmarking, which can be used by an organization progressively to stimulate the improvement process. These are: internal benchmarking, competitive benchmarking and comparative benchmarking. With benchmarking, employees in the organizations can determine the best practices in the industry and organization can become best with the implementation (Zangwill, 1995; Dhawan, 1996). However, the Indian automobile sector has not effectively used this tool. Only 35% of the organizations are using benchmarking tool to improve performance (Figure 3.9).

Pareto Diagram

This is also one of the seven quality control tools. It is mainly a prioritization tool attributed to Vilfredo Pareto, an Italian economist (1848-1923). Pareto principle was first used by Juran in 1950 in relation to quality. He termed 20%, important causes 'the vital few', and 80%, less important, 'the trivial many'. A plot for Pareto analysis is a ranked frequency distribution of defects in a certain output based on type of causes (Spenley, 1992). The survey indicates that 66% of the Indian automobile organizations are using this tool (Figure 3.9). To be competitive globally, Indian automobile organizations have to prevent the problems from recurring. Organizations are required to do root cause analysis to prevent the problems from recurring.

5S Activities

5S is a foundation of the majority of improvement activities. Ever growing customer demands for quality product is forcing organizations to rethink about the workplaces. This phenomenon has been understood as product improvements cannot be done in filthy organizations and people cannot work to their maximum potential under such dismal environment. Therefore, 5S has gained worldwide importance (Hirano, 1995). This is one of the major reasons, despite 62% of automobile sector claim to be following TQM philosophy, why organizations have not been able to sustain improvement activities. This is also confirmed by the low percentage of Indian automobile organizations focusing on 5S activities. As can be seen from Figure 3.9, only 43% of the organizations are using 5S activities.

Business Process Re-engineering (BPR)

The definition of BPR is "the fundamental rethinking and radical redesign of business process to achieve dramatic improvements in business performance" (Hammer and Champy, 1993). Worldwide organizations are using BPR as an innovative tool for dramatic improvement. American automotive industry, which was in depression in early 1980s got benefited through this technique. Ford Motor achieved a 75% reduction in head count in their accounts payable departments. Reengineering should be deployed when a need exists for heavy blasting (Davenport and Short, 1990; Hammer, 1990; Business Today, 1997). However, in the Indian automobile sector only 16% of the organizations are using this tool to achieve higher performance results (Figure 3.9). If Indian automobile sector wants to be globally competitive it must focus on this vital tool.

3.4.2.1 Indian Automobile Sector Perception of Weightages on TQM Variables Elements for Effective Implementation of TQM in the Organizations

The characteristics of world-class organizations are that they offer products and services capable of capturing and retaining world-wide market share on the basis of superior performance and lower price, besides exceeding customers' expectations. The success of the Deming Prize as a catalyst for spreading quality awareness in Japan and MBNQA criteria in America, Australian Quality Award (AQA) Model and EQA Model gave momentum to the organizations in achieving performance excellence in their respective countries.

Various award models are in practice in India like CII-Exim Award Model based on EQA Model, Golden Peacock National Quality Award Model, RGNQA Model, and Manufacturers Association of Information Technologies (MAIT). Agrawal (1999) states that these models and their implementation lack comprehensiveness and transparency and these have not been aligned to Indian socio-cultural value system. Based on Indian socio-cultural value system he proposed Business Excellence Model suited for the Indian organizations and same model has been adopted for assessment of the Indian automobile sector. The perception of weightages on twelve TQM variables/elements were sought from the Indian automobile sector and same has been compiled and shown in Table 3.8.

Table 3.8: Weightages of TQM variables for effective implementation of TQM in organizations based on automobile sector perception

TQM variables/elements	***Maximum score based on Agrawal's model***	***Automobile manufacturers average score***	***Suppliers average score***	***Sub-contractors average score***	***Automobile sector average score***	***Percentage of error over maximum score***
Leadership	125	100	119	159	126	1%
Strategic Planning	100	81	100	148	110	10%
Information Management	60	87	85	55	76	27%
Human Resource Focus	95	77	84	86	82	14%
Customer and Market Focus	110	88	95	108	97	12%
Supplier Focus	30	50	51	15	39	30%
Process Management	80	93	95	87	92	15%
Score of Enablers	**600**	**576**	**629**	**658**	**622**	**4%**
Impact on Society	70	75	40	35	50	29%
Human Resource Satisfaction	100	95	85	66	82	18%
Customer Satisfaction	115	135	119	83	112	3%
Supplier Satisfaction	40	58	46	25	43	8%
Organization-Specific Business Results	75	61	81	133	91	23%
Score of Results	**400**	**424**	**371**	**342**	**378**	**5%**
Total score	**1000**	**1000**	**1000**	**1000**	**1000**	

The average variation against each variable/element is less than 30% against the maximum score of each variable/element. Incidentally, this also matches with the adjustment limit of 30% adapted during evaluation by the different MBNQA award examiners. Board of examiners for MBNQA award reviews applications in a four-stage process. First, each application is reviewed independently by at least five examiners, wherein the strengths and weaknesses of the assessees are examined. Each examiner assigns numerical score to each examination item. Organizations unable to go to the next stage are provided with a complete feedback report. In the examination the approach deployment and results are used in awarding numerical scores based on scoring guidelines. Applicants are required to provide information on these dimensions. In the second stage, consensus review is undertaken. If the difference between highest and lowest assigned score by each examiner is up to 30%, the lead examiner will allocate a final value for each item. If the difference is higher than 30%, then discussions are held among examiners to achieve consensus score. In the discussion, issues for site visit and agenda for management discussions are also identified. These discussions also form the basis of the feedback report. This normally includes comments on strengths, and areas for improvement. Typically a score of 750 or so takes an organization to site visit stage. In a site visit, five to eight examiners including at least one senior examiner are included. The objective is to verify the information and clarify the issues and questions highlighted at the review stage. Interview with the management and employees, review and examination of the applicable records and information are the key features of a site visit. The final plan as agreed by the organization and examiners are sent in advance. In the third stage, site visit is undertaken. After the site visit, the findings are submitted to a panel of judges. A full panel of judges reviews the last stage of the award procedure. The judges recommend two winners for each category and the award administrating authority does the final approval. To maintain the integrity of the award, rigorous record checks are carried out by award administrating authority. There is a check for compliance with environmental, public health and safety regulations and other relevant records. This ensures that the award winners are appropriate role models.

Since average variation in each variable/element is less than 30% as shown in Table 3.8, Agrawal's (Agrawal, 1999) TQM variables/elements weightages have been taken as it is. Analysis of the Section-II of the questionnaire would be presented now.

3.4.3 Response Analysis of the Questionnaire

The response has been statistically analyzed and a total score for each organization is calculated. It has been found that the senior management has been liberal in self-assessment of their own organization. This leads to a bias in assessment of own achievement. Therefore, the absolute score based on this analysis has been suitably adjusted in each element/ variable to minimize the bias. To arrive at the final score, the average score of each variable/element against maximum 5-point scale has been converted against maximum score assigned to each variable/element. The total of all individual variable/element score gives the self-assessment score of the organization.

In order to adjust the score obtained, MBNQA award criteria qualifying score is assumed as the guiding factor. Literature review revealed (Brown *et al.*, 1994; Van der Wiele *et al.*, 1996a) that organizations getting around 600 score in the MBNQA criteria are considered as a serious contenders for the award and site visit is undertaken for such organizations. After compilation, self-assessment data reveals that 27% of the organizations have rated themselves higher than 800. Their average score has been found to be around 869. Considering that these organizations could qualify as serious contenders for the MBNQA award assessment, their average score of 869 could be considered as 600. This means self-assessment rating is to be adjusted by [869-600/869 = 30.9%] say 30%.

Incidentally, this adjustment rating also matches with the result of Agrawal (Agrawal, 1999). Absolute score obtained therefore, has been adjusted by 30%. To get an indicative feel of the maturity level of organizations, the moderated score can be compared with the levels given in Table 3.9, 3.10 and 3.11 below. The tables are based on the results of Caravatta, Siow and, Chin and Pun (Caravatta, 1997; Siow *et al.*, 2001; Chin and Pun, 2002).

Table 3.9: Relationship of score with organizational maturity (Caravatta, 1997)

Score Range	*Characteristics*	*Description*
1000	World-class quality performance	Excellent approaches, full deployment, processes continuously improved, sustained results.
800	Superior quality accomplishment	Good systematic, effective approaches have been refined and are deployed through out most of the company. Results are good to excellent in most key areas. Continuous improvements are in place. Trends show positive improvement.

Contd....

600	Strong quality implementation	Strong, systematic and effective approaches to quality are in place. Good results and/or improvement trends in most key areas. No major gaps in development.
400	Quality awareness	Organization is aware and needs to begin to formalize its quality efforts. No systematic approaches, results are weak and poor.
200	Traditional find and fix	Main emphasis is quarterly profit maximization, cost containment and reduction.
0	No quality awareness	—

Table 3.10: Relationship of score with organizational maturity (Siow *et al.*, 2001)

Evaluation Criteria	***Evaluation Definition***	***Grades***
World-class	Comprehensive evidence of a systematic approach to succession plans. Clear evidence that these plans are being regularly reviewed, leading to improved business effectiveness.	1.0
Award winners	Extensive evidence of a systematic approach to succession plans. Clear evidence is available that these plans are being regularly reviewed and refined.	0.75
Improvers	Evidence of a systematic approach to succession plans is available. Clear evidence is available that these plans are being regularly reviewed.	0.50
Drifters	Little evidence of a systematic approach to succession plans. There is clear evidence that these plans are being occasionally reviewed.	0.25
Uncommitted	No evidence of a systematic approach to succession plans. No plans are reviewed.	0

Table 3.11: Relationship of score with organizational maturity (Chin and Pun, 2002)

TQM status	*Descriptions of TQM status*	*Score*
Achiever	Organizations have reached a point of TQM maturity. The kind of culture, values, trust, capabilities, relationship and employee involvement required to attain the internationally or recognized standards specific quality excellence awards have been developed. Continuous improvement has become total in nature.	≥ 70
Improver	Organizations are those who are moving in the right direction and have made real progress, but they have still a long way to go. The process of improvement is typically not self-sustaining, and the TQM efforts may not be internalized throughout the organization. These organizations are often vulnerable to short-term pressures and unexpected difficulties.	≥ 40 but < 70
Initiator	Organizations are those who have become aware of continuous improvement in their organization, but there are still no clear guidance of what to do in order to facilitate the TQM adoption process.	≥ 20 but < 40
Uncommitted	Organizations are those with some understanding (or misunderstanding) of TQM and have decided that the principles and practices underpinning the concept are not for them. For instance, they may give an impression that they have adopted TQM, but no real changes have been made.	< 20
Unaware	Organizations are those not familiar with the concept, practices and tools and techniques of continuous improvement. Some may be registered to ISO 9001 or ISO 9002, but they are unaware of the wider issues and mechanisms of continuous improvement and TQM.	0.

A statistical analysis of the response/score of 48 organizations has been carried out. An average score of 48 organizations can be considered as the national automobile sector average. The national automobile sector average is determined as 484 (moderated by a level of 70%). This average is slightly less than national average i.e. 491 (Agrawal, 1999). This also matches indirectly with the result given in Tables 3.12 and 3.13. The table is based on the results of Sharma (Sharma, 1997).

Table 3.12: Development status in TQM

Relative grade/Rating	***Industry***
(a) Outstanding	Heavy Engineering
(b) Very Good	Automobile Industry
(c) Good	Light Engineering, Chemicals
(d) Satisfactory	Electronics
(e) Poor	Textiles

In terms of point scores, the order obtained is: Textiles < Electronics < Light Engineering < Chemicals < Automobile < Heavy Engineering.

Table 3.13: Overall rating of the organizations based on total composite score on attributes of TQM

	Electronics	***Light Engg.***	***Heavy Engg.***	***Auto-mobile***	***Chemicals***	***Textiles***
Composite point score	86.24	91.51	107.83	101.30	86.8	73.03
Maximum applicable point score	150	150	150	150	140	140
Score percent	57.49	61.00	71.89	67.53	62.00	52.16

Sharma (1997) study reveals that the automobile score has been 675 against 1000 maximum score. After moderation of this score @70% to minimize the factor of self-bias, the score obtained has been 473. This score almost matches with the automobile score of 484 computed by this study. Based on these results it is revealed that there has been very slow improvement in TQM since 1997 in the automobile sector. After comparing 484 score against Table 3.9, it can be assumed that the situation in Indian automobile sector is little more than quality awareness. The Indian automobile sector is in the category of improver when 484 score is compared against Tables 3.10 and 3.11. This implies that the Indian automobile sector is aware about the need for improving quality. However, systematic approaches are not yet in place and efforts for improvement are not yielding sufficient results. As per Sakaria (1995), India's performance has been abysmal among the 41 countries whose products and services were ranked by the World Competitive Report 1994. India occupies a lowly 38th place on TQM practices and price to quality ratio of India is 3.47 as against 7.03 of Japan on a 10-point scale. Same report of 1996 and 2001 (IMD, 2002) also shows that India has slid several places on all parameters even against 1994 rankings. The composite score of 484 when compared with the earlier results of Sharma (1997) and Agrawal (1999) reveal that there is no significant progress in TQM. It implies that there has been no significant progress in TQM since 1994 in the automobile sector. This also dispels the notion that an ISO 9000/QS 9000/ISO 14001 certified organization means excellence. These certificates may only mean commitment on the part of top management and beginning of the journey towards performance excellence. However, the Indian automobile sector has to go a long way as far as development of TQM philosophy is concerned.

The relationship of score among different automobile categories reveals that the weakest link among the three categories is the sub-contractor category. The average score of sub-contractor category is 401 against 536 and 495 of automobile manufacturers and suppliers categories, respectively. The comparative results are shown in Table 3.14. It is evident from Table 3.14 that both categories i.e. automobile manufacturers and suppliers seem to be working hard to achieve 600 score. This implies that both are working hard to deploy TQM philosophy to achieve strong, systematic and effective approaches to quality. To succeed, in the automobile sector as a whole much development work has to be done in sub-contractor category. In this regard automobile manufacturers and suppliers have to take lead in systematic development of the sub-contractor category.

3.5 INDIVIDUAL ELEMENT ANALYSIS

3.5.1 Leadership

In early 80's, some of liberal policy changes were announced by Government of India, making a turning point for the automobile sector. Maruti Udyog Limited (MUL), a joint venture with Suzuki Motors Ltd. of Japan was set up. Other Indo-Japanese joint ventures were set up in two-wheeler industry like Hero Honda, TVS Suzuki, Escorts Yamaha, Kinetic Honda etc. Further the delicensing of auto sector in 1993 opened up the gates to a virtual flood of international automakers into the country to

Table 3.14: Comparative score among automobile manufacturer, supplier, sub-contractor categories and national composite score of automobile sector

S. No.	Category/elements	Maximum score	Normalized average score			
			Automobile manufacturers category	***Suppliers category***	***Sub-contractors category***	***Automobile sector (after moderation)***
I	**Enablers**					
1	Leadership	125	66	66	58	63
2	Strategic planning	100	57	53	46	52
3	Information management	60	33	29	24	29
4	Human Resource Focus	95	49	45	36	45
5	Customer and market focus	110	60	55	45	55
6	Supplier focus	30	15	13	11	13
7	Process management	80	44	38	28	38
	Total enablers	**600**	**324**	**299**	**248**	**295**

Contd....

II	Results					
8	Impact on society	70	38	31	24	31
9	Human resource satisfaction	100	52	47	36	45
10	Customer satisfaction	115	60	59	49	57
11	Supplier satisfaction	40	22	18	13	18
12	Organization specific business results	75	40	41	31	38
	Total results	**400**	**212**	**196**	**153**	**189**
	Maximum score	**1000**	**536**	**495**	**401**	**484**

tap the large population base of more than one billion people. This revolution brought a greater systems emphasis, more market orientation/ customer focus, continuous improvement culture, latest tools and practices of TQM and top management commitment towards quality. This is evident by the average score of 2.52 of the Indian automobile sector on leadership as shown in Table 3.15. It is particularly more predominant in case of automobile manufacturer and supplier categories where average score is 2.63 and 2.66 respectively on a 5-point scale.

All ISO 9000/QS 9000 certified organizations have developed and communicated quality policy and objectives. The key value emphasized is the importance of the customer focus, continuous improvement, teamwork, data-based decisions, mutual contributions and open communication. Some organizations developed core values, vision and mission statement also. This is evident by the higher average score of 2.82. Lowest score is assigned to the aspect, "the top management gives effective consideration to quality of work in appraisal system". This score is 2.57 in automobile manufacturer category, 2.64 in supplier category and only 2.10 in sub-contractor category on a 5-point scale. This implies that most of the organizations are not giving due consideration to the performance appraisal system with the quality of work. Another weak area is for the aspect, "benchmarking the organization's performance against the best performer." The average score is 2.45, 2.58 and 1.54 in case of automobile manufacturer, supplier and sub-contractor categories, respectively.

Table 3.15: Leadership

1. Leadership	*Normalized average score*			
	Automobile manufacturers category	*Supplier category*	*Sub-contractor category*	*Automobile sector*
1.1 Top Management a. The top management is having personnel valuable involvement in all aspects of quality management	2.80	2.96	2.24	2.78
b. The top management trains the members of the core team (constituted of senior level managers) on group jobs. Always active in providing and receiving training	2.68	2.64	1.82	2.48
c. The top management actively involve them-	2.63	2.61	2.31	2.51

Contd....

selves in timely recognition and appreciation of individual's/team's contribution				
d. The top management encourages the core team to set high performance goals and provide appropriate resources	2.63	2.82	1.82	1.98
e. The top management gives effective consideration to quality of work in appraisal systems	2.57	2.64	2.10	2.51
f. The top management encourages core team to monitor and evaluate the level of performance and assess its effectiveness	2.68	2.74	1.96	2.57
g. The top management respect and value all employees and encourage open communication and exchange of information among different teams for enhancing innovativeness and creativeness in each individual	2.92	2.64	2.24	2.58
h. The top management is supportive and pay sufficient attention to the needs of the people and maintain comparative status with other similar organizations	2.57	2.56	1.96	2.44
i. The top management show trust and confidence in their subordinates and empower them to take decision	2.63	2.77	2.10	2.60
1.2 Top Management Commitment				
a. The top management commits itself to the organi-	2.80	2.88	2.73	2.82

Contd....

zation's vision and mission and informs everyone down the line				
b. The top management views customers and suppliers as an integral part of value chain	2.74	2.96	2.73	2.86
c. The top management gives importance to the suggestions made by the employees and encourages to take up incremental improvement efforts	2.68	2.70	3.01	2.76
1.3 Change Management				
a. The top management is committed to change management through				
• Benchmarking the organization's performance against the 'best performer'	2.45	2.58	1.54	2.33
• Challenges due to changes in the environmental factors	2.45	2.45	2.03	2.44
• Poor performance of the organization due to internal factors	2.21	1.97	2.66	2.17
Total	**39.43**	**39.92**	**33.25**	**37.81**
Average (normalized score)	**2.63**	**2.66**	**2.22**	**2.52**

Visible change management is weak due to internal factors as is evident from the average score of 2.17 on a 5-point scale. However the appreciation that quality management is not a 'quick fix' but requires a long-term commitment for continuous improvement is very much there. Deming (1993), Juran (1986) and Agrawal *et al.* (1998) also give great emphasis on developing leadership.

3.5.2 Strategic Planning

The average score of strategic planning is 2.64 on a 5-point scale and is shown in Table 3.16. This implies that all responding organizations are having strategic planning. Automobile manufacturer category is very strong in strategic planning with average score of 2.83 on a 5-point scale and weakest among these is sub-contractor category with average score of 2.31 on a 5-point scale. Most companies have realized that unless strategic planning is put into practice, they will not be able to compete under the present competitive market scenario. This is in contrast to the pre-liberalization era when only two car models were available i.e. Ambassador and Premier Padmini. Now the automobile sector is realizing that they have to compete on different models, features, quality cost and delivery.

This has brought the following into the focus: new technology, involvement of people, teamwork, putting into action long-term strategy rather than short-term gains. The appreciation that potential growth is possible only through world-class quality is forcing the automobile sector to continuously improve and implement strategic planning. QS 9000 (1998), Barclay (1993) and Lascelles and Dale (1989) also give great emphasis on developing business plan.

Table 3.16: Strategic planning

2. Strategic Planning	***Normalized average score***			
	Automobile manufacturers category	***Supplier category***	***Sub-contractor category***	***Automobile sector***
a. The top management is committed to spend enough time for understanding the changing business scenario and its implications	2.74	2.80	2.24	2.67
b. The organization is ready to create a high level vision and mission of what it can be like in future in the changing business scenario	2.80	2.74	2.38	2.68
c. The organization's strategic planning incorporates the needs of customers after a thorough understanding of their needs, market trends and address realignment of work process to improve customer focus and operational performance	2.80	2.72	2.38	2.67

Contd....

d. The profile of organization's strengths, weak ness, opportunities and threats forms the basis of strategies.	2.86	2.39	2.38	2.51
e. Efforts are made to integrate quality i.e., quality planning, quality control and quality improvement with business strategies	2.86	2.64	2.38	2.64
f. The organization's strategies are targeted for quantified measurable improvement in quality, cycle/response time and waste reduction	2.80	2.70	2.38	2.65
g. Long-term perspective is more important than short-term gains	2.80	2.67	1.96	2.56
h. Commitment of resources for new facilities, process improvements and training is done considering long term objectives	2.98	2.72	2.38	2.72
Total	**22.63**	**21.37**	**18.48**	**21.10**
Average (normalized score)	**2.83**	**2.67**	**2.31**	**2.64**

3.5.3 Information Management

The organizations should have effective information management system. They should be using techniques for continuous improvement of processes and quality projects across the organization. They should achieve this through team work and cross-functional teams. Networking should be actively promoted and information should be easily accessible to all. QS 9000 (1998) also gives emphasis on Electronic Communication and Shipment Notification System and also gives emphasis on continuous improvement based on the analysis of company level data. The average score of 2.44 on a 5-point scale is indicated in Table 3.17. This implies that shared information and information technology is providing adequate technological support and communication.

Automobile manufacturer category is very strong with average score of 2.92 on a 5-point scale against a question "Information Technology (IT) is being used to improve the co-ordination and information access across various departments." This is an area of concern for supplier and sub-contractor categories with average score of 2.29 and 1.61 on a 5-point scale, respectively.

Automobile manufacturer category is very strong with average score of 2.80 on a 5-point scale against a question "IT is being used to connect two parties (internal or external) within a process that would otherwise communicate through intermediaries." But this is an area of concern for supplier and sub-contractor categories with an average score of 1.72 and 1.47 on a 5-point scale, respectively.

Another strong area in the automobile sector against a question is "organization uses information on product performance, customer feedback/complaints etc. for quality improvement" with average score of 2.91 on a 5-point scale.

Another area of concern is assigned to the question "employees usually feel free to share information with their managers and/or colleagues." The average score 2.45 on a 5-point scale implies that there is a lack of environment for employees to feel free to share information with their managers and/or colleagues.

Another area of concern is assigned to the question "organization's information management system is easily accessible throughout the organization." The average score of 2.39 on a 5-point scale implies that there is a lack of transparency in accessibility of the information. The growing use of information technology is a good sign. As this will result in effective transformation of raw knowledge into useful data by an increased use of information processing capabilities of computer and value-adding capabilities of human resources (Agrawal *et al.,* 1998).

Worldwide, there is emphasis on the use of information technology. In Indian ISO 9000/QS 9000 certified automobile organizations, the use of past performance data to improve understanding of the processes is very limited. This is indicated by the modest average score of 2.51 on a 5-point scale.

Another area of concern is that the organization's working system and procedures do not promote easy upward flow of information. This is indicated by the modest average score of 2.48 on a 5-point scale. Ishikawa (1985) and John (1995) also give great emphasis on developing information management.

Table 3.17: Information management

3. Information Management	*Normalized average score*			
	Automobile manufacturers category	*Supplier category*	*Sub-contractor category*	*Automobile sector*
3.1 Information Technology (IT)				
a. IT is being used to improve the co-ordination and information access across various departments	2.92	2.29	1.61	2.30
b. It has transformed unstructured processes into routine transactions through shared databases	2.74	2.13	1.61	2.17
c. IT is being used to transfer information rapidly and easily across large distances, making the process independent of geography	2.68	2.16	1.47	2.14
d. IT is being used to connect two parties (internal or external) within a process that would otherwise communicate through intermediaries	2.80	1.72	1.47	2.17
e. IT and communication technologies are used to spread information and to reduce time lag	2.68	2.23	1.40	2.17
3.1 Shared Information				
a. Organization's working system and procedures promote easy upward flow of information	2.68	2.48	2.24	2.48
b. Employees usually feel free to share information with their managers and/or colleagues	2.80	2.45	2.03	2.45
c. Organization uses information on product performance, customer feedback/complaints etc. for quality improvement	2.98	2.83	3.01	2.91
d. Organization reviews and updates all data before	2.63	2.64	2.10	2.52

Contd....

integrating in process improvement plans				
e. Organization uses supplier performance related data for quality improvement efforts	2.68	2.53	2.59	2.58
f. Organization's information management system is easily accessible throughout the organization	2.68	2.51	1.75	2.39
g. Organization uses past performance data to improve understanding of processes	2.63	2.72	1.82	2.51
h. Organization periodically evaluates and improves its processes so as to further improve overall performance	2.86	2.64	2.24	2.61
i. Organization gives priority to product quality improvements decision vis-à-vis financial performance	2.80	2.68	2.52	2.67
Total	**38.55**	**33.69**	**27.86**	**34.07**
Average (normalized score)	**2.75**	**2.43**	**1.99**	**2.44**

3.5.4 Human Resource Focus

Human resource foçus is an improvement enabler in the business excellence model. The organization should keep focus on the needs and expectations of its employees to utilize their full potential. This will help in the development of TQM philosophy in the organization. The environment should be open and trustworthy. Recognition and reward schemes should reflect contribution of individuals and teams based on performance and should be transparent (Choppin, 1991; Stratton, 1991; Harber *et al.*, 1991).

There is an improvement in human resource focus in the organizations. This is evident with an average score of 2.36 on a 5-point scale in the automobile sector. Emphasis on education and training is improving with an average score of 2.52 on a 5-point scale. Though this is still an area of concern for sub-contractor category with average score of 1.89 on a 5-point scale (Table 3.18). Employees are empowered to reduce the non-value adding activities. This is evident by average score of 2.67 on a 5-point scale.

In order to improve the performance of the organizations, the organizations should consider employees as their most valuable asset. Worldwide, there is a trend to offer stress control programme for the employees to improve the quality of their work life. However, in the Indian automobile sector this is not happening. The average score of 1.94 on a 5-point scale corroborates the same. In order to improve the quality and productivity in the organizations, health, safety and ergonomics considerations of the employees are must and this is evident with the organization's growing concern about well being of the employees. The average score of 2.46 on a 5-point scale corroborates the same.

In order to make use of the full potential of employees, efforts are made to recognize and reward the accomplishment of the employees. This is evident by the average score of 2.39 on a 5-point scale. However, this is a weak area as far as sub-contractor category is concerned with an average score of 1.96 on a 5-point scale. Another area of concern is timely and sincere recognition and award to the deserving employees. This is evident by a low average score of 2.07 on a 5-point scale. Other areas of concern are recognition and reward for the team-oriented behaviour. If human resource focus is not systematically sustained, it will become difficult to survive and grow. Gryna (1991), Juran and Gryna (1995) also give great emphasis on developing human resource focus.

Table 3.18: Human resource focus

4. Human resource focus	***Normalized average score***			
	Automobile manufacturers category	***Supplier category***	***Sub-contractor category***	***Automobile sector***
4.1 Human Resource Development				
a. Organization's business plan consider human resources capabilities for addressing quality leadership opportunities	2.57	2.42	2.03	2.39
b. The investment in education and training is decided considering employee needs and future business needs	2.92	2.58	1.89	2.52
c. Employees are encouraged to write, follow and improve upon the standard operating procedures	2.63	2.37	2.10	2.38

Contd....

d. Employees are empowered to reduce the non-value adding activities	2.92	2.64	2.45	2.67
e. Employees are encouraged to involve and participate in decision making of major policy changes, that enable to soften the resistance to change	2.57	2.32	1.61	2.23
f. Employees are encouraged to develop multi skills and capabilities (through job rotation)	2.57	2.29	2.31	2.51
g. Organization evaluates and improves its human resource planning using employee's feedback	2.28	2.26	1.89	2.19
h. Organization encourages employees to bring their problems without any hesitation to the seniors for resolution	2.68	2.58	1.61	2.41
i. Organization makes effort to integrate employees job performance with key quality improvement targets and business results	2.68	2.56	2.24	2.52
j. Organization offers stress control programmes for the employees so as to improve quality of their work life	2.28	1.97	1.47	1.94
k. Organization is concerned about employee well being (health, safety and ergonomics)	2.74	2.42	2.24	2.46
4.2 Employee Involvement				
a. Employees are enthusiastic in supporting the vision and mission of the organization	2.57	2.53	1.82	2.39
b. Each and every employee contributes significantly for the success of organization	2.78	2.56	2.17	2.52

Contd....

c. Employees are responsible in maintaining safe working environment	2.86	2.53	1.89	2.48
4.3 Shared Information				
a. Efforts are made to recognize and reward the accomplishments of the employees	2.63	2.45	1.96	2.39
b. The recognition and rewards to the employees are timely and sincere	2.39	2.04	1.75	2.07
c. Efforts are made to recognize and reward the team oriented behaviour	2.68	2.16	1.68	2.19
d. Efforts are made to understand the family and home life of the employees	1.98	1.83	1.26	1.75
Total	**46.71**	**42.51**	**33.95**	**42.41**
Average (normalized score)	**2.60**	**2.36**	**1.88**	**2.36**

3.5.5 Customer and Market Focus

It is very important to understand the concept of internal and external customer. The desired results cannot be achieved in case of external customer unless internal customer is focused. The supplier/customer relationships should be systematically managed to secure clear understanding of requirements (Day, 1993; Akao, 2002; Akao and GlennH, 2003). Average score of 2.47 on a 5-point scale corroborates that there is an increase in the emphasis on customer and market focus. There is an increasing emphasis on the determination of customers' current requirements and expectations regularly. This is evident by the average score of 2.81 on a 5-point scale (Table 3.19). Some organizations regularly evaluate and improve upon their processes based on the changing customer expectations. This is evident by an average score of 2.67 on a 5-point scale. An organization regularly evaluates and improves the commitments for service performance to match customer expectations. This is evident by average score of 2.54 on a 5-point scale. Band (1991) and Peters (1988) also give great emphasis on developing customer and market focus.

Table 3.19: Customer and market focus

5. Customer and Market Focus	***Normalized average score***			
	Automobile manufacturers category	***Supplier category***	***Sub-contractor category***	***Automobile sector***
5.1 Customer Knowledge				
a. Organization regularly determines customer's requirements and expectations	3.03	2.83	2.52	2.81
b. Organization selects customer groups/ market segments with intention of adding quality-conscious customers	2.57	2.58	2.24	2.51
c. Organization determines specific product features and their relative importance using customer listening techniques like QFD etc.	2.63	2.02	1.54	2.06
d. Organization analyses and uses information on customer loss/gain and product performance to develop future strategies	2.57	2.45	2.45	2.48
e. Organization addresses future needs taking into account competitors, customer, and changing market segments	2.86	2.53	2.03	2.45
f. Organization regularly evaluates and improves upon its processes based on changing customer expectations	2.86	2.69	2.38	2.67
5.2 Customer Relationship				
a. Commitment like guarantee/warrantee etc. are simple and are effectively communicated to the customers	2.68	2.48	1.68	2.37

Contd...

b. Organization regularly evaluates and improves their commitments for service performance to match customer expectations	2.92	2.58	1.96	2.54
c. Organization follow up with customers on product performance and builds long-term relationship	2.86	2.72	2.10	2.63
d. Organization has an effective system to reward and motivate customer-contact employees	2.22	1.97	1.61	1.95
e. Organization regularly evaluates and uses the customer feedback to improve performance standards	2.74	2.86	2.24	2.70
Total	**29.93**	**27.71**	**22.75**	**27.17**
Average (normalized score)	**2.72**	**2.52**	**2.06**	**2.47**

3.5.6 Supplier Focus

Supplier should be treated as partners in the process of improvement. Supplier rating system, supplier training and development, understanding of supplier's needs etc. should be an ongoing activity. QS 9000 (1998) also emphasizes the same.

Efforts in the area of supplier quality management have been initiated by the Indian automobile sector. Awareness is growing. Activities like supplier quality system audits, supplier rating and qualification system, supplier training and supplier recognition programmes are being initiated. But still they are at very low level. This is evident by the low average score of 2.10 on a 5-point scale (Table 3.20). Thus, there is a need for the Indian automobile sector to seriously focus in this area.

There is a lack of co-ordination on a question "members of the major suppliers work jointly in teams on issues like new product development, resource saving and energy conservation." This is evident by the low average score of 2.04 on a 5-point scale. Another area of concern is lack of organizations sharing of the resources and system with major suppliers like financial and accounting system, financial resources, information expertise and training facilities. This is evident by consistent low score on a 5-point scale against each above point. The average score range from 1.63

to 2.39. Thus, there is a greater need to share resources for mutual benefit and improving quality, lowering cost and delivery. This could become an effective basis for implementation of Just-in-Time (JIT).

The average score of 2.64 on a 5-point scale indicates growing implementation of vendor rating system (based on quality, price and delivery schedule). Another area of strength has emerged against the question "the organization has a goal to develop the suppliers". This is evident by the average score of 2.60 on a 5-point scale. But the weakest link seems to be the sub-contractor category that has yet to take the task of further development of their suppliers. Low involvement of sub-contractors in the development of their vendors is evident with low average score of 1.54 on a 5-point scale.

In the surveyed organizations the supplier focus seems to be quite low. Thus there is a need to improve supplier focus in the Indian automobile sector. Suppliers should be considered as business partners and should be given due and appropriate focus. This is the need of the hour under the present liberalized economy for the survival and growth of the Indian automobile sector. Literature survey revealed that there is no systematic study which has been carried out to analyze the impact of supplier quality management (Froker *et al.,* 1997). Lascelles and Dale (1989) and Imai (1996) also give great emphasis on developing supplier focus.

Table 3.20: Supplier focus

	Normalized average score			
6. Supplier Focus	***Automobile manufacturers category***	***Supplier category avg.***	***Sub-contractor category***	***Automobile sector avg.***
a. Members of the major suppliers work jointly in teams on issues like new product development, resource saving and energy conservation	2.45	1.97	1.75	2.04
b. The organization shares the following resources and system with major suppliers				
• Financial and accounting system	1.75	1.72	1.26	1.63

Contd....

• Financial resources	1.98	1.81	1.26	1.74
• Information system	2.63	1.97	1.68	2.07
• Production planning system	2.80	2.10	2.52	2.37
• Quality system	2.80	2.42	1.82	2.39
• Technical expertise	2.57	2.37	1.89	2.32
• Training facilities	2.28	1.83	1.26	1.82
c. Material supplied by vendors is accepted:				
• By 100% inspection	2.80	3.07	1.40	2.65
• By thumb rule inspection	3.21	3.28	3.15	3.24
• By sampling inspection	2.74	2.72	1.75	2.52
• By certification of the vendor	2.16	1.53	1.96	1.78
d. The assessment of the strength of supplier is based on:				
• Vendor rating system (based on quality, price and delivery schedule)	2.92	2.83	1.82	2.64
• Technical competence	2.51	2.04	2.10	2.17
• Overall management competence	2.10	1.78	1.96	1.89
e. The organization has a goal to develop the suppliers	2.98	2.56	1.54	2.60
Total	**40.19**	**35.42**	**27.93**	**33.69**
Average (normalized score)	**2.51**	**2.21**	**1.75**	**2.10**

3.5.7 Process Management

ISO 9000/QS 9000 quality system implementation helps in improving the understanding of the processes through structured documentation. Quality system should integrate with continuous improvement for all products and services. 5S, Kaizen, Poka-yoke, cross-functional teams (CFT), quality circles and TPM should be used to improve processes. Process improvement targets should be measurable. These include project activities, corrective and preventive actions, opportunities for using SQC techniques, cost of quality, supplier auditing, competitive benchmarking and measuring customer satisfaction and dissatisfaction. Effective use of PDCA cycle can help the Indian automobile sector in developing the continuous improvement culture.

Average score of 2.35 on a 5-point scale indicates the awareness regarding process management. Many organizations are working to improve product design considering customers' stated and implied needs. This is evident by the average score of 2.32 on a 5-point scale (Table 3.21).

Table 3.21: Process management

	Normalized average score			
7. Process Management	***Automobile manufacturers category***	***Supplier category***	***Sub-contractor category***	***Automobile sector***
7.1 Product management				
a. Organization's product design considers customer's implied and future likely needs also	2.86	2.37	1.54	2.32
b. Organization validates its product designs taking into account performance, process and supplier capabilities	2.68	2.26	1.75	2.26
c. Company evaluates and improves design and design processes so as to improve product quality and cycle/ response time	2.68	2.26	1.68	2.25
d. Organization determines the cause of variations, makes corrections and integrates them into the process using statistical techniques etc.	2.86	2.45	1.82	2.42
7.2 Process management				
a. Organization regularly evaluates and maintains the key business process, their requirements, quality and operational performance	2.80	2.61	2.10	2.56

Contd....

b. Organization makes use of benchmarking/customers information for business and support service process improvement	2.68	2.51	1.68	2.38
c. Organization effectively uses alternative technology, process research and testing for business process improvement	2.74	2.32	1.75	2.30
Total	**19.30**	**16.77**	**12.32**	**16.49**
Average (normalized score)	**2.76**	**2.39**	**1.76**	**2.35**

The average score of 2.56 on a 5-point scale is quite encouraging against the question "organization regularly evaluates and maintains the key business process, their requirements, quality and operational performance". Another area of strength against the question is "organization determines the cause of variations, makes corrections and integrates them into the process using statistical techniques etc." The average score of 2.42 on a 5-point scale corroborates the same. However, sub-contractors are using very limited knowledge of SPC as is evident by the low average score of 1.82 on a 5-point scale. The knowledge of workers in using SPC is very limited in the sub-contractor category.

Benchmarking is being done in most of the organizations. This is evident by the average score of 2.68 and 2.51 in case of automobile manufacturer and supplier categories, respectively. This is a good beginning to improve the processes and performance. However, this is an area of concern as far as sub-contractor category is concerned. This is evident through low average score of 1.68 on a 5-point scale. This can be detrimental in sustaining quality in the long run by the automobile manufacturers.

Overall, there is a need for improving process management for getting better results. Due to lack of effective process management, some problems keep on repeating time and again. The present efforts for process management/improvement are not satisfactory. Systematic approach is therefore, required to overcome this weakness. Ishikawa (1985) and Smith (1995) also give great emphasis on developing process management.

3.5.8 Impact on Society

All employees should value and promote their organization within the community. The organization should have well-established prevention-based systems for environmental management (OHSAS 18001, 1999). Automobile manufacturers are encouraging their suppliers to go for ISO

14001 Environmental Management System. The organizations are required to follow all regulatory requirements mandatorily.

Some organizations have started taking interest in societal responsibilities, but generally there is a lack of awareness towards promoting this aspect. This is evident by the low average score of 2.21 on a 5-point scale (Table 3.22).

Table 3.22: Impact on society

8. Impact on Society	*Normalized average score*			
	Automobile manufacturers category	*Supplier category*	*Sub-contractor category*	*Automobile sector*
a. Organization is effectively satisfying the needs and expectations of the society at large	2.86	2.26	2.45	2.45
b. Organization effectively evaluates possible impacts of its products and operations on society	2.92	2.32	1.40	2.28
c. Adequate efforts are done in the alignment of work plans with the available resources	2.74	2.42	2.10	2.37
d. Organization effectively promotes ethical conduct in all activities that it does and organization's ad-campaigns are truthful and reflects facts	2.86	2.42	2.59	2.17
e. Organization effectively considers quality of work-life while deciding service conditions of employees.	2.63	2.07	1.40	2.07
f. Organization effectively considers energy conservation and preservation of Global Resources/Raw Materials	2.86	2.48	1.33	2.33
g. Organization considers utilization of the recycled materials and makes effective efforts to improve upon it.	2.51	2.32	1.54	2.21

Contd....

h. Organization makes efforts to impart education and training to community at large/ neighbourhood with respect to its products and services	2.28	1.81	1.12	1.78
Total	**21.64**	**18.09**	**13.93**	**17.66**
Average (normalized score)	**2.70**	**2.26**	**1.74**	**2.21**

Very few organizations effectively evaluate possible impacts of its products and operations on society. This is evident by the low average score of 2.28 on a 5-point scale. In this regard the worst hit is sub-contractor category with average score of 1.40 on a 5-point scale.

Another area of concern is the lack of efforts on the part of organizations to impart education and training to community at large/neighbourhood with respect to its products and services. The low average score of 1.78 on a 5-point scale corroborates this. The overall results indicate that the Indian automobile sector is yet to work in a significant way in this direction. Present contribution of the automobile sector for society is not satisfactory and needs concerted efforts to make improvement in this direction. ISO 14001 (1996) also gives great emphasis on developing impact on society.

3.5.9 Human Resource Satisfaction

The major constraint in the Indian automobile sector is to make full use of the potential of all employees. Generally there has been lack of seriousness in the process of recruitment, training, development, motivation and involvement. Employees have less faith and trust on the recognition and award system. Lack of interest on the part of human resource reflects in managing the shop floor. By and large, workers have general grievance against management and this is evident on the shop floor the way key resources are handled. Management is required to recognize this very critical area and initiate trust building measures. A low average score of 2.29 on a 5-point scale indicates this aspect, which is shown in Table 3.23.

There is a growing need to improve industrial relations and sort out differences/demands across the table without keeping any issues pending. This is evident through a high average score of 2.73 on a 5-point scale. This is very encouraging and quite a contrast to the past.

Another strong area has been that there is a growing realization on the part of the employees in superior quality and services. This is also evident through average score of 2.74 and 2.58 on a 5-point scale in case of automobile manufacturers and suppliers, respectively. But the same point is a matter of concern for a sub-contractor category. This is evident with a low score of 1.96 on a 5-point scale. Unless serious efforts are made to develop sub-contractor category, maintaining quality of products and services on the part of automobile manufacturers cannot be sustained in the long run. Another area of concern is employees satisfaction level, which is not regularly reviewed and corrective action taken. This is evident through a low average score of 1.93 on a 5-point scale. Thus lot need to be done to improve the human resource satisfaction. This will help the Indian automobile sector to survive and grow in the liberalized economy. ISO/TS 16949 (2002) and Imai (1996) also give emphasis on developing human resource satisfaction.

Table 3.23: Human resource satisfaction

9. Human Resource Satisfaction	***Normalized average score***			
	Automobile manufacturers category	***Supplier category***	***Sub-contractor category***	***Automobile sector***
a. Employees satisfaction level is regularly reviewed and corrective action taken	2.39	1.86	1.54	1.93
b. Existing system of incentive and reward are adequate for maximum employee contribution	2.45	2.10	1.54	2.07
c. Efforts are made by the organization to improve job skills of the employees and improvements are visible	2.80	2.39	1.75	2.37
d. The employees' motivation level is very high and consistently high performance is effectively rewarded	2.45	2.21	1.61	2.14
e. Organization's image as an employer is good and organization is able to attract best talent from market	2.33	2.42	1.61	2.23
9.1 Team Work				
a. The team members trust one another	2.74	2.42	1.75	2.37
b. The team members appreciate constructive criticism	2.57	2.32	1.75	2.26

Contd....

c. There is intense communication within the teams to generate good and great ideas, about potential changes and solutions to problems	2.39	2.29	1.82	2.22
d. Team members are exposed to training on benchmarking, project management and other tools and techniques to carry out the change effort successfully	2.57	2.29	1.75	2.25
e. The team members create their performance measurement system	2.51	2.23	1.54	2.16
9.2 Value				
a. Employees in the organization understand that each and every job is essential and important and every individual makes a difference	2.51	2.35	1.96	2.30
b. Employees believe in accepting the ownership of problems and solve them	2.63	2.29	1.96	2.30
c. Employees in the organization believe that "We succeed or fail together as a team not as individuals"	2.51	2.24	1.54	2.17
d. Employees believe in superior quality and service	2.74	2.58	1.96	2.49
9.3 Industrial Relations				
a. The organization has cordial and good industrial relations between the labour and management	2.92	2.72	2.10	2.64
b. There is discussion across the table on the demands made by either side to sort out the issues, without keeping any issue pending	2.78	2.72	2.73	2.73
Total	**41.29**	**37.44**	**28.91**	**36.62**
Average (normalized score)	**2.58**	**2.34**	**1.81**	**2.29**

3.5.10 Customer Satisfaction

Customer Satisfaction means the internal and external customers are satisfied. The increase in realization of customer focus is reflected by the average score of 2.49 on a 5-point scale (Table 3.24).

Now organizations effectively determine customer satisfaction and make efforts to improve it further. This is evident through average score of 2.77 on a 5-point scale. Now management teams and customers regularly discuss on key policy issues, which is evident through average score of 2.55 on a 5-point scale. Area of concern is that customer satisfaction level is not effectively compared with that of key competitors based on in-house scientific studies. This is evident through a low average score of 2.09. ISO/TS 16949 (2002) and Akao (2002) also give emphasis on developing human resource satisfaction.

Table 3.24: Customer satisfaction

10. Customer Satisfaction	***Normalized average score***			
	Automobile manufacturers category	***Supplier category***	***Sub-contractor category***	***Automobile sector***
a. Organization effectively determines customer satisfaction and makes effective efforts to improve it further	2. 80	2.86	2.52	2.77
b. Customer satisfaction level is effectively compared with that of key competitors based on in house scientific studies	2.39	2.21	1.40	2.09
c. Customer satisfaction level is effectively compared with that of key competitors by using independent survey	2.45	2.02	1.40	2.00
d. Customers' feedback is collected and used to improve the products and customer service	2.80	2.74	2.73	2.76
e. Efforts are made to anticipate the customers' needs, requests and probable complaints that will enable the company to respond in real time	2.63	2.56	1.96	2.45

Contd....

f. Management team and regular customers discuss on key policy issues	2.57	2.74	2.03	2.55
g. Top management executives base their decisions on the customers data base analysis rather than their previous experience in business	2.51	2.61	2.31	2.52
h. Customers have a 'single point of contact' in the organization	2.74	2.56	2.73	2.64
i. Service to internal customers is improved by actively involving different functional departments and units	2.63	2.67	1.96	2.51
j. The organization collects and analyses the data on customer dissatisfaction concerning:				
• Organization's service	2.63	2.56	1.68	2.39
• Organization's products	2.86	2.64	2.80	2.73
Total	**29.01**	**28.15**	**23.52**	**27.41**
Average (normalized score)	**2.64**	**2.56**	**2.14**	**2.49**

3.5.11 Supplier Satisfaction

A TQM system does not support receiving inspection but this would work only if the processes of the suppliers are under control. Supplier processes should produce consistent quality parts and most of their parts should be self-certified. Therefore many organizations have programme to improve supplier's performance. These include supplier quality audits, supplier rating and qualification systems, training and supplier recognition programmes. A low average score of 2.28 on a 5-point scale (Table 3.25) for supplier satisfaction is a matter of concern.

Table 3.25: Supplier satisfaction

11. Supplier satisfaction	***Normalized average score***			
	Automobile manufacturers category	***Supplier category***	***Sub-contractor category***	***Automobile sector***
a. What is the level of the quality of your supplier	2.80	2.21	1.54	2.22

Contd....

performance as compared to supplier of your key competitors?				
b. Organization constantly endeavours for development of capabilities of its suppliers	2.80	2.43	1.54	2.33
Total	**5.60**	**4.64**	**3.08**	**4.55**
Average (normalized score)	**2.80**	**2.32**	**1.54**	**2.28**

3.5.12 Company Specific Business Results

A balanced view of company-specific business results is important to understand whether the company is becoming good or merely looking good. An assessment against this criterion confirms the organization's approaches have successfully ingrained the core values into the main streams of the enterprise. Efforts in the area of improving product quality significantly over last financial year have been initiated. This is evident through an average score of 2.80 on a 5-point scale (Table 3.26).

Table 3.26: Company-specific business results

	Normalized average score			
12. Company specific business results	***Automobile manufacturers category***	***Supplier category***	***Sub-contractor category***	***Automobile sector***
a. Organization enjoys product quality leadership for the range of products it deals with	2.63	2.74	1.68	2.49
b. Organization has significantly improved the product quality from last financial year	2.92	2.83	2.59	2.80
c. Organization has significantly reduced the product quality from last financial year	2.45	2.58	1.75	2.38
d. Organization has significantly improved the pro-				

Contd....

duct from the viewpoint of production cycle/response-time from last financial year	2.63	2.58	2.17	2.51
Total	**10.62**	**10.74**	**8.19**	**10.18**
Average (normalized score)	**2.65**	**2.69**	**2.05**	**2.55**

3.6 EMERGING ISSUES

The analysis indicates strengths as well as weaknesses in the TQM-related approaches of respondent organizations. The overall scenario in the automobile sector's indicates that TQM philosophy is in infancy stage. Indian automobile sector average score indicates that this sector is aware about the need for improving quality. After liberalization, the scene is fast changing and organizations are trying hard to imbibe continuous improvement culture through adopting TQM as a guiding philosophy. However, there are many vital areas for improvement.

The response analysis indicates that sub-contractor category is still not responding to the changing needs of the market scenario. Major steps have not been taken for cost reduction by this category. Corrective and preventive actions arc weak thus leading to very high rejections. The cost of quality has not been understood as an important analytical tool to drive continuous improvement in a prioritized manner. The overall awareness of quality models lacks in all categories and the worst hit is sub-contractor category. In many organizations, people are trained for quality tools, but softer part of the quality integration i.e. quality culture and team working have not been well appreciated.

Another weak area is top management involvement in training the members of the core team which is reflected in low morale of the people. The strategic planning is generally not done on the basis of organization's strengths, weaknesses, opportunities and threats. Generally, strategic plans are not being monitored regularly. Though information management system has been developed, information sharing among employees is very weak. Information is not easily accessible throughout the organization. The top management also sets too many priorities resulting in lack of focus. There is generally a lack of communication of goals throughout the organization. Past performance data is not shared in setting objectives and goals and neither is it effectively deployed.

In many organizations, environment is not conducive to make full use of the potential of employees. There is lack of transparency in award and recognition of the employees. Lack of using customer listening techniques like QFD is a weak area and thus customer and market focus lacks depth.

Consequently, roles for all levels of management and technical staff in quality improvement based on customer perception are not developed.

Suppliers are generally not treated as business partners in the process of improvement. Thus many objectives of improving quality, lowering cost and delivery lack direction and organizations are forced to keep inventory to ward off these problems. Processes are generally not benchmarked to drive continuous improvement culture. It has been analyzed that there is general lack of interest in societal responsibilities. Very few organizations effectively evaluate possible impacts of its products and operations on society.

It is realized that TQM programmes cannot achieve desired results, unless everybody right from top to bottom is involved. The analysis reveals that in spite of above weaknesses the overall quality scenario in the automobile sector is improving. More and more organizations are focusing on TQM as a strategy to survive and grow.

3.7 CONCLUSIONS

The actual TQM activities started in the automobile sector after liberalization. The de-licensing of the auto sector in India opened the gates to a virtual flood of international automakers into the country. This revolution brought a greater system emphasis, more market orientation/ customer focus and continuous improvement culture. This has a positive effect on the automobile sector. The response of the questionnaire provided significant insights into TQM scenario in the automobile sector. It provided an opportunity to understand the best practices being followed by leading quality conscious organizations and also throws light on the way these are implementing TQM philosophy. A survey has been undertaken with a view to obtain general status of TQM practices followed in the automobile sector. Subsequently the results would be used to develop a simulation model using system dynamics. The next chapter focuses on developing a causal relationship for TQM index in the Indian automobile sector.

4

Chapter

TQM Modeling of the Automobile Manufacturing Sector

4.1 INTRODUCTION

Before the start of liberalization of the market in the early 1990s, the growth of the automobile-manufacturing sector in India had been relatively slow and there were only a few indigenous auto manufacturers. One significant event – the start of a new era for the Indian automobile manufacturing - was when, in 1983, Maruti, one of the few auto companies, was taken over by the Government of India and subsequently entered into a joint venture agreement with Suzuki of Japan. The policy of economic liberalization initiated by the Government of India in 1991 gave a further impetus to the growth of this sector. Major auto manufacturers such as General Motors, Hyundai, Fiat, Honda, etc. set up manufacturing bases in India. With liberalization came increased competition and manufacturers came under pressure to improve quality. Soon after the liberalization of markets, manufacturers started to implement formal quality improvement programmes, including total quality management (TQM).

Though there has been steady growth in the automobile sector, India is still a player of little consequence in the world auto market. This lack of international market penetration has been mirrored by a lack of continuing development of TQM. The Indian automobile sector contributes only 5 percent of the country's industrial output, as compared to the 8-10 percent range in other developing countries like Mexico and Brazil, and a much higher 15-17 percent range in developed countries like the USA and Germany (Sharma, 2000). Bridging the wide gap between the "best in class" and the present ranking of India on different competitive parameters provides an enormous challenge, but must be done if India is to realize its potential for economic growth.

National Quality Awards (NQA) (such as the Deming Prize, the Malcolm Baldrige National Quality Award (MBNQA), the Australian Quality Award (AQA) and the European Quality Award (EQA) models) have contributed significantly to an understanding of business excellence in countries like Japan, the USA, Australia and European nations (Mody, 1996; McAdam and O'Neill, 1999; Bester, 2000). Such models may be helpful in assisting the Indian automobile industry to become more competitive in the global market. This chapter addresses issues relating to the identification of TQM variables, which would be used in the development of a causal loop diagram, which may be helpful in taking proactive action in implementing the TQM philosophy. This chapter begins with the identification of the TQM variables that are used as the building blocks of the causal loop diagram.

Quality can be defined and described in a variety of ways, from a variety of perspectives. A precise meaning depends on the context within which "quality" is being used. It has been defined as excellence (Peters and Waterman, 1995), value (Feigenbaum, 1951), fitness for use (Juran and Gryna, 1988), conformance to requirements (Crosby, 1979), defect avoidance (Crosby, 1984), meeting and/or exceeding customers' expectations (Parasuraman *et al.*, 1985). Though there is a wide variety of concepts surrounding the term "quality", all writers agree that quality is one of the important "critical success factors" to achieve competitiveness. This is also true for the Indian automobile sector. One of the major reasons for the dismal performance of the Indian automobile sector in world markets is the lack of effective quality management systems (Rao, *et al.*, 1997; Mohanty, 1995).

TQM initiatives often fail due to a lack of essential quality measures to monitor important factors such as customer satisfaction, supplier satisfaction, management leadership, product quality and employee morale. It is the feedback on such measures via appropriate measurement that allows the success of quality initiatives to be assessed – and the quality programmes to be refined and modified.

Most authors describe TQM as a "system" but the dynamic interaction among its subsystems has not received due attention in the literature. SD methodology has been extensively used for modeling policy issues and operational problems. However, one of the reasons for the limited use of SD for modeling TQM is the fact that the philosophical concept of TQM sometimes leads it to abstraction and subjectivity. The complex interactions among seven "enablers" variables and five "results" variables have been developed and their interactions have been discussed in this chapter and present chapter is also focused on the long-term effect of these interactions.

This chapter has been organized as follows: it starts with identification of TQM variables, an explanation of the system dynamics methodology, causal loop diagram for a TQM inolex, system dynamics modeling and its structural details. Based on the SD approach, TQM model is developed for automobile sector. The chapter ends with model results, validation and conclusions.

4.2 IDENTIFICATION OF TQM VARIABLES

Many authors describe TQM as "a system" but the dynamic interactions among its subsystems have not received due attention in the literature. Application of system dynamics in deriving a "TQM index" has a tremendous potential. TQM index is an aggregate "score" of TQM variables that are clustered under "enablers" and "results". One reason for using system dynamics in modeling TQM is that the TQM philosophy shares many abstract concepts (Kumar, 1995).

A generic framework for a NQA model can be divided into two parts: enablers and results. Such an analysis rightly suggests that the existence of "good" enablers underpins better results. A simple, pictorial representation of this quality framework model is shown in Figure 4.1.

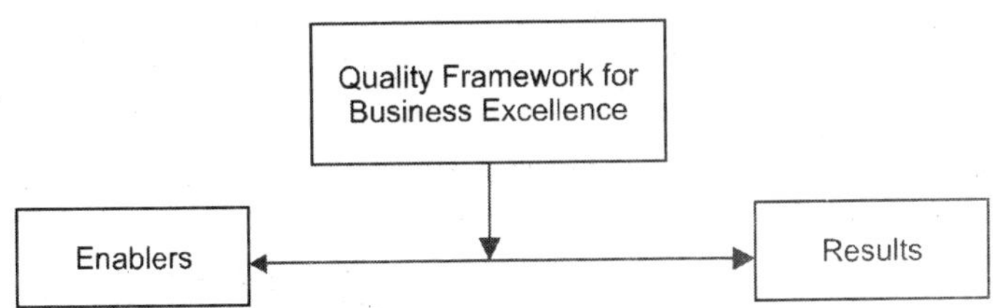

Fig. 4.1: Quality framework model

By using the MBNQA model and modifying it to suit Indian conditions, twelve TQM variables have been identified. Seven of these variables have been identified as enablers and five variables have been identified as results.

4.2.1 Identification of TQM Variables: Enablers

Within the context of Indian socio-cultural values, the seven enablers have been identified as: leadership, strategic planning, human resource focus, customer and market focus, supplier focus, process management and information management (Agrawal, 1999).

Information management provides the foundation on which all enablers rest while information acts as "the glue" as shown in Figure 4.2.

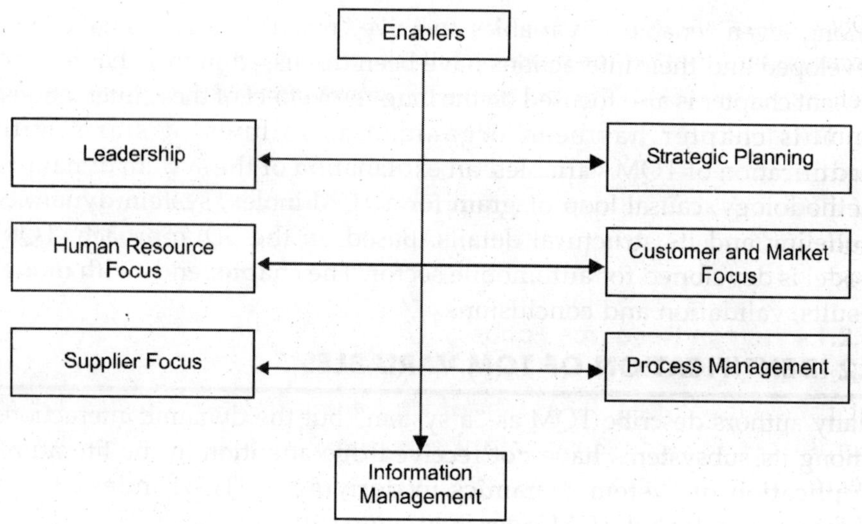

Fig. 4.2: Identification of TQM enablers

4.2.1.1 Leadership

One of the important roles of the senior managers is to provide clear vision and values that promote total quality. The top management needs to spell a clear quality policy or mission as the underpinning process to realize the value and vision (Waldman and Gopalakrishnan, 1996; Leonard and Sasser, 1982; Gryna, 1991). The top management needs to build culture, and progressively remove cross-departmental barriers. It needs to act as facilitators to improve the ways things are done by encouraging participation, involvement and development of employees. Leaders need to become a part of the team to pursue customer satisfaction both internal and external.

4.2.1.2 Strategic Planning

Business strategies need to incorporate long-term goals and objectives for the organization. For this purpose, one should consider changing customer and market expectations. Overall strategy with a focus on critical success factors and critical processes can lead to individuals and departments towards clear mission, purpose, statements and goals arrived at by the participation. Long-term view of the future should be clearly identified and effectively communicated within the organization (Peters, 1988; Tillery and Rutledge, 1991).

4.2.1.3 Information Management

The organizations need to have effective information management system for taking timely and proactive actions (Crosby, 1979; Deming, 1986; Juran,

1986). Important attributes of information management are: a) timely and accurate information for process control, and avoiding the production of defectives; b) availability and usage of information where it is needed for immediate action (Flynn *et al.,* 1994). Effective information measurement and communication system need to be in place for continuous improvement of all processes. The role of information filters should continuously be reduced by eliminating barriers and improving response time (Ishikawa, 1985; John, 1995).

4.2.1.4 Human Resource Focus

The organizations are required to focus on the needs and expectations of their employees. They should maximize opportunities for all employees to secure use of full potential through the processes of recruitment, training, development, motivation, and involvement (Leonard and Sasser, 1982; Gryna, 1991). Recognition and reward schemes should reflect contribution of individuals and teams based on the performance. Career progression should promote values and the organizational requirements must propel it towards becoming a house of integrity (Juran and Gryna, 1995).

4.2.1.5 Customer and Market Focus

Customer and market focus organizations are required to understand the concept of internal and external customers. The supplier/customer relationships can be systematically managed to secure clear understanding of requirements. Measures of customer satisfaction and financial performance need to be communicated back, to focus resources on process improvements and secure improved design and performance, in the long-term (ISO/TS 16949, 2002; Band, 1991; Peters, 1988).

4.2.1.6 Supplier Focus

TQM principles advocate that suppliers should be treated as partners in the process of improvement. Supplier rating system, supplier training and development, understanding of supplier's need should, therefore, be an ongoing activity (ISO/TS 16949, 2002; Lascelles and Dale, 1989).

4.2.1.7 Process Management

The organizations need to have systems approach to control all operations, using documented systems. Continuous improvement should be done for all products and services, with the use of various tools such as quality circles, 5S, Kaizen, fool-proofing and Total Productive Maintenance (TPM). Effective measures should be designed to quantify results (and targets) in process improvement. ISO 9000/QS 9000 quality system implementation also helps in improving the understanding of the processes and their improvement (Smith, 1995; Mody, 1995).

4.2.2 Identification of TQM Variables: Results

Results are the measures of the level of output and outcome. Results are emphasized in all the examined award models. It is observed that quality (in the form of high levels of customer satisfaction) is achieved through leadership driving strategic planning, keeping a focus on its people, customers, markets and suppliers and effectively managing the processes leading ultimately to better business results (Spitzer, 1995). In terms of "results" this translates into a series of complementary measures such as impact on society; human resource satisfaction; customer satisfaction; supplier satisfaction and company-specific business results as shown in Figure 4.3.

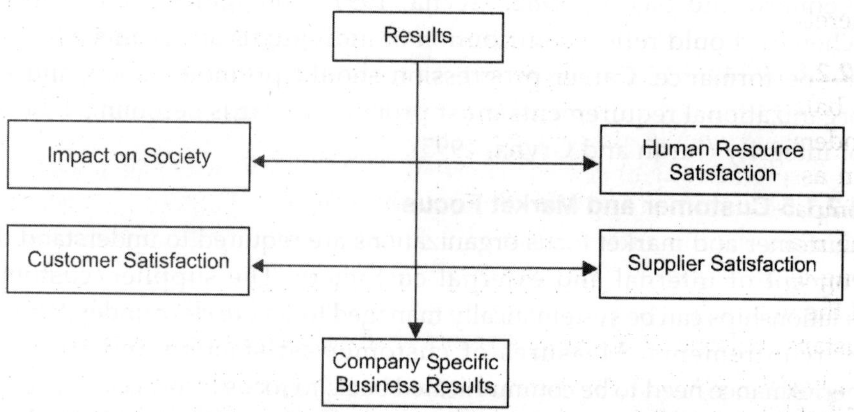

Fig. 4.3: Identification of TQM variables of results

4.2.2.1 Impact on Society

All employees are required to value and promote their organization within the community. The organization should balance its societal responsibilities with the demands of its stakeholders. The organization should have well-established prevention-based systems for environmental management. The organization should also follow all regulatory requirements. The organization should not be seen breaking any societal moral values (ISO 14001, 1996; OHSAS 18001, 1999).

4.2.2.2 Human Resource Satisfaction

Human resource satisfaction means the organization has been able to make use of full potential of all employees. This demonstrates the effectiveness of the processes of recruitment, training, development and motivation. Employees have faith on the recognition and reward schemes. They have faith and trust on management. Performance appraisal system should be encouraging co-operation rather than competition among employees (ISO/TS 16949, 2002; IS/ISO 9000, 2000).

4.2.2.3 Customer Satisfaction

Customer satisfaction means that the internal and external customers are satisfied, the customer base is improving and organizations are getting repeat orders. Service standards and results are shared with customers and regularly improved and updated. Customers' complaints are systematically monitored and properly addressed (Akao, 2002; ISO/TS 16949, 2002).

4.2.2.4 Supplier Satisfaction

Customers treat their suppliers as partners. Suppliers are generally satisfied. They want to do repeat business and are serious to maintain long-term relationship with their customers. Customers pursue regular training and development of suppliers. The understanding of supplier's need is, therefore, an ongoing activity (ISO/TS 16949, 2002).

4.2.2.5 Company-specific Business Results

A balanced view of company-specific business result is important to understand whether the company is becoming good or merely looking good. An assessment against this criterion confirms the extent to which the company's approaches have successfully ingrained the core values into the main streams of the enterprise. A composite view of short-term and long-term performance provides substantive insight into the core values of the organization. Focusing on issues that matters most are necessary to sustain competitive advantage (Neves and Nakhai, 1995; Stratton, 1991).

4.3 SYSTEM DYNAMICS MODELING REVIEW

System Dynamics (SD) is the methodology for understanding the behavior of complex, dynamic social-technological-economic and political (S-T-E-P) systems to show how system structures and the policies used in decision-making govern the behavior of the system. System dynamics was pioneered in 1959 by Forrester (1961), who combined the cybernetics and information feedback concepts put forth by Wiener (1948), and showed the new methodology that could be applied to problems which were very difficult to be solved earlier. Within a few years of its conception, system dynamics was applied to a wide range of problems, such as managing a research and development project, combating urban stagnation and decay (Forrester, 1968, 1969), understanding the implications of exponential growth in a world of finite and declining natural resources (Forrester, 1971b) etc. Dyson (1990) described system dynamics as a way of abstracting a system by means of material and information flows, delays and information feedback control structure.

Riddalls and Bennett (2002) developed the modeling and control of aggregated production-inventory systems. Smith and Ackere (2002) stated that interest in applying SD to business policy and strategy problems have been growing due to the availability of user friendly, high level graphical simulation software such as *ithink, Powersim* and *Vensim*. They further stated that with the accessibility of books describing the SD approach such as those authored by Senge (1991), Morecroft and Sterman (1994), Sterman (2000) etc. have also played a key role in enhancing the interest in applying system dynamics in strategy problems.

Morecroft (1992) emphasized that system dynamics should use formal quantitative computer models. A repetitive experimentation with the system, testing assumptions or altering the management policies can lead to better insight. Richardson and Pugh (1981) clarified that the problems one addresses from the perspective of system dynamics have at least two features in common. First they are dynamic i.e. they involve quantities which change over time. They can be expressed in terms of graph of variables over time. Skill in defining problems dynamically is a first step towards learning the system dynamics approach. A second feature of the problems to which the system dynamics perspective applies involves the notion of feedback.

Goodman (1983) explained that some of the examples of a feedback system are servo-mechanisms as used in the NC machines and close-loop control systems. All human systems are basically feedback systems. The fundamental element of feedback structures is the relationship between two variables. The arrow indicates the direction of the influence. Coyle (1983) stated that a formal model has two advantages over the informal, the so-called mental models on which most human decisions are based. First, formal models are more explicit and communicable. A system dynamics model exposes its assumptions about a problem for criticism for better understanding the problem. A mental model, on the other hand, is fuzzy. The implicit nature of mental models is the cause of occasional misunderstandings, miscommunications, and misapplications.

Richardson and Pugh (1981) emphasized on the need of constructing flow diagrams based on causal loop relationship. The inter-relationships among the model variables are represented in a system dynamics flow diagram. Two fundamental elements, used in flow diagrams, to represent each feedback loop of the causal diagram are levels and rates of flow. The level (or state) variables describe the condition of the system at any particular time. The rate (action) variables, determine how fast the levels are changing. They represent the activities and decision functions in the system. Another type of variable is the auxiliary variables by separately representing different processes in the system.

Goodman (1983) identified the three basic steps of system dynamics procedure, which consists of:

1. formulation and verbal description of a mental model and its representation through diagram,
2. development of flow diagram based on the casual relationships of Step 1 and
3. transformation of flow diagrams to a set of equations in the form of computer simulation language.

Sushil (1993) underlined a need to understand the usefulness of a dynamic model in comparison with mental and descriptive models. He further underlined the need to use specialized software packages due to the following reasons:

- Specialized software packages need almost no programming skills. These are user friendly and interactive. These help the user to effectively build the model.
- Special functions such as table function and delays etc are in-built in any SD software.
- SD model are developed iteratively as results of simulation and provide insight about the system conceptualization and model development.
- SD model is basically a set of equations to be solved in a particular order and there is a requirement of sequencing the equations. User will have to concentrate only on nature of equations.
- The SD models result into a dynamic simulation of the systems and time response of variables are plotted to study the trends. The graphics module for SD modeling is imperative, which is difficult with general purpose programming languages.

Lee (1997) in his paper showed that system modeling enhances the system performance analysis and illustrated the causality functions and feedback loops. Lyons *et al.* (1996) built their model to investigate the present and future service demand. Pfahl and Lebsanft (1999) identified that by combining system dynamics modeling with already existing and commonly used static modeling methods we can solve the problems in the software engineering community. However, despite having many strengths, system dynamics has been subjected to severe criticism and controversy in the past. Some main criticisms of SD models are listed below:

- As per Kalman (1978) the internal structure with too many variables can make the system difficult to understand the causal behaviour.
- Keloharju (1983) observed that system dynamics methodology is difficult and require higher demand of professionalism than other methodologies.
- Although, endogenisation was considered to be a strength in the system dynamics models yet the need to cover structural

deficiencies resulted in some sort of untraceable chaos in these models (Kamlan, 1978).

4.4 SYSTEM DYNAMICS METHODOLOGY

The genesis of SD and the general systems theory can be traced to the 1940s (Bertalanffy, 1969). It is explained for different applications by Forrester (1961), Dutta and Mohapatra (1968), etc. The objective of SD approach is to capture the dynamic interaction of different system variables and to analyze their impact on policy decisions over a long-term horizon. This requires, first, system boundaries to be defined and a model of the system to be built. The systematic procedural steps in SD modeling include the following (Roberts, 1978):

(1) Define the problems to be solved and goals to be achieved.
(2) Describe the system with a causal loop/influence diagram.
(3) Formulate structure of the model, i.e. develop flow diagrams and associated mathematical models that represent rates of change through different interactions.
(4) Collect the initial data needed for operation of the model either from historical data and/or from discussion with the executives/planners having knowledge and experience of the system under study. These are the initial values of all the level variables, constants, multipliers etc.
(5) Validate the model using appropriate criteria to establish sufficient confidence in the model.
(6) Use the model to test various actions to find the best way to achieve prescribed goals.

4.5 DEVELOPING A CAUSAL LOOP DIAGRAM FOR A TQM INDEX

System dynamics focuses on the structure and behavior of the systems composed of interacting feedback loops. A "causal loop diagram" is a system dynamic tool, which helps the modeler to conceptualize the real world system in terms of feedback loops.

In a causal loop diagram, the arrows indicate the direction of influence and plus/minus signs indicate the type of influence. All other things being equal, if a change in one variable generates a change in the same direction in the second variable, relative to its prior value, the relationships between the two variables is referred to as positive. If the change in the second variable takes place in the opposite direction, the relationship is negative (Forrester, 1985; Goodman, 1983).

4.5.1 Positive Feedback Loops

When a feedback loop response to a variable reinforces the original perturbation, it is called as positive feedback loop. In a positive feedback loop, a variable continually feeds back upon itself to reinforce its own growth or decay. Expected system behaviors in positive feedback structure are exponential growth or exponential decay.

4.5.2 Negative Feedback Loops

When a feedback loop response to a change of variable opposes the original perturbation, the loop is negative or goal seeking. Negative feedback is characterized by goal-directed or goal-oriented behavior. The concept of control itself entails goal orientation. Expected behavior of a system in negative feedback structures is an asymptotic growth or asymptotic decline directed towards the goal (Goodman, 1983).

4.5.3 Assumptions in Developing the Causal Loop Diagram

The following assumptions have been made in developing the casual loop diagram for a TQM index of automobile sector in India.

1. Organizations are aware of the importance of TQM philosophy in enhancing competitiveness.
2. Total quality, essentially, is a way of business that values intellectual capital and satisfaction of customers through the involvement and empowerment of people.
3. Organizations are aware that NQA models have contributed significantly to business excellence in countries like Japan, the USA, Australia and European nations.
4. Organizations are aware that customer satisfaction, people (employee) satisfaction and impact on society are achieved through leadership driving policy and strategy, people management, resources and processes leading ultimately to excellence in business results.
5. ISO 9000, QS-9000 and ISO 14001 certification is a journey towards TQM but not an end in itself.

The definition of the full set of variables, which includes the seven enablers and five results variables, is shown in Tables 4.1 to 4.3.

Table 4.1: Definition of variables for enablers

TQM variables: enablers		
Variables	***References***	***Remarks***
Leadership (lds)	(Crosby, 1981; Deming, 1993)	Senior managers who provide clear vision and values that promote total quality. The most important TQM enabler for driving a TQM culture.
Strategic Planning (stp)	(Ishikawa, 1985; Mody, 1996)	Business strategies incorporate long-term and short-term goals based on customer and market expectations.

Contd....

Information Management (inm)	(Ishikawa, 1985; John, 1995)	Effective information and communication systems for continuous improvement of all work.
Human Resource Focus (hrf)	(Juran and Gryna, 1995)	Maximize opportunities for all employees to realize their full potential.
Customer and Market Focus (cmf)	(Day, 1993; Bossert, 1990)	Customer (internal and external customer) relationships must be managed to secure clear understanding of requirements.
Suppliers Focus (suf)	(IS/ISO 9000, 2000; ISO/TS 16949, 2002)	Suppliers are treated as partners in the process of improvement.
Process Management (prm)	(Mody, 1995)	Systems approach to quality in control of all operations including appropriate use of "quality tools".

Table 4.2: Definition of variables for results

TQM variables: enablers		
Variables	***References***	***Remarks***
Impact on Society (ios)	(ISO 14001, 1996; OHSAS 18001, 1999)	Societal responsibilities / environmental management.
Human Resource Satisfaction (hrs)	(ISO/IS 9000, 2000; ISO/ TS 16949, 2002)	All employees are motivated and dedicated to continuous improvement–feeling empowered and valued.
Customer Satisfaction (cus)	(Day, 1993; ISO/IS 9000, 2000; Akao, 2002)	Internal and external customers know that their needs are important – and addressed.
Supplier Satisfaction (sus)	(Imai, 1996; Khanna, 1999;)	Suppliers want to do repeat business – as partners.
Company Specific Business Results (bsr)	(Mody, 1996)	Do the company's results demonstrate effective performance?

Table 4.3: Definition of other variables

Other Variables	*Remarks*
Total quality management index (TQMI)	Aggregate results of TQM variables: enablers and results.
Gap in customer satisfaction (gcus)	Difference between desired customer satisfaction and actual customer satisfaction.
Gap in business results (gbsr)	Difference between desired business results and actual results.
Gap in impact on society (gios)	Difference between desired impact on society and actual impact on society.
Gap in supplier satisfaction (gsus)	Difference between desired supplier satisfaction and actual supplier satisfaction.
Gap in human resource satisfaction (ghrs)	Difference between desired human resource satisfaction and actual human resource satisfaction.
Actual customer satisfaction (acus)	Actual customer satisfaction achieved by the organization
Actual business results (absr)	Actual performance achieved by the organization.
Actual human resource satisfaction (ahrs)	Actual human resource satisfaction achieved by the organization
Actual supplier satisfaction (asus)	Actual supplier satisfaction achieved by the organization
Actual impact on society (aios)	Actual societal impact achieved by the organization.
Desired customer satisfaction (dcus)	Desired target for customer satisfaction for competitive advantage set by the organization.
Desired business results (dbsr)	Desired target for business results to sustain and grow and become competitive, set by the organization.
Desired supplier satisfaction (dsus)	Desired supplier satisfaction target set by the organization.
Desired impact on society (dios)	Desired impact on society target set by the organization.
Desired human resource satisfaction (dhrs)	Desired human resource satisfaction target set by the organization.

4.5.4 Representing Causal-Loop Relationships

A causal loop diagram for the TQM index has been developed after detailed discussions with TQM experts, practising executives and academicians and is shown in Figure 4.4. Various positive and negative feedback loops are shown in this figure. Combinations of positive and negative feedbacks that maintain the balance of the system's model are synthesized in this relationship.

It has been assumed that effective leadership modulates the implementation of TQM and thus enhances the TQM index. Only top management can influence and alter the system, thus its role is crucial. Leadership must guide every system, strategy and method for achieving excellence. Thus an "increase" in leadership causes an increase in the TQM index in the auto sector. A "decrease" in leadership has the opposite effect. Therefore, the feedback loop between leadership and TQM index variables is positive.

Similarly, customers are the final judges of how well an organization performs - what customers say, counts. It is their perception that will determine whether they remain loyal or seek an alternative. Customer-focused leadership drives employees to: listen to customers and act quickly on what they say; listen specifically to dissatisfied customers for they often deliver the most valuable information. The resulting increase in "customer and market focus" means that the organization will set high desired customer satisfaction as a particular goal. This may, if no other action is taken, increase the "gap" in customer satisfaction (the difference between desired customer satisfaction and actual customer satisfaction).

Any increased gap in customer satisfaction will have a negative effect on leadership. Thus the feedback loop between the variables of leadership, customer and market focus, desired customer satisfaction and the gap in customer satisfaction is negative. As the gap in customer satisfaction increases, it will also have a negative effect on customer and market focus. Thus the feedback loop between the variables of customer and market focus, desired customer satisfaction and gap in customer satisfaction is also negative.

What follows now is a detailed examination of the various interrelationships among the TQM variables – to establish whether the various connecting feedback loops are positive or negative. This detailed examination is essential to gain a full understanding of the interactions.

Improved (increased) leadership will tend to increase customer and market focus, which in turn will increase actual customer satisfaction. Increase in actual customer satisfaction will reduce the gap in customer satisfaction, which in turn will increase leadership. Thus the feedback loop between leadership, customer and market focus, actual customer satisfaction and gap in customer satisfaction variables is positive. An increase in the gap in customer satisfaction will also tend to reduce customer and market focus. Thus the feedback loop between customer and market focus, actual customer satisfaction and the gap in customer satisfaction is positive.

Company-specific business results are very important for the survival and growth of any (auto sector) organization. It is assumed here that an increase in leadership will tend to increase customer and market focus. This, in turn, will increase actual customer satisfaction. An increase in actual customer satisfaction will tend to increase actual company-specific business results, which in turn will reduce the gap in company-specific business results. Any increase in the gap in company-specific business results will have a negative effect on leadership and also on customer and market focus. Thus the feedback loop among the variables of leadership, customer and market focus, actual customer satisfaction, actual company-specific business results and the gap in company-specific business results is positive. Also, the feedback loop among the variables of customer and market focus, actual customer satisfaction, actual company-specific business results and the gap in company-specific business results is positive.

An increase in desired customer satisfaction will tend to increase desired company-specific business results, which in turn will increase the gap in company-specific business results. An increase in the gap in company-specific business results will have a negative effect on leadership and customer and market focus. Thus the feedback loop among the variables of leadership, customer and market focus, desired customer satisfaction, desired company-specific business results and gap in company-specific business results is negative. Similarly, the feedback loop among customer and market focus, desired customer satisfaction, desired company-specific business results and the gap in company-specific business results is negative.

An increase in leadership will tend to increase customer and market focus, which in turn will increase actual customer satisfaction. An increase in actual customer satisfaction will tend to increase the TQM index, which in turn will increase leadership. An increase in customer and market focus will also have a positive effect on the TQM index. Thus the feedback loop among leadership, customer and market focus, actual customer satisfaction and the TQM index is positive. Also the feedback loop among leadership, customer and market focus and the TQM index is positive.

An increase in leadership will tend to increase customer and market focus, which in turn will increase actual customer satisfaction. An increase in actual customer satisfaction will tend to increase actual company-specific business results, which in turn will increase the TQM index. An increase in the TQM index will have a positive effect on leadership, customer and market focus and actual customer satisfaction. Thus the feedback loop among leadership, customer and market focus, actual customer satisfaction, actual company-specific business results and the TQM index is positive. The feedback loop among customer and market focus, actual customer satisfaction, actual company-specific business results and the TQM index is also positive, as is the feedback loop among actual customer satisfaction, actual company-specific business results and the TQM index.

An increase in leadership will tend to increase customer and market focus, which in turn will increase desired customer satisfaction. An increase in desired customer satisfaction will tend to increase desired company-specific business results goal, which in turn will increase the gap in company-specific business results. An increase in the gap in company-specific business results will have a negative effect on actual impact on society, which in turn will reduce the TQM index. To remain competitive it is very important that all employees must promote their organization within the community. The organization must have well-established prevention-based systems for environmental management. The feedback loop among leadership, customer and market focus, desired customer satisfaction, desired company-specific business results, gap in company-specific business results, actual impact on society and the TQM index is negative. Similarly, the feedback loop among leadership, customer and market focus, actual customer satisfaction, actual company-specific business results, the gap in company-specific business results, actual impact on society and the TQM index is positive. Also the feedback loop connecting the variables of TQM index, customer and market focus, actual customer satisfaction, actual company-specific business results, the gap in company-specific business results and actual impact on society is positive. The feedback loop among the variables of the TQM index, actual customer satisfaction, actual company-specific business results, the gap in company-specific business results and actual impact on society variables is also positive.

An increase in leadership rate will tend to increase the TQM index, which in turn will increase actual impact on society. An increase in actual impact on society will tend to reduce the gap in impact on society (the difference between desired impact on society and actual impact on society). An increase in the gap in impact on society will tend to reduce leadership. Thus the feedback loop connecting leadership, TQM index, actual impact on society and the gap in impact on society is positive.

An increase in leadership causes an increase in strategic planning. To remain competitive, a set of measurable goals and a long-range view of the future must guide every organization. These measurable goals, emerging from the strategic planning, serve to align the work of everyone in the organization. An increase in strategic planning causes an increase in information management, which in turn increases process management. Effective management is the cornerstone of effective planning, improved decision making, and better leadership. People take decisions everyday. Without information, however, decisions are based on intuition or gut feeling. People routinely make decisions of enormous consequence about customers, strategies, goals and employees, with little or no data. This is detrimental to the TQM philosophy. Effective information management improves decision quality.

Equally important in terms of raising the TQM index is process management. Effective measures should be designed to quantify results (and targets) in process improvement. An increase the process management will tend to increase the TQM index, which in turn will further reinforce leadership. Thus the feedback loop among the variables of leadership, strategic planning, information management, process management and the TQM index is positive.

An increase in leadership will tend to increase strategic planning, which in turn will increase information management, which will further increase process management. An increase in process management will help the organization to set a desired goal for impact on society, which in turn will increase the gap in impact on society (the difference between desired impact on society and actual impact on society). An increase in this gap in impact on society will have a negative effect on leadership.

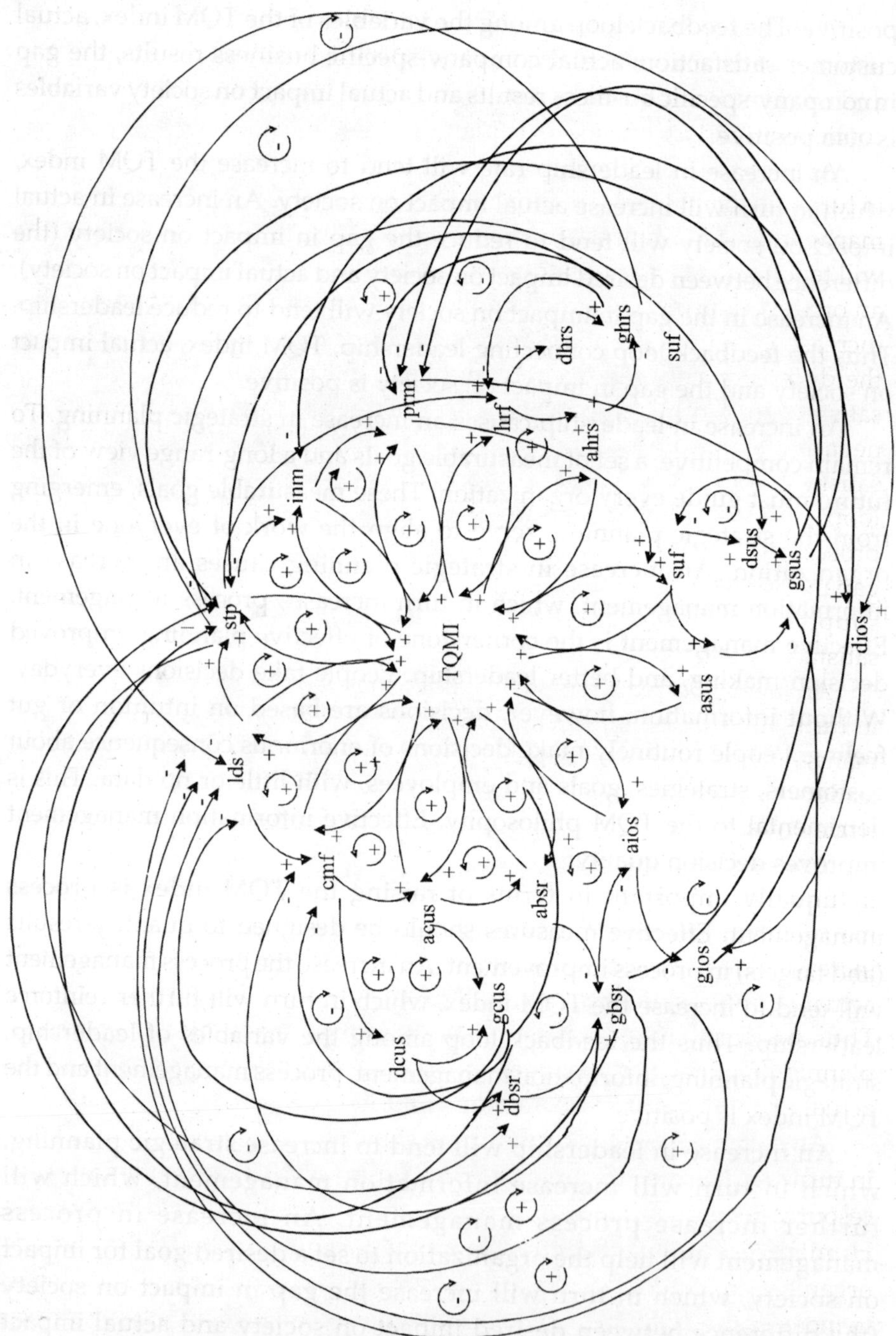

Fig. 4.4: Causal loop diagram for TQM index

Thus the feedback loop connecting leadership, strategic planning, information management, process management, desired impact on society and the gap in impact on society is negative. Similarly, the feedback loop connecting leadership, strategic planning and the TQM index is positive.

An increase in leadership will tend to increase strategic planning, which in turn will increase information management and further increase process management. An increase in strategic planning and process management will tend to increase supplier focus. An increase in supplier focus will help an organization set a desired supplier satisfaction goal, which in turn will increase the gap in supplier satisfaction. The gap in supplier satisfaction is the difference between desired supplier satisfaction and actual supplier satisfaction. An increase in this gap in supplier satisfaction will have a negative effect on leadership. Also an increase in the gap in supplier satisfaction will have negative effect on supplier focus. Thus the feedback loop among leadership, strategic planning, information management, process management, supplier focus, desired supplier satisfaction and the gap in supplier satisfaction is negative. Similarly, the feedback loop among supplier focus, desired supplier satisfaction and the gap in supplier satisfaction is negative.

An increase in leadership will tend to increase strategic planning, which in turn will increase information management. An increase in information management will tend to increase the TQM index, which in turn will increase leadership. Thus the feedback loop connecting the variables of leadership, strategic planning, information management and the TQM index is positive.

An increase in leadership will tend to increase strategic planning, which in turn will increase information management. An increase in information management will tend to increase process management, which in turn will increase supplier focus. An increase in supplier focus will tend to increase actual supplier satisfaction, which in turn will increase the TQM index. Thus the feedback loop among the variables of leadership, strategic planning, information management, process management, supplier focus, actual supplier satisfaction and the TQM index is positive.

An increase in leadership will tend to increase strategic planning, which in turn will increase the human resource focus. An increase in the human resource focus will tend to increase actual human resource satisfaction. Human resource satisfaction is an important success factor for any organization. An increase in actual human resource satisfaction will tend to increase the TQM index, which will have a positive effect on leadership. An increase in actual human resource satisfaction will also reduce the gap in human resource satisfaction, which in turn will have a positive effect on human resource focus. An increase in the gap in human resource satisfaction will tend to reduce leadership. Thus the feedback loop connecting leadership, strategic planning, human resource focus, actual human resource satisfaction and the TQM index is positive. The feedback loop connecting human resource focus, actual human resource satisfaction and the gap in human resource satisfaction is positive. (The gap in human resource satisfaction is the difference between desired human resource satisfaction and actual human resource satisfaction). The feedback loop among leadership, strategic planning, human resource focus, actual human resource satisfaction and the gap in human resource satisfaction is positive. Similarly, the feedback loop among leadership, strategic planning, human resource focus, desired human resource satisfaction and the gap in human resource satisfaction variables is negative.

An increase in leadership will tend to increase strategic planning, which in turn will help organizations to set desired supplier satisfaction goals. An increase in desired supplier satisfaction will increase the gap in supplier satisfaction, which in turn will have a negative effect on leadership. Thus the feedback loop among leadership, strategic planning, desired supplier satisfaction and the gap in supplier satisfaction is negative.

An increase in leadership will tend to increase strategic planning, which in turn will help organizations to set a goal for the desired impact on society. An increase in the desired impact on society will tend to increase the gap in impact on society, which in turn will have a negative effect on leadership. Thus the feedback loop among leadership, strategic planning, desired impact on society and the gap in impact on society is negative.

An increase in strategic planning will tend to increase the TQM index, which in turn will further increase strategic planning. Thus the feedback loop between strategic planning and the TQM index is positive. Similarly, all feedback loops between strategic planning, information management, human resource focus, actual human resource satisfaction, supplier focus, actual supplier satisfaction, actual impact on society, actual company-specific business results, actual customer satisfaction, customer and market focus, process management and TQM index variables are positive.

The causal loop diagram, which is developed in this chapter, provides an insight into understanding the dynamic interactions among subsystems of TQM variables. Though working through the various causal relationships and feedback loops takes some time, it does build an understanding of those relationships, and it allows an organization to take proactive action to ensure the effective implementation of the TQM philosophy. The causal loop diagram has been used for TQM modeling of auto sector in the next chapter using system dynamic approach. This model can be used for evaluating long-term strategies – to ensure more effective implementation of the TQM philosophy and an enhanced TQM index.

4.6 SYSTEM DYNAMICS MODELING

SD focuses on the structure and behavior of systems composed of interacting feedback loops.

4.6.1 Structural Details of System Dynamics Modeling

Causal loop diagrams characterize the initial view of the system and basically serve the purpose of communication between the modeler and the policy maker. However, the formulation of an operational model of the system is based on more specific structural details, like rates or policy variables, accumulation of level, auxiliaries, constants, information flows and delays. Flow diagrams represent such details and specific aspects of the model structure (Forrester, 1961; Richardson and Pugh, 1981).

Rate variables, indicating rate of change, are often complicated functions of level variables, indicating a particular state in time. For ease of expression, the rates are subdivided into various auxiliary variables. An auxiliary is a computation based on information in a feedback system, and aids in formulation of rate equation. Both rates and auxiliaries depend on some constant terms, which do not change within the time frame under consideration. A model of a feedback system must trace the significant flow of material and information throughout the system. Delays are an integral part of large systems. Delays could be in real physical terms, in information or just in perception.

This model structure leads to a simple system of equations that suffices for representing information feedback systems. The equations tell how to generate the system conditions for a new point in time, given the conditions of the model are evaluated repeatedly to generate a sequence of steps equally spaced in time. The interval of time between successive solutions is relatively short, which is determined by the dynamic characteristics of the modeled system.

4.7 SYSTEM DYNAMICS MODEL FOR THE INDIAN AUTOMOBILE SECTOR

The complex interactions among the TQM related enablers, results and other variables have been developed and analyzed in this chapter based on a causal-loop diagram. Further extension of this work is to capture the time-dependent trends and their associated managerial implications.

4.7.1 Variables of the Model

Key variables of a TQM system and their time, response or reference mode are identified to define the problem dynamically. Key variables have been identified on the basis of a survey of selected companies and a review of the TQM literature and discussion with experts in academia and industries. The key variables for a typical TQM system have been identified and discussed in this chapter. These are: leadership (lds), strategic planning (stp), information management (inm), human resource focus (hrf), customer and market focus (cmf), supplier focus (suf), process management (prm), impact on society (ios), human resource satisfaction (hrs), customer satisfaction (cus), supplier satisfaction (sus), company-specific business results (bsr), total quality management index (TQMI), gap in customer satisfaction (gcus), gap in business results (gbsr), gap in impact on society (gios), gap in supplier satisfaction (gsus), gap in human resource satisfaction (ghrs), actual customer satisfaction (acus), actual business results (absr), actual human resource satisfaction (ahrs), actual supplier satisfaction (asus), actual impact on society (aios), desired customer satisfaction (dcus), desired human resource satisfaction (dhrs), desired business results (dbsr), desired supplier satisfaction (dsus), desired impact on society (dios).

4.7.2 Weightages of TQM Variables for Effective Implementation of TQM

The weightages of TQM variables for effective implementation of TQM in organizations based on automobile sector perceptions have been identified and are indicated in Table 4.4.

Table 4.4: TQM variables and maximum score against each variable

S.N.	*Category/variables*	*Maximum score*
I: Enablers		
1.	Leadership	125
2.	Strategic planning	100
3.	Information management	60
4.	Human resource focus	95
5.	Customer and market focus	110
6.	Supplier focus	30
7.	Process management	80
Total of enablers		**600**
II: Results		
8.	Impact on society	70
9.	Human resource satisfaction	100
10.	Customer satisfaction	115

Contd....

11. 12.	Supplier satisfaction Company specific business results	40 75
Total of results		**400**
Maximum TQMI score		**1000**

Indian auto organizations have been asked in the research to self-assess the performance of the organization against each variable. A literature review revealed that organizations getting a score of around 600 against the MBNQA criteria are considered as serious contenders for the award (Brown *et al.,* 1994). This has provided a base for site visits to these organizations only. Scores have been normalized as per the scheme mentioned in Chapter 3.

The purpose of modeling TQM using the system dynamics methodology is to understand the strengths and weaknesses against each variable and to devise alternative policies to maximize the total quality management index, which is aimed to provide a direction to move towards world-class performance.

4.7.3 Flow Diagrams

The causal loop for the TQM index model has been converted into a flow diagram with the help of the ithink 7.0.2 ANALYST software 2001 (Richmond, 2001). Level variables, rate variables, decision factors and decision points are inter-connected. The SD equations have been generated in the model to represent the dynamics of the systems encapsulating the rate of changes with each interaction. The resulting flow diagram is shown in Figure 4.5.

4.7.4 Base Model for Total Quality Management Index (TQMI)

The TQM is the sum of enablers and results of the business processes of the automobile sector. This model recognizes the fact that there has to be good enablers for better results (Pannirselvam and Ferguson, 2001). The TQM index of any automobile organization can be improved provided that there is improvement in leadership, strategic planning, information management, process management, supplier focus, customer and market focus and human resource focus of the organization. Strategically, organizations are required to focus on improving the enablers.

For illustration purposes, representations of associated SD equations are represented below. In these representations, "A" denotes auxiliary equations and K denotes system state at a time K. For example, the first equation in the following set implies that TQM index at time K is the sum of enablers and results at time K.

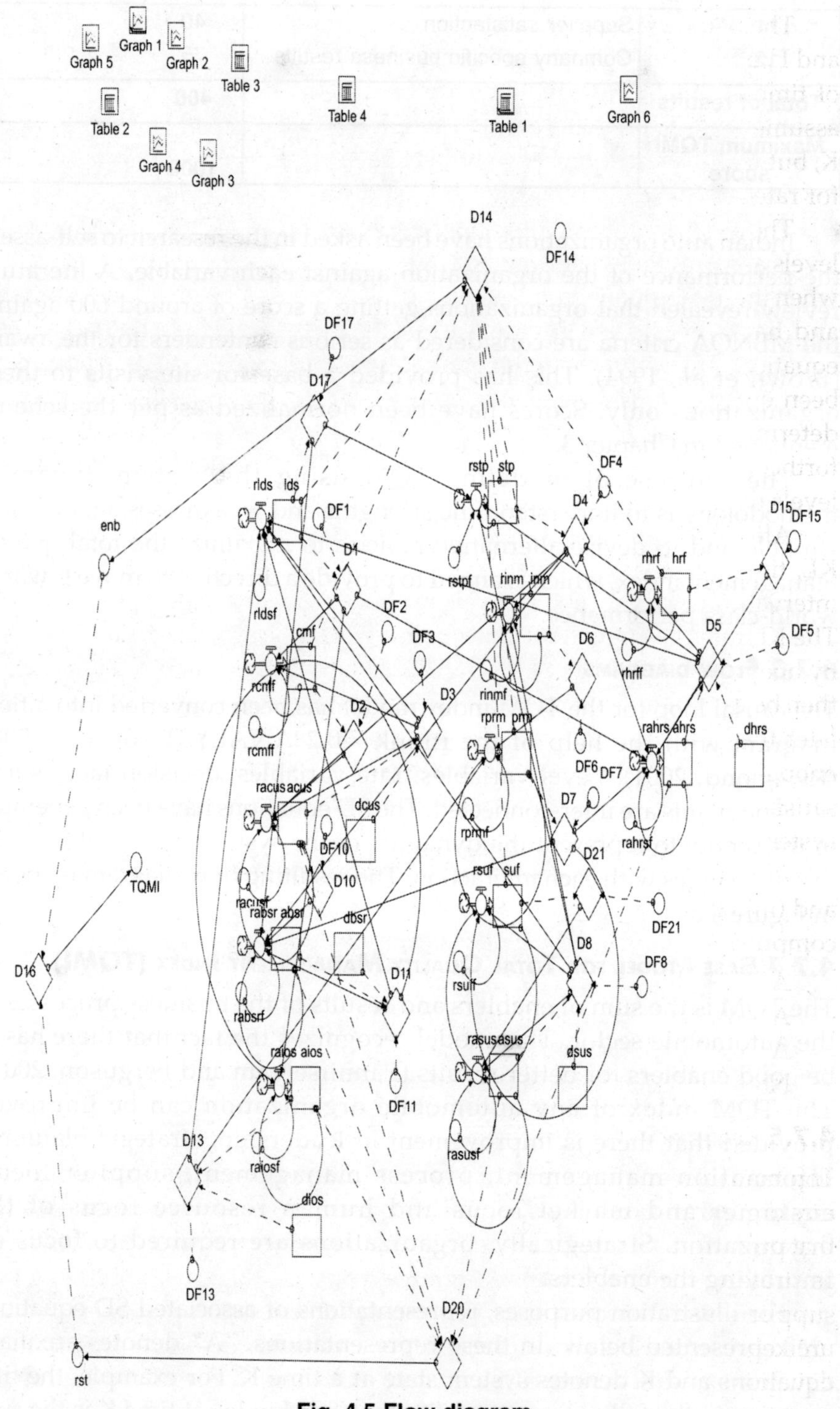

Fig. 4.5 Flow diagram

The equations are written in terms of the generalized time steps J, K, and L, using the arbitrary convention that K represents the "present" point of time at which the equations are being evaluated. In other words, we assume that the progress of the solution has just reached to a stage at time K, but that the equations have not yet been solved for levels at time K, nor for rates over the interval, say KL.

The level equations show how to obtain levels at time K, based on (i) levels at a previous time J, and (ii) rates over the interval JK. At the time K, when the level equations are evaluated, all necessary information is available and has been carried forward from the preceding time step. The rate equations are evaluated at the present time K after the level equations have been evaluated. The values determined by the rate (decision) equations determine the rates that represent the actions that will be taken over the forthcoming interval KL. Constant rates imply a constant rate of change in levels during a time interval.

After evaluation of the levels at time K and the rates for the interval KL, time is "indexed". That is, the J, K, L positions are moved one time interval to the right. The K levels just calculated are relabeled as J levels. The KL rates become the JK rates. Time K, "the present", is thus advanced by one interval of time of DT length. The entire computation sequence can then be repeated to obtain a new state of the system at a time that is one DT later than the previous state. By definition this DT interval must be short enough so that it represents constant rates of flow over the interval as a satisfactory approximation to continuously varying rates in the actual system (Forrester, 1961).

ithink software denotes (i) time K as time (t), (ii) time J as time (t – dt), and (iii) time interval DT as dt. A set of sample flow diagram equations as computed by *ithink* software has been represented below:

A TQMI.(t) = enb.(t) + rst.(t)

A enb.(t) = lds.(t) + stp.(t) + inm.(t) + prm.(t) + suf.(t) + cmf.(t) + hrf.(t)

A rst.(t) = ios.(t) + hrs.(t) + cus.(t) + sus.(t) + bsr.(t)

Now we discuss some of the basis for developing logics for flow equations.

4.7.5 Leadership

Top management leadership is of paramount importance to the success of any organization. Unless top managers provide a clear vision and values that promote total quality in the organization, other enabling variables (such as strategic planning, human resource focus, customer and market focus, supplier focus, process management and information management) are unlikely to make a positive impact. Thus, for the success of any organization, developing leadership attributes and skills should be at the top of the management agenda (Deming, 1993).

Each level equation requires a base year to set the initial value. Here, the base year for the initial value of "leadership" has been set as 1998 based on actual feedback from one of the auto organizations. The initial value of leadership has been set as 33 on the basis of a self-assessment of the organization that has been adopted for this case study. The SD equations for leadership are represented in the following set. Here, "L" denotes level equations and "N" denotes initial value. Accordingly the SD equations for leadership are represented in the following set. Here, "L" denotes level equations and "N" denotes initial value.

L lds.(t) = lds.(t – dt) + (rlds) * dt
N lds = 33
lds Leadership (Numbers)
rlds Leadership Rate (Numbers/Year).

For the company in this case study, we have taken "leadership level" to a variable accumulating up to a maximum level of 125 (Table 4.4). We can represent leadership as a closed loop and we assume that the leadership rate depends entirely on the level of leadership, the gap in company-specific business results, the gap in customer satisfaction, the gap in human resource satisfaction, the gap in impact on society and the gap in supplier satisfaction as discussed in section 4.5.4. As suggested in section 4.2.1.1, an increase in "leadership" depends mainly on the top management commitment being translated into effective decision-making and management action.

Senior managers must assess performance gaps and intervene to fill such gaps and steer the company to greater heights of growth and progress. This involves the revision and updating of both long-term and short-term plans, and ensuring that:

- those plans are properly communicated, and that they are understood by those who must implement them; and
- the plans are then acted upon in a timely and effective manner.

In the following set of SD equations "R" denotes a rate variables equation.

R rlds.(dt) = (lds*rldsf + (dsus – asus)*DF8 + (dhrs – ahrs)*DF5 + (dcus – acus)* DF3 + (dios – aios)*DF13 + (dbsr – absr)*DF11)/year

A gcus.(t) = (dcus.(t) – acus.(t))
A gbsr.(t) = (dbsr.(t) – absr.(t))
A gios.(t) = (dios.(t) – aios.(t))
A ghrs.(t) = (dhrs.(t) – ahrs.(t))
A gsus.(t) = (dsus.(t) – asus.(t))
rldsf - Leadership Rate Fraction

DF3, DF5, DF8, DF11 and DF13 are Decision Fractions.

Decision fraction, DF3, DF5, DF8, DF11 and DF13 are constant and decided by self-assessment team for initializing the simulation runs. The explanation of the decision fraction is encapsulated into the rate equations of the system dynamics models. For example let us consider the rate equation for the leadership.

Here, left hand side is the rate of leadership for the forthcoming period (dt). Each simulation run is for a time interval (dt), which is very-very small. In other words, it is going to generate the initial value of leadership-rate (rlds.(dt)) for the next experiment.

The right hand side of the equation is the sum of two types effects. First is the term (lds*rldsf). This indicates the increase in the leadership variables at time (t) due to the effort of the company to improve by say a fraction of rldsf. The second set of terms is (DF3*gcus.(t) + DF11*gbsr.(t) + DF13*gios.(t) + DF5*ghrs.(t) + DF8* gsus.(t)). This indicates the impact of different variables (related to gap in results) towards the change in leadership-rate. For example (DF3*gcus.(t)) means that the gap in customer satisfaction at time (t) (i.e., gcus.(t)) helps to improve leadership rate by a decision faction of DF3. There are other structural equations in the model that normalize the values of different variables during interactions. Similarly, other terms of second set could be interpreted.

Values of decision fraction in structural equation (say DF3 = 0.04) are the initialization of the model so that the rate of leadership (rlds(dt)) is calculated for the second run. It is important to note here that a large number of simulation runs are involved for the reported time period of ten years. The complex dynamic interaction of all the variables has been captured and simulated on *ithink software 7.0.2 Analyst.* Over such a long period of time, the insights that we get from the system dynamics models remain similar even if the model is initialized with slightly different values of decision fraction, as the model quickly picks up the dynamic interaction of the different variables that are represented through all the structural equations.

Similarly other set of equations has been developed across the range of factors and interactions that impact on the TQM index. This builds a "model" of the situation that can be used to explore the efficacy of alternative improvement strategies.

4.7.6 Strategic Planning

Increase in the top management leadership helps the organization to set strategic planning in place. Strategic planning should incorporate long-term goals and objectives for the organization. Overall strategy should be to focus on "critical success factors" and "critical processes" to achieve the objectives and goals of the organization (Mody, 1996; Ishikawa, 1985).

Each level equation requires a base year to set the initial value. Here, the base year for the initial value of "strategic planning" has been set as 1998 based on actual feedback from one of the auto organizations. The initial value of strategic planning has been set as 44 on the basis of a self-assessment of the organization that has been adopted for this case study. The SD equations for strategic planning are represented in the following set.

L stp.(t) = stp.(t – dt) + (rstp)*dt

N stp = 44

stp - Strategic Planning (Numbers)

rstp - Strategic Planning Rate (Number/Year).

For the company in this case study, we have taken "strategic planning level" to be a variable accumulating up to a maximum level of 100 (Table 4.4). We can represent strategic planning as a closed loop and we assume that the strategic planning rate depends entirely on the level of strategic planning, leadership, the gap in human resource satisfaction and the gap in supplier satisfaction. The rate equation of strategic planning is given below:

R rstp.(dt) = stp* rstpf + lds*DF17 + (dhrs – ahrs)*DF5 + (dsus – asus)*DF8

rstpf - Strategic Planning Rate Fraction

DF5, DF8 and DF17 are Decision Fractions.

4.7.7 Information Management

Increase in leadership has positive effect on strategic planning and information management. Effective information measurement and communication system need to be in place for continuous improvement of all work. Information management acts as a glue for all enablers. Thus, information management is very important for the top management to take strategic decisions (Ishikawa, 1985; John, 1995).

Each level equation requires a base year to set the initial value. Here, the base year for the initial value of "information management" has been set as 1998 based on actual feedback from one of the auto organizations. The initial value of information management has been set as 19 on the basis of a self-assessment of the organization that has been adopted for this case study. The SD equations for information management are represented in the following set.

L inm.(t) = inm.(t - dt) + (rinm)*dt

N inm = 19

inm - Information Management (Number)

rinm - Information Management Rate (Number/Year).

For the company in this case study, we have taken "information management level" to be a variable accumulating up to a maximum level of 60 (Table 4.4). We can represent information management as a closed loop and we assume that the information management rate depends entirely on the level of information management, strategic planning, and the gap in supplier satisfaction. The rate equation of information management is given below:

R rinm (dt) = inm*rinmf + stp*DF4 + (dsus – asus)*DF8

rinmf - Information Management Rate Fraction

DF4 and DF8 are Decision Fractions.

4.7.8 Process Management

The increase in process management means an increase in system approach to control all operations, using documented traceable systems. This helps in achieving continuous improvement for all products and services. Use of quality tools such as quality circles, 5S, Kaizen, fool proofing and TPM will help the organizations to improve their processes continuously. Thus, for the success of any organization, developing system approach and improvemental culture should be at the top of the management agenda (Smith, 1995; Mody, 1995).

Each level equation requires a base year to set the initial value. Here, the base year for the initial value of "process management" has been set as 1998 based on actual feedback from one of the auto organizations. The initial value of process management has been set as 22 on the basis of a self-assessment of the organization that has been adopted for this case study. The SD equations for process management are represented in the following set.

L prm.(t) = prm.(t-dt) + (rprm)*dt

N prm = 22

prm - Process Management (Number)

rprm - Process Management Rate (Number/Year).

For the company in this case study, we have taken "process management level" to be a variable accumulating up to a maximum level of 80 (Table 4.4). We can represent process management as a closed loop and we assume that the process management rate depends entirely on the level of process management, information management and the gap in impact on society. The rate equation of process management is given below:

R rprm.(dt) = prm*rprmf + inm*DF6 + (dios – aios)*DF13

rprmf - Process Management Rate Fraction

DF6 and DF13 are Decision Fractions.

4.7.9 Human Resource Focus

Human resource focus plays an important role for the success of any organization. It focuses on the needs and expectations of its employees and thus maximizes opportunities for all employees to secure full use of their potential. The effective process of recruitment, training, development, motivation and involvement of people will help in achieving the same (Juran and Gryna, 1995).

Each level equation requires a base year to set the initial value. Here, the base year for the initial value of "human resource focus" has been set as 1998 based on actual feedback from one of the auto organizations. The initial value of human resource focus has been set as 23 on the basis of a self-assessment of the organization that has been adopted for this case study. The SD equations for human resource focus are represented in the following set.

L hrf.(t) = hrf.(t-dt) + (rhrf)*dt
N hrf = 23
hrf - Human Resource Focus (Number)
rhrf - Human Resource Focus Rate (Number/Year).

For the company in this case study, we have taken "human resource focus level" to be a variable accumulating up to a maximum level of 95 (Table 4.4). We can represent human resource focus as a closed loop and we assume that the human resource focus rate depends entirely on the level of human resource focus, strategic planning and the gap in human resource satisfaction. The rate equation of human resource focus is given below:

R rhrf(dt) = hrf*rhrff + stp*DF4 + (dhrs – ahrs)*DF5
rhrff - Human Resource Focus Rate Fraction
DF4 and DF5 are Decision Fractions.

4.7.10 Supplier Focus

Supplier focus plays a vital rate for the success of any organization. Suppliers are treated as partners in the process of improvement. Supplier rating system, supplier training and development, and understanding of supplier's need become an ongoing activity (Imai, 1986; Khanna, 1999).

Each level equation requires a base year to set the initial value. Here, the base year for the initial value of "supplier focus" has been set as 1998 based on actual feedback from one of the auto organizations. The initial value of supplier focus has been set as 8 on the basis of a self-assessment of the organization that has been adopted for this case study. The SD equations for supplier focus are represented in the following set.

L suf.(t) = suf.(t – dt) + (rsuf)*dt
N suf = 8
suf - Supplier Focus (Number)
rsuf - Supplier Focus Rate (Number/Year).

For the company in this case study, we have taken "supplier focus level" to be a variable accumulating up to a maximum level of 30 (Table 4.4). We can represent supplier focus as a closed loop and we assume that the supplier focus rate depends entirely on the level of supplier focus, process management and the gap in supplier satisfaction. The rate equation of supplier focus is given below:

R rsuf.(dt) = suf*rsuff + prm*DF7 + (dsus – asus)*DF8
rsuff - Supplier Focus Rate Fraction
DF7 and DF8 are Decision Fractions.

4.7.11 Customer and Market Focus

Customer and market focus is very important to understand the requirements of internal and external customers. It helps in understanding the supplier customer relationships to secure clear understanding of requirements. Thus for the success of any organization, customer and market focus should be at the top of the management agenda (Bosert, 1990; Day, 1993; Akao, 2002).

Each level equation requires a base year to set the initial value. Here, the base year for the initial value of "customer and market focus" has been set as 1998 based on actual feedback from one of the auto organizations. The initial value of customer and market focus has been set as 41 on the basis of a self-assessment of the organization that has been adopted for this case study. The SD equations for customer and market focus are represented in the following set.

L cmf.(t) = cmf.(t – dt) + (rcmf)*dt

N cmf = 41

cmf - Customer and Market Focus (Number)

rcmf - Customer and Market Focus Rate (Number/Year).

For the company in this case study, we have taken "customer and market focus level" to be a variable accumulating up to a maximum level of 110 (Table 4.4). We can represent customer and market focus as a closed loop and we assume that the customer and market focus rate depends entirely on the level of customer and market focus, leadership and the gap in customer satisfaction. The rate equation of customer and market focus is given below:

R rcmf.(dt) = cmf*rcmff + lds*DF1 + (dcus – acus)*DF3

rcmff - Customer and Market Focus Rate Fraction

DF1 and DF3 are Decision Fractions.

4.7.12 Customer Satisfaction

Customer satisfaction is of paramount importance to the success of any organization. Customer satisfaction means that the internal and external customers are satisfied and customers' complaints are systematically monitored and these are addressed properly (Bossert, 1990; Day, 1993).

Each level equation requires a base year to set the initial value. Here, the base year for the initial value of "customer satisfaction" has been set as 1998 based on actual feedback from one of the auto organizations. The initial value of customer satisfaction has been set as 32 on the basis of a self-assessment of the organization that has been adopted for this case study. The SD equations for customer satisfaction are represented in the following set.

L acus.(t) = acus.(t – dt) + (racus)*dt

N cus = 32

acus - Actual Customer Satisfaction (Number)
racus - Actual Customer Satisfaction Rate (Number/Year).

For the company in this case study, we have taken "customer satisfaction level" to be a variable accumulating up to a maximum level of 115 (Table 4.4). We can represent customer satisfaction as a closed loop and we assume that the customer satisfaction rate depends entirely on the level of actual customer satisfaction, customer and market focus, strategic planning and the gap in customer satisfaction. The rate equation of customer satisfaction is given below:

R racus.(dt) = acus*racusf + cmf*DF2 + stp*DF4 + (dcus – acus)*DF3

racusf - Actual Customer Satisfaction Rate Fraction

DF2, DF3 and DF4 are Decision Fractions.

4.7.13 Human Resource Satisfaction

Human resource satisfaction is a must for the survival and growth of any organization under present competitive market scenario. Unless human resource focus is systematically managed, actual human resource satisfaction cannot be improved. Human resource satisfaction means the organization has been able to make use of the full potential of all employees. Employees have faith and trust on management (ISO/TS 16949, 2002).

Each level equation requires a base year to set the initial value. Here, the base year for the initial value of "human resource satisfaction" has been set as 1998 based on actual feedback from one of the auto organizations. The initial value of human resource satisfaction has been set as 25 on the basis of a self-assessment of the organization that has been adopted for this case study. The SD equations for human resource satisfaction are represented in the following set.

L ahrs.(t) = ahrs.(t – dt) + (rahrs)*dt
N hrs = 25
ahrs - Actual Human Resource Satisfaction (Number)
rahrs - Actual Human Resource Satisfaction Rate (Number/Year).

For the company in this case study, we have taken "human resource satisfaction level" to be a variable accumulating up to a maximum level of 100 (Table 4.4). We can represent human resource satisfaction as a closed loop and we assume that the human resource satisfaction rate depends entirely on the level of actual human resource satisfaction, human resource focus, leadership, strategic planning, process management and the gap in human resource satisfaction. The rate equation of human resource satisfaction is given below:

R rahrs(dt) = ahrs*rahrsf + hrf*DF15 + lds*DF1 + stp*DF4 + prm*DF7 + (dhrs – ahrs)*DF5

rahrsf - Actual Human Resource Satisfaction Rate Fraction
DF1, DF4, DF5, DF7 and DF15 are Decision Fractions.

4.7.14 Supplier Satisfaction

Supplier satisfaction is a must for the survival and growth of any organization. Suppliers are required to be treated as partners and long-term relationship with suppliers should be established to achieve continuous improvement in the products and services (Imai, 1986).

Each level equation requires a base year to set the initial value. Here, the base year for the initial value of "supplier satisfaction" has been set as 1998 based on actual feedback from one of the auto organizations. The initial value of supplier satisfaction has been set as 11 on the basis of a self-assessment of the organization that has been adopted for this case study. The SD equations for supplier satisfaction are represented in the following set.

L asus.(t) = asus.(t – dt) + (rasus)*dt
N sus = 11
asus - Actual Supplier Satisfaction (Number)
rasus - Actual Supplier Satisfaction Rate (Number/Year).

For the company in this case study, we have taken "supplier satisfaction level" to be a variable accumulating up to a maximum level of 40 (Table 4.4). We can represent supplier satisfaction as a closed loop and we assume that the supplier satisfaction rate depends entirely on the level of actual supplier satisfaction, supplier focus and the gap in supplier satisfaction. The rate equation of supplier satisfaction is given below:

R rasus.(dt) = asus*rasusf + suf*DF21 + (dsus – asus)*DF8
rasusf - Actual Supplier Satisfaction Rate Fraction
DF8 and DF21 are Decision Fractions.

4.7.15 Impact on Society

Impact on society is very important for the success of any organization. All employees should value and promote their organization within the community. The organization should have well-established prevention-based systems for environment management (ISO 14001, 1996).

Each level equation requires a base year to set the initial value. Here, the base year for the initial value of "impact on society" has been set as 1998 based on actual feedback from one of the auto organizations. The initial value of impact on society has been set as 25 on the basis of a self-assessment of the organization that has been adopted for this case study. The SD equations for impact on society are represented in the following set.

L aios.(t) = aios.(t – dt) + (raios)*dt
N ios = 25
aios - Actual Impact on Society (Number)
raios - Actual Impact on Society Rate (Number/Year).

For the company in this case study, we have taken "impact on society level" to be a variable accumulating up to a maximum level of 70 (Table 4.4). We can represent impact on society as a closed loop and we assume that the impact on society rate depends entirely on the level of actual impact on society, leadership and the gap in company-specific business results. The rate equation of impact on society is given below:

R raios.(dt) = aios*raiosf + lds*DF1 + (dbsr – absr)*DF11

raiosf - Actual Impact on Society Rate Fraction

DF1 and DF11 are Decision Fractions.

4.7.16 Company-Specific Business Results

Improved company-specific business results are a must for the survival and growth of any auto organization. A balanced view of company-specific business results is important to understand the overall performance of the organization (Neves and Nakhai, 1995; Steeples, 1993).

Each level equation requires a base year to set the initial value. Here, the base year for the initial value of "company-specific business results" has been set as 1998 based on actual feedback from one of the auto organizations. The initial value of company-specific business results has been set as 32 on the basis of a self-assessment of the organization that has been adopted for this case study. The SD equations for company-specific business results are represented in the following set.

L absr.(t) = absr.(t – dt) + (rabsr)*dt

N bsr = 32

absr - Actual Company Specific Business Result (Number)

rabsr - Actual Company Specific Business Results Rate (Number/ Year).

For the company in this case study, we have taken "company-specific business results level" to be a variable accumulating up to a maximum level of 75 (Table 4.4). We can represent company-specific business results as a closed loop and we assume that the company-specific business results rate depends entirely on the level of actual company-specific business results, actual customer satisfaction, process management, leadership, strategic planning and the gap in company-specific business results. The rate equation of company-specific business results is given below:

R rabsr.(dt) = absr*rabsrf + acus*DF10 + prm*DF7 + lds*DF17 + stp*DF4 + (dbsr – absr)*DF11

rabsrf - Actual Company Specific Business Results Rate Fraction

DF4, DF7, DF10, DF11 and DF17 are Decision Fractions.

4.8 MODEL RESULTS

Figure 4.6 shows the relationship among enablers, results and the TQM index. The base year for the model calculations was taken to be 1998. The simulation time interval (DT) was selected as one year and simulation time period as ten years. Table 4.5 shows the results of analysis against short-term, mid-term and long-term perspectives. Enablers in the first two years do not increase the results in the same proportion and thus the TQM index increases at a relatively slow rate.

Table 4.5: Comparative scores against short-term, mid-term and long-term perspectives

Variables	*Score of variables on a scale of 0-1000*		
	Short-term perspective (1-2 years)	Mid-term perspective (3–6 years)	Long-term perspective (7-10 years)
Enablers	319.03	510.71	567.35
Results	171.72	273.29	320.10
TQM index	490.47	784	887.45

However, the rates of increase for enablers, results and the resulting TQM index are highest in the three to six year periods. From the seventh year onwards, the model stabilizes and the rates of change of enablers, results and the TQM are reduced substantially – the graphs flatten. However, within this flattening, it can be seen that up to the sixth year, the rates of increase in enablers and results remain almost the same, but from the seventh year onwards the performance of results increases proportionally much higher than the rate of increase for the enablers.

The trend charts for the result and enabler variables are shown in Figure 4.7 and 4.8.

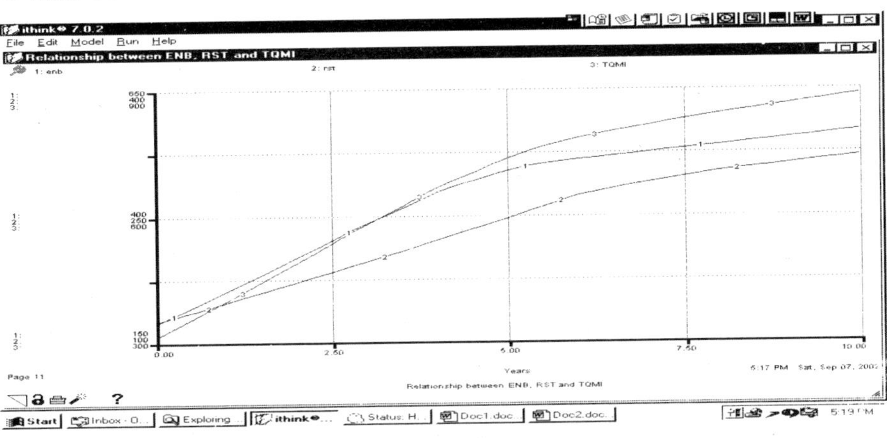

Fig. 4.6: Relationship among enb, rst and TQMI (1. enb, 2. rst, 3. TQMI)

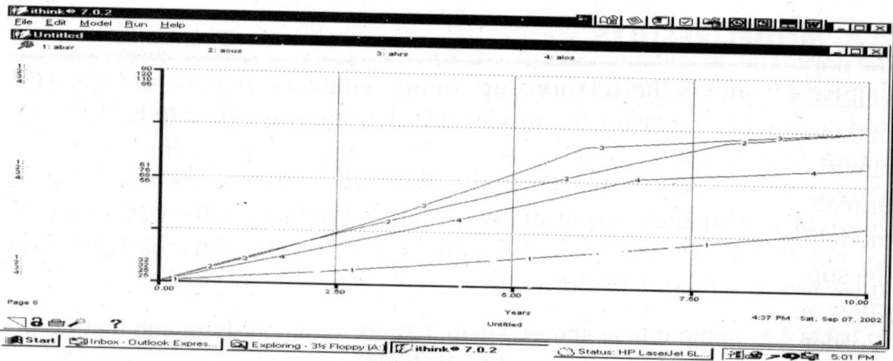

Fig. 4.7: Relationship among variables of result (1. absr, 2. acus, 3. ahrs, 4. aios)

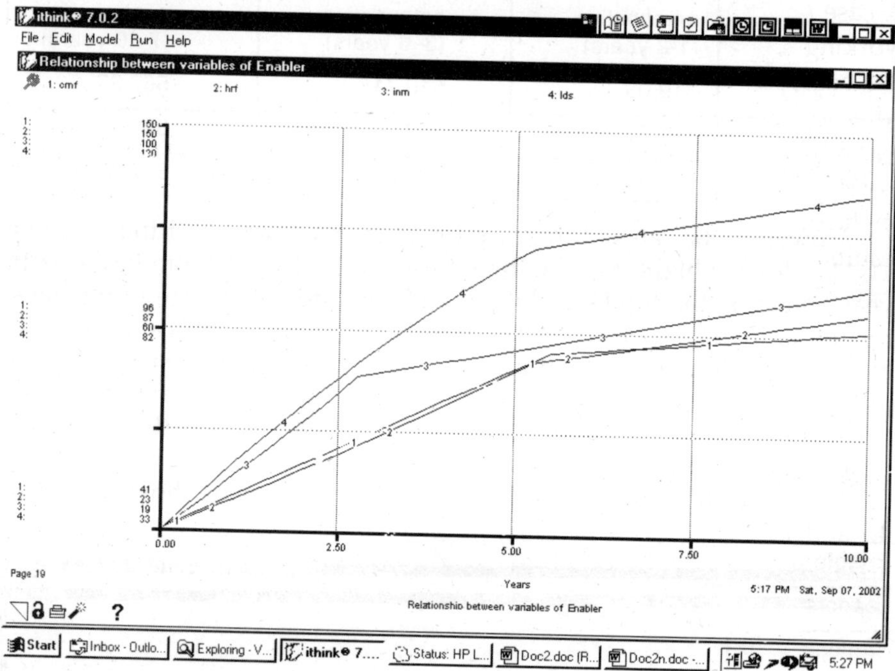

Fig. 4.8: Relationship among variables of enabler (1. cmf, 2. hrf, 3. inm, 4. lds)

4.9 MODEL VALIDATION

Validation of any system dynamics model is necessary to establish necessary confidence in the model according to some chosen criteria with respect to the organization/system under study. According to Forrester (1961), Coyle (1979) and Wright (1971), the significance of a model depends on how well it serves its purpose. Thirteen subjective criteria have been suggested by these authors for validation of the model. Generally, there is a serious criticism for the popular validation techniques due to their overemphasis on quantitative validation rather than the usefulness of the model to guide further decision-making. Also, the validation techniques and processes often pay insufficient attention to the underlying assumptions, which often remain hidden and unrealistic. Huntington *et al.* (1982), state that the primary goal of policy modeling should be the insights that quantitative models can provide, not the supposedly precise projections (i.e. numbers) they can produce for any given scenario. Forrester and Senge (1980), Bell and Senge (1980) and Wolstenholme and Coyle (1983) have emphasized the development of system dynamics as a methodology for system description and qualitative analysis.

Case Study

A case study has been carried out in an organization, which has been working on projects to implement TQM. Our SD model discussed earlier has been populated with the initial data collected for this organization. After four years of efforts in implementing TQM, a survey questionnaire was administrated in a workshop environment to four different groups to assess performance against the TQM variables. The average score based on the questionnaire was then compared with the system dynamics model results and the outcomes are presented in Table 4.6. These results have been used to validate the performance of the system dynamics model.

Table 4.6:Validation of results based on comparison questionnaire and SD model result in the fourth year of TQM implementation

TQM variables	*Average score based on questionnaire*	*Results based on system dynamic model*	*Percent deviation from system dynamics prediction*
Enablers			
Leadership	85	88.38	3.9
Strategic planning	78	79.76	2.2
Information management	48	53.17	10.7
Human resource focus	59	63.03	6.8
Customer and market focus	80	76.59	-4.2
Supplier focus	18	20.33	12.9
Process management	50	65.54	3.1

Contd....

Total score of enablers	**418**	**446.81**	**6.9**
Results			
Impact on society	40	42.98	7.4
Human resource satisfaction	54	59.80	10.7
Customer satisfaction	71	64.34	-9.3
Supplier satisfaction	16	16.32	2.0
Company specific business results	42	37.68	-10.2
Total score of results	223	221.13	-0.8
TQM index	**641**	**667.94**	**4.2**

Since maximum variation has been observed to be around 10 percent, the SD model fairly replicates the dynamic behavior of the TQM system and thus validates the interrelationships. The percentage deviation that is reported in Table 4.6 can be attributed to following reasons:

- A limitation in capturing all the dependent and independent variables of the model,
- Despite efforts in this research to normalize the score, there are limitations due to some leftover bias in the self-assessment scores during different stages of the model,
- Some gaps in computing the data for the model,
- Gap arising due to simplification in the interactions, which are sometimes necessary due to time limit for this research and limitation of the researcher in modeling the entire interactions of this model, and
- Difficulty in the quantification of some of the subjective factors such as resistance to change, motivation, etc. However, implications of this have been taken into account when determining the rate of change of these variables considered under results. Yet there are limitations in exact conversion of subjective estimates into quantitative measures.

Tests replicate well for the "pattern prediction" and for the "event prediction" as compared to "point prediction" focusing on a value on a specific date. The results obtained are validated through testing in the case organization.

4.10 CONCLUSIONS

Different sets of strategies need to be adopted at different stages of TQM implementation. In discussing TQM, the MBNQA model has been used as the basis of the framework identified in this chapter. Leadership is the most important enabler for improving the TQM index. The assumption here is that effective leadership modulates the implementation of TQM and thus enhances the TQM index for the auto-manufacturing sector. Top management has a significant influence on, and the ability to make changes to, the system. Thus its role is crucial. Leadership must guide every system, strategy and method for achieving excellence. Thus the feedback loop between leadership and the TQM index is positive. However, there is a total of seven enablers of TQM in auto sector: leadership, strategic planning, human resource focus, customer and market focus, supplier focus, process management and information management. These influence five results: impact on society, human resource satisfaction, customer satisfaction, supplier satisfaction and company-specific business results. Causal relationships have been developed between these sets of enablers and results. These are 62 feedback loops, which have been identified and discussed. The resulting dynamic interactions indicate that 43 feedback loops are positive and 19 are negative. Gaps in customer satisfaction, supplier satisfaction, impact on society, human resource satisfaction and business results have been identified as goal-seeking loops.

The primary purpose of developing a SD model for the TQM index is to bring improvement in the automobile manufacturing sector of India. The self-assessment by various teams has been conducted through a questionnaire, which provides a snapshot picture of the organization, usually expressed in terms of strengths and areas for improvement, and a score. The proposed SD model can predict the rate of improvement on different TQM variables based on the specific strength and gaps of the organization. The SD model helps managers to continuously monitor their TQM efforts and related performance, and take corrective measures on key problem areas. The model also helps the organization to take policy decisions arising out of the dynamic nature of the system. The model does not take decisions – but it does support them. Real improvement then depends on the effective implementation of insights that are derived from this model. The Indian auto sector is required to design its own strategies to improve its scores and bridge the identified gaps. The model presented in this chapter has the capability to help in identifying the future scenarios resulting from different policy level changes through a combination of actions enforcing fast, moderate or slow improvement. These scenarios can be modeled through reinforcement or relaxation of selected enablers of the system. The related experimentations would be presented in Chapter 5.

5

Chapter

Scenario Building and Policy Experimentation

5.1 INTRODUCTION

System dynamics modeling of TQM has been developed and validated in Chapter 4 to understand the system behavior with respect to different variables in the category of enablers and results. In this chapter, three sub-models would be developed. Few policy experimentations have been attempted to examine the applicability of these sub-models. Finally, the policy experimentations are used to generate scenario building. Optimistic and pessimistic scenarios, based on a set of positive and negative assumptions about the market situations for improving total quality management index (TQMI) in the Indian automobile sector, have been analyzed in this chapter.

5.2 MARKET SCENARIOS

Based on the emerging market scenarios, following four scenarios have been identified:

(i) External enabler strong (EES)
(ii) External enabler moderate (EEM)
(iii) External enabler weak (EEW)
(iv) External enabler crash (EEC)

5.2.1 External Enabler Strong (EES)

This is the most optimistic scenario when government policies are very much favourable for the growth of the Indian automobile sector and organizations are under a protective environment. Customers do not have much choice and it is a sellers market, which leads the organizations to have consistent growth and strong results. Customer is likely to suffer the most, as he/she has to pay extra cost for the inefficiency of the total chain. This is a representation of pre-liberalization era particularly during 1980's of the Indian automobile sector.

5.2.2 External Enabler Moderate (EEM)

In this scenario, some of the government policies are in contrast to what automobile sector is expecting. Government is in the process of opening up the economy in a phased manner leading to the growth of competition among different automakers. Liberalization has brought many major car manufacturers such as General Motors, Hyundai, Daewoo, Fiat, Honda etc. in the Indian market. Since competition is growing, customers are getting more choices and thus becoming more demanding. This scenario is forcing the auto supply chain to shed off the inefficiency and therefore, the automobile manufacturers are taking steps to develop their suppliers and going for faster improvements. Supplier category still enjoys protection from their automobile manufacturers. This is the initial phase of a post-liberalization era of Indian automobile sector.

5.2.3 External Enabler Weak (EEW)

In this scenario, there is negligible protection to the automobile sector by government and by and large the market has matured after liberalization. Latest models of automobiles are flooding the market. Competition has become very stiff and customers demand the highest quality. This leads to weak results of the organizations with the same strategy that are deployed during "external enabler strong" or "external enabler moderate" market scenario. This is a notional representation of the present phase of post-liberalization era of the Indian automobile sector.

5.2.4 External Enabler Crash (EEC)

This is the most pessimistic scenario when no protection is available to the automobile sector by government. Customer is the king and has a liberty to buy from anywhere and has the freedom to buy any kind of vehicle including second hand vehicle at a very competitive price. With the stiff competition, customer is so demanding that automobile manufacturers are in no position to provide protection to either suppliers or sub-contractors. Performance is the only criteria for the survival of automobile manufacturers, suppliers and sub-contractors. Competitors are on the lookout for high talent from the market and by and large employees and suppliers are also very hard pressed to perform. The effect of this market scenario is the most severe on the performance of the organizations.

The organizations, which are doing so good under the market scenarios "external enabler strong", "external enabler moderate" and "external enabler weak", the moment protection is totally withdrawn, some of the organization's performance crash to bottom and their survival becomes very difficult. This era of competition is yet to come in the Indian automobile sector.

As discussed above, first three scenarios are unique, however, if the transition phase of these three scenarios are not handled effectively, at any stage, this may lead to EEC. It is therefore important to understand its implications. To understand the market implications effectively, we have considered following three sub-models.

(i) Sub model 1: External enabler strong (EES)
(ii) Sub model 2: External enabler moderate (EEM)
(iii) Sub model 3: External enabler weak (EEW)

5.2.5 Sub-model 1: External Enabler Strong (EES)

Sub-model 1 has been developed for "external enabler strong" market scenario. Different experiments have been carried out to see the effect of "external enabler strong" market scenario and the effect of transition from "external enabler strong" to "external enabler moderate" market scenario. Policy experimentations have been conducted using system dynamics methodology. System dynamics methodology has, therefore, been used in this chapter for deriving better insight to handle the transition phase and to understand the behaviour of different categories of organizations.

5.2.6 Sub-model 2: External Enabler Moderate (EEM)

Sub-model 2 has been developed for "external enabler moderate" market scenario. Different experiments have been carried out to see the effect of "external enabler moderate" market scenario and the effect of transition from "external enabler moderate" to "external enabler weak". Policy experimentations have been conducted using system dynamics methodology. System dynamics methodology has, therefore, been used in this chapter for deriving better insight to handle the transition phase and to understand the behaviour of different categories of organizations.

5.2.7 Sub-model 3: External Enabler Weak (EEW)

Sub-model 3 has been developed for "external enabler weak" market scenario. Different experiments have been carried out to see the effect of "external enabler weak" market scenario and the effect of transition from "external enabler weak" to "external enabler crash". Policy experimentations have been conducted using system dynamics methodology. System dynamics methodology has, therefore, been used in this chapter for deriving better insight to handle the transition phase and to understand the behaviour of different categories of organizations.

In order to capture the implications of above mentioned sub-models, it is important to map the real situation of companies to understand their position with respect to TQM implementation.

5.3 MAPPING OF REAL COMPANIES SITUATION

Organizations have been categorized into four types namely: *quitter, slipper, disillusioned* and *climber*. These are dependent on the status of their performance and the resulting status has been shown in the enabler–result grid-graph in Figure 5.1.

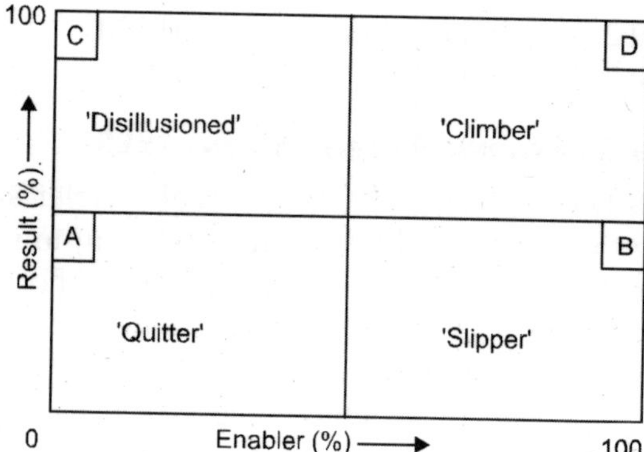

Fig. 5.1: Enabler – result response grid

5.3.1 Type 'A' Organizations: Quitter

The groups of organizations falling in this category are weak in deploying enablers, resulting into low results and thus leading to low TQM index. Under severe competition when there is no protection from customers, such organizations do not survive and the performance of such organizations crashes to the bottom. It has been assumed here that low enablers would yield poor results.

5.3.2 Type 'B' Organizations: Slipper

The groups of organizations that fall in this category are aware of the need to strongly deploy enablers in the organization for their survival and growth. But these enablers are not effective in achieving the desired results. It has been assumed here that such organizations achieve low results in spite of higher enablers. Either implementation process of such groups of organizations is faulty or they believe in only ISO 9000 certification route.

5.3.3 Type 'C' organizations: Disillusioned

This group of organizations is weak in deploying enablers. However, the results of these organizations are quite high. It has been assumed here that low enablers yield high results. Normally, such organizations are able to survive only under protected environment. Most of such organizations normally believe that nothing is going to happen to these organizations so long as good results are coming.

5.3.4 Type 'D' organizations: Climber

Such groups of organizations are the real proactive organizations. They believe in the strategy of implementing high enablers to achieve high results. They have high conviction that there is a direct relationship among enablers, results and TQM index. Though, they have gone for ISO/QS certification, yet they believe that this is a small step towards TQM journey and there is no quick fix to achieve the TQM maturity level. Such organizations have high commitment from top management. There is an involvement of each and everyone in the organization to achieve the TQM maturity level to sustain the survival and growth.

5.4 FRAMEWORK FOR EXPERIMENTATION

Experimentation has been done for all the three sub-models as stated above. The experimentation has been done for the most pessimistic, most likely, and most optimistic scenarios of each sub-model. The most pessimistic scenario has been when effectiveness of enablers is 0%. Most likely scenario has been conceived when effectiveness of enablers is 100%, and most optimistic scenario has been assumed when effectiveness of enablers is 160%. These frameworks for experimentations have been shown in Figure 5.2.

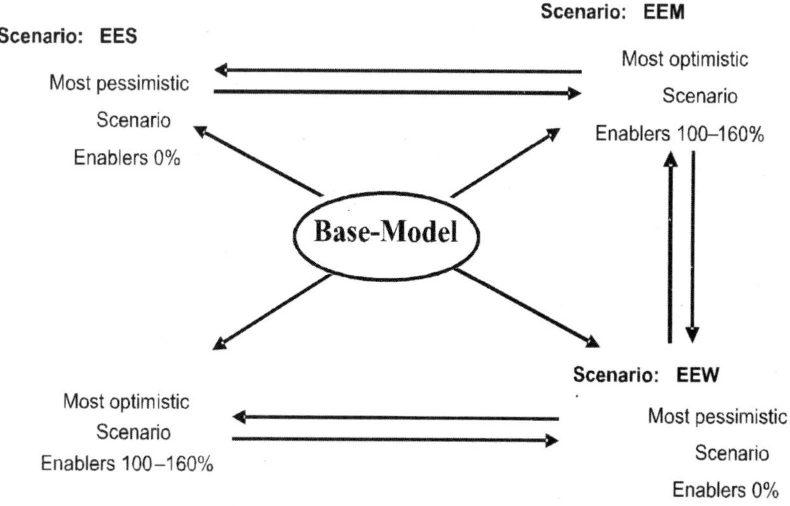

Fig. 5.2: Experimentation framework

5.4.1 Weightage of TQM Variables for Effective Implementation of TQM

Indian auto organizations are required to self-assess the performance of the organization against each variable. To get an indicative feel of the level of organizational maturity, the score can be compared with the levels given in Table 5.1. The table is based on the results of Siow (Siow *et al.,* 2001).

Table 5.1: Relationship of score with organizational maturity (Siow *et al.,* 2001)

Evaluation criteria	*Evaluation definition*	*Grades*
World-class	Comprehensive evidence of a systematic approach to succession plans. Clear evidence that these plans are being regularly reviewed, leading to improved business effectiveness.	1.0
Award winners	Extensive evidence of a systematic approach to succession plans. Clear evidence that these plans are being regularly reviewed and refined.	0.75
Improvers	Evidence of a systematic approach to succession plans. Clear evidence that these plans are being regularly reviewed.	0.50
Drifters	Little evidence of a systematic approach to succession plans. Clear evidence that these plans are being occasionally reviewed.	0.25
Uncommitted	No evidence of a systematic approach to succession plans. Any plans are not reviewed.	0

Based on the input from the above table, results from Caravatta (1997) and Chin and Pun (2002), the TQM maturity level has been considered around 880 score of TQM index. Such organizations are very serious contenders to become world-class. As per Table 5.1 such organizations fall between award winners and world-class. The term TQM index has been developed to indicate the level of TQM status of the organizations.

TQM variables and maximum score against each variable and initial value for experimentation have been shown in Table 5.2. As discussed in Section 4.9, a survey questionnaire was administrated in a workshop environment to four different groups of case organizations to assess the performance against the TQM variables. Based on the self-assessment of these groups, initial values have been decided. Maximum score against each TQM variable has been taken based on business excellence model developed by Agrawal (Agrawal, 1999). In this model, it has been assumed that TQM index has a maximum value of 1000.

Table 5.2: Comparison of maximum score of enablers, results and TQMI with initial values for experimentation

Category/Variables	*Maximum score*	*Initial value/Base value*
I: Enablers		
Leadership (*lds*)	125	33
Strategic Planning (*stp*)	100	44
Information Management (*inm*)	60	9
Human Resource Focus (*hrf*)	95	23
Customer and Market Focus (*cmf*)	110	41
Supplier Focus (*suf*)	30	8
Process Management (*prm*)	80	22
Total of Enablers	600	190
II: Results		
Impact on Society (*ios*)	70	25
Human Resource Satisfaction (*hrs*)	100	25
Customer Satisfaction (*cus*)	115	32
Supplier Satisfaction (*sus*)	40	11
Organization Specific Business Results (*bsr*)	75	32
Total of Results	**400**	**125**
TQM Index (TQMI)	**1000**	**315**

As discussed in Section 5.2, different market scenarios will have different levels of competition, thus efforts of the organization should accordingly be commensurate for the survival and growth of the organizations. The primary purpose of developing a SD model for the TQM index is to drive improvement —here, in the automobile manufacturing sector. The self-assessment by various teams via a questionnaire provides a snapshot picture of the organization, usually expressed in terms of strengths and areas for improvement, and a score. The model can predict the rate of improvement on different TQM variables based on the specific strength and gaps of the organizations. The SD model helps managers to continuously monitor the TQM performance and take corrective measures on problem areas. The model helps the organization to take policy decisions arising out of the dynamic nature of the system. Therefore, policy experimentation and scenario building would be done to see the effect of individual market scenario and transition phases in different market scenarios. The results of these experimentations and scenario building may help the organizations to take timely action to avoid a crashing effect on the performance. The crashing effect on the performance has been defined as a situation when organizations continue to remain at base value with enabler value at 190, result value at 125 and TQM index at 315. It has been assumed that if transition is not effectively handled in market scenarios such as from 'external enabler strong" to "external enabler moderate", from "external enabler moderate" to 'external enabler weak", and from "external enabler weak" to "external enabler crash", it will have a crashing effect on the performance of the organizations. Thus the transition phase, if not managed effectively, has been generally denoted in this book as a "crash" situation. In this chapter, any crash situation from one market scenario to another has been considered as the outcome of a "external enabler crash" market scenario, irrespective of the level of transition phase. In this chapter, policy experimentation and scenario building have been attempted for deriving better insight so that timely actions can be taken to bring the organization on a right path of TQM journey.

5.5 SENSITIVITY ANALYSIS

Sensitivity tests are carried out by identifying the variables, which affect the behavior of the model developed for the growth of TQM index. In the Indian automobile sector, TQM index growth is affected by some major variables like enablers and results. The enabler variables are leadership, strategic planning, information management, human resource focus, customer and market focus, supplier focus and process management. The result variables are impact on society, human resource satisfaction, supplier satisfaction, customer satisfaction and company-specific business results. The SD model recognizes the fact that there has to be good enablers for better results. TQM index is an aggregation of enablers and result variables.

5.5.1 Run Specification with EES-scenario for Group of Companies under Categories 'Quitter', 'Disillusioned' and 'Climber'

Quitter organizations are weak in deploying enablers, resulting into low results. Under severe competition when protection from customers is withdrawn, such organizations will find it very difficult to survive. These organizations will be forced to quit the market if they continue to remain in this category. *Disillusioned* organizations are weak in deploying enablers however, the results of the companies are very strong. Such organizations are able to survive only under protected environment. Such organizations live in the disillusionment that nothing is going to happen. *Climber* organizations are the real proactive organizations. They believe in the strategy of implementing high enablers to achieve high results. Such organizations consistently climb on the ladder of success.

Different experiments have been carried out from 0% effectiveness of enablers to 160% effectiveness of enablers. These experiments have been conducted to analyze the effect on enabler variables, result variables and TQM index during "external enabler strong" market scenario. The details of the run specification are given in Table 5.3A to 5.3C.

Different experiments have been carried out from 0% effectiveness of enablers to 160% effectiveness of enablers. These experiments have been conducted to analyze the effect on enabler variables, result variables, and TQM index during the transition phase from a "external enabler strong" scenario to a "external enabler moderate" market scenario. The effect of the same has been assumed as the outcome of a "external enabler crash" market scenario. The details of the run specification during "external enabler crash" market scenario is given in Table 5.3B.

Table 5.3A: Run specification for sensitivity analysis during EES market scenario (Runs 1 to 17 – Scenario for group of companies 'disillusioned' and 'climber')

Run No.	*Run details*	*Initial values/ Base values*	*Experimentation to determine impact on variables*
1	Effectiveness of enablers: 0%	**Base value**	**Seven Enablers**
2	Effectiveness of enablers: 10%	cmf: 41	cmf
3	Effectiveness of enablers: 20%	hrf: 23	hrf
4	Effectiveness of enablers: 30%	inm: 9	inm
5	Effectiveness of enablers: 40%	lds: 33	lds
6	Effectiveness of enablers: 50%	prm: 22	prm
7	Effectiveness of enablers: 60%	stp: 44	stp
8	Effectiveness of enablers: 70%	suf: 8	suf
9	Effectiveness of enablers: 80%	Sub-total of	
10	Effectiveness of enablers: 90%	enabler:190	+
11	Effectiveness of enablers: 100%	**Base value of**	**Five Result**
12	Effectiveness of enablers: 110%	**results**	absr
13	Effectiveness of enablers: 120%	absr: 32	acus
14	Effectiveness of enablers: 130%	acus: 32	ahrs
15	Effectiveness of enablers: 140%	ahrs: 25	aios
16	Effectiveness of enablers: 150%	aios: 25	asus
17	Effectiveness of enablers: 160%	asus: 11	+
		Sub-total of result: 125 **Base value of TQMI** Sub-total of enablers:190 Sub-total of results: 125TQMI: 315	**TQMI**

Table 5.3B: Run specification for sensitivity analysis during EEC market scenario (transition phase from EES to EEM, Runs 18 to 34 – Scenario for group of companies 'quitter' and 'climber'

Run No.	*Run details*	*Initial values/ Base values*	*Experimentation to determine impact on variables*
18	Effectiveness of enablers: 0%	**Base value** cmf: 41 hrf: 23 inm: 9 lds: 33 prm: 22 stp: 44 suf: 8 Sub-total of enabler:190 **Base value of results** absr: 32 acus: 32 ahrs: 25 aios: 25 asus: 11 Sub-total of result: 125 **Base value of TQMI** Sub-total of enablers:190 Sub-total of results:	**Seven Enablers** cmf hrf inm lds prm stp suf + **Five Result** absr acus ahrs aios asus + **TQMI**
19	Effectiveness of enablers: 10%		
20	Effectiveness of enablers: 20%		
21	Effectiveness of enablers: 30%		
22	Effectiveness of enablers: 40%		
23	Effectiveness of enablers: 50%		
24	Effectiveness of enablers: 60%		
25	Effectiveness of enablers: 70%		
26	Effectiveness of enablers: 80%		
27	Effectiveness of enablers: 90%		
28	Effectiveness of enablers: 100%		
29	Effectiveness of enablers: 110%		
30	Effectiveness of enablers: 120%		
31	Effectiveness of enablers: 130%		
32	Effectiveness of enablers: 140%		
33	Effectiveness of enablers: 150%		
34	Effectiveness of enablers: 160%		

125TQMI: 315Different experiments have been carried out to see the effect of individual and combination of enablers on TQM index. The details of run specification are given in Table 5.3C.

Table 5.3C: The effect of individual and combination of enablers on TQMI (Runs 35 to 41 - Scenario for groups of companies under category of 'quitter' and 'climber')

Run No.	*Run details*	*Initial values/*	*Experimentation to determine impact on variables*
35	**A.** lds affecting TQMI. Effectiveness of lds: 0%; rest: 100%	**Base value** cmf: 41 hrf: 23 inm: 9 lds: 33	**Seven Enablers** cmf hrf inm lds
36	**B.** lds and stp affecting TQMI. Effectiveness of lds/stp: 0% rest: 100%		

37	**C.** lds, stp and cmf affecting TQMI. Effectiveness of lds/stp/ cmf: 0%; rest: 100%	prm: 22 stp: 44 suf: 8	prm stp suf
38	**D.** lds, stp, cmf and hrf affecting TQMI. Effectiveness of lds/stp/c-mf/ hrf : 0%; rest: 100%	Sub-total of enabler:190 **Base value of**	+ **Five Result**
39	**E.** lds, stp, cmf, hrf and prm affecting TQMI. Effectiveness of lds/stp/cmf/hrf/ prm: 0%; rest: 100%	**results** absr: 32 acus: 32 ahrs: 25	absr acus ahrs aios
40	**F.** lds, stp, cmf, hrf, prm and inm affecting TQMI. Effectiveness of lds/stp/cmf/hrf/ prm/inm: 0%; rest: 100%	aios: 25 + asus: 11	asus Sub-total of **TQMI**
41	**G.** lds, stp, cmf, hrf, prm, inm and suf affecting TQMI. Effectiveness of lds/stp/cmf/hrf/ prm/inm/suf: 0%	result: 125 **Base value of TQMI** Sub-total of enablers:190 Sub-total of results: 125TQMI: 315	

Experiments are conducted for comparing EES and EEC at the same level of effectiveness of enablers. Performance levels at 0% to 100% of the effectiveness are reported for both the market scenarios in Table 5.4. Zero percent and 100% effectiveness of enablers show two extreme situations. Zero percent effectiveness of enablers indicates that organization is not at all serious about implementing the enabler variables. Hundred percent effectiveness of enablers indicates that the organization is very serious in implementing the enabler variables. Ten percent to 90% effectiveness of enablers indicates that the organizations fall in between these two extreme situations. Zero percent to 160% effectiveness of enablers means that organizations rate of increase of enablers is 0, 0.1, 0.2, 0.3, 0.4, 0.5, 0.6, 0.7, 0.8, 0.9, 1, 1.1, 1.2, 1.3, 1.4, 1.5 and 1.6 respectively.

5.5.1.1 Learning and Insight

During a scenario of "external enabler strong" it is revealed that at 100% effectiveness of enablers, such group of organizations produce very strong results resulting into high TQM index. From Table 5.4 it can be seen from the simulated results at 100% effectiveness of enablers that enabler score is 538, result score is 345 and TQM index is 883 in both the market scenarios. As per Table 5.1 such organizations fall between award winners and world-class. This situation reveals the excellent handing of the transition phase from "external enabler strong" to "external enabler moderate". Such groups of organizations take about 10 years to achieve the TQM maturity level as is evident from Table 5.4. Hundred percent effectiveness of enablers is a notional representation of organizations that are able to deploy the enablers at an optimum level. This insight helps the organization to decide about the time period required by the organizations to achieve the TQM maturity level. The time period to achieve

Table 5.4: Comparison between scenario of EES and EEC at same level from 0% to 160% effectiveness of enablers in the interval of 10% increase

EES					EEC (transition phase from EES to EEM)					
Simulated Run	*%age of effectiveness (enb)*	*enb*	*rst*	*TQMI after 10 years*	*Years to achieve*	*Simulated Run*	*enb*	*rst*	*TQMI after 10 years*	*TQM maturity*
Run 1	0	190	299	489	>50	Run 18	190	125	315	Never
Run 2	10	230	306	537	40	Run 19	242	145	387	>50
Run 3	20	274	313	587	29	Run 20	295	168	464	35
Run 4	30	320	320	641	22	Run 21	349	194	543	25
Run 5	40	366	324	690	18	Run 22	397	222	619	20
Run 6	50	408	327	736	16	Run 23	435	252	687	17
Run 7	60	445	333	779	14	Run 24	470	276	747	15
Run 8	70	482	336	819	12	Run 25	496	301	797	13
Run 9	80	505	339	845	11	Run 26	514	318	833	12
Run 10	90	524	341	865	11	Run 27	529	333	862	11
Run 11	100	538	345	883	10	Run 28	538	345	883	10
Run 12	110	550	351	901	9	Run 29	550	351	901	9
Run 13	120	559	350	909	9	Run 30	559	350	909	9
Run 14	130	565	352	918	8	Run 31	565	352	918	8
Run 15	140	575	356	932	8	Run 32	575	356	932	8
Run 16	150	574	356	930	8	Run 33	574	356	930	8
Run 17	160	579	359	938	8	Run 34	579	359	938	8

the TQM maturity level depends on the effectiveness of the strategic planning. Depending on the organization's strategic plan, the TQM maturity level can either be achieved faster or slower than what is stated above. The results show that such groups of organizations fall under *'climber'* category i.e. high enablers resulting into high results, which are the most desirable case. Increase in the effectiveness of enablers from 130% to 160% reveals that the years to achieve the TQM maturity level come down from about 10 years to about 8 years and remain constant at this level even with a further increase in the effectiveness of enablers. It establishes the fact that there is no quick fix to achieve the TQM maturity level. It takes minimum 8-10 years to achieve the TQM maturity level with consistent efforts and focus. When effectiveness of enablers is reduced, though there is an appreciable drop in the enablers but results do not fall appreciably during "external enabler strong" market scenario. From Table 5.4 it can be observed that at 0% effectiveness of enablers, total enabler value falls to the base value of 190 whereas results are still at a much higher value of 299. This is a case of protection either from the customer or it is a monopoly situation. Such groups of organizations fall under the *'disillusioned'* category i.e., low enablers resulting into high results. This is a dicey situation where such groups of organizations live under disillusionment that organizations are doing very well. During the transition of market scenarios from "external enabler strong" to "external enabler moderate", same group of organizations who are doing very well under a scenario of "external enabler strong" (result value 299), crash to an original base value at 0% effectiveness of enablers (result value 125). The crash situation has been denoted when organization's performance continue to remain at base value with enabler value 190, result value 125 and TQM index 315. From Table 5.4, it can be observed that at 0% effectiveness of enablers, enabler and result value continue to remain at a base value of 190 and 125, respectively and therefore, such organizations will find it very difficult to achieve the TQM maturity level if they continue with the same effectiveness of enablers. After comparison of this performance against Table 5.1, it is revealed that such organizations fall between drifters and improvers. Zero percent effectiveness is a notional representation that the organization's deployment of enablers is very poor. Such groups of organizations fall under the category of *'quitter'*. Therefore, the learning is that organization's should handle this transition phase with careful planning to ward-off such a crash situation. They should maintain the performance level that was achieved at 100% effectiveness of enablers. The organization should be able to differentiate whether it is really doing well or pretending to do so. Such organizations should be careful regarding personal biases in the self-assessment of the organization.

Figure 5.3 shows the trend of increase in result and TQM index at 0% effectiveness of enablers with "external enabler strong" market scenario. At 0% effectiveness of enablers, enabler value is constant at base value of 190. However, result and TQM index are still on the increase. Such organizations fall under the group of *'disillusioned'* companies.

The performance of the trend shown in Figure 5.3 can be explained from Table 5.5, which shows increase in result and TQM index after the initiation of TQM programme. It is evident from this table that though enabler value is at a base value of 190, result value and TQM index increases to 299 and 489, respectively in 10 years. This kind of performance is possible only under a protected market.

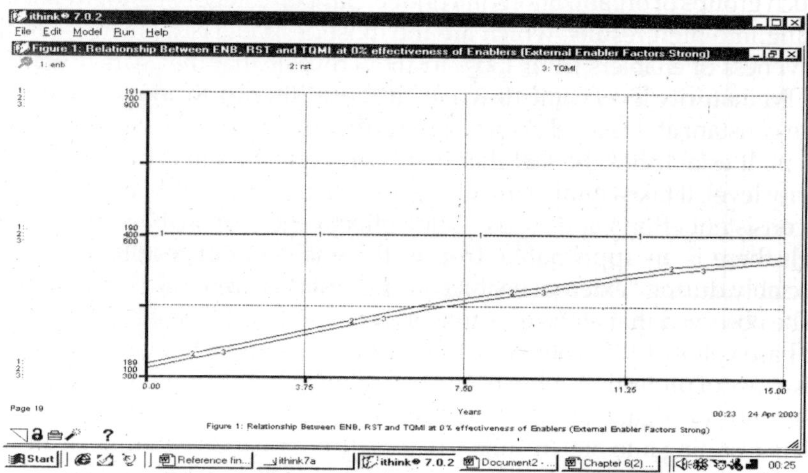

Fig. 5.3: Relationship among enb, rst and TQMI at 0% effectiveness of enablers during "external enabler strong" market scenario

Figure 5.4 shows the trend of increase in enabler, result and TQM index at 100% effectiveness of enablers. The trend shows that increase in the enabler is instrumental in the increase of result and TQM index. Such organizations fall under the category *'climber'*. Still, it can be highly deceptive for the organizations. Such organizations therefore, should judge their performance in totality by keeping in mind the external factors.

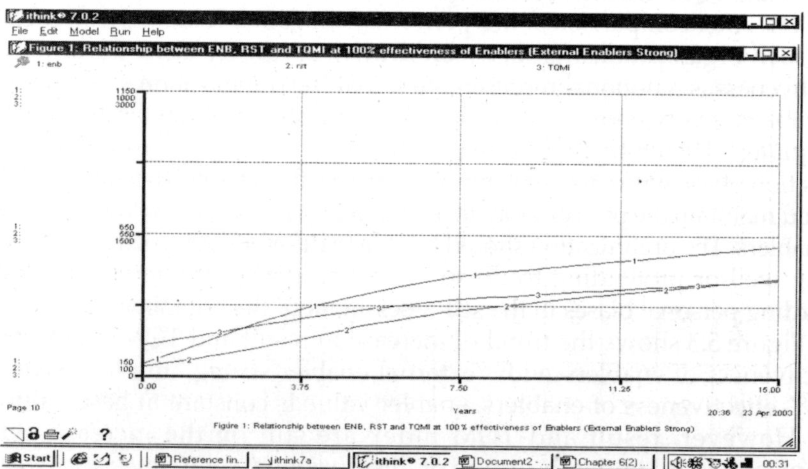

Fig. 5.4: Relationship among enb, rst and TQMI at 100% effectiveness of enablers during "external enabler strong" market scenario

Table 5.5: Relationship among enb, rst and TQMI at 0% effectiveness of enablers during "external enabler strong" market scenario

Years	*absr*	*acus*	*ahrs*	*aios*	*asus*	*cmf*	*hrf*	*inm*	*lds*	*prm*	*stp*	*suf*	enb	rst	TQMI
Initial	32	32	25	25	11	41	23	19	33	22	44	8	190	125	315
0	34	41	29	27	12	41	23	19	33	22	44	8	190	144	334
1	36	50	33	29	14	41	23	19	33	22	44	8	190	163	353
2	38	59	37	31	15	41	23	19	33	22	44	8	190	182	372
3	40	68	42	33	16	41	23	19	33	22	44	8	190	202	392
4	42	77	46	36	18	41	23	19	33	22	44	8	190	221	411
5	44	86	51	38	19	41	23	19	33	22	44	8	190	240	430
6	47	93	55	41	21	41	23	19	33	22	44	8	190	258	448
7	49	95	60	43	22	41	23	19	33	22	44	8	190	272	462
8	51	98	65	46	23	41	23	19	33	22	44	8	190	285	475
9	53	101	70	49	24	41	23	19	33	22	44	8	190	299	489

The performance of the trend shown in Figure 5.4 can be explained from Table 5.6, which shows increase in enabler, result and TQM index after the initiation of TQM programme. It is evident from this table that with the increase of enabler, both result and TQM index continue to increase. At the end of 10th year, these organizations achieve the TQM maturity level resulting into enabler value, result value and TQM index to 538, 345 and 883 respectively. This kind of unchallenged and gradual rate of performance is possible only under a protected market.

The organizations, which do not effectively handle the transition phase from "external enabler strong" to "external enabler moderate", would crash to the base value at 0% effectiveness of the enablers. Such a situation is shown in Figure 5.5. Such organizations fall under the group *'quitter'* i.e., when low enablers resulting low results.

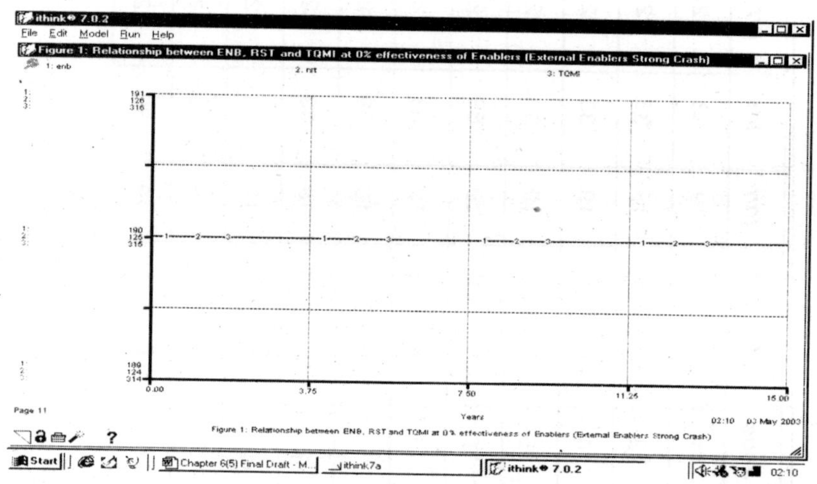

Fig. 5.5: Relationship among enb, rst and TQMI at 0% effectiveness of enabler (transition phase from EES to EEM)

The combined picture of individual results and enablers, total enablers, results and TQMI from 0% effectiveness of enablers to 100% effectiveness of enablers in the interval of 10% increase is shown in Table 5.7.

The Figure 5.6 shows the trend of group of *'quitter' 'disillusioned'* and *'climber'* category organizations with "external enabler strong" and "external enabler crash" market scenario. Though correlation exists between enabler and result in case of *'disillusioned'* group of companies, the relationship is very weak. However, the relationship between enabler and result under *'quitter'* and *'climber'* group of organizations

Table 5.6: Relationship among enb, rst and TQMI at 100% effectiveness of enablers during "external enabler strong" market scenario

Years	*absr*	*acus*	*ahrs*	*aios*	*asus*	*cmf*	*hrf*	*inm*	*lds*	*prm*	*stp*	*suf*	*enb*	*rst*	*TQMI*
Initial	**32**	**32**	**25**	**25**	**11**	**41**	**23**	**19**	**33**	**22**	**44**	**8**	**190**	**125**	**315**
0	34	41	29	27	12	49	29	29	46	25	52	9	242	145	387
1	37	52	34	29	14	58	35	40	58	29	61	11	295	168	463
2	40	64	41	31	15	66	42	50	68	35	70	13	347	193	541
3	44	77	48	346	17	74	49	53	78	41	80	15	393	221	614
4	48	90	57	37	18	82	55	55	86	48	81	18	428	252	680
5	52	95	66	40	20	89	62	58	92	56	82	20	462	275	738
6	56	98	77	43	21	90	68	60	98	63	84	23	489	298	788
7	61	101	81	47	23	92	74	63	101	67	85	25	509	315	824
8	66	103	83	50	25	93	78	66	104	68	86	25	524	330	854
9	72	106	85	54	26	95	82	63	107	70	87	26	538	345	883

are very strong. In such a situation, high enablers produce high results, which is the most desirable for the survival and growth of the organizations under severe competitive market scenario. The learning is that organizations under *'disillusioned'* category should move towards the *'climber'* category.

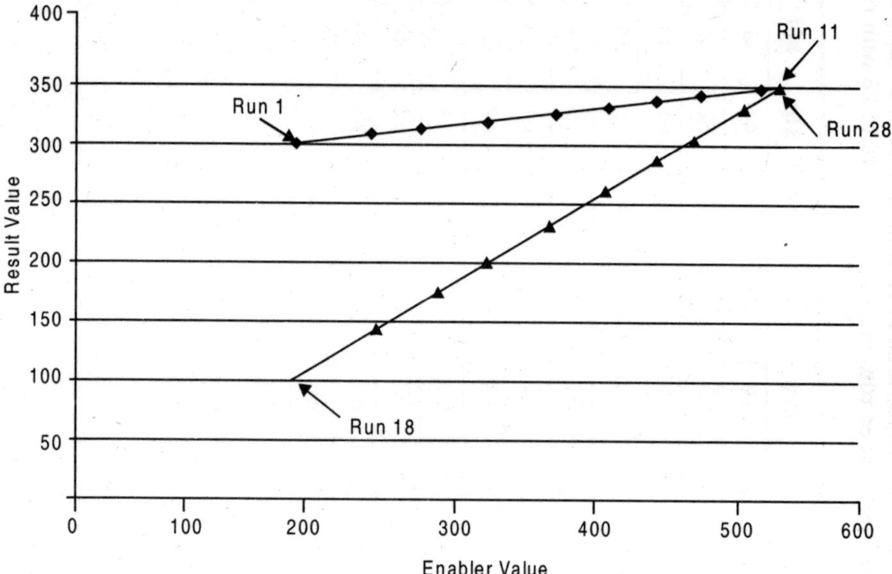

Fig. 5.6: Relationship among enabler, result and TQMI from 0% effectiveness of enabler to 100% at an interval of 10% increase during EES and EEC

5.5.2 Run Specification During "External Enabler Strong" and "Transition Phase from EES to EEM" (Runs 35 to 41)

5.5.2.1 Run Specification During External Enabler Strong Market Scenario to See the Effect of Individual and Combination of Enablers at 0% Effectiveness of Enablers

Run specifications to see the effect of individual and combination of enablers on enabler, result and TQM index during "external enabler strong" market scenario are listed in Table 5.3A and 5.3C. The effect of lds, lds/stp, lds/stp/cmf, lds/stp/cmf/hrf, lds/stp/cmf/hrf/prm, lds/stp/cmf/hrf/prm/inm and lds/stp/cmf/hrf/prm/inm/suf at 0% effectiveness of enabler, result and TQM index are shown in Table 5.8.

Table 5.7: Combined picture of individual results and enablers, total enablers, results and TQMI from 0% effectiveness of enablers to 100% effectiveness of enablers in the interval of 10% increase (Runs 18 to 28 with reference to Table 5.3B)

% of effect-iveness	*absr*	*acus*	*ahrs*	*aios*	*asus*	*cmf*	*hrf*	*inm*	*lds*	*prm*	*stp*	*suf*	*enb*	*rst*	*TQMI*
0	32	32	25	25	11	41	23	19	33	22	44	8	190	125	315
10	34	42	29	27	12	49	29	29	46	25	52	9	242	145	387
20	37	52	34	29	14	58	35	41	57	30	61	11	295	168	464
30	40	64	41	31	15	66	42	51	68	35	70	13	349	194	543
40	44	77	48	34	17	74	49	57	77	42	80	15	397	222	619
50	48	90	57	37	18	81	55	60	85	49	82	18	435	252	687
60	52	96	67	40	20	88	62	63	92	57	84	21	470	276	747
70	57	100	77	43	21	90	68	64	97	64	85	24	496	301	797
80	61	102	83	47	23	92	74	65	101	67	86	25	514	318	833
90	67	104	85	50	25	94	79	67	105	69	87	25	529	333	862
100	72	106	85	54	26	95	82	68	107	70	87	26	538	345	883

Table 5.8: Relationship among enabler, result and TQMI at 0% effectiveness of enablers during "external enabler strong" market scenario (Runs 11, 35 to 41 with reference to Tables 5.3A and 5.3C)

Run No.	***Enablers***	***enb***	***rst***	***TQMI after 10th Year***
11	Effectiveness of enablers: 100%	538	345	883
35	Effectiveness of lds: 0%	463	328	792
36	Effectiveness of lds/stp: 0%	407	317	725
37	Effectiveness of lds/stp/cmf: 0%	353	316	669
38	Effectiveness of lds/stp/cmf/hrf: 0%	304	308	613
39	Effectiveness of lds/stp/cmf/hrf/ prm: 0%	253	301	554
40	Effectiveness of lds/stp/cmf/hrf/prm/inm: 0%	204	301	505
41	Effectiveness of lds/stp/cmf/hrf/prm/inm/suf: 0%	190	299	489

The trend of relationship among enabler, result and TQM index at 0% effectiveness of different combination of enablers is shown in Figure 5.7.

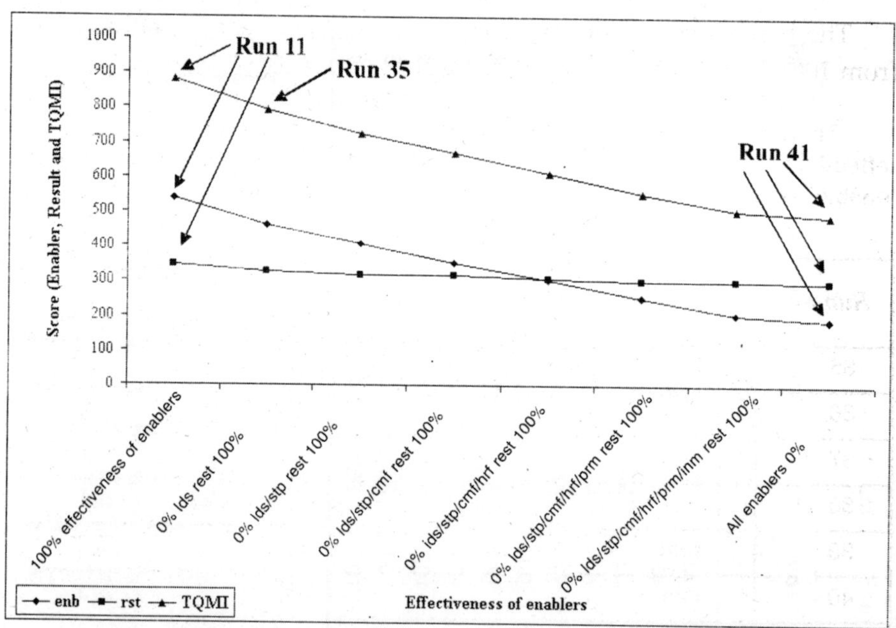

Fig. 5.7: Relationship trend among enabler, result and TQMI at 0% effectiveness of different combination of enablers during "external enabler strong" market scenario

The percent reduction in enabler, result and TQM index from 100% effectiveness to 0% effectiveness of various enablers is shown in Table 5.9.

Table 5.9: Percent reduction in enabler, result and TQMI from 100% effectiveness to 0% effectiveness of various enablers during "external enabler strong" market scenario (Runs 35 to 41 with reference to Tables 5.3A and 5.3C)

Run No.	Effectiveness of enablers: 0%	% Reduction		
		enb	rst	TQMI
35	lds	13.9	4.9	10.3
36	lds/stp	24.3	8.1	17.9
37	lds/stp/cmf	34.4	8.4	24.2
38	lds/stp/cmf/hrf	43.5	10.7	30.6
39	lds/stp/cmf/hrf/prm	53.0	12.8	37.3
40	lds/stp/cmf/hrf/prm/inm	62.0	12.8	42.8
41	lds/stp/cmf/hrf/prm/inm/suf	64.7	13.3	44.6

The percent reduction due to individual enabler at 0% effectiveness from 100% effectiveness of enablers is shown in Table 5.10.

Table 5.10: Percent reduction in enabler, result and TQMI from 100% effectiveness to 0% effectiveness due to individual enablers during "external enabler strong" market scenario (Runs 35 to 41 with reference to Tables 5.3A and 5.3C)

Run No.	Effectiveness of enablers: 0%	% Reduction		
		enb	rst	TQMI
35	lds	13.9	4.9	10.3
36	stp	10.4	3.2	7.6
37	cmf	10.1	0.3	6.3
38	hrf	9.1	2.3	6.4
39	prm	9.5	2.1	6.7
40	inm	9.0	0	5.5
41	suf	2.7	0.5	1.8

The percent reduction in TQM index at 0% effectiveness of individual enablers and their % wise contribution is shown in Table 5.11.

Table 5.11: Percent reduction in TQMI at 0% effectiveness of individual enablers and their contribution in % during "external enabler strong" market scenario (Runs 35 to 41 with reference to Tables 5.3A and 5.3C)

Run No.	*Effectiveness of enablers: 0%*	*0% Reduction TQMI*	*% Contribution*	*Cumulative% contribution*
35	lds	10.3	23.2	23.2
36	stp	7.6	17.1	40.3
37	prm	6.7	15.0	55.3
38	hrf	6.4	14.3	69.6
39	cmf	6.3	14.1	83.7
40	inm	5.5	12.3	96.0
41	suf	1.8	4.0	100
	Total	**44.6**	**100**	

5.5.2.2 Run Specification During External Enabler Crash Market Scenario (Transition Phase from EES to EEM) to See the Effect of Individual and Combination of Enablers at 0% Effectiveness of Enablers

Run specification to see the effect of individual and combination of enablers on enabler, result and TQM index with EEC market scenario. The effect of lds, lds/stp, lds/stp/cmf, lds/stp/cmf/hrf, lds/stp/cmf/hrf/prm, lds/stp/cmf/hrf/prm/inm and lds/stp/cmf/hrf/prm/inm/suf at 0% effectiveness of enabler, result and TQM index are shown in Table 5.12.

Table 5.12: Relationship among enabler, result and TQMI at 0% effectiveness of enablers during "external enabler crash" market scenario (Runs 28, 35 to 41 with reference to Tables 5.3B and 5.3C)

Run No.	*Enablers*	*enb*	*rst*	*TQMI after 10th Year*
28	Effectiveness of enablers: 100%	538	345	883
35	Effectiveness of lds: 0%	465	298	763
36	Effectiveness of lds/stp: 0%	416	245	661
37	Effectiveness of lds/stp/cmf: 0%	362	206	568
38	Effectiveness of lds/stp/cmf/hrf: 0%	306	175	482
39	Effectiveness of lds/stp/cmf/hrf/ prm: 0%	255	154	409
40	Effectiveness of lds/stp/cmf/hrf/ prm/inm: 0%	205	144	350
41	Effectiveness of lds/stp/cmf/hrf/prm/inm/ suf: 0%	190	125	315

The trend of relationship among enabler, result and TQM index at 0% effectiveness of different combination of enablers is shown in Figure 5.8.

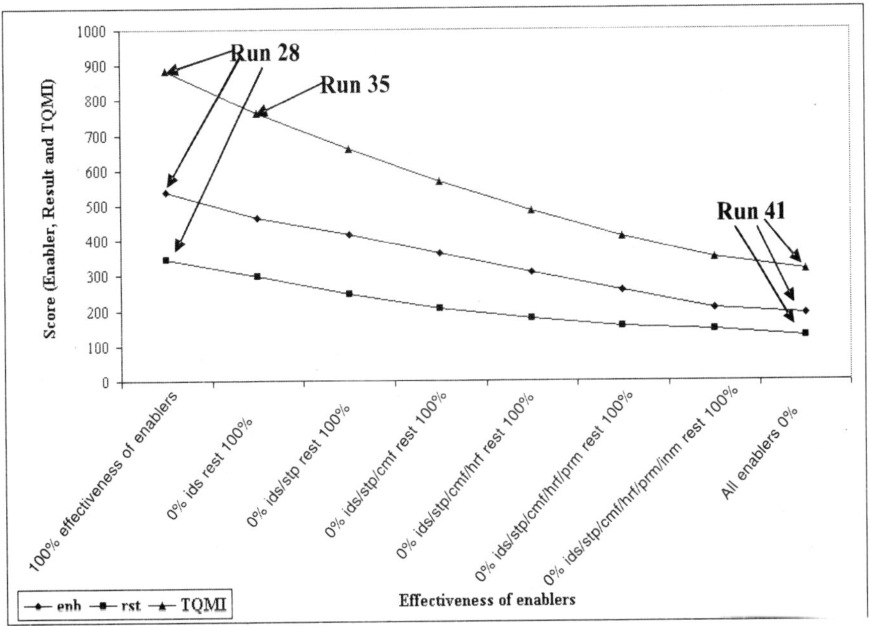

Fig. 5.8: Relationship trend among enabler, result and TQMI at 0% effectiveness of different combination of enablers during "external enabler crash" market scenario

The percent reduction in enabler, result and TQM index from 100% effectiveness to 0% effectiveness of various enablers is shown in Table 5.13.

Table 5.13: Percent reduction in enabler, result and TQMI from 100% effectiveness to 0% effectiveness of various enablers during "external enabler crash" market scenario (Runs 35 to 41 with reference to Tables 5.3B and 5.3C)

Run No.	***Effectiveness of enablers: 0%***	***% Reduction***		
		enb	***rst***	***TQMI***
35	Ids	13.6	13.6	13.6
36	Ids/stp	22.8	28.8	25.1
37	Ids/stp/cmf	32.6	40.3	35.6
38	Ids/stp/cmf/hrf	43.0	49.2	45.4
39	Ids/stp/cmf/hrf/prm	52.6	55.3	53.6
40	Ids/stp/cmf/hrf/prm/inm	61.8	58.1	60.4
41	Ids/stp/cmf/hrf/prm/inm/suf	64.7	63.8	64.4

The percent reduction due to individual enabler at 0% effectiveness from 100% effectiveness of enablers is shown in Table 5.14.

Table 5.14: Percent reduction in enabler, result and TQMI from 100% effectiveness to 0% effectiveness due to individual enablers during "external enabler crash" market scenario (Runs 35 to 41 with reference to Tables 5.3B and 5.3C)

Run No.	*Effectiveness of enablers: 0%*	*% Reduction*		
		enb	*rst*	*TQMI*
35	lds	13.6	13.6	13.6
36	stp	9.2	15.2	11.5
37	cmf	9.8	11.5	10.5
38	hrf	10.4	8.9	9.8
39	prm	9.6	6.1	8.2
40	inm	9.2	2.8	6.8
41	suf	2.9	5.7	4.0

The percent reduction in TQM index at 0% effectiveness of individual enablers and their % wise contribution is shown in Table 5.15.

Table 5.15: Percent reduction in TQMI at 0% effectiveness of individual enablers and their contribution in % during "external enabler crash" market scenario (Runs 35 to 41 with reference to Tables 5.3B and 5.3C)

Run No.	*Effectiveness of enablers: 0%*	*% Reduction TQMI*	*% Contribution*	*Cumulative % contribution*
35	lds	13.6	21.1	21.1
36	stp	11.5	17.9	39
37	cmf	10.5	16.3	55.3
38	hrf	9.8	15.2	70.5
39	prm	8.2	12.7	83.2
40	inm	6.8	10.6	93.8
41	suf	4.0	6.2	100
	Total	64.4	100	

5.5.2.3 Learning and Insight

From Table 5.11, it is evident that leadership, strategic planning, process management, and human resource focus contribute to 69.6% of total TQM index reduction from 100% effectiveness of enablers during "external enabler strong" market scenario. In other words, it is evident that leadership, strategic planning, process management and human resource focus contribute 69.6% in achieving the TQM maturity level at 100% effectiveness of the enablers. The maximum contributor is from variable leadership with a 23.2% contribution followed by strategic planning (17.1%), followed by process management (15.0%), and human resource focus (14.3%). The above result shows that the organizations should best focus on leadership, strategic planning, process management and human resource focus for the survival and growth when they face a market scenario of "external enabler strong".

From Table 5.15, it is also evident that leadership, strategic planning, customer and market focus, and human resource focus contribute 70.5% of total TQM index reduction from 100% effectiveness of enablers during the transition phase from "external enabler strong" to "external enabler moderate" market scenario. In other words it is evident that leadership, strategic planning, customer and market focus, and human resource focus contribute 70.5% in achieving the TQM maturity level at 100% effectiveness of the enablers. The maximum contributor is from leadership (21.1%), followed by strategic planning (17.9%), customer and market focus (16.3%) and human resource focus (15.2%). These results show that the major contributors for the success of any organization in achieving the TQM maturity level are leadership, strategic planning, customer and market focus, and human resource focus. The organizations, therefore, have to focus primarily on leadership, strategic planning, customer and market focus, and human resource focus for the survival and growth of the organizations during a transition phase from "external enabler strong" to "external enabler moderate" market scenario. If organizations are not achieving the TQM maturity level within 10 years, then leadership, strategic planning, customer and market focus, and human resource focus are possibly lacking.

5.5.3 Run Specification with EEM–Scenario for Group of Companies under Categories of 'Quitter' 'Disillusioned' and 'Climber'

Different experiments have been carried out from 0% effectiveness of enablers to 160% effectiveness of enablers. These experiments have been conducted to analyze the effect on enablers variables, results variables, and TQM index during the "external enabler moderate" market scenario. The details of run specification are given in Table 5.16A to 5.16C.

Different experiments have been carried out from 0% effectiveness of enablers to 160% effectiveness of enablers. These experiments have been conducted to analyze the effect on enabler variables, result variables and TQM index during a transition phase from "external enabler moderate" to "external enabler weak" market scenario. The effect of the same has been assumed as the outcome of "external enabler crash" market scenario. The details of run specification during "external enabler crash" market scenario is given in Table 5.16B.

Different experiments have been carried out to judge the effect of individual and combination of enablers on TQM index. The details of run specification are given in Table 5.16C.

Table 5.16A: Run specification for sensitivity analysis during EEM market scenario (Runs 42 to 58 – Scenario for group of companies 'disillusioned' and 'climber')

Run	*Run details*	*Initial values*	*Experimentation to determine impact on variables*
42	Effectiveness of enablers: 0%	**Base value**	**Seven Enablers**
43	Effectiveness of enablers: 10%	cmf: 41	cmf
44	Effectiveness of enablers: 20%	hrf: 23	hrf
45	Effectiveness of enablers: 30%	inm: 9	inm
46	Effectiveness of enablers: 40%	lds: 33	lds
47	Effectiveness of enablers: 50%	prm: 22	prm
48	Effectiveness of enablers: 60%	stp: 44	stp
49	Effectiveness of enablers: 70%	suf: 8	suf
50	Effectiveness of enablers: 80%	Sub-total of	
51	Effectiveness of enablers: 90%	enabler:190	+
52	Effectiveness of enablers: 100%	**Base value of**	**Five Result**
53	Effectiveness of enablers: 110%	**results**	absr
54	Effectiveness of enablers: 120%	absr: 32	acus
55	Effectiveness of enablers: 130%	acus: 32	ahrs
56	Effectiveness of enablers: 140%	ahrs: 25	aios
57	Effectiveness of enablers: 150%	aios: 25	asus
58	Effectiveness of enablers: 160%	asus: 11	+
		Sub-total of result: 125 **Base value of TQMI** Sub-total of enablers:190 Sub-total of results: 125TQMI: 315	**TQMI**

Table 5.16B: Run specification for sensitivity analysis during EEC market scenario (transition phase from EEM to EEW, Runs 59 to 75 – Scenario for group of companies 'quitter' and 'climber')

Run	*Run details*	*Initial values*	*Experimentation to determine impact on variables*
59	Effectiveness of enablers: 0%	**Base value**	**Seven Enablers**
60	Effectiveness of enablers: 10%	cmf: 41	cmf
61	Effectiveness of enablers: 20%	hrf: 23	hrf
62	Effectiveness of enablers: 30%	inm: 9	inm
63	Effectiveness of enablers: 40%	lds: 33	lds
64	Effectiveness of enablers: 50%	prm: 22	prm
65	Effectiveness of enablers: 60%	stp: 44	stp

66	Effectiveness of enablers: 70%	suf: 8	suf
67	Effectiveness of enablers: 80%	Sub-total of	
68	Effectiveness of enablers: 90%	enabler:190	+
69	Effectiveness of enablers: 100%	**Base value of**	**Five Result**
70	Effectiveness of enablers: 110%	**results**	absr
71	Effectiveness of enablers: 120%	absr: 32	acus
72	Effectiveness of enablers: 130%	acus: 32	ahrs
73	Effectiveness of enablers: 140%	ahrs: 25	aios
74	Effectiveness of enablers: 150%	aios: 25	asus
75	Effectiveness of enablers: 160%	asus: 11	+
		Sub-total of result: 125 **Base value** **of TQMI** Sub-total of enablers:190 Sub-total of results: 125TQMI: 315	**TQMI**

Table 5.16C: The effect of individual and combination of enablers on TQMI (Runs 76 to 82 - Scenario for groups of companies under category of 'quitter' and 'climber')

Run	*Run details*	*Initial values*	*Experimentation to determine impact on variables*
76	**A.** lds affecting TQMI. Effectiveness of lds: 0%; rest: 100%	**Base value** cmf: 41	**Seven Enablers** cmf
77	**B.** lds and stp affecting TQMI. Effectiveness of lds/stp: 0% rest: 100%	hrf: 23 inm: 9 lds: 33	hrf inm lds
78	**C.** lds, stp and cmf affecting TQMI. Effectiveness of lds/stp/cmf: 0%; rest: 100%	prm: 22 stp: 44 suf: 8	prm stp suf
79	**D.** lds, stp, cmf and hrf affecting TQMI. Effectiveness of lds/stp/c-mf/ hrf : 0%; rest: 100%	Sub-total of enabler:190 **Base value of**	 + **Five Result**
80	**E.** lds, stp, cmf, hrf and prm affecting TQMI. Effectiveness of lds/stp/cmf/hrf/ prm: 0%; rest: 100%	**results** absr: 32 acus: 32 ahrs: 25	absr acus ahrs aios
81	**F.** lds, stp, cmf, hrf, prm and inm affecting TQMI. Effectiveness of lds/stp/cmf/hrf/ prm/inm: 0%; rest: 100%	aios: 25 + asus: 11	asus Sub-total of **TQMI**
82	**G.** lds, stp, cmf, hrf, prm, inm and suf affecting TQMI. Effectiveness of lds/stp/cmf/hrf/ prm/inm/suf: 0%	result: 125 **Base value** **of TQMI**	
		Sub-total of enablers:190 Sub-total of results: 125TQMI: 315	

Experiments are further conducted for comparing EEM and EEC at same effectiveness for different enablers. Performance levels at 0% to 160% of the effectiveness have been reported for the both the market scenarios in Table 5.17.

5.5.3.1 Learning and Insight

During "external enabler moderate" market scenario, it has been observed that at 100% effectiveness of enablers, such group of organizations find it very difficult to attain the same result as compared to what they achieved during "external enabler strong" market scenario. From Table 5.17, it can be seen from the simulated results at 100% effectiveness of enablers that enabler score is 540 and result score is 295. Thus, TQM index is 835 in both the market scenarios. As shown in Table 5.1, such organizations fall between an award winner organization and a world-class organization. Present situation reveals that a meticulous handling of the transition phase from "external enabler moderate" to "external enabler weak" is must. Such groups of organizations take around 13 years to achieve the TQM maturity level. Hundred percent effectiveness of enablers is a notional representation that the organizations have been able to deploy the enablers at an optimum level. This obtained insight helps the organization to decide about the minimum time period required by an organization to achieve the TQM maturity level. The time period to achieve the TQM maturity level depends on the effectiveness of the strategic planning. Depending on the organization's strategic plan, the TQM maturity level can either be achieved faster or slower than what is stated above. The results show that organizations that fall under a *'climber'* category are the most desirable organizations. Increase in the effectiveness of enablers from 130% to 160% reveals that the years to achieve the TQM maturity level come down from 13 years to 10 years and remain static at almost 10 years even though there is a further increase in the effectiveness of enablers. It establishes the fact that there is no quick fix to achieve the TQM maturity level. It takes minimum 10-13 years to achieve the TQM maturity level during the market scenario when external enabler is moderate. The results are mainly affected by the stiff competition in comparison to the results achieved during "external enabler strong" market scenario. When effectiveness of enablers is reduced, though there is an appreciable drop in the enabler, results do not fall that appreciably. From Table 5.17, it can be observed that at 0% effectiveness of enablers, enabler falls to a base value of 190 whereas results are still at much higher value of 257 as compared to a base value of 125 during "external enabler moderate" market scenario. The results are comparatively less than what has been achieved during the scenario of "external enabler strong". It has been assumed that with the increase of competition there has been reduction in the results. This shows that though protection from customer has come down, yet it is not totally withdrawn. Such groups of organizations fall under the *'disillusioned'* category

Table 5.17: Comparison of scenario of EEM and EEC at same level from 0% to 160% effectiveness of enablers in the interval of 10% increase

		EEM				EEC (transition phase from EEM to EEW)				
Run No.	***%age of effectiveness (enb)***	***enb***	***rst***	***TQMI after 10 years***	***Years to achieve TQMI maturity***	***Run No.***	***enb***	***rst***	***TQMI after 10 years***	***Years to achieve TQMI maturity***
42	0	190	257	447	>50	59	190	125	315	Never
43	10	232	262	495	>50	60	242	142	384	>50
44	20	278	269	548	41	61	296	162	458	37
45	30	327	276	603	30	62	350	183	534	27
46	40	373	283	657	24	63	400	207	607	22
47	50	417	289	706	20	64	439	233	672	20
48	60	455	292	747	17	65	474	254	729	17
49	70	489	291	781	16	66	502	270	773	16
50	80	514	293	808	14	67	518	287	805	15
51	90	529	293	823	13	68	532	291	823	14
52	100	540	295	836	13	69	540	295	835	13
53	110	554	295	850	10	70	554	295	850	10
54	120	557	295	853	10	71	557	295	853	10
55	130	563	296	860	10	72	563	296	860	10
56	140	573	294	868	10	73	573	294	868	10
57	150	578	297	875	10	74	578	297	875	10
58	160	581	295	876.	10	75	581	295	876	10

of organizations, where low enablers produce high results. These organizations believe that good results can be assured only through certification. Based on ISO certification, such organizations get initial protection from customers. This is a dicey situation where such groups of organizations live under a disillusionment that organizations are doing very well under competitive market scenario whereas in reality they may not be doing so. During transition period from a scenario of "external enabler moderate" to "external enabler weak", the same group of organizations, which were doing well under a scenario of "external enabler moderate" (result value 257), crash to their original base value at 0% effectiveness of enablers (with result value as 125). This crash situation has been observed when organizations performance continue to remain at the base value with enabler value 190, result value 125 and TQM index 315 (Table 5.17). A replication of this situation was observed during the initial setback of Maruti Udyog Limited (an Indian automobile company), when it came into red for the first time with a loss of Rs. 269 crore in 2000-01 (Soni and Pandya, 2002). After comparison of this performance against Table 5.1, it is revealed that such organizations fall between drifters and improvers. Zero percent effectiveness is a notional representation that the organization's deployment of enablers is very poor. Therefore, the learning is that organizations should effectively handle this transition to ward-off such crash situations and should and maintain the performance level of 100% effectiveness of enablers. However, the level of competition during scenarios of "strong", "moderate" or "weak" is quite different. It is very important that the organizations should safeguard themselves from individual biases in making self-assessment for quality measures.

Comparison of performance between scenario of "external enabler strong" and "external enabler moderate" at 0% effectiveness of enablers is shown in Table 5.18.

Table 5.18: Comparison of performance between EES and EEM enabler factors at 0% effectiveness

Run No.	*External enabler*	*enb*	*rst*	*TQMI after 10th year*	*Years to achieve TQMI maturity*
1	Strong	190	299	489	>50
42	Moderate	190	257	447	>50

Comparison of performance between scenario of "external enabler strong" and "external enabler moderate" at 100% effectiveness of enablers is shown in Table 5.19.

Table 5.19: Comparison of performance between EES and EEM enabler factors at 100% effectiveness

Run No.	*External enabler*	*enb*	*rst*	*TQMI after 10th year*	*Years to achieve TQMI maturity*
11	Strong	538	345	883	10
52	Moderate	540	295	835	13

From Tables 5.18 and 5.19, it is evident that in a competitive market scenario, even better focus on enabler cannot maintain the same result unless strategies are meticulously deployed. Any slackness in the implementation of enablers can lead to disaster for the concerned organizations. Therefore, organizations should benchmark against better performing competitors before deciding the strategy. It takes about 10 years to achieve the TQM maturity level when external enabler is strong and it takes about 13 years to achieve the TQM maturity level in case of external enabler is moderate.

Comparison of performance between scenarios of "external enabler strong" and "external enabler moderate" during transition phase at 0% effectiveness of enablers is shown in Table 5.20.

Table 5.20: Comparison of performance during transition phase at 0% effectiveness of enablers (Runs 18 and 59)

Run No.	*Transition phase*	*enb*	*rst*	*TQMI after 10th year*	*Years to achieve TQMI maturity*
18	Strong to moderate	190	125	315	Never
59	Moderate to weak	190	125	315	Never

From Table 5.20 it is evident that if transition from "external enabler strong" to "external enabler moderate" and from "external enabler moderate" to "external enabler weak" market scenario is not effectively handled, it will be having a crashing effect on the performance of the organizations. In such situations, enabler and result would crash to a base value of 190 and 125, respectively at 0% effectiveness of enablers. It is therefore, recognized that organizations should take proactive actions during transition phase to avoid a crash situation.

Figure 5.9 shows the trend in the increase of result and TQM index at 0% effectiveness of enablers during "external enabler moderate" market scenario. At 0% effectiveness of enablers, enabler value is constant at base value of 190. However, result and TQM index are still on the increase. Such organizations fall under *'disillusioned'* group of category.

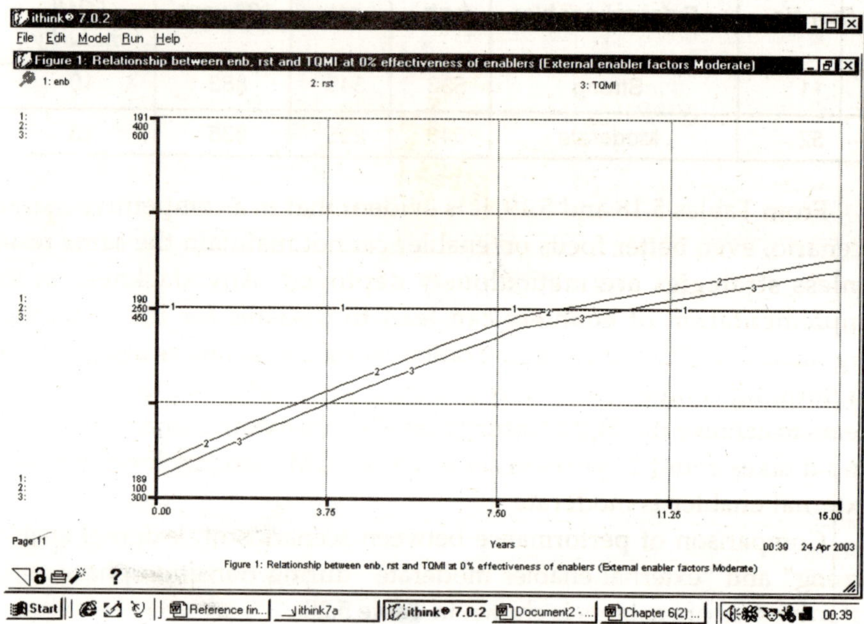

Fig. 5.9: Relationship among enb, rst and TQMI at 0% effectiveness of enablers during "external enabler moderate" market scenario

The trend shown in Figure 5.9 can be explained from Table 5.21. The increase in result and TQM index each year after the initiation of TQM programme is shown in Table 5.21. It is evident from this table that though enabler value is at a base value of 190, result value and TQM index increases to 277 and 467, respectively after about 13 years. These values of result and TQM index are much less than what has been achieved during "external enabler strong" market scenario. Therefore, the competition has an adverse affect on the performance of the organization.

Figure 5.10 shows the trend of increase in enabler, result and TQM index at 100% effectiveness of enablers. The trend shows that an increase in the enabler is instrumental in the increase of result and TQM index. Such organizations fall under the category of *'climber'* but it can also be highly deceptive for the organizations. Organizations therefore, should judge their performance in totality, keeping in mind the external factors.

Table 5.21: Relationship among enb, rst and TQMI at 0% effectiveness of enablers during "external enabler moderate" market scenario

Years	*absr*	*acus*	*ahrs*	*aios*	*asus*	*cmf*	*hrs*	*inm*	*lds*	*prm*	*stp*	*suf*	*enb*	*rst*	*TQMI*
Initial	32	32	25	25	11	41	23	19	33	22	44	8	190	125	315
0	33	40	28	25	12	41	23	19	33	22	44	8	190	141	331
1	35	49	31	26	13	41	23	19	33	22	44	8	190	157	347
2	37	57	35	27	14	41	23	19	33	22	44	8	190	172	362
3	39	65	38	27	15	41	23	19	33	22	44	8	190	187	377
4	41	72	42	28	17	41	23	19	33	22	44	8	190	202	392
5	43	79	45	29	18	41	23	19	33	22	44	8	190	216	406
6	45	86	48	29	19	41	23	19	33	22	44	8	190	230	420
7	47	93	52	30	20	41	23	19	33	22	44	8	190	244	434
8	49	93	55	31	21	41	23	19	33	22	44	8	190	250	440
9	51	93	59	31	21	41	23	19	33	22	44	8	190	257	447
10	53	93	62	32	22	41	23	19	33	22	44	8	190	264	454
11	55	93	65	32	23	41	23	19	33	22	44	8	190	270	460
12	57	93	69	33	24	41	23	19	33	22	44	8	190	277	467

Table 5.22: Relationship among enb, rst and TQMI at 100% effectiveness of enablers during "external enabler moderate" market scenario

Years	*absr*	*acus*	*ahrs*	*aios*	*asus*	*cmf*	*hrs*	*inm*	*lds*	*prm*	*stp*	*suf*	*enb*	*rst*	*TQMI*
Initial	32	32	25	25	11	41	23	19	33	22	44	8	190	125	315
0	34	41	28	25	12	49	29	29	46	25	52	9	242	142	384
1	36	51	33	26	13	58	35	40	58	29	61	11	296	161	457
2	39	61	38	27	14	67	42	50	69	35	70	13	349	183	532
3	43	73	45	28	16	75	49	53	79	42	80	15	395	206	602
4	47	85	52	29	17	83	56	55	88	49	81	18	432	232	664
5	51	94	60	31	18	88	63	58	95	56	83	20	466	255	722
6	55	94	69	32	19	90	69	61	101	64	84	24	495	271	767
7	60	94	79	33	21	91	76	63	104	66	85	24	512	288	801
8	60	94	82	34	22	93	79	66	107	67	87	25	526	293	820
9	60	94	82	35	23	94	82	68	110	69	88	26	540	295	835
10	60	94	82	37	24	96	86	71	113	71	89	26	555	298	853
11	60	94	82	38	25	97	89	74	115	73	91	27	569	300	869
12	60.	94	82	39	27	99	93	76	118	75	92	28	583	303	886

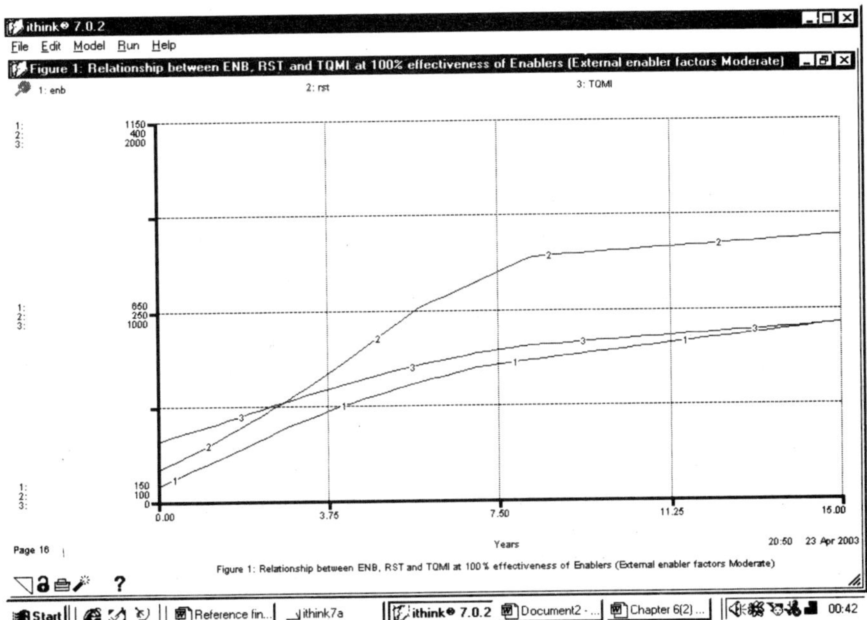

Fig. 5.10: Relationship among enb, rst and TQMI at 100% effectiveness of enablers during "external enabler moderate" market scenario

The trend shown in Figure 5.10 can be explained from Table 5.22, which shows increase in enabler, result and TQM index each year after the initiation of TQM programme. It is evident from this table that with the increase of enabler, result and TQM index continue to gradually increase till the 8th year. Due to competition, the organizations find it very difficult to attain same kind of result and TQM index, as they had achieved during "external enabler strong". From the 8th year onwards, the rate of increase in results substantially comes down even with an increase in enablers as the competitive market scenario prevents the results to surface. The organization however, achieves the TQM maturity level after about 13 years with enabler, result and TQM index value at 583, 303 and 886, respectively.

If the transition phase from "external enabler moderate" to "external enabler weak" not handled properly, the enabler, result and TQM index would crash to the base value at 0% effectiveness of enablers. Such groups of organizations fall under the category of *'quitter'* i.e. low enablers produce low results. The resulting situation is shown in Figure 5.11.

The combined picture of individual results and enablers, total enablers, results and TQMI from 0% effectiveness of enablers to 100% effectiveness of enablers in the interval of 10% increase are shown in Table 5.23.

Table 5.23: Combined picture of individual results and enablers, total enablers, results and TQMI from 0% effectiveness of enablers to 100% effectiveness of enablers in the interval of 10% increase (Runs 59 to 69 with reference to Table 5.16B)

% of effectiveness	*absr*	*acus*	*ahrs*	*aios*	*asus*	*cmf*	*hrf*	*inm*	*lds*	*prm*	*stp*	*suf*	*enb*	*rst*	*TQMI*
0	32	32	25	25	11	41	23	19	33	22	44	8	190	125	315
10	34	41	28	25	12	49	29	29	46	25	52	9	242	142	384
20	36	51	33	26	13	58	35	41	58	30	61	11	296	162	458
30	39	62	39	27	14	67	42	51	69	35	70	13	350	183	534
40	43	73	45	28	16	75	49	57	79	42	80	15	400	207	607
50	47	85	52	29	17	82	56	60	87	49	83	18	439	233	672
60	51	92	60	31	18	88	63	63	94	57	85	21	474	254	729
70	55	92	69	32	19	91	69	64	100	65	86	24	502	270	773
80	60	92	79	33	21	92	76	65	104	66	87	25	518	287	805
90	60	92	80	34	22	94	80	67	107	68	88	25	532	291	823
100	60	94	82	35	23	94	82	68	110	69	88	26	540	295	835

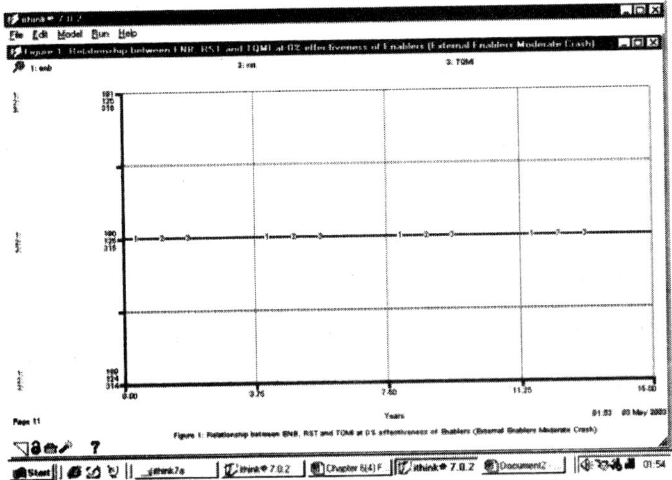

Fig. 5.11: Relationship among enb, rst and TQMI at 0% effectiveness of enabler (transition phase from EEM to EEW)

Figure 5.12 shows the trend of *'quitter', 'disillusioned'* and *'climber'* category organizations with "external enabler moderate" and "external enabler crash" market scenario. Though a correlation appears to exist between enabler and result in the case of group of *'disillusioned'* organizations, the relationship is very weak. The relationship between enabler and result under *'quitter'* and *'climber'* organizations appears to be very strong. Management may like to effectively deploy enablers to produce high results. This is highly desirable for the survival and growth of the organizations under severe competition.

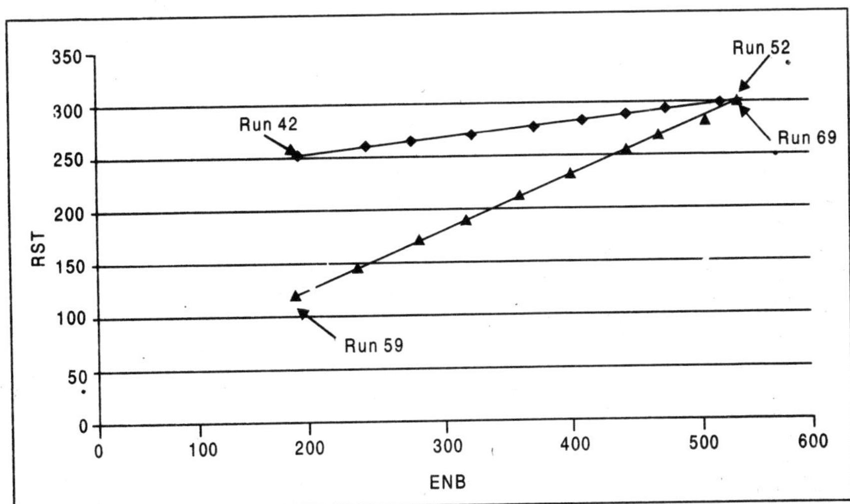

Fig. 5.12: Relationship between enabler and result from 0% effectiveness of enabler to 100% at the interval of 10% increase (Runs 42 to 52 and 59 to 69) during EEM and EEL

5.5.4 Run Specification During "External Enabler Moderate" and "Transition Phase from EEM to EEW" (Runs 76 to 82)

5.5.4.1 Run Specification During External Enabler Moderate Market Scenario to See the Effect of Individual and Combination of Enablers at 0% Effectiveness of Enablers

Run specification to see the effect of individual and combination of enablers on enabler, result and TQM index during "external enabler moderate" market scenario. The effect of lds, lds/stp, lds/stp/cmf, lds/stp/cmf/hrf, lds/stp/cmf/hrf/prm, lds/stp/cmf/hrf/ prm/inm and lds/stp/cmf/hrf/ prm/inm/suf at 0% effectiveness on enabler, result and TQM index are shown in Table 5.24.

Table 5.24: Relationship among enabler, result and TQMI at 0% effectiveness of enablers during "external enabler moderate" market scenario (Runs 52, 76 to 82 with reference to Tables 5.16A and 5.16C)

Run No.	Enablers	*enb*	*rst*	*TQMI after 10th Year*
52	Effectiveness of enablers: 100%	540	295	836
76	Effectiveness of lds: 0%	463	287	751
77	Effectiveness of lds/stp: 0%	409	279	688
78	Effectiveness of lds/stp/cmf: %	355	279	634
79	Effectiveness of lds/stp/cmf/ hrf: 0%	305	266	571
80	Effectiveness of lds/stp/cmf/ hrf/prm: 0%	253	258	512
81	Effectiveness of lds/stp/cmf/hrf/prm/ inm: 0%	204	258	463
82	Effectiveness of lds/stp/cmf/hrf/prm/ inm/suf: 0%	190	257	447

The trend of relationship among enabler, result and TQMI at 0% effectiveness of enablers is shown in Figure 5.13.

The percent reduction due to individual enabler at 0% effectiveness from 100% effectiveness of enablers is shown in Table 5.26.

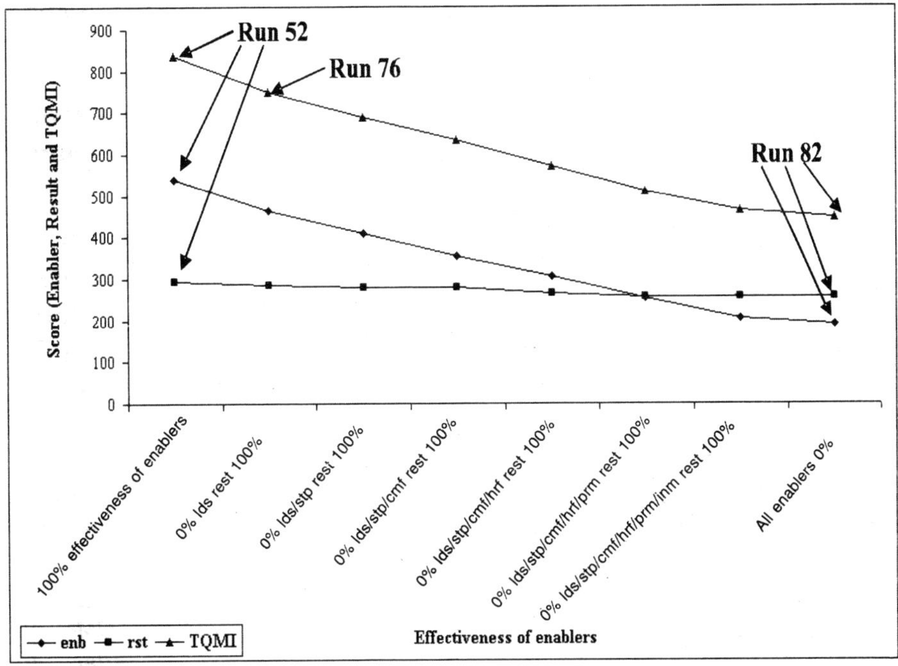

Fig. 5.13: Relationship trend among enb, rst and TQMI at 0% effectiveness of different combination of enablers during "external enabler moderate" market scenario

The percent reduction in enabler, result and TQM index from 100% effectiveness to 0% effectiveness of various enablers is shown in Table 5.25.

Table 5.25: Percent reduction in enabler, result and TQMI from 100% effectiveness to 0% effectiveness of various enablers during "external enabler moderate" market scenario (Runs 76 to 82 with reference to Tables 5.16A and 5.16C)

Run No.	***Effectiveness of enablers: 0%***	***% Reduction***		
		enb	***Rst***	***TQMI***
76	lds	14.3	2.7	10.2
77	lds/stp	24.3	5.4	17.7
78	lds/stp/cmf	34.3	5.4	24.2
79	lds/stp/cmf/hrf	43.5	9.8	31.7
80	lds/stp/cmf/hrf/prm	53.1	12.5	38.8
81	lds/stp/cmf/hrf/prm/inm	62.2	12.5	44.6
82	lds/stp/cmf/hrf/prm/inm/suf	64.8	12.9	46.5

Table 5.26: Percent reduction in enabler, result and TQMI from 100% effectiveness to 0% effectiveness due to individual enablers during "external enabler moderate" market scenario (Runs 76 to 82 with reference to Tables 5.16A and 5.16C)

Run No.	*Effectiveness of enablers: 0%*	*% Reduction* enb	Rst	TQMI
76	lds	14.3	2.7	10.2
77	stp	10.0	2.7	7.5
78	cmf	10.0	0	6.5
79	hrf	9.2	4.4	7.5
80	prm	9.6	2.7	7.1
81	inm	9.1	0	5.8
82	suf	2.6	0.4	1.9

The percent reduction in TQM index at 0% effectiveness of individual enablers and % wise there contribution is shown in Table 5.27.

Table 5.27: Percent reduction in TQMI at 0% effectiveness of individual enablers and their contribution in % during "external enabler moderate" market scenario (Runs 76 to 82 with reference to Tables 5.16A and 5.16C)

Run No.	*Effectiveness of enablers: 0%*	*% Reduction TQMI*	*% Contribution*	*Cumulative % contribution*
76	lds	10.2	21.9	21.9
77	stp	7.5	16.1	38.0
78	hrf	7.5	16.1	54.1
79	prm	7.1	15.3	69.4
80	cmf	6.5	14.0	83.4
81	inm	5.8	12.5	95.9
82	suf	1.9	4.1	100
	Total	46.5	100	

5.5.4.2 Run Specification During External Enabler Crash Market Scenario (Transition Phase from EEM to EEW) to See the Effect of Individual and Combination of Enablers at 0% Effectiveness of Enablers

Run specification to see the effect of individual and combination of enablers on enabler, result and TQM index during a market scenario of "external enabler crash". The effect of lds, lds/stp, lds/stp/cmf,.lds/stp/cmf/hrf, lds/stp/cmf/hrf/prm, lds/stp/cmf/hrf/ prm/inm and lds/stp/cmf/hrf/ prm/inm/suf at 0% effectiveness on enabler, result and TQM index is shown in Table 5.28.

Table 5.28: Relationship among enabler, result and TQMI at 0% effectiveness of enablers during "external enabler crash" market scenario (Runs 69, 76 to 82 with reference to Table 5.16B and 5.16C)

Run No.	*Enablers*	*enb*	*rst*	*TQMI after 10th Year*
69	Effectiveness of enablers: 100%	540	295	836
76	Effectiveness of lds: 0%	465	271	737
77	Effectiveness of lds/stp: 0%	417	225	643
78	Effectiveness of lds/stp/cmf: %	363	193	556
79	Effectiveness of lds/stp/cmf/hrf: 0%	305	167	472
80	Effectiveness of lds/stp/cmf/hrf/prm: 0%	255	149	404
81	Effectiveness of lds/stp/cmf/hrf/prm/inm: 0%	205	141	347
82	Effectiveness of lds/stp/cmf/hrf/prm/inm/suf: 0%	190	125	315

The trend of relationship among enabler, result and TQMI at 0% effectiveness of enablers is shown in Figure 5.14.

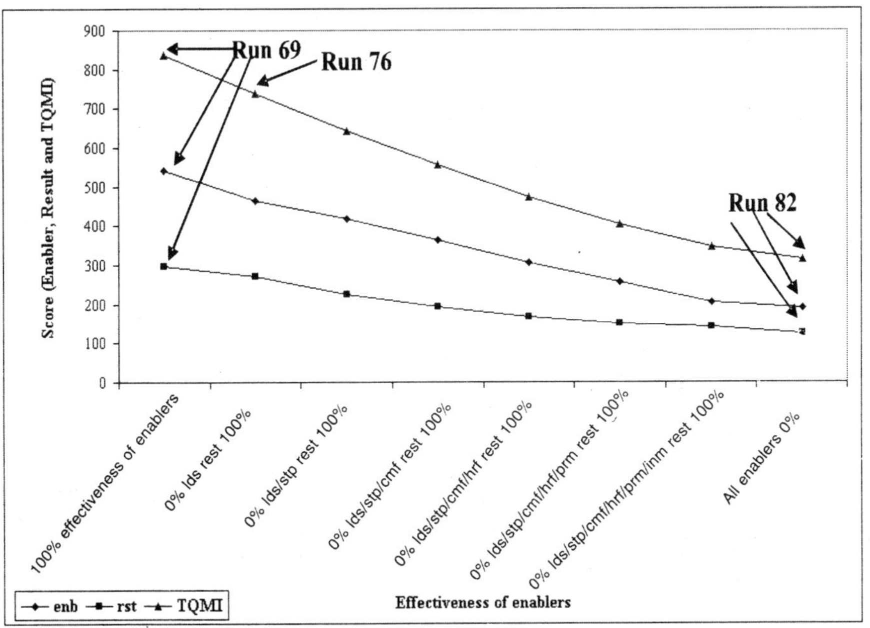

Fig. 5.14: Relationship trend among enabler, result and TQMI at 0% effectiveness of different combination of enablers during "external enabler crash" market scenario

The percent reduction in enabler, result and TQM index from 100% effectiveness to 0% effectiveness of various enablers is shown in Table 5.29.

Table 5.29: Percent reduction in enabler, result and TQMI from 100% effectiveness to 0% effectiveness of various enablers during "external enabler crash" market scenario (Runs 76 to 82 with reference to Table 5.16 B and 5.16C)

Run No.	Effectiveness of enablers: 0%	% Reduction enb	Rst	TQMI
76	lds	14.0	8.1	12.0
77	lds/stp	22.8	23.7	23.0
78	lds/stp/cmf	32.8	34.7	33.4
79	lds/stp/cmf/hrf	43.5	43.6	43.5
80	lds/stp/cmf/hrf/prm	52.8	49.5	51.6
81	lds/stp/cmf/hrf/prm/inm	61.9	52.2	58.5
82	lds/stp/cmf/hrf/prm/inm/suf	64.9	57.8	62.4

The percent reduction due to individual enabler at 0% effectiveness from 100% effectiveness of enablers is shown in Table 5.30.

Table 5.30: Percent reduction in enabler, result and TQMI from 100% effectiveness to 0% effectiveness due to individual enablers during "external enabler crash" market scenario (Runs 76 to 82 with reference to Tables 5.16B and 5.16C)

Run No.	Effectiveness of enablers: 0%	% Reduction enb	Rst	TQMI
76	lds	14.0	8.1	12.0
77	stp	8.8	15.6	11.0
78	cmf	10.0	11.0	10.4
79	hrf	10.7	8.9	10.1
80	prm	9.3	5.9	8.1
81	inm	9.1	2.7	6.9
82	suf	3.0	5.3	3.9

The percent reduction in TQM index at 0% effectiveness of individual enablers and % wise their contribution is shown in Table 5.31.

Table 5.31: Percent reduction in TQMI at 0% effectiveness of individual enablers and their contribution in % during "external enabler crash" market scenario (Runs 76 to 82 with reference to Tables 5.16B and 5.16C)

Run No.	*Effectiveness of enablers: 0%*	*% Reduction TQMI*	*% Contribution*	*Cumulative % contribution*
76	lds	12.0	19.2	19.2
77	stp	11.0	17.6	36.8
78	cmf	10.4	16.7	53.5
79	hrf	10.1	16.2	69.7
80	prm	8.1	13.0	82.7
81	inm	6.9	11.1	93.8
82	suf	3.9	6.2	100
	Total	62	100	

5.5.4.3 Learning and Insight

From Table 5.27, it is evident that leadership, strategic planning, human resource focus and process management contribute to 69.4% of total TQM index reduction from 100% effectiveness of enablers during "external enabler moderate" market scenario. In other words, leadership, strategic planning, human resource focus and process management contribute 69.4% in achieving the TQM maturity level at 100% effectiveness of enablers. The maximum contributor is leadership with 21.9%, followed by strategic planning with 16.1%, human resource focus with 16.1%, and process management with 15.3%. The results show that the organizations should better focus on leadership, strategic planning, human resource focus and process management for achieving the success during "external enabler moderate" market scenario. If organizations are not achieving the TQM maturity level within 13 years, then leadership, strategic planning, human resource focus and process management are really lacking.

From Table 5.31, it is evident that leadership, strategic planning, customer and market focus, and human resource focus contribute to 69.7% of total reduction in TQM index from 100% effectiveness of enablers during transition phase from "external enabler moderate" to "external enabler weak". In other words, leadership, strategic planning, customer and market focus, and human resource focus contribute 69.7% in achieving the TQM maturity level at 100% effectiveness of enablers. The maximum contributor is leadership with 19.2% contribution followed by strategic planning with 17.6%, customer and market focus with 16.7%, and human resource focus with 16.2%. The results show that the organizations should better focus on leadership, strategic planning, customer and market focus, and human resource focus for achieving the success during transition phase from "external enabler moderate" to "external enabler weak". If organizations are not achieving the TQM maturity level within 13 years then leadership is certainly lacking.

Comparison of performance among enabler, result and TQM index at 0% effectiveness of individuals, and combination of enablers during transition phases from "external enabler strong" to "external enabler moderate" and "external enabler moderate" to "external enabler weak" is given in Table 5.32.

Table 5.32: Comparison among enabler, result and TQMI at 0% effectiveness during transition phases from EES to EEM and EEM to EEW (Run 28, 35 to 41 and 69, 76 to 82)

Effectiveness of enablers	***Transition phases***					
	Strong – Moderate			***Moderate – Weak***		
	enb	***rst***	***TQMI***	***enb***	***rst***	***TQMI***
Effectiveness of enablers: 100%	538	345	883	540	295	835
Effectiveness of enablers: 0%						
Ids	465	298	763	465	271	737
Ids/stp	416	245	661	417	225	643
Ids/stp/cmf	362	206	568	363	193	556
Ids/stp/cmf/hrf	306	175	482	305	167	472
Ids/stp/cmf/hrf/prm	255	154	409	255	149	404
Ids/stp/cmf/hrf/prm/inm	205	14	350	205	141	347
Ids/stp/cmf/hrf/prm/inm/suf	190	125	315	190	125	315

From Table 5.32 it is evident that in spite of higher enabler during transition phase from "external enabler moderate" to "external enabler weak", the desired results are poorly achieved in comparison to what could have been achieved during the transition phase from "external enabler strong" to "external enabler moderate". The lesson therefore, is that the organizations which do not prepare themselves for the effective transition from "external enabler moderate" to "external enabler weak" would find it difficult to survive and grow even after reinforcing the enablers.

Comparison of % contribution towards reduction in TQM index at 0% effectiveness of individual enablers during transition phases from "external enabler strong" to "external enabler moderate" and from "external enabler moderate" to "external enabler weak" is shown in Table 5.33.

From Table 5.33, it is quite evident that leadership, strategic planning, customer and market focus, and human resource focus are the main contributors towards the reduction in TQM index from 100% effectiveness of enablers during both the transition phases from "external enabler strong" to "external enabler moderate" and from "external enabler moderate" to "external enabler weak". To ward-off a crash and for achieving the TQM maturity level, the management must focus on leadership, strategic planning, customer and market focus, and human resource focus during these transition phases.

Table 5.33: Comparison in % contribution in reduction of TQMI at 0% effectiveness of individual enablers during transition phase from EES to EEM and from EEM to EEW (Run 35 to 41 and 76 to 82)

Effectiveness of 0% enablers:	*Transition phase*	
	Strong to moderate (% Contribution in TQMI reduction)	*Moderate to weak (% Contribution in TQMI reduction)*
lds	21.1	19.2
stp	17.9	17.6
cmf	16.3	16.7
hrf	15.2	16.2
prm	12.7	13.0
inm	10.6	11.1
suf	6.2	6.2
Total	100	100

5.5.5 Run Specification with EEW – Scenario for Group of Companies under Category 'Quitter', 'Disillusioned' and 'Climber'

Different experiments have been conducted from 0% effectiveness of enablers to 160% effectiveness of enablers. These experiments have been conducted to analyze the effect on enablers variables, results variables and TQM index during "external enabler weak" market scenario. The details of the run specification are given in Table 5.34A to 5.34C.

Table 5.34A: Run specification for sensitivity analysis during EEW market scenario (Runs 83 to 99 – Scenario for group of companies 'disillusioned' and 'climber')

Run No.	*Run details*	*Initial values/ Base Values*	*Experimentation to determine impact on variables*
83	Effectiveness of enablers: 0%	**Base value**	**Seven enablers**
84	Effectiveness of enablers: 10%	cmf: 41	cmf
85	Effectiveness of enablers: 20%	hrf: 23	hrf
86	Effectiveness of enablers: 30%	inm: 9	inm
87	Effectiveness of enablers: 40%	lds: 33	lds
88	Effectiveness of enablers: 50%	prm: 22	prm
89	Effectiveness of enablers: 60%	stp: 44	stp

Contd....

90	Effectiveness of enablers: 70%	suf: 8	suf
91	Effectiveness of enablers: 80%	Sub-total of	
92	Effectiveness of enablers: 90%	enabler:190	+
93	Effectiveness of enablers: 100%	**Base value of**	**Five Result**
94	Effectiveness of enablers: 110%	**results**	absr
95	Effectiveness of enablers: 120%	absr: 32	acus
96	Effectiveness of enablers: 130%	acus: 32	ahrs
97	Effectiveness of enablers: 140%	ahrs: 25	aios
98	Effectiveness of enablers: 150%	aios: 25	asus
99	Effectiveness of enablers: 160%	asus: 11	+
		Sub-total of result: 125 **Base value of TQMI** Sub-total of enablers:190 Sub-total of results: 125TQMI: 315	**TQMI**

Different experiments have been conducted for 0% effectiveness of enablers to 160% effectiveness of enablers. These experiments have been conducted to analyze the effect on enabler variables, result variables and TQM index during transition phase from "external enabler weak" to "external enabler crash" market scenario. The effect of the same has been assumed as the outcome of "external enabler crash" market scenario. The details of run specification during "external enabler crash" market scenario are given in Table 5.34B.

Table 5.34B: Run specification for sensitivity analysis during EEC market scenario (transition phase from EEW to EEC, Runs 100 to 116 – Scenario for group of companies 'quitter' and 'climber')

Run No.	***Run details***	***Initial values/ Base values***	***Experimentation to determine impact on variables***
100	Effectiveness of enablers: 0%	**Base value**	**Seven enablers**
101	Effectiveness of enablers: 10%	cmf: 41	cmf
102	Effectiveness of enablers: 20%	hrf: 23	hrf
103	Effectiveness of enablers: 30%	inm: 9	inm

Contd....

104	Effectiveness of enablers: 40%	lds: 33	lds
105	Effectiveness of enablers: 50%	prm: 22	prm
106	Effectiveness of enablers: 60%	stp: 44	stp
107	Effectiveness of enablers: 70%	suf: 8	suf
108	Effectiveness of enabiers: 80%	Sub-total of	
109	Effectiveness of enablers: 90%	enabler:190	+
110	Effectiveness of enablers: 100%	**Base value of**	**Five Result**
111	Effectiveness of enablers: 110%	**results**	absr
112	Effectiveness of enablers: 120%	absr: 32	acus
113	Effectiveness of enablers: 130%	acus: 32	ahrs
114	Effectiveness of enablers: 140%	ahrs: 25	aios
115	Effectiveness of enablers: 150%	aios: 25	asus
116	Effectiveness of enablers: 160%	asus: 11	+
		Sub-total of result: 125	**TQMI**
		Base value of TQMI Sub-total of enablers:190 Sub-total of results: 125TQMI: 315	

Different experiments have been carried out to see the effect of individual and combination of enablers on TQM index. The details of run specification are given in Table 5.34C.

Table 5.34C: The effect of individual and combination of enablers on TQMI (Runs 117 to 123 - Scenario for groups of companies under category of 'quitter' and 'climber')

Run No.	*Run details*	*Initial values/ Base values*	*Experimentation to determine impact on variables*
117	**A.** lds affecting TQMI. Effectiveness of lds: 0%; rest: 100%	**Base value** cmf: 41	**Seven enablers** cmf
118	**B.** lds and stp affecting TQMI. Effectiveness of lds/stp: 0% rest: 100%	hrf: 23 inm: 9 lds: 33	hrf inm lds
119	**C.** lds, stp and cmf affecting	prm: 22	prm

Contd....

	TQMI. Effectiveness of lds/stp/ cmf: 0%; rest: 100%	stp: 44 suf: 8	stp suf
120	**D.** lds, stp, cmf and hrf affecting TQMI. Effectiveness of lds/stp/c-mf/ hrf : 0%; rest: 100%	Sub-total of enabler:190 **Base value of**	+ **Five Result**
121	**E.** lds, stp, cmf, hrf and prm affecting TQMI. Effectiveness of lds/stp/cmf/hrf/ prm: 0%; rest: 100%	**results** absr: 32 acus: 32 ahrs: 25	absr acus ahrs aios
122	**F.** lds, stp, cmf, hrf, prm and inm affecting TQMI. Effectiveness of lds/stp/cmf/hrf/ prm/inm: 0%; rest: 100%	aios: 25 + asus: 11	asus Sub-total of **TQMI**
123	**G.** lds, stp, cmf, hrf, prm, inm and suf affecting TQMI. Effectiveness of lds/stp/cmf/hrf/prm/inm/suf: 0%	result: 125 **Base value of TQMI** Sub-total of enablers:190 Sub-total of results: 125TQMI: 315	

Experiments are further conducted for comparing EEW and EEC at same effectiveness for different enablers. Performance levels at 0% to 160% of the effectiveness have been reported for the both the market scenarios in Table 5.35.

5.5.5.1 Learning and Insight

During the market scenario of "external enabler weak", it has been observed that at 100% effectiveness of enablers, such group of organizations find it very difficult to attain same results that they have achieved during "external enabler strong" or "external enabler moderate" market scenario. From Table 5.35, it can be seen from the simulated results at 100% effectiveness of enablers, the enabler score is 552 and result score is 276 and thus TQM index is 829 in both the market scenarios. As per Table 5.1, such organizations fall between award winners and world-class. This situation reveals the excellent handling of the transition phase from "external enabler weak" to "external enabler crash". More efforts are still required to match with the performance achieved during "external enabler strong" or "external enabler moderate" market scenario. Such groups of organizations take about 13 years to achieve the TQM maturity level. Hundred percent effectiveness of enablers is a notional representation of that

Table 5.35: Comparison between scenarios of EEW Vs EEC (transition phase from EEW to EEC) at same level from 0% to 160% effectiveness of enablers in the interval of 10% increase

EEM						***EEC***				
Run No.	***%age of effectiveness (enb)***	***enb***	***rst***	***TQMI after 10 years***	***Years to achieve TQMI maturity***	***Run No.***	***enb***	***rst***	***TQMI after 10 years***	***Years to achieve TQMI maturity***
83	0	190	161	351	>50	100	190	125	315	Never
84	10	241	174	416	>50	101	243	129	372	>50
85	20	296	188	485	39	102	300	136	437	38
86	30	352	203	556	29	103	359	146	506	28
87	40	405	219	625	23	104	414	160	574	23
88	50	449	234	684	20	105	459	176	636	20
89	60	484	246	731	17	106	489	195	685	17
90	70	512	256	768	16	107	514	216	730	16
91	80	529	267	796	15	108	530	238	769	15
92	90	543	274	817	14	109	542	260	803	14
93	100	552	276	829	13	110	552	276	829	13
94	110	561	276	837	13	111	561	276	837	13
95	120	567	276	844	12	112	567	276	844	12
96	130	570	274	845	11	113	570	274	845	11
97	140	576	278	855	11	114	576	278	855	11
98	150	582	278	861	11	115	582	278	861	11
99	160	587	278	865	11	116	587	278	865	11

the organizations have been able to deploy the enablers at optimum level. This insight helps the organizations to decide about the time period required by the organizations to achieve the TQM maturity level. The time period to achieve the TQM maturity level depends on the effectiveness of the strategic planning. Depending on the organization's strategic plan, the TQM maturity level can either be achieved faster or slower than what is stated above. The results show that such groups of organizations fall under *'climber'* category, which is a most desirable case. Increase in the effectiveness of enablers from 130% to 160% shows that years to achieve the TQM maturity level come down from about 13 years to about 11 years and remain constant at this level even with further increase in the effectiveness of enablers. It establishes the fact that there is no quick fix to achieve the TQM maturity level. It takes minimum 11-13 years to achieve the TQM maturity level during "external enabler weak" market scenario and it cannot be compressed further. The results are affected by the stiff global competition. When effectiveness of enablers is reduced though there is appreciable drop in the level of enabler but does not result in an appreciable drop in results. From Table 5.35, it can be observed that at 0% effectiveness of enablers, enablers fall to the base value of 190 whereas results are still at much higher value of 161 during "external enabler weak" market scenario. Though results are comparatively less than those achieved during the scenarios of "external enabler strong" and "external enabler moderate", results are still at a higher value than the base value. This shows that though protection from customer has substantially come down, still little protection is continuing to the suppliers from automobile manufacturers. Such groups of organizations also fall under *'disillusioned'* category where enabler is less but produced results are high. Such groups of organizations also believe in ISO 9000/QS 9000-certification route and are convinced that good results could be assured only through certification. This is a dicey situation when such group of organizations live under disillusionment that organizations are doing very well under a competitive market scenario where actually situation seems to be different. During transition of market scenarios from "external enabler weak" to "external enabler crash", same group of organizations who were doing reasonably well under a scenario of "external enabler weak" (result value 161), crash to the original base value at 0% effectiveness of enablers (result value 125). The crash situation has been denoted when organization's performance continue to remain at base value with enabler value 190, result value 125 and TQM index 315. From Table 6.35, it can be observed that at 0% effectiveness of enablers, enabler and result value continue to remain at the base value of 190 and 125, respectively and such organizations will find it very difficult to achieve the TQM maturity level if they continue with the same effectiveness of enablers.

After comparing this performance against Table 5.1, it is revealed that such organizations fall between drifters and improvers. Therefore, the learning is that organizations should handle the transition phase effectively to ward-off such crash situation, and maintain the performance level of 100% effectiveness of enablers. The organizations should safeguard themselves from the individual biases in making self-assessment of the organization.

Comparison of performance among scenarios of "strong", "moderate" and "weak" at 0% effectiveness of enablers is shown in Table 5.36.

Comparison of performance among scenarios of "strong", "moderate" and "weak" at 100% effectiveness of enablers is shown in Table 5.37.

Table 5.36: Comparison of performance among scenarios of EES, EEM and EEW enabler at 0% effectiveness

Run No.	*External enabler*	*enb*	*rst*	*TQMI after 10th year*	*Years to achieve TQMI maturity*
1	Strong	190	299	489	>50
42	Moderate	190	257	447	>50
83	Weak	190	161	351	>50

Table 5.37: Comparison of performance among scenarios of EES, EEM and EEW enabler at 100% effectiveness

Run No.	*External enabler*	*enb*	*rst*	*TQMI after 10th year*	*Years to achieve TQMI maturity*
11	Strong	538	345	883	10
52	Moderate	540	295	836	13
93	Weak	552	276	829	13

From Tables 5.36 and 5.37, it is revealed that during the "external enabler weak" market scenario, organizations cannot sustain the same performance what they have achieved during the scenario of "external enabler strong" or "external enabler moderate" despite having higher values for enabler. Therefore, it is required that organizations should work strategically to deploy the enablers to achieve the optimum results and this should ideally take place much before the arrival of transition phases. Any slackness in the timely deployment of enablers can lead to disaster. Therefore, organizations should develop strategy by taking into account the external market scenario. At 0%

effectiveness of enablers, the organizations will find it very difficult to achieve the TQM maturity level with the same effectiveness of enablers. At 100% effectiveness of enablers, it takes about 10 years to achieve the TQM maturity level during "external enabler strong" market scenario and 13 years during "external enabler moderate" market scenario and "external enabler weak" market scenario. However, from the above results, it has been observed that exogenous factors do not contribute much in delaying the TQM maturity level. Most of the factors detrimental to the TQM maturity level are within the organization's control and can be controlled by the top management leadership and through strategic planning.

Comparison of performance among scenarios of "strong", "moderate" and "weak" at 0% effectiveness of enablers during transition phase is shown in Table 5.38.

Table 5.38: Comparison of performance during transition phases at 0% effectiveness of enablers

Run No.	***Transition phase***	***enb***	***rst***	***TQMI after 10th year***	***Years to achieve TQMI maturity***
18	Strong to moderate	190	125	315	Never
59	Moderate to weak	190	125	315	Never
100	Weak to crash	190	125	315	Never

From Table 5.38, it is evident that if transitions of scenario are not effectively managed, the same organizations may crash to a base level. This means, that for the selected data set for the experimentation, it crashes to a base value of 190 for enabler and 125 for result. It is therefore, required that organizations should effectively deploy strategic planning to avoid the crash effect on the performance during a transition phase.

Figure 5.15 shows the trend of increase in result and TQM index at 0% effectiveness of enablers during "external enabler weak" market scenario. At 0% effectiveness of enablers, enabler value is constant at a base value of 190. However, result value and TQM index still increase at a low rate. Such groups of organizations fall under *'disillusioned'* category. Figure 5.16 shows the trend of increase in enablers, results and TQM index at 100% effectiveness of enablers. The trend shows that increase in enablers is instrumental in the increase of results and TQM index. Such groups of organizations fall under category of *'quitter'* and *'climber'* defined earlier.

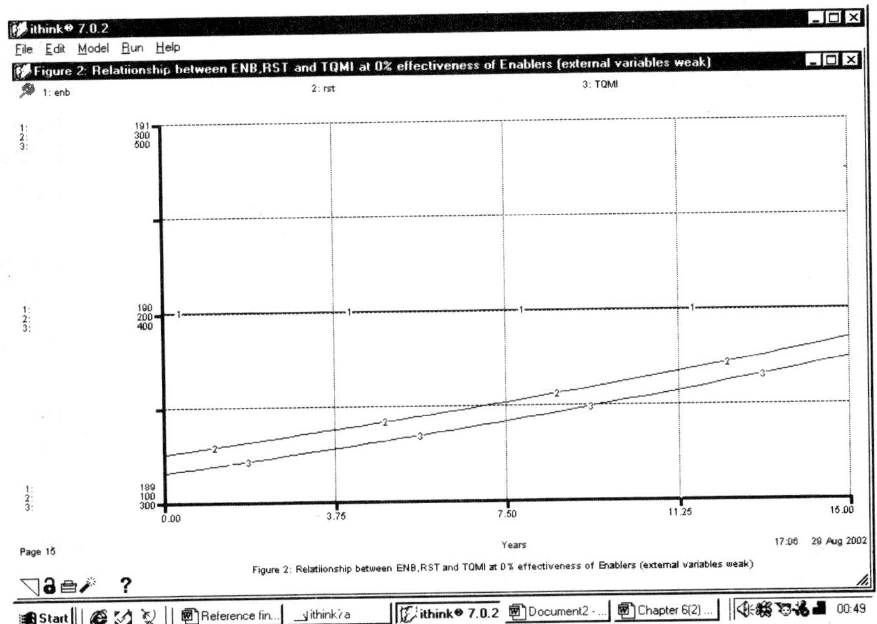

Fig. 5.15: Relationship among enb, rst and TQMI at 0% effectiveness of enablers during "external enabler weak" market scenario

The performance of the trend shown in Figure 5.15 can be explained from Table 5.39, which shows increase in result and TQM index after the initiation of TQM programme. It is evident from this table that though the enabler value is at a base value of 190, result value and TQM index increase to 161 and 351, respectively at the end of 10th year. These values are much less than what has been achieved during "external enabler moderate" market scenario (Table 5.36). The stiff competition has an adverse affect on the performance of the result and TQM index.

Figure 5.16 shows the trend in increase in enabler, result and TQM index at 100% effectiveness of enablers. The trend shows that increase in the enabler is instrumental in the increase of result and TQM index. Such organizations fall under the *'climber'* category but this situation can be highly deceptive for the organizations. Organizations therefore, should judge their performance in totality and must keep in mind the external factors.

The performance of the trend shown in Figure 5.16 can be explained from Table 5.40, which shows increase in enabler, result and TQM index each year after the initiation of TQM programme. It is evident from this table that with an increase of enablers, the rate of increase in results and TQM index is very slow till 6th year. At the end of 6th year, enabler value, result value and TQM index reaches to 481, 194 and 675, respectively. Due to stiff competition, the

Table 5.39: Relationship among enb, rst and TQMI at 0% effectiveness of enablers during "external enabler weak" market scenario

Years	*absr*	*acus*	*ahrs*	*aios*	*asus*	*cmf*	*hrs*	*inm*	*lds*	*prm*	*stp*	*suf*	*enb*	*rst*	*TQMI*
Initial	32	32	25	25	11	41	23	19	33	22	44	8	190	125	315
0	33	32	26	25	11	41	23	19	33	22	44	8	190	128	318
1	35	33	27	25	11	41	23	19	33	22	44	8	190	131	321
2	36	34	28	25	11	41	23	19	33	22	44	8	190	134	324
3	38	34	29	25	11	41	23	19	33	22	44	8	190	138	328
4	39	35	30	25	11	41	23	19	33	22	44	8	190	141	331
5	41	36	31	25	11	41	23	19	33	22	44	8	190	145	335
6	42	37	32	25	11	41	23	19	33	22	44	8	190	149	339
7	44	38	33	25	11	41	23	19	33	22	44	8	190	153	343
8	46	39	35	25	11	41	23	19	33	22	44	8	190	157	347
9	47	40	36	25	11	41	23	19	33	22	44	8	190	161	351

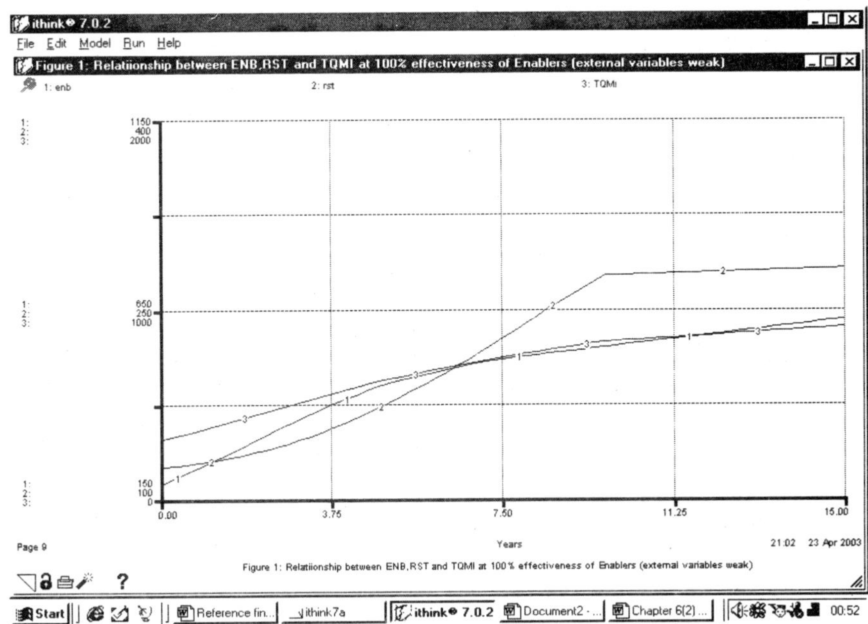

Fig. 5.16: Relationship among enb, rst and TQMI at 100% effectiveness of enablers during "external enabler weak" market scenario

organizations find it very difficult to attain same kind of result and TQM index as compared to what has been achieved during "external enabler moderate" market scenario. With consistent efforts in deploying enablers, the rate of increase in result increases till 10th year. At the end of 10th year enabler value, result value and TQM index reaches to 552, 276 and 829, respectively. From 10th year onwards, the rate of increase of results reduces considerably. This rate of decrease can be attributed to inept handling of stiff competition. The organizations however, achieves the TQM maturity level in 13 years with enabler, result and TQM index value of 594, 279 and 874, respectively.

During transition phase from "external enabler weak" to "external enabler crash", the organizations crash to a base value at 0% effectiveness of enablers. This means that for the selected data set for the experimentation it crashes to a base value of 190 for enabler and 125 for result. It is therefore, required that organizations should deploy strategic planning to avoid crash effect during a transition phase. Such group of organizations fall under *'quitter'* category i.e. when low enabler means low results. The resulting effect has been shown in Figure 5.17.

Table 5.40: Relationship among enb, rst and TQMI at 100% effectiveness of enablers during "external enabler weak" market scenario

Years	*absr*	*acus*	*ahrs*	*aios*	*asus*	*cmf*	*hrs*	*inm*	*lds*	*prm*	*stp*	*suf*	*enb*	*rst*	*TQMI*
Initial	32	32	25	25	11	41	23	19	33	22	44	8	190	125	315
0	33	33	26	25	11	50	29	29	46	25	52	9	242	129	372
1	34	35	28	25	12	59	35	41	59	29	61	11	299	135	435
2	38	38	31	25	12	70	42	51	73	35	71	13	358	145	504
3	42	44	34	25	12	80	50	54	85	42	82	15	411	159	570
4	44	50	41	26	13	88	57	56	97	49	83	18	452	175	628
5	49	57	46	27	13	90	65	59	102	56	84	21	481	194	675
6	54	65	54	27	13	91	72	61	105	64	86	24	508	215	723
7	57	74	64	28	13	93	78	64	108	66	87	25	524	238	762
8	59	83	73	29	14	94	81	67	111	68	88	26	538	260	798
9	59	91	81	30	14	96	84	69	114	70	90	26	552	276	829
10	59	91	81	31	14	97	88	72	117	72	91	27	566	277	844
11	59	91	81	32	14	99	91	74	120	73	92	28	580	278	859
12	59	91	81	32	15	100	95	77	123	75	94	28	594	279	874

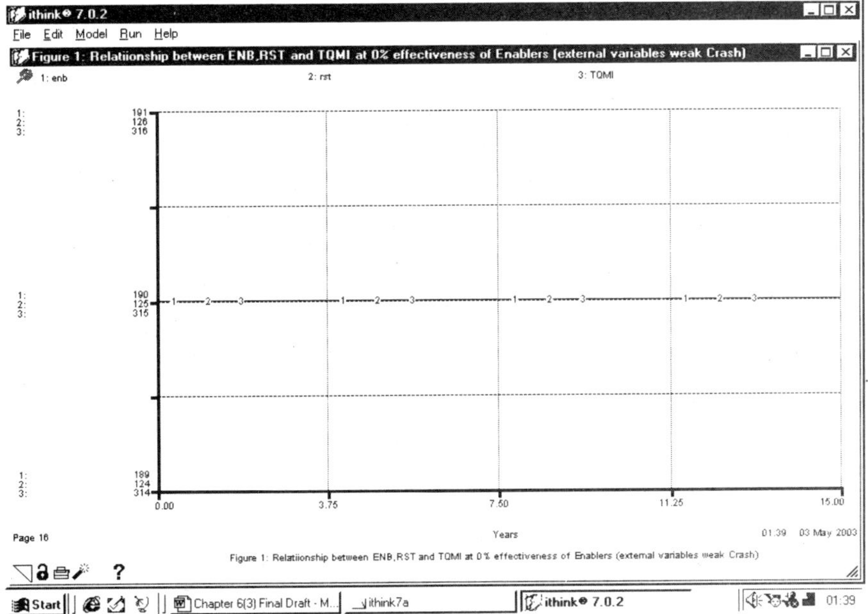

Fig. 5.17: Relationship among enb, rst and TQMI at 0% effectiveness of enabler (transition phase from EEW to EEC)

Figure 5.17 shows that enabler, result and TQM index continue to remain at the base value of 190, 125 and 315, respectively for the simulated period of 15 years. The combined picture of individual results and enablers, total enablers, results and TQMI from 0% effectiveness of enablers to 100% effectiveness of enablers in the interval of 10% increase is shown in Table 5.41.

TQM status level has been shown in Table 5.42 based on comparing the data in Tables 5.6, 5.22 and 5.40 against Table 5.1.

Table 5.41: TQM Status level during market scenarios strong, moderate and weak against Table 5.1

	External enabler		
	Strong	***Moderate***	***Weak***
	Years to achieve TQM status		
Improvers	3	3	3
Award winners	7	7	8
World-class	10	13	13

Table 5.42: Combined picture of individual results and enablers, total enablers, results and TQMI from 0% effectiveness of enablers to 100% effectiveness of enablers in the interval of 10% increase (Runs 100 to 110 with reference to Table 5.34B)

% of effect.	*absr*	*acus*	*ahrs*	*aios*	*asus*	*cmf*	*hrf*	*inm*	*lds*	*prm*	*stp*	*suf*	*enb*	*rst*	*TQMI*
0	32	32	25	25	11	41	23	19	33	22	44	8	190	125	315
10	33	33	26	25	11	50	29	29	46	25	52	9	243	129	372
20	35	35	28	25	12	59	35	41	59	30	61	11	300	136	437
30	38	38	31	25	12	70	42	52	72	36	71	13	359	146	506
40	42	45	35	25	12	80	50	58	85	42	80	15	414	160	574
50	44	50	41	26	13	89	57	61	97	50	84	18	459	176	636
60	48	58	48	27	13	91	65	63	103	57	85	21	489	195	685
70	53	65	56	27	13	92	72	65	107	64	86	24	514	216	730
80	57	74	64	28	13	94	78	66	111	67	87	25	530	238	769
90	59	83	73	29	14	95	82	68	113	68	87	26	542	260	803
100	59	91	81	30	14	96	84	69	114	70	90	26	552	276	829

It is evident from Table 5.42 that improvers, award winners, and world-class performance status is attained in 3 years, 7-8 years, and 10-13 years depending on the external enabler market scenario with the optimum deployment of enablers.

Figure 5.18 shows the trend of *'quitter', 'disillusioned'* and *'climber'* companies with "external enabler weak" market scenario and "external enabler crash" market scenario.

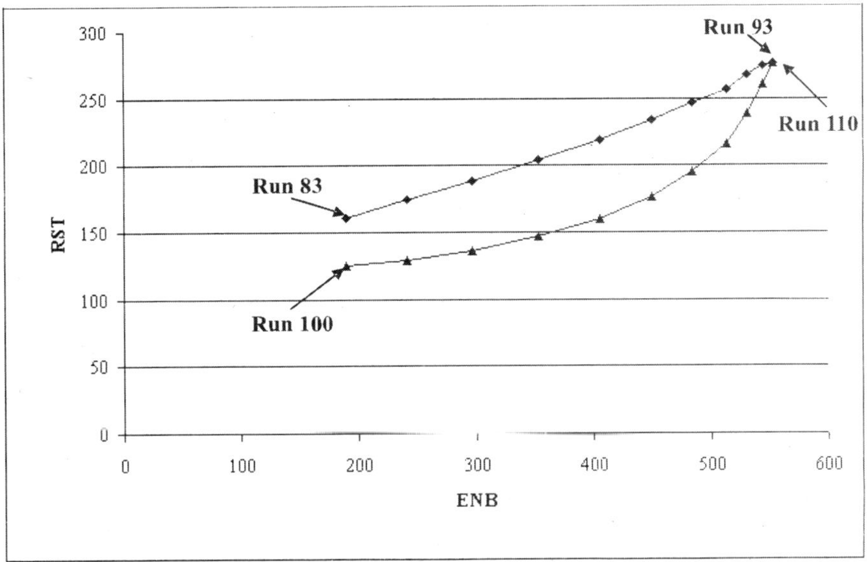

Fig. 5.18: Relationship between enabler and result from 0% effectiveness of enabler to 100% at the interval of 10% increase (Run 83 to 93 and 100 to 110)

At 0% effectiveness of enablers, the results do not crash to the base value which is still at higher value during "external enabler weak" market scenario. Such group of organizations falls under the category of *'disillusioned'*. Though correlation exists between enabler and result, relationship is very weak. At 0% effectiveness of enablers the results also crash to the base value during "external enabler crash" market scenario and at 100% effectiveness of enablers the results also increases. Such group of organizations falls under *'quitter'* and *'climber'* category. The relationship between enabler and result in *'quitter'* and *'climber'* categories is very strong. Initially the rate of increase in results is slow till 400 values of enablers. But with consistent efforts to increase the enablers, high rate of increase in the results is achieved. This establishes the fact that there is no shortcut to achieve the TQM maturity level. In competitive market scenario, initial efforts on enablers may not be converted into sufficient results due to very high expectation of customers and initial resistance to change from within.

Sustaining the efforts on enablers will tend to reduce the resistance from within and rate of increase in results will pickup in due course of time. Effective leadership will help in sustaining the efforts on enablers in spite of initial setback in achieving the results and this stage is most desirable for the survival and growth of the organizations under severe global competitive market scenario. The learning lesson is that the organization in *'disillusioned'* category should move towards *'climber'* category.

5.5.6 Run Specification During "External Enabler Weak" and "Transition Phase from EEW to EEC" (Runs 117 to 123)

5.5.6.1 Run Specification During External Enabler Weak Market Scenario to See the Effect of Individual and Combination of Enablers at 0% Effectiveness of Enablers

Run specification to see the effect of individual enablers on other enabler, result and TQM index during "external enabler weak" market scenario is presented now. The effect of lds, lds/stp, lds/stp/cmf, lds/stp/cmf/hrf, lds/stp/cmf/hrf/prm, lds/stp/cmf/hrf/prm/inm and lds/stp/cmf/hrf/prm/inm/suf at 0% effectiveness on enabler, result and TQM index is shown in Table 5.43.

Table 5.43: Relationship among enabler, result and TQMI at 0% effectiveness of enablers during "external enabler weak" market scenario (Runs 110, 117 to 123 with reference to Tables 5.34A and 5.34C)

Run No.	*Enablers*	*enb*	*rst*	*TQMI after 10th Year*
93	Effectiveness of enablers: 100%	552	276	829
117	Effectiveness of lds: 0%	470	266	737
118	Effectiveness of lds/stp: 0%	417	214	632
119	Effectiveness of lds/stp/cmf: %	363	183	546
120	Effectiveness of lds/stp/cmf/hrf: 0%	313	175	488
121	Effectiveness of lds/stp/cmf/hrf/ prm: 0%	263	175	438
122	Effectiveness of lds/stp/cmf/hrf/prm/inm: 0%	247	175	422.
123	Effectiveness of lds/stp/cmf/hrf/prm/inm/suf: 0%	190	161	351

The trend of relationship among enabler, result and TQM index at 0% effectiveness of enablers during "external enabler crash" market scenario is shown in Figure 5.19.

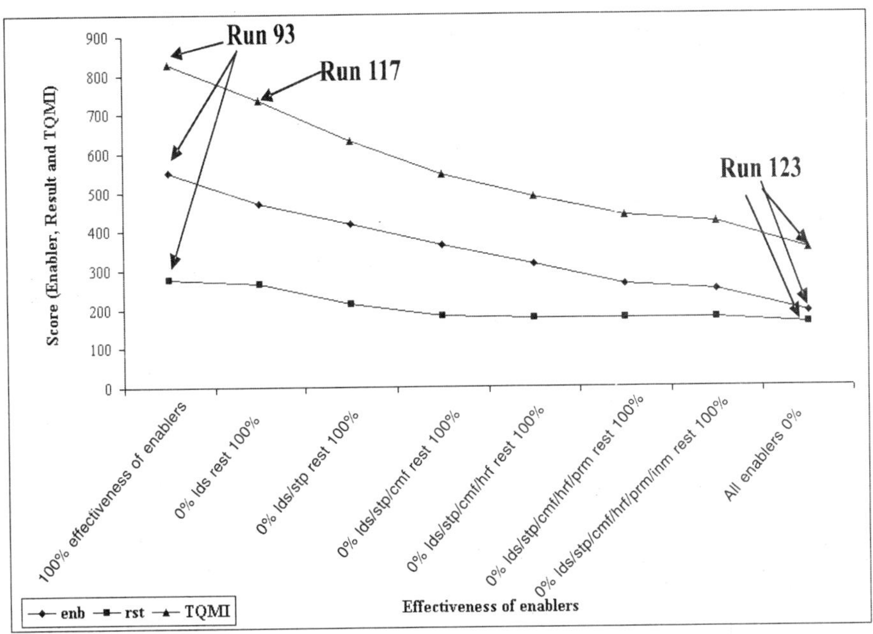

Fig. 5.19: Relationship trend among enabler, result and TQMI at 0% effectiveness of different combination of enablers during "external enabler weak" market scenario

The percent reduction in enabler, result and TQM index from 100% effectiveness to 0% effectiveness of various enablers is shown in Table 5.44.

Table 5.44: Percent reduction in enabler, result and TQMI from 100% effectiveness to 0% effectiveness of various enablers during "external enabler weak" market scenario (Runs 117 to 123 with reference to Table 5.34A and 5.34C)

Run No.	*Effectiveness of enablers: 0%*	*% Reduction*		
		enb	*Rst*	*TQMI*
117	lds	14.9	3.6	11.1
118	lds/stp	24.5	22.5	23.8
119	lds/stp/cmf	34.2	33.7	34.1
120	lds/stp/cmf/hrf	43.3	36.6	41.1
121	lds/stp/cmf/hrf/prm	52.4	36.6	47.2
122	lds/stp/cmf/hrf/prm/inm	55.3	36.6	49.1
123	lds/stp/cmf/hrf/prm/inm/suf	66.6	41.7	57.7

The percent reduction due to individual enabler at 0% effectiveness from 100% effectiveness of enablers is shown in Table 5.45.

Table 5.45: Percent reduction in enabler, result and TQMI from 100% effectiveness to 0% effectiveness due to individual enablers during "external enabler weak" market scenario (Runs 117 to 123 with reference to Tables 5.34A and 5.34C)

Run No.	*Effectiveness of enablers: 0%*	*% Reduction*		
		enb	*Rst*	*TQMI*
117	lds	14.9	3.6	11.1
118	stp	9.6	18.8	12.7
119	cmf	9.8	11.2	10.4
120	hrf	9.1	2.9	7.00
121	prm	9.1	0	6.00
122	inm	2.9	0	1.9
123	suf	10.3	5.1	8.6

The percent reduction in TQM index at 0% effectiveness of individual enablers and their contribution % wise is shown in Table 5.46.

Table 5.46: Percent reduction in TQMI at 0% effectiveness of individual enablers and their contribution in % during "external enabler weak" market scenario (Runs 117 to 123 with reference to Tables 5.34A and 5.34C)

Run No.	*Effectiveness of enablers: 0%*	*% Reduction TQMI*	*% Contribution*	*Cumulative % contribution*
117	stp	12.7	21.9	21.9
118	lds	11.1	19.3	41.2
119	hrf	10.4	18.0	59.2
120	cmf	8.6	14.8	74.0
121	prm	7.0	12.1	86.1
122	inm	6.0	10.5	96.6
123	suf	1.9	3.4	100
	Total	57.7	100	

5.5.6.2 Run Specification During External Enabler Crash Market Scenario (Transition Phase from EEW to EEC) to See the Effect of Individual and Combination of Enablers at 0% Effectiveness of Enablers

Run specification to see the effect of individual enablers on enabler, result and TQM index during "external enabler crash" market scenario is presented now. The effect of lds, lds/stp, lds/stp/cmf, lds/stp/cmf/hrf, lds/stp/cmf/hrf/prm, lds/stp/cmf/hrf/prm/inm and lds/stp/cmf/hrf/prm/inm/suf at 0% effectiveness on enabler, result and TQM index is shown in Table 5.47.

Table 5.47: Relationship among enabler, result and TQMI at 0% effectiveness of enablers during "external enabler crash" market scenario (Runs 110, 117 to 123 with reference to Table 5.34B and 5.34C)

Run No.	*Enablers*	*enb*	*rst*	*TQMI after 10th Year*
110	Effectiveness of enablers: 100%	552	276	829
117	Effectiveness of lds: 0%	472	220	692
118	Effectiveness of lds/stp: 0%	418	167	585
119	Effectiveness of lds/stp/cmf: %	363	149	513
120	Effectiveness of lds/stp/cmf/hrf: 0%	306	134	441
121	Effectiveness of lds/stp/cmf/hrf/ prm: 0%	255	129	385
122	Effectiveness of lds/stp/cmf/hrf/prm/inm: 0%	206	128	334
123	Effectiveness of lds/stp/cmf/hrf/prm/inm/suf: 0%	190	125	315

The trend of relationship among enabler, result and TQM index at 0% effectiveness of enablers during "external enabler crash" market scenario is shown in Figure 5.20.

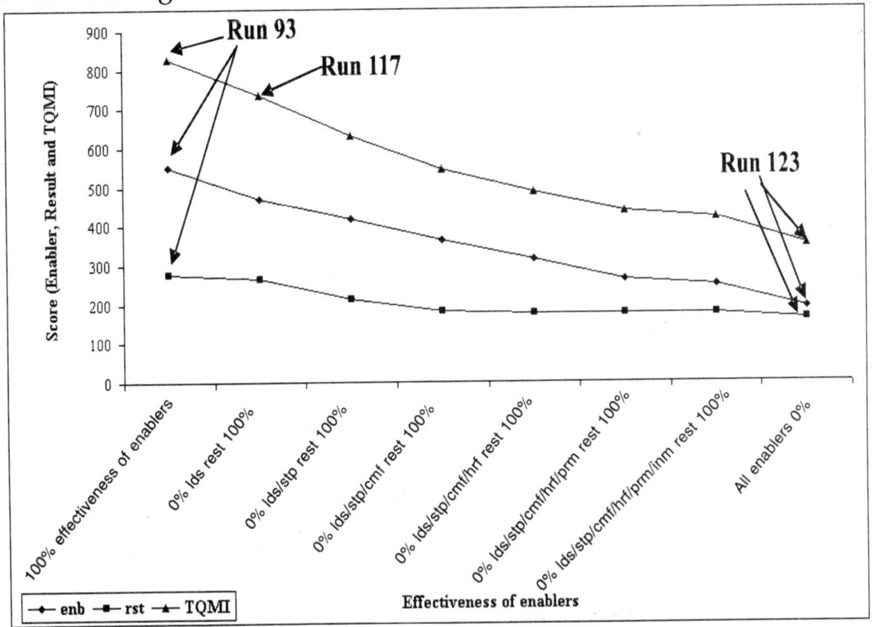

Fig. 5.20: Relationship trend among enabler, result and TQMI at 0% effectiveness of different combination of enablers during "external enabler crash" market scenario

The percent reduction in enabler, result and TQM index from 100% effectiveness to 0% effectiveness of various enablers is shown in Table 5.48.

Table 5.48: Percent reduction in enabler, result and TQMI from 100% effectiveness to 0% effectiveness of various enablers during "external enabler crash" (Runs 117 to 123 with reference to Tables 5.34B and 5.34C)

Run No.	*Effectiveness of enablers: 0%*	*% Reduction*		
		enb	*rst*	*TQMI*
117	lds	14.5	20.4	16.5
118	lds/stp	24.2	39.6	29.4
119	lds/stp/cmf	34.2	45.9	38.1
120	lds/stp/cmf/hrf	44.6	51.2	46.8
121	lds/stp/cmf/hrf/prm	53.7	53.1	53.5
122	lds/stp/cmf/hrf/prm/inm	62.7	53.7	59.7
123	lds/stp/cmf/hrf/prm/inm/suf	65.6	54.8	62.0

The percent reduction due to individual enabler at 0% effectiveness from 100% effectiveness of enablers is shown in Table 5.49.

Table 5.49: Percent reduction in enabler, result and TQMI from 100% effectiveness to 0% effectiveness due to individual enablers during "external enabler crash" (Runs 117 to 123 with reference to Tables 5.34B and 5.34C)

Run No.	*Effectiveness of enablers: 0%*	*% Reduction*		
		enb	*rst*	*TQMI*
117	lds	14.5	20.4	16.5
118	stp	9.7	19.2	12.9
119	cmf	10.0	6.3	8.7
120	hrf	10.4	5.3	8.7
121	prm	9.1	1.9	6.7
122	inm	9.0	0.6	6.2
123	suf	2.9	1.1	2.3

The percent reduction in TQM index at 0% effectiveness of individual enablers and their contribution % wise is shown in Table 5.50.

Table 5.50: Percent reduction in TQMI at 0% effectiveness of individual enablers and their contribution in % during "external enabler crash" (Runs 117 to 123 with reference to Tables 5.34B and 5.34C)

Run No.	*Effectiveness of enablers: 0%*	*% Reduction TQMI*	*% Contribution*	*Cumulative % contribution*
117	lds	16.5	26.6	26.6
118	stp	12.9	20.8	47.4

Contd....

119	cmf	8.7	14.0	61.4
120	hrf	8.7	14.0	75.4
121	prm	6.7	10.9	86.3
122	inm	6.2	10.0	96.3
123	suf	2.3	3.7	100
	Total	62.0	100	

5.5.6.3 Learning and Insight

From Table 5.46 it is evident that strategic planning, leadership, human resource focus and customer and market focus contribute towards 74.0% of total TQM index reduction from the 100% effectiveness of enablers during "external enabler weak" market scenario. In other words, strategic planning, leadership, human resource focus and customer and market focus contribute to 74.0% in achieving the TQM maturity level. The maximum contributor is with strategic planning (21.9%) followed by leadership (19.3%), human resource focus (18%), and customer and market focus (14.8%). The results show that the organizations should focus on strategic planning, leadership, human resource focus and customer and market focus for the survival and growth of the organizations during "external enabler weak" market scenario. If organizations are not achieving the TQM maturity level within 13 years, then strategic planning and leadership should be lacking.

From Table 5.50 it is evident that leadership, strategic planning, customer and market focus, and human resource focus contribute to 75.4% of total TQM index reduction from 100% effectiveness of enablers during transition phase from "external enabler weak" to "external enabler crash". In other words, leadership, strategic planning, customer and market focus, and human resource focus contribute to 75.4% in achieving the TQM maturity level. The maximum contributor is from leadership (26.6%) followed by strategic planning (20.8%), customer and market focus (14.0%), and human resource focus (14.0%). The results show that the organizations have to focus maximum on leadership, strategic planning, customer and market focus, and human resource focus for the survival and growth of the organizations during transition phase from "external enabler weak" to "external enabler crash". If organizations are not achieving the TQM maturity level within 13 years, then leadership and strategic planning should be lacking.

To sustain a TQM maturity level during "external enabler weak" market scenario, it is very important to focus on key variables like strategic planning, leadership, human resource focus and customer and market focus in the same order of priority. However, to sustain a TQM maturity level during "external enabler crash" market scenario, it is very important to focus on key variables like leadership, strategic planning, customer and market focus, and human resource focus in the same order of priority. Out of these four key variables, leadership and strategic planning demand much more attention during "external enabler crash" market scenario.

Validation of results

Indian automobile sector is at present passing through "external enabler weak" market scenario phase and in near future it is likely to enter into a "external enabler crash" market scenario phase. To validate the results, a survey questionnaire was administrated in a workshop environment to five different groups to assess the effect of each variable on TQM index, assuming very low effectiveness of each variable. The team members of these groups had requisite knowledge and experience in implementing TQM in their organization. The groups were asked to assess the effect of each variable on TQM index in these two different market scenarios. The differences between these two scenarios were clearly explained to all the team members before assessing the effect of each variable on TQM index. The average score, based on the questionnaire, was compared with the results of system dynamics model. Outcomes are presented in Tables 5.51 and 5.52. These results validate the performance of the system dynamics model.

Table 5.51: Validation of results based on comparison of questionnaire and SD model result (percent reduction in TQMI from 100% effectiveness to 0% effectiveness due to individual enablers during "external enabler weak" market scenario)

S. No.	***Effectiveness of enablers: 0%***	***% reduction in TQMI***		***Percent deviation from system dynamics results***
		Based on questionnaire	***Based on system dynamics model***	
1	stp	23.00	21.94	4.8
2	lds	20.00	19.30	3.6
3	hrf	16.00	18.00	11.1
4	cmf	15.00	14.84	1.1
5	prm	14.00	12.11	15.6
6	inm	9.00	10.47	14.0
7	suf	3.00	3.34	10.2
	Total	100	100	

Table 5.52: Validation of results based on comparison of questionnaire and SD model result (percent reduction in TQMI from 100% effectiveness to 0% effectiveness due to individual enablers during "external enabler crash" market scenario)

S. No.	*Effectiveness of enablers: 0%*	*% reduction in TQMI*		*Percent deviation from system dynamics results*
		Based on questionnaire	*Based on system dynamics model*	
1	lds	30.00	26.6	12.8
2	stp	20.00	20.8	3.8
3	cmf	15.00	14.0	7.1
4	hrf	12.00	14.0	14.3
5	prm	10.00	10.9	8.2
6	inm	10.00	10.0	0
7	suf	3.00	3.7	1.9
	Total	100	100	

Since maximum variation has been observed to be around 15% in both the market scenarios, the system dynamics result fairly replicates the mental model perception of different teams. This model can be used for better insight and can help the organizations to improve the TQM index.

Comparison of performance among enabler, result and TQM index at 0% effectiveness of individuals and combination of enablers during transition phases from "external enabler strong" to "external enabler moderate", "external enabler moderate" to "external enabler weak" and "external enabler weak" to external enabler crash" is given in Table 5.53.

Table 5.53: Comparison among enabler, result and TQMI at 0% effectiveness during transition phases from EES to EEM, EEM to EEW and EEW to EEC (Run 28, 35 to 41, 69, 76 to 82 and 110, 117 to 123)

Effectiveness of enablers	*Transition phases*								
	Strong – Moderate			*Moderate – Weak*			*Weak – Crash*		
	enb	*rst*	*TQMI*	*enb*	*rst*	*TQMI*	*enb*	*rst*	*TQMI*
Effectiveness: 100%	538	345	883	540	295	836	552	276	829
Effectiveness of enablers : 0%									

Contd....

lds	465	298	763	465	271	737	472	220	629
lds/stp	416	245	661	417	225	643	418	167	585
lds/stp/cmf	362	206	568	363	193	556	363	149	513
lds/stp/cmf/hrf	306	175	482	305	167	472	306	134	441
lds/stp/cmf/hrf/prm	255	154	409	255	149	404	255	129	385
lds/stp/cmf/hrf/prm/inm	205	144	350	205	141	347	206	128	334
lds/stp/cmf/hrf/prm/ inm/suf	190	125	315	190	125	315	190	125	315

From Table 5.53, it is evident that in spite of higher enabler during the transition phase from "external enabler weak" to "external enabler crash" in comparison to the transition phases from "external enabler strong" to "external enabler moderate" and "external enabler moderate" to "external enabler weak", the desired results achieved during a transition phase from "external enabler weak" to "external enabler crash" is much less than what has been achieved during the transition phases from "external enabler strong" to "external enabler moderate" and "external enabler moderate" to "external enabler weak". The organizations, which have not taken proactive actions to manage the transition phase from "external enabler weak" to "external enabler crash" would find it difficult to survive and grow even after increasing the enablers in comparison to the enablers deployed during the earlier transition phases. The hasty deployment of enablers is not going to ensure effective results. It is therefore, always desirable for the organizations to proactively meet such market challenges to achieve better results and the TQM maturity level.

Comparison in % contribution towards reduction of TQM index at 0% effectiveness of individual enablers during transition phases from "external enabler strong" to "external enabler moderate", "external enabler moderate" to "external enabler weak" and from "external enabler weak" to "external enabler crash" is shown in Table 5.54.

Table 5.54: Comparison in % contribution in reduction of TQMI at 0% effectiveness of individual enablers during transition phase from EES to EEM, EEM to EEW and from EEW to EEC (Run 35 to 41, 76 to 82 and 117 to 123)

	Transition phases		
Effectiveness of enablers: 0%	***Strong-moderate (% Contribution in TQMI reduction)***	***Moderate-weak (% Contribution in TQMI reduction)***	***Weak-crash (% Contribution in TQMI reduction)***
lds	21.1	19.2	26.6
stp	17.9	17.6	20.8

Contd....

cmf	16.3	16.7	14
hrf	15.2	16.2	14
prm	12.7	13.0	10.9
inm	10.6	11.1	10
suf	6.2	6.2	3.7
Total	100	100	100

From Table 5.54, it is evident that leadership and strategic planning are the main contributors for maintaining TQM index during the transition phase from "external enabler weak" to "external enabler crash" market scenario. They contribute to 47.4% in achieving the TQM maturity level. To ward-off the crash situation in global competitive scenario, management must focus on leadership and strategic planning more than any other enabler. These two enablers would help in sustaining other enablers. Thus the organizations growth and survival mainly depends on leadership and strategic planning during competitive market scenario. However, the main contributors for achieving TQM index at 100% effectiveness of enablers (leadership, strategic planning, customer and market focus, and human resource focus) are same during all the three transition phases.

5.5.7 Run Specification with EEW - Scenario for Group of Companies under Category Quitter, Slipper and Disillusioned

Different experiments have been carried out from 0% effectiveness of enablers to 100% effectiveness of enablers. These experiments have been conducted to get an insight regarding *'quitter', 'slipper'* and *'disillusioned'* group of companies during "external enabler weak" market scenario. The details of run specification are given in Table 5.55A and 5.55B.

Table 5.55A: Sensitivity analysis for TQMI of Auto sector EEW (Runs 124 to 134 -Scenario for group of companies under category *'Quitter'* and *'Slipper'*)

Run	***Run details***	***Initial values/ Base values***	***Experimentation to determine impact on variables***
124	Effectiveness of enablers: 0%	**Base value**	**Seven Enablers**
125	Effectiveness of enablers: 10%	cmf: 41	cmf
126	Effectiveness of enablers: 20%	hrf: 23	hrf
127	Effectiveness of enablers: 30%	inm: 9	inm
128	Effectiveness of enablers: 40%	lds: 33	lds
129	Effectiveness of enablers: 50%	prm: 22	prm

Contd....

130	Effectiveness of enablers: 60%	stp: 44	stp
131	Effectiveness of enablers: 70%	suf: 8	suf
132	Effectiveness of enablers: 80%	Sub-total of	
133	Effectiveness of enablers: 90%	enabler:190	+
134	Effectiveness of enablers: 100%	**Base value of**	**Five Result**
		results	absr
		absr: 32	acus
		acus: 32	ahrs
		ahrs: 25	aios
		aios: 25	asus
		asus: 11	+
		Sub-total of	**TQMI**
		result: 125	
		Base value	
		of TQMI	
		Sub-total of	
		enablers:190	
		Sub-total of	
		results:	
		125TQMI: 315	

Table 5.55B: Sensitivity analysis for TQMI of Auto sector EEW (Runs 135 to 145 -Scenario for group of companies under category *'Disillusioned'* and *'Slipper'*)

Run No.	*Run details*	*Initial values*	*Experimentation to determine impact on variables*
135	Effectiveness of enablers: 0%	**Base value**	**Seven Enablers**
136	Effectiveness of enablers: 10%	cmf: 41	cmf
137	Effectiveness of enablers: 20%	hrf: 23	hrf
138	Effectiveness of enablers: 30%	inm: 9	inm
139	Effectiveness of enablers: 40%	lds: 33	lds
140	Effectiveness of enablers: 50%	prm: 22	prm
141	Effectiveness of enablers: 60%	stp: 44	stp
142	Effectiveness of enablers: 70%	suf: 8	suf
143	Effectiveness of enablers: 80%	Sub-total of	
144	Effectiveness of enablers: 90%	enabler:190	+
145	Effectiveness of enablers: 100%	**Base value of**	**Five Result**

Contd....

	results absr: 32 acus: 32 ahrs: 25 aios: 25 asus: 11 Sub-total of result: 125 Base value of TQMI Sub-total of enablers:190 Sub-total of results:125 **TQMI: 135**	absr acus ahrs aios asus + **TQMI**

Table 5.56 shows the simulated result of group of *'quitter'* and *'slipper'* organizations, where at 0% effectiveness of enablers, the enabler value is at a base value of 190 and corresponding result value is poor at a score of 136, which is very close to the base value of result. Such organizations fall under *'quitter'* category where low enabler yields low result. Increase in the effectiveness of enablers from 0% to 100% does not make any appreciable change in results. Though enabler value increases to 557 at 100% effectiveness of enablers, corresponding value of result is still low at a value of 180. Such group of organizations falls under *'slipper'* category where increase in enablers does not increase results.

Table 5.56: EEW- Scenario for group of companies *'Quitter'* and *'Slipper'*

Run No.	***Effectiveness of enablers***	***enb***	***rst***	***TQMI after 10th year***	***Years to achieve TQMI maturity level***
124	0	190	136	326	Never
125	10	243	139	383	Never
126	20	301	143	444	36
127	30	362	146	509	28
128	40	419	150	569	24
129	50	466	155	621	22

Contd....

130	60	494	160	655	20
131	70	521	167	688	19
132	80	535	171	706	18
133	90	548	175	724	17
134	100	557	180	738	17

Figure 5.21 shows the trend of enabler and result from 0% to 100% effectiveness of enablers.

Table 5.57 shows the simulated result of group of *'disillusioned'* and *'slipper'* organizations where at 0% effectiveness of enablers, the enabler value is at a base value 190 and corresponding result value is comparatively at much higher value than the base value (226). Such organizations fall under *'disillusioned'* category where low enabler is instrumental for high results. Increase in the effectiveness of enablers from 0% to 100% with 10% increase also does not make any appreciable change in the results. Though enabler value increases to 552 at 100% effectiveness of enablers, corresponding value of result remain stagnant at 226. Such group of organizations falls under *'slipper'* category where increase in enablers does not increase results.

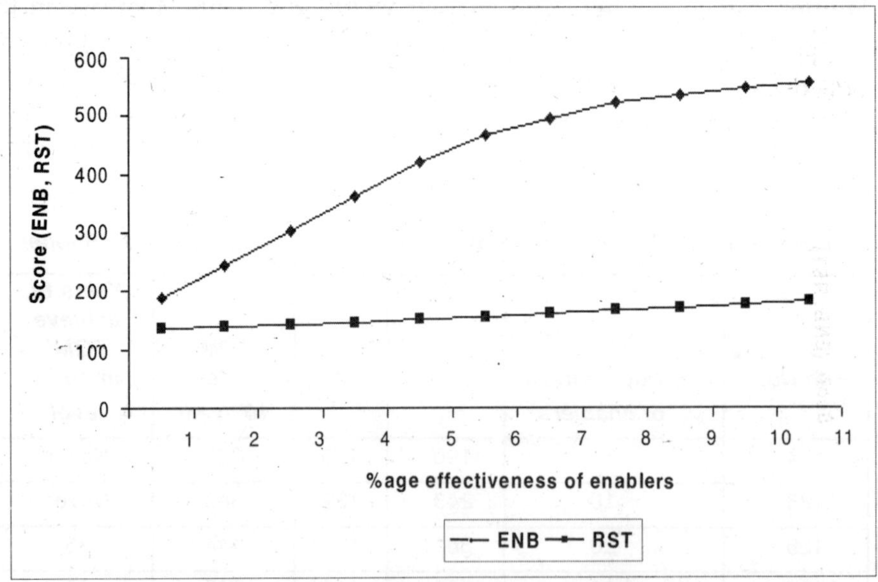

Fig. 5.21: Trend of enabler and result from 0% to 100% effectiveness of enablers at 10% increase in enablers (Run 124 to 134)

Table 5.57: EEW - Scenario for group of companies *'Slipper'* and *'Disillusioned'*

Run No.	***Effectiveness of enablers***	***enb***	***rst***	***TQMI after 10th year***	***Years to achieve TQMI maturity level***
135	0	190	226	416	Never
136	10	235	227	463	50
137	20	285	227	513	34
138	30	339	227	566	27
139	40	390	227	618	22
140	50	434	227	662	20
141	60	477	227	704	18
142	70	510	227	738	17
143	80	527	227	755	16
144	90	542	225	767	16
145	100	552	226	778	15

Figure 5.22 shows the trend of enabler and result from 0% to 100% effectiveness of enablers.

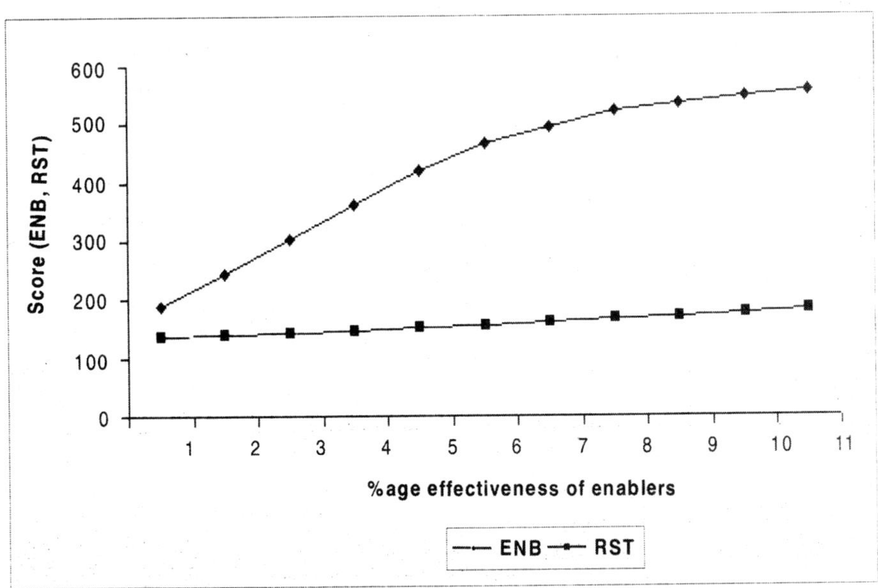

Fig. 5.22: Trend of enabler and result from 0% to 100% effectiveness of enablers at 10% increase in enablers (Run 135 to 145)

5.5.7.1 Learning and Insight

From Table 5.56 and Figure 5.21, it is observed that with the increase in the effectiveness of enablers from 0% to 100%, there is a very slow increase in the corresponding value of results. At 0% and 100% effectiveness of enablers, the value of enablers increase from 190 to 557 but the corresponding results value increases very slow. Such groups of organization fall under *'slipper'* category, where increase in enabler does not increase the results. However, at 0% effectiveness of enablers, the result value is poor (at 136), which is very close to the base value of result i.e., 125. Such groups of organizations fall under *'quitter'* category where low enabler yields low results. Such groups of organizations are forced to quit the market if they continue to remain in *'quitter'* category. Still, such organizations hope to achieve the TQM maturity level at 100% effectiveness of enablers in around 17 years as shown in Table 6.56. This may be detrimental for the survival of the organizations. Such groups of organizations should learn from their mistakes and should increase the effectiveness of enablers to produce high results The inherent learning would be that organizations should move from *'quitter'* category to *'climber'* category rather than ending up at *'slipper'* category. This is only possible if top management leadership is committed and organization understands that ISO 9000 certification is a small step towards TQM journey.

From Table 5.57 and Figure 5.22, it is observed that with an increase in the effectiveness of enablers from 0% to 100%, there is hardly any increase in the corresponding value of results. At 0% and 100% effectiveness of enablers, the value of enablers increase from 190 to 552 but the corresponding results value remain stagnant at 226. Such groups of organizations fall under *'slipper'* category, however, at 0% effectiveness of enablers, the results value is still high at 226. This establishes the fact that such groups of organizations also fall under the *'disillusioned'* category but fail to utilize the protection provided by customers. Such groups of organizations become complacent after initial good results. Survival becomes difficult when customers support is withdrawn. With changes in market scenario and pressure from customers, such group of *'disillusioned'* organizations pretend to change by taking ISO 9000 certification route but end up at *'slipper'* category. The reason for low results can be attributed to half-hearted attempts by these organizations to work for ISO certificate only. Such groups of *'slipper'* organizations believe that they will be able to achieve the TQM maturity level in 15 years (Table 5.57). In reality this is not possible if organizations continue with the same set of strategy. The lesson for such groups of organizations is to consolidate results through effective strategic planning. This will help the organizations to move from *'disillusioned'* category to *'climber'* category rather than ending up at *'slipper'* category.

5.6 MAJOR INSIGHTS FROM EXPERIMENTATIONS

In this research, more than 145 experimentations have been conducted. These have been presented in the previous sections of this chapter. Some of these experimentations provide valuable insights for the practitioners. These are provided in a summarized form in Tables 5.58 and 5.59.

Table 5.58: Summary of insights from experimentations related to scenario building

S. No.	*Scenario developed*	*Reference*	*Insights*
1.	Most pessimistic scenario	Runs 1 to 17, Table 5.3A and 5.5, Figure 5.3 Runs 42 to 58, Table 5.16A and 5.21, Figure 5.9 Runs 83 to 99, Table 5.34 A and 5.39, Figure 5.15 Runs 35 to 41, Table 5.3A, 5.3C and 5.11 Runs 76 to 82, Table 5. 16A, 5.16C and 5.27 Runs 117 to 123, Table 5.34A, 5.34C and 5.46 Runs 124 to 134, Table 5.55A and 5.56, Figure 5.21 Runs 135 to 145, Table 5.55B and 5.57, Figure 5.22	• 1 Organizations will find it difficult to survive during transition phases, such as withdrawal of patronage from customer unless prioritized attention is paid on most contributing enablers. • 2 Organizations, which were getting result despite inadequate attention on quality-related enablers, would find it difficult to avert a serious crash in their result during transition phases such as the one when government policy changes towards liberalization and open-market, or customers support is withdrawn due to emergence of alternative products/services. • 3 There is no quick-fix to achieve the TQM maturity

Contd....

			level as such organizations should focus on leadership, strategic planning, process management and human resource focus when competition is quite low. But as competition grows organizations must focus on leadership, strategic planning, customer and market focus, and human resource focus
2.	Most likely scenario	Runs 1 to 17, Table 5.3A and 5.6, Figure 5.4 Runs 42 to 58, Table 5.16A and 5.22, Figure 6.10 Runs 83 to 99, Table 5.34A and 5.40, Figure 5.16 Runs 35 to 41, Table 5.3A, 5.3C and 5.11 Runs 76 to 82, Table 5.16A, 5.16C and 5.27 Runs 117 to 123, Table 5.34A, 5.34C and 5.46, Runs 124 to 134, Table 5.55A and 5.56, Figure 5.21	•1 Organizations can achieve award winner and world class status provided organizations focus on leadership, strategic planning, customer and market focus, and human resource focus • 2 Organizations should achieve TQM maturity level in about 10-13 years. If organizations fail to do so then organization's focus on leadership and strategic planning is lacking
3.	Most optimistic scenario	Runs 1 to 17, Table 5.3A Runs 42 to 58, Table 5.16A Runs 83 to 99, Table 5.34A	• 1 Organizations can achieve award winner and world class status in about 8-10 years with an increase in the effectiveness of the key enablers such as leadership, strategic planning, customer and market focus, and human resource focus • 2 Without proper deployment of key enablers, the organization performance is likely to crash

Table 5.59: Summary of insights from experimentations related to transition phases

S. No.	*Transition phases*	*Reference*	*Insights*
1.	Most pessimistic scenario	Runs 18 to 34, Table 5.3B, Figure 5.5 Runs 59 to 75, Table 5.16B, Figure 5.11 Runs 100 to 116, Table 5.34B, Figure 5.17 Run No. 35 to 41, Table 5.3B, 5.3C and 5.15 Run No. 76 to 82, Table 5.16B, 5.16C and 5.31 Run No. 117 to 123, Table 5.34B, 5.34C and 5.50	• 1 Organization will find it difficult to achieve the TQM maturity level, if it continues to work with the same strategy as deployed during the days of customer patronage. • 2 Survival of the organizations would become difficult if strategic planning of the organization does not change in accordance with the level of intensified competition during different transition phases. • 3 Organization can achieve the status of award winner and world class, provided it focuses on key enablers such as leadership, strategic planning, customer and market focus, and human resource focus.
2.	Most likely scenario	Runs 18 to 34, Table 5.3B and 5.6, Figure 5.4 Runs 59 to 75, Table 5.16B and 5.22, Figure 5.10 Runs 100 to 116, Table 5.34B and 5.40, Figure 5.16, Runs 35 to 41, Table 5.3B, 5.3C and 6.15 Run No. 76 to 82, Table 5.16B, 5.16C and 5.31 Runs 117 to 123, Table	• 1 Organizations can continue to achieve award winner and world-class status provided the deployment of the key variables commensurate with the level of competition during different transitions in market scenarios. • 2 There is no quick fix to achieve the TQM maturity level. Organizations are required to focus on leadership, strategic

Contd....

	5.34B, 5.34C and 5.50	planning, customer and market focus, and human resource focus to achieve the TQM maturity level within 10-13 years.
3. Most optimistic scenario	Runs18 to 34, Table 5.3B Runs 59 to 75, Table 5.16B Runs 100 to 116, Table 5.34B	• 1 Organizations can achieve award winner and world class status in about 8-10 years with an increase in the effectiveness of the key enablers such as leadership, strategic planning, customer and market focus, and human resource focus.

5.7 CONCLUSIONS

System dynamics modeling of TQM has been used to understand the system behavior with respect to enablers and results under different market scenarios. In this chapter a total of 145 simulated runs have been attempted to understand the model behavior and mapping of real situations. The simulated run has been conducted for 15 years. Organizations have been categorized into four types namely: *'quitter'*, *'slipper'*, *'disillusioned'* and *'climber'*. *'Climber'* group of organizations have high top management commitment and is characterized by the involvement of everyone in the organization to achieve the TQM maturity level. Experimentation has been conducted for three sub-models. The experimentation has been done for the most pessimistic, most likely and most optimistic scenarios of each sub-model. It is revealed during experimentation that there is no quick fix to achieve the TQM maturity level. It takes about 10 years to achieve the TQM maturity level during a scenario when external enabler are strong and about 13 years when it is moderate or weak with the best possible effectiveness of enablers (i.e. 100% effectiveness of enablers). It is also evident after comparison that organizations attain the status of improvers, award winners and world-class performers in 3 years, 7-8 years, and 10-13 years depending on the market scenario. At low effectiveness of enablers (0% effectiveness of enablers), enabler and result value continue to remain at the base value during different stages of transition phases. The organizations therefore, will find it very difficult to achieve the TQM maturity level with low effectiveness of enablers in any of the market scenarios. During experimentation, it is revealed that effective management of transition phases in market scenarios through strategic planning is very important to avoid the crashing effect on the performance of the organizations. Different market scenarios have different levels of competition, thus efforts of the organization should commensurate accordingly. It is concluded that though level of competition would be quite different during different market scenarios, its effect would be indifferent if in case enablers are not properly managed according to the need of the undergoing transition. During experimentation, it is revealed that the main contributor variables to achieve the TQM maturity level in any organization during transition phases are leadership, strategic planning, customer and market focus, and human resource focus. Therefore, organizations must focus on these enablers for survival and growth. During transition phases of different market scenarios, leadership and strategic planning are the key variables. Top management leadership should be committed and should take ISO 9000/QS-9000 certification only as a small step towards TQM journey. There is always a need to evolve very effective strategic planning and monitoring system for getting optimum results.

A summary of insights from different experimentation has been presented in this chapter.

6

Chapter

TQM Implementation Strategies

6.1 INTRODUCTION

Basics of TQM, its different models, design of measurement of TQM Index under different market scenarios and their implications on TQM index under different market scenarios have been presented in the preceding chapters. However, success of TQM will lie in integrating measurement and implementation efforts, commitment and involvement of top management and employees of the organization. A clear understanding of the TQM objectives is a prerequisite for organizational success. It should be ensured that objectives are achievable, measurable, simple to understand and consistent with the organization's mission and goals. This chapter highlights the need and imperative of an effective organization for achieving TQM Index to become a world-class company.

An effective Total Quality Management (TQM) system comprises of an organizational structure, procedures, processes and resources to meet the TQM policy objectives. It is primarily designed to satisfy the internal managerial needs of the organization and, therefore, it may vary from one organization to another.

TQM should be viewed as a formal integrated process. Edosomwan (1987) defines it as an integrated process involving both management and employees with the ultimate goal of managing the design, development, production, transfer and the use of various types of products or services in both the work environment and the market place. TQM, under the systems approach also assumes a broader perspective. Sumanth (1984) defines it as formal management process involving all levels of management and employees. TQM calls for a planned, systematic and formally structured approach in planning, development and usage of several resources to achieve system performance. It calls for systematic evaluation so as to identify areas for improvement and a control mechanism to monitor progress of implementation programmes to achieve improvements in identified areas.

Improvement in TQM is possible through systematic planning process, associated with a monitoring plan and well-crafted implementation strategies. These issues are elaborated in this chapter.

6.2 PHASES OF TQM IMPLEMENTATION

TQM comprises of six phases, which contain 18 major steps as shown in Figure 6.1. The process starts with a Start up and Commitment Phase and proceeds through Strategy Phase, Systems and Protocols Development Phase, Practice Phase, Monitoring Phase and Growth Phase. At the end of the last stage, it is the start of a new cycle to stage one. It, therefore, becomes a continuous exercise of implementation, achieving results of enhanced TQM and setting new values of performance objectives. It is an ongoing process with a well-defined purpose, approach and strategy. Implementation can be carried out in six phases in any organisation.

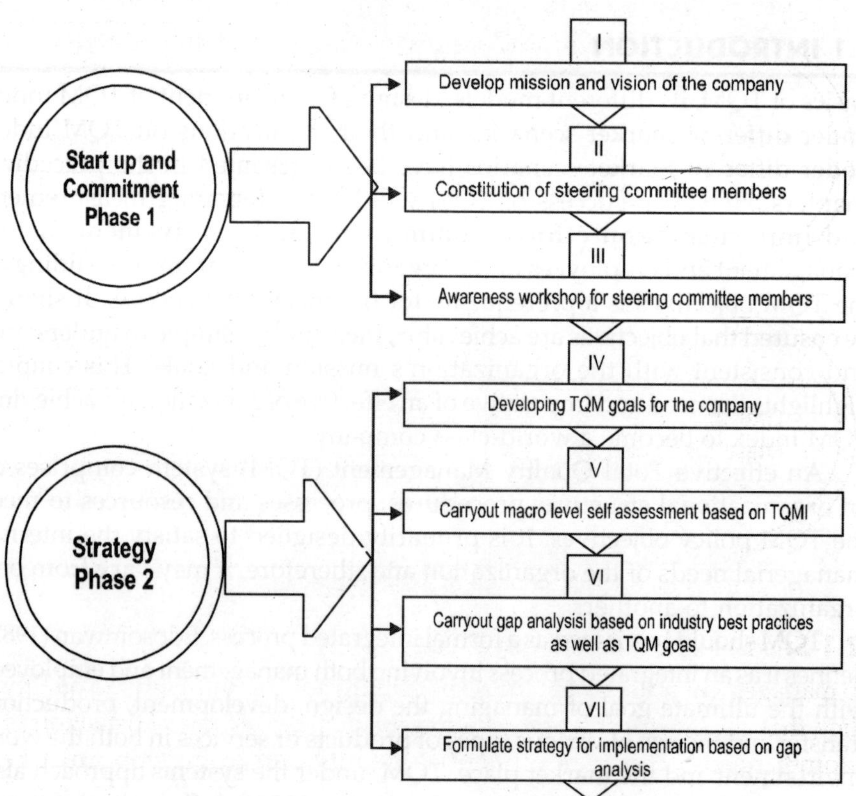

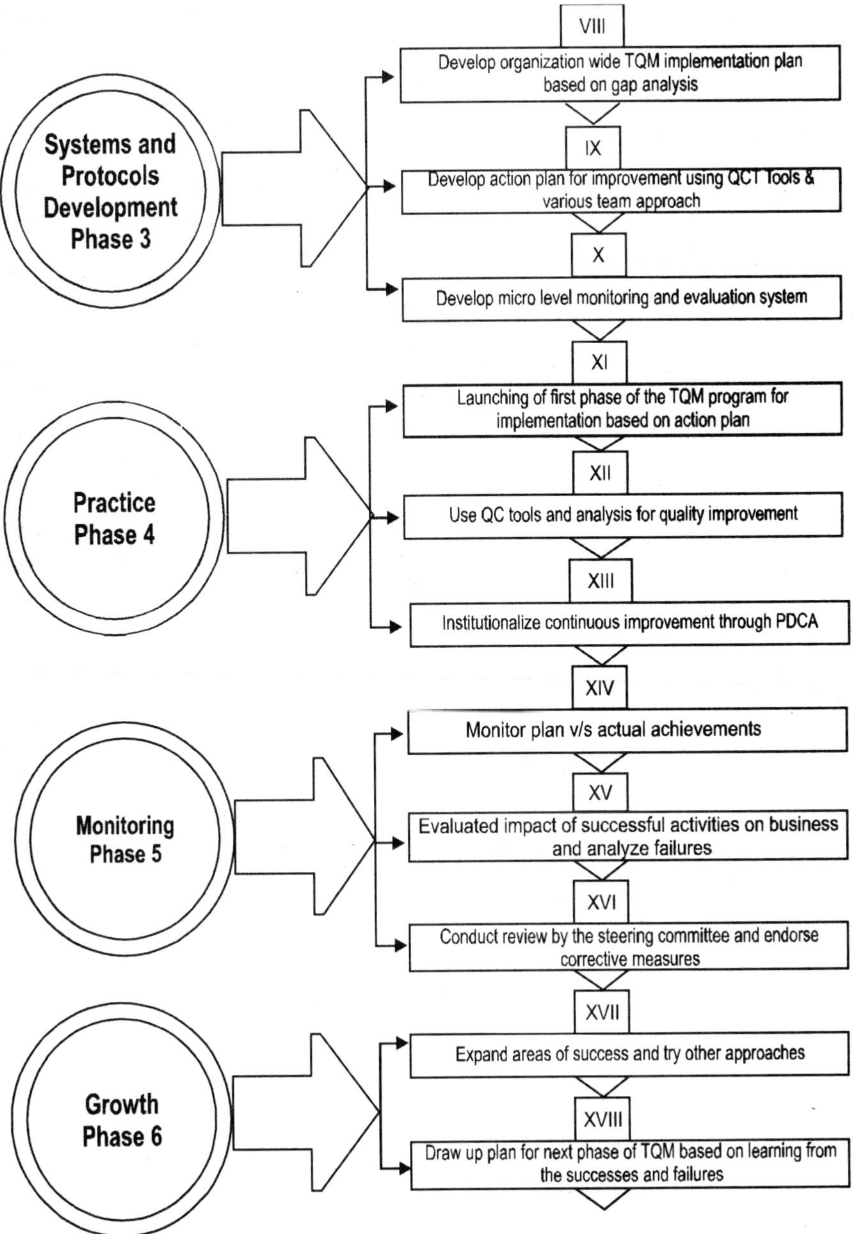

Fig. 6.1: Six phases of TQM implementation

6.2.1 Start up and Commitment Phase

Top management must accept the responsibility for commitment to a quality policy that deals with the organization for quality and the satisfaction of customer needs. This commitment to quality and leadership must be demonstrated by developing and communicating the vision organization-wide. Commitment of top management is achieved when the rewards of implementing TQM are realized. That is, the tangible business and operating benefits of TQM must be realized by top management as a prerequisite for their serious commitment.

To manage the quality journey, a steering committee led by the Senior operations manager such as General Manager may be set up who may be supported by a full time executive for this job. External consultants are often very effective at this stage as they bring in outside perspective needed during the development of system and protocol. Advantage of having external consultant lies with the fact that he supports out-of-the-box thinking which is often ignored in the day-to-day working of the organization. Consultant helps in arranging awareness workshops for the steering committee members for their commitment towards TQM journey.

Senior managers who are members of the steering committee are responsible for developing a comprehensive policy based on clear vision and mission statements, including the quality goals deployed effectively at all levels of the organization. This unites the efforts of all employees and determines the corporate expectations. This comprehensive quality policy should be communicated effectively to ensure common understanding of the organization's expectations and direction to achieve organization-wide commitment.

At the departmental level, quality committees headed by the department heads are established to implement the quality policy to achieve the organization's goals. These committees have a direct reporting relationship with the steering committee through committees' heads.

Six phases of TQM deployment (Figure 6.1) represent what organizations must do to delight the customer by consistently meeting customer requirements, and then achieve a reputation of excellence. TQM must be truly organization-wide to be successful in achieving business efficiency and effectiveness. It must start with the top management leadership. Leaders establish unity of purpose and direction of the organization. They should create and maintain the internal environment in which people can become fully involved in achieving the organization's objectives. This requires following steps:

1. Establish long-term vision.
2. Enlist others in a common vision by appealing to their values, interests, hopes and dreams.
3. Search for challenging opportunities to change, grow, innovate and improve.

4. Evaluate risk and learning from the past mistakes.
5. Foster collaboration by promoting cooperative goals and building trust.
6. Strengthening others by sharing information and power and increasing their discretion and visibility.
7. Set an example by behaving in the ways that is consistent with the stated values.
8. Plan small wins that promote consistent progress and build commitment.
9. Recognize individual contributions to the success of every project.
10. Communicate the start-up activities to all the employees.

6.2.1.1 Develop Vision and Mission of the Company

This indeed is a very crucial exercise. It clarifies as to what is considered important by the management. It provides vision to the business environment. It provides direction, guidance and leadership to the employees to work collectively. It also spells out the current status of the company to meet the competition.

Requisite TQM vision and mission statement is based on the following prerequisites:

Consensus

A consensus must exist among the executives. The agreement on vision and mission statement must be arrived through open, free and frank discussion. This is not possible in large groups. The facilitator should therefore organize small group discussions involving not more than five to seven executives in a group. The consensus built up in a group can be shared by other groups to disseminate it in the organization in order to have a shared perception.

Feasible

The policies so framed should be realistic, practical and feasible. The implementation of the policies should lead to visible operational improvement in the organization. It is also desirable that the policies should be in quantitative terms so that there is no ambiguity to measure the results of performance. This however does not preclude exclusion of qualitative policies.

The policies can be evolved from two prominent sources:

(i) Data of past performances of the organization and the feedback as obtained through self assessment and TQM audit. An analysis is carried out and gap is established.

(ii) Data and analysis of the competition and benchmarking.

Resources

It should be fully ensured that implementation does not fall through on account of non-availability of resources. It is desirable that before formal pronouncement of TQM vision and mission is made it should be vetted thoroughly and resources required are determined and availability ensured. Dropping of implementation of any objectives and goals midway can affect the attitudes, morale and enthusiasm of employees in a big way and commitment of top management towards TQM may be doubted. It is better to dilute or exclude some of the policies which cannot be pursued on account of financial constraints.

Similarly, some of the policies may call for availability of suitable skills, know-how or problem-solving abilities such as professional expertise etc. This can be a major requirement of resource wherever upgradation of technology is called for. Care is needed to properly evaluate the likelihood of availability of this type of resource before firming up the policies.

Technology factor

Technology is the single factor responsible for largest increase in TQM. Technology encompasses several areas. It represents the knowledge, techniques and the methodology to carry-out the process of transformation in a production or service system. Technology can lead to more production in the same time, same production in lesser time, generation of lesser defects, errors or rejections, increased plant life with reduced expense on breakdowns, repairs and maintenance, consistency and repeatability in processes, reduced wastages, reduced fatigue to operators and others engaged in the production process.

Foremost, technology is represented in the selection of appropriate plant and machinery. Automation brings in increased rate of production. Computer aided devices have helped in increased productivity and reduction in rejections. The net effect is reduced cost of production. Technology also encompasses use of appropriate manufacturing methods, process engineering, production planning and control, production scheduling, tool engineering etc. Techniques relating to improving the effectiveness of work are generally classified as industrial engineering techniques. Most of these techniques are well described in literature on industrial engineering and management. It is not within the scope of this book to go through, even briefly all these techniques and to illustrate their application.

Technology factor also covers use of appropriate techniques in the area of inventory management, materials planning, quality control, value analysis, and in selection of appropriate inputs of raw materials. Technology factor is relevant in the selection of a product design or in carrying out product research. The product design has an impact on the life of the machine tools or processing machinery, cost of production, the rejection rate, generation of wastages and productivity.

Very often, alternative technologies are also available. The new technology to be selected has to be evaluated against several criteria, such as the rate of defect generation, the maintenance cost, the employment level etc. It is not always the latest technology that is to be selected but very often it is the appropriate technology which is to be chosen in the interest of total system goals.

Vision

The world over, just one thing has fired the imagination of people: A vision of a future. A vision is a vividly descriptive image of what an organization wants to become or wants to be known for. An organizational vision offers a compelling method for forging employees into an empowered, highly motivated team. Customer-driven vision statements are given below. HDFC: Develop close relationships with individual households, maintain position as the premier housing finance institution in the country, and transform ideas into viable and creative solutions. Colgate Palmolive: To be the company of first choice in oral and personal hygiene by continuously caring for consumers and partners. Anderson Consulting: To help our clients change to be more successful.

The core function of an organizational vision is to ignite people into thinking beyond the company's existing capabilities and present environment. Only a shared vision can achieve this. The impact of vision could be product quality, organizational growth, market performance, sense of belonging, shareholders value etc.

Mission

A statement of intent of what a company wants to achieve and through which lines of business over a period of time.

Embrace a single clear quality philosophy. Without one, the company is like a ship without a rudder. It will loose its way and self-destruct in the midst of global opportunities and problems. The mission statement is a primary expression of quality philosophy, more powerful and enduring than any body in the organization.

Quality Policies

Review all systems, policies, and procedures in the organization and check their harmony with your quality mission. These include organizational structures, manufacturing and purchasing policies, quality control procedures, HR policies, and incentive systems. Immediately discard all existing systems or structures that are not consistent with the corporate quality philosophy/mission.

6.2.1.2 Constitution of Steering Committee Members

(1) Establish a steering committee. The objectives of establishing the steering committee are to:
   - Provide strategic direction on TQM for the organization.
   - Establish plans for TQM implementation.
   - Review and revise quality plans for implementation.

Make sure that the committee is headed by the general manager with all senior managers being members. Whenever possible, include some middle managers as members in the council.

(2) Nominate a quality-related manager to provide support in the planning and implementation of TQM.

(3) Demonstrate visibility of senior managers' commitment to quality and customer satisfaction. This requires:

- Serving at the steering committee.
- Participating in developing a comprehensive quality policy.
- Developing quality management system.
- Attending training courses with staff.
- Delivering training courses to staff.
- Conducting face-to-face regular meetings with staff.
- Communicating the vision and mission to staff.
- Conducting benchmarking visits to other organizations.
- Participating in celebrating successful quality achievements.
- Participating in social gatherings and events.
- Rewarding and recognizing team successes.
- Keeping regular contacts with customers.
- Reviewing quality issues at management meetings.
- Using quality techniques and tools in their daily activities.

(4) Communicate the mission statement consistently. Communicate the mission statement and the objectives defining the quality values, expectations and focus to all employees. An early implementation step must be the clear widespread communication of the mission. This requires:

- Demonstrating top management commitment and acceptance of the mission.
- Using face-to-face communication by conducting meetings with all employees. If not possible, meet with groups of 50-60 each time. If not possible, use a cascade approach.
- Conduct question/answer sessions with employees.
- Encourage open discussions.
- Reinforce face-to-face communication of the mission by other communication modes such as Posters and in-house magazine.

6.2.1.3 Awareness Workshop for Steering Committee Members

(1) Steering committee must develop a clear belief in the benefits that TQM can bring in to the organization. This requires investing time and effort learning about TQM through:

- Reading about TQM.
- Attending training courses.
- Attending conferences.
- Consulting experts.
- Visiting other organizations for benchmarking purposes.

(2) Ensure consensus agreement of all senior managers. This involves all senior managers having belief in the tangible benefits that TQM can bring to the organization. This leads to gaining consensus agreement among senior managers concerning planning to implement TQM. This requires:
- All senior managers serve at the steering committee as members.
- Attending training courses.
- Attending conferences.
- Reading about TQM.
- Visiting other organizations for benchmarking purposes.

6.2.2 Strategy Phase

This is the cornerstone of the programme on TQM and is crucial for its success. At this stage all factors which affect an organization are considered, the strengths and weaknesses are taken into account and consensus arrived at in selecting the performance objectives. The exercise comprises of arriving at the achievable values of performance objectives which become targets for performance. These objectives have to be realistic, representative of the system TQM as a whole and should project the potential performance of the organization.

Strategy phase need to develop TQM goals for the company. The goal of the company should be to become a world-class company. During this phase self-assessment exercises and TQM index should be arrived at based on average score of different assessment groups. Gap analysis should be done based on industry best practices as weil as against TQM goal. For this purpose, one should consider changing customer and market expectations. Long-term view of the future should be clearly identified and effectively communicated within the organization.

The most senior directors and management must all demonstrate that they are serious about quality. This requires involving everyone in the organization in quality improvement. Therefore, management must enable all employees to participate in the strategic planning preparation, implementation and evaluation of improvement activities. This is important as top and middle management have a major role to play, since they must not only grasp the principles of TQM, but they must also go to explain them to those for whom they are responsible, and ensure that their commitment is communicated. For an organization to be successful in the marketplace, each part of it must work properly together towards the same goals, recognizing that each person and each activity affects, and in turn is affected by others. This means focusing on business processes that add value to customer satisfaction. The continuous improvement of existing products, services and processes is fundamental for continuous customer satisfaction.

6.2.2.1 Developing TQM Goals for the Company

It is recommended that TQM vision and mission should form the basis to draw up three time-frame goals:

(i) Short term goals
(ii) Medium term goals
(iii) Long term goals

Short-term goals

These are the goals which are 'fixed type' and are required to be completed over a predetermined time period, which should not exceed a period of twelve months. These short term goals are in clear, precise quantitative terms with no ambiguity. There is normally no change till the time period specified expires. It is normally expected that performance level should exceed a success rate of 90%. There is a built-in urgency for their completion.

Medium-term goals

These are the goals which have a time frame of completion varying from twelve to twenty months. Many of these goals are built around the organization's plan for future growth. The goals are usually rolling type. The completed tasks are replaced with new objectives. Similarly, the incomplete ones are carried forward to the next term. Often there is a review of these goals and objectives with a view to provide for extra resources as the same are not fully and accurately determined at the time of drawing up of goals and objectives.

Long-term goals

These belong to areas where new investments are called for and there is considerable gestation period involved. Change of product technology through new designs, collaboration with third parties, upgradation, new processing facilities, new tooling to cut down manufacturing costs, plant re-layouts are some examples. Organizational changes such as structural redesign, training and development, work culture and work environment, resources planning for future growth are some other areas which require long term policies.

6.2.2.2 Carry Out Macro Level Self-assessment Based on TQMI

Steering committee should form different teams to carry out the self-assessment against questionnaire (Annexure A1 and A2). These teams should assess the organization's performance against the TQM variables and results. TQM index should be computed based on the average score of these different teams. Different teams should be encouraged for the self-assessment to remove the individual biases. TQM index reflects the present status of the organization. This gives input to the organization as to what path to adopt to bridge the gap.

6.2.2.3 Carry Out Gap Analysis Based on Industry Best Practices As Well As TQM Goal

The genesis of improvement lies in the right identification of weak areas against a level to which the organization would like to reach. The destination of the organization by no means should be less than the world-class level. In Chapter 4 we have explained different components of enablers and results, which contribute towards building the world-class organization. We have also suggested the TQM index needed to compete at this level. By comparing, the organization may find the gaps that exist at different components of enablers and results. An illustration of the gap identification for enablers and results are shown in Figure 6.2 and 6.3.

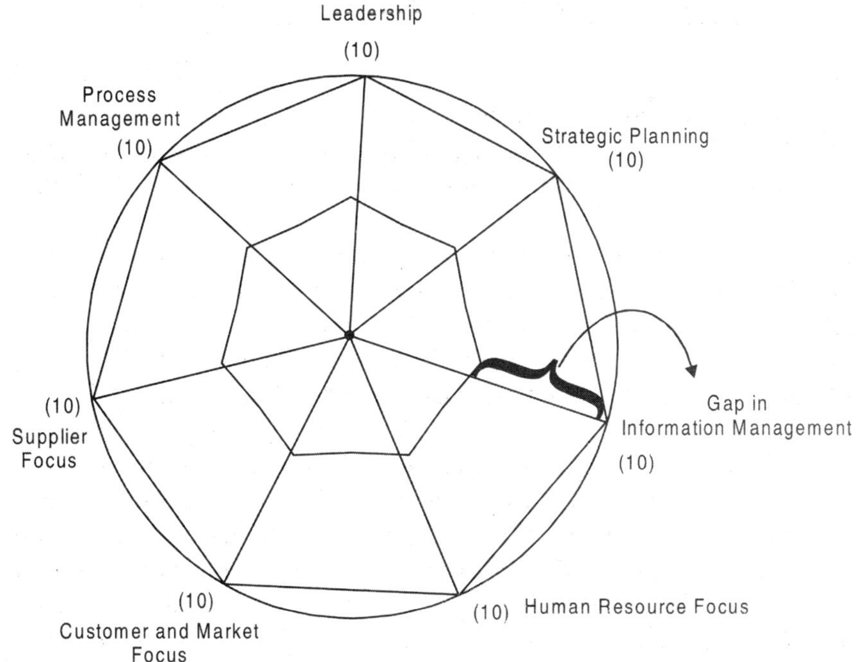

Fig. 6.2: Radar chart for gap analysis in enablers

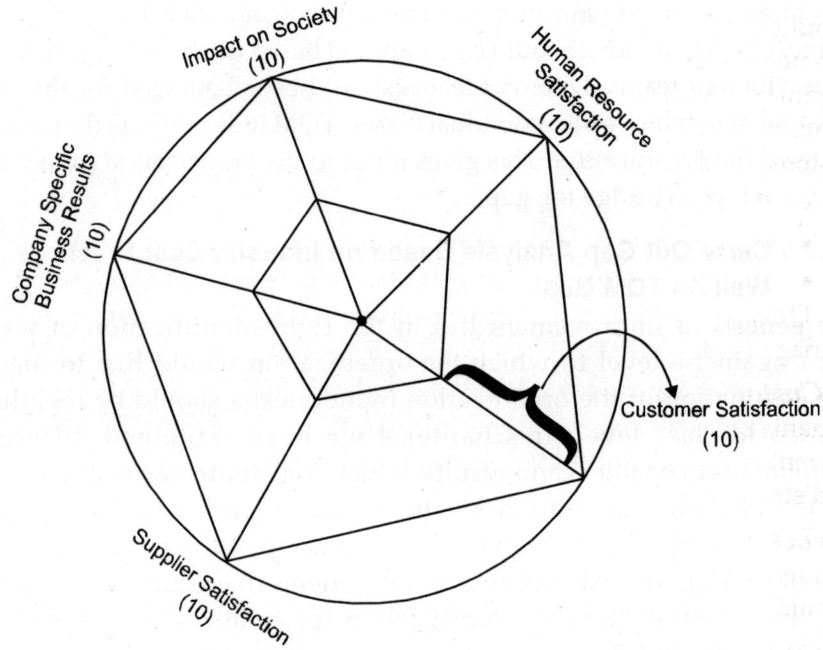

Fig. 6.3: Radar chart for gap analysis in results

6.2.2.4 Formulate Strategy for Implementation Based on Gap Analysis

Steering committee should involve departmental quality committee members in formulating strategy to bridge the identified gap areas. Steering committee should encourage departmental quality committees to prioritize the goal and make action plan.

Steering committee based on the inputs from all quality committees should prepare a road map for monitoring the overall progress. This will help the steering committee to estimate the approximate time frame for achieving the world-class status and they can readjust the road map based on organization's goal. Based on road map departmental quality committees should be asked to prepare short-term, medium-term and long-term goals. These goals should be deployed at each level of the organization. Actions based on strategy should help the organization to attain the world-class status.

6.2.3 Systems and Protocols Development Phase

During this phase, the organization should develop quality management system as a base to achieve world-class status. Apart from this, the organization should develop action plan for improving the organization's performance using various QC tools. Efforts should be made to encourage group activities in each and every department for the implementation of 5S, Kaizen, Quality Circle and TPM. It is very important to use these activities across the whole plant. It is extremely important that each team should be encouraged to soil their own hands. This will help in achieving the needed cultural change for effective bridging of the gap against organization goal. Apart from this, the organization should develop micro level monitoring and evaluation system to track the progress. Quality system should provide the base for:

- Continuous improvement
- Emphasizing defect prevention, and
- The reduction of variation and waste in the supply chain

Quality system should be established based on eight quality management principles.

(i) Customer focused organization

Organizations depend on their customers and therefore, should understand current and future customer needs, should meet customer requirements and strive to exceed customer expectations.

(ii) Leadership

Leaders establish unity of purpose and direction of the organization. They should create and maintain the internal environment in which people can become fully involved in achieving the organization's objectives.

(iii) Involvement of people

People at all levels are the essence of an organization and their full involvement enables their abilities to be used for the organization's benefit.

(iv) Process approach

A desired result is achieved more efficienciently when activities and related resources are managed as a process.

(v) System approach to management

Identifying, understanding and managing interrelated processes as a system contributes to the organization's effectiveness and efficiency in achieving its objectives.

(vi) Continual improvement

Continual improvement of the organization's overall performance should be a permanent objective of the organization.

(vii) Factual approach to decision making

Effective decisions are based on the analysis of data and information.

(viii) Mutually beneficial supplier relationship

An organization and its suppliers are interdependent and a mutually beneficial relationship enhances the ability of both to create value.

The ISO 9000 Documentation Standards

ISO 9000 is a set of standards governing documentation of a quality program. Companies become certified by proving to a qualified external examiner that they have complied with all the requirements. Once certified, companies are listed in a directory so that potential customers can see which companies have been certified and to what level. Compliance with ISO 9000 standards says *nothing* about the actual quality of a product. Rather, it indicates to customers that companies can provide documentation to support whatever claims they make about quality.

Managing by a quality management system will enable the objectives set out in the quality policy to be achieved. In this regard, the ISO 9000:2000 series set out methods by which a system can be implemented to ensure that the specified customer requirements are met. The quality management system should apply to, and interact with, processes in the organization. Therefore, managing by customer-driven systems and processes requires deploying the human and other resources along the processes to add values for customer satisfaction.

This approach of managing by customer-driven systems and processes is associated with the concept of the internal customer–supplier relationship. Throughout the organizations there are a series of internal suppliers and customers. These form the quality chain, which is considered as the core of company-wide improvement (Oakland, 2000). The internal customer–supplier relationships must be managed to add value to customer satisfaction, which makes measurement of capability vital.

Many TQM writers have pointed out the importance of focusing on system processes and internal customer–supplier relationships and their management. They emphasized that TQM is centered on the effective management of processes and continuous customer satisfaction (Kanji, 1995; Zairi, 1994; Oakland, 2000; Braganza & Mayers, 1997; Beskese & Cebeci, 2001; Kolka, 2002; Stahan, 2002).

An early stage in the implementation process is to seek certification of a formal documented quality system to determine the assembly of components, such as the organizational structure, responsibilities, processes and resources for implementing total quality management. This also requires a comprehensive identification of customers and customer needs and the alignment of processes to satisfy the needs. The effort involves promoting internal customer–supplier relationships in the quality chain, recognizing that each person and each activity affects, and in turn is affected by others to deliver values for the customer. In this regard, it is very important to understand the core processes and gain process sponsorship to ensure that appropriate resources are made available to map, investigate and improve the process. Moreover, it is important to break down the core processes into sub processes, activities and tasks. This requires understanding customer needs at each level.

Quality has to be managed–it will not just happen (Oakland, 2000). This means that it must involve everyone in the process and be applied throughout the organization. Many people in the support functions of organizations never see, experience or touch the products or services that their organizations buy or provide, but they do handle or produce things such as purchase orders or invoices. If every fourth invoice carries at least one error, what image of quality is transmitted (Oakland, 2000)? This makes the application of total quality approach to the management of support services and business processes important.

The setting up of performance measurement procedures to track the performance of the processes and for their continuous improvement is a vital component of this construct. Clearly, suppliers need to be evaluated and selected on their ability to supply the product or service in accordance with the organization's requirement.

ISO 14000 – An Environmental Management System

The ISO 14001 documentation standards require participating companies to keep track of their raw materials use and their generation, treatment, and disposal of hazardous wastes. Although not specifying what each company is allowed to emit, the standards require companies to prepare a plan for ongoing improvement in their environmental performance. ISO 14000 is a series of five standards that cover a number of areas, including the following:

- ***Environmental Management System:*** Requires a plan to improve performance in resource use and pollutant output.
- ***Environmental Performance Evaluation:*** Specifies guidelines for the certification of companies.
- ***Environmental Labeling:*** Defines terms such as *recyclable, energy efficient,* and *safe for the ozone layer.*
- ***Life-Cycle Assessment:*** Evaluates the lifetime environmental impact from the manufacturer, use, and disposal of a product.

Seek certification of a formal documented quality management system to ensure that specified customer requirements are met. Ensure that the quality management system applies to, and interacts with, all processes in the organization. Ensure that the quality management is determined by the nature of the process carried out to add value to the customer satisfaction. To maintain their certification, companies must be inspected by outside, private auditors on a regular basis.

Implementation Stage

(1) Identify customer and customer needs. Identify customers in terms of internal and external customers. This requires that everyone understands the concept of the internal customer. Ensure that the requirements of the external customer are identified. This requires using various sources of information.

- Sales people and marketing personnel provide inputs.
- Customer surveys.
- Customer complaints.
- Focus groups.

Ensure that everyone in the organization knows his or her internal customer. This requires each person to interrogate every interface as follows:

- Who are my immediate customers?
- What are their true requirements?
- Do I have the necessary capability to meet the requirements? (If not, then what must change to improve the capability?)
- Who are my immediate suppliers?
- What are my true requirements?
- Do my suppliers have the capability to meet my requirements?

(2) Ensure that everyone understands the concept of quality chain of internal customer–supplier relationship. Introduce the concept of internal customer–supplier at the early stages of implementation so that the entire organization understands that each individual and each process has internal customers and suppliers. Ensure that this concept is used to add value to customer satisfaction.

(3) Apply the total quality approach to the management of support services and business processes. Ensure that everyone understands that quality management requires the involvement of everyone in the process and is applied throughout the organization. Emphasize that failure to meet customer requirements in one part of the system creates multiple problems elsewhere.

The key to lasting success lies right at the start of journey i.e. how the programme is initiated and implemented. That will also decide whether employees adapt for the continuous change or develop resistance for the change.

There are two schools of thoughts. One saying; "People Welcome Change" while other saying; "People generally resist change". The first school of thought is based on MASLOW'S hierarchy of needs, by which people should welcome changes, as (a) It provides a new challenge. People often become bored with the routine tasks and begin to look for something more challenging and satisfying. (b) People wish to participate and involve themselves for recognition and for self fulfillment of their potential.

During this phase, mindset of the people should be changed through organizing training programmes on TQM concepts and its tools and techniques. A platform for the people to be recognized should be created by the formation of quality circle, 5S teams and TPM teams. Develop monitoring system for self-assessment and establish a mechanism for inputs and mutual support for attainment.

elop Organization-wide TQM Implementation Plan Based ìap Analysis

' organization to focus on deciding priority related to quality, cost, flexibility, delivery, safety, market leadership and morale ,zation. This needs to be dovetailed into proper system and .eliver the result and operational level. Department-wise action be needed for the purpose.

Ensure that the entire workforce understands and is committed to the vision, values and quality goals of the organization. Communicate the vision, values and quality goals to all employees emphasizing the need for a management system that is based on total quality management. This requires:

- Gathering all employees to attend a face-to-face meeting to announce the need for the quality management system. If it is not possible to gather all employees, meet employees in groups of 50-60; if this is not possible, use the cascade approach.
- Gather all employees to attend a face-to-face meeting to communicate the vision, mission, values, expectations and the quality goals of the organization. This, of course, can be done in the same meeting to announce the need for the quality system. If it is not possible to meet with all employees, meet with employees in groups of 50-60; if not possible, use the cascade approach.
- Provide TQM awareness workshops on the concepts and philosophies of TQM.

(2) Provide training for employees in interactive skills. Manage the training programme to provide systematic training for employees to improve their communication skills, effective meeting skills and empowerment and leading skills.

(3) Provide training for employees in problem identification and solving skills, quality improvement skills and other technical skills. Provide training in problem identification and solving skills, teamwork and decision making to foster continuous improvement. This requires the establishment of a systematic approach to quality training which ensures that training for quality should have an appreciation of the personal responsibility for meeting customer requirements by everyone from the most senior manager to the most junior employee. This demands reviewing the effectiveness of quality training programmes on a continuous basis and to establish and maintain procedures for the identification of the training needs and the provision of the actual training itself.

Human Resource Focus

1. Employees must be treated with dignity and respect.
2. They must be trained to build competence where req
3. Each employee must know what exactly is required to where possible, must be able to assess the quality of
4. Fear must be totally removed from the organization an must be encouraged to bring out weakness in the syster
5. Empower employees to take appropriate action in their are for improvement.
6. In case of a mistake, examine the system rather than the man to prevent its recurrence.
7. Involve employees in quality plans and draw upon their intimate knowledge of processes for improvement.
8. Assess employees' satisfaction level and take appropriate measures to improve their morale so that they take pride in belonging to the company.

Employees – The doer in to TQM

The greatest contributions to the process of TQM are made by the people who make the organization. People – who share the vision? Intellectual capital and knowledge are more and more the true assets of any organization. In its Japanese context, Total Quality refers not only to the quality of management which ultimately produces quality goods and services, but to the quality of human behavior, skills and commitment necessary to accomplish our business objectives. This not only makes good business sense, it also reflects a deeper yearning of the human spirit to be of service, to build loving, caring relationships, to affirm our interdependence, and to bring value, beauty, and benefit into the world.The human quality should always include the following three components:

1. Creativity – The joy of thinking
2. Physical activity – The joy of working with sweat on the forehead.
3. Sociality – The joy of working together.

In a survey conducted by National Productivity Council (NPC) (1983), inefficient utilization of human resources constitutes the single largest factor (36.3%) for low level of productivity in Indian companies. The role of human resource in TQM has been well recognized by a number of authors and researchers. It is now well known that the successful organizations are essentially people oriented. The human resource includes employee at all levels: executives, engineers, blue and white collar workers. The key element is, therefore, human resource development to achieve improvements in TQM. A number of techniques: financial incentives, fringe benefits, promotions, job enrichment, job enlargement, job rotation, employee on, skill enhancement, management by objectives, learning curve, ation, working condition improvement, training, education, role recognition etc.

nce to human resource development is that human resources motivated and developed to handle the tasks entrusted. The motivation has received attention of behavioral scientists and a of motivation techniques have been proposed in the last few es. TQM improvement strategies based on human resource opment can be grouped under the following classifications:

Organization Development (OD)

OD calls for changing the systems, the culture and the behavior of an organization in a planned and systematic manner in order to improve the organization's effectiveness. An organization is more effective if the employees carry a conviction that their goals are integrated with the goals of the organization. In order to achieve these objectives an organization should create a work environment conductive to participatory management, a transparent and an open approach to solve all problems and a philosophy that interests of employees and the organization are in unison rather than in conflict with each other.

Employee Participation

The involvement of employees in the process of management creates a right climate and a work attitude towards improvement of TQM. Participation is vital equally in planning, target setting and implementation. Employees can be involved through several ways: Quality circles, task forces, brain-storming, suggestion schemes, meetings and through formal and informal discussions.

Employee Motivation

A positive attitude creates a right atmosphere to achieve results in the desired direction. A motivated employee considers his work as a meaningful activity and he sees this as an opportunity to achieve self-fulfillment. A motivated environment is characterized by:

1. An atmosphere of trust
2. Protection and security (health, safety, welfare)
3. Opportunities to grow
4. Professional development

6.2.3.2 Develop Action Plan for Improvement Using QC Tools & Various Team Approach

In order to ensure the commitment and involvement of everyone in the organization in the quality improvement, top management must enable all employees in the preparation, implementation and evaluation of improvement activities.

Practical assistance, training, recognition and participation given to ensure that all employees, in order to attain the qual the organization, acquire the relevant knowledge and expe issue of employee commitment and involvement is a critical q for success.

As employees become committed and involved and the entire understands, and is committed to, the vision, values and quali the organization, empowerment becomes a necessity. Employees be aware of the TQM concepts, trained to improve interactive skills, pro identification and solving skills, and technical skills. Employees need to informed about the quality initiative and participate in the improvement activities and through top-down and bottom-up communication. Teamwork skills are needed to have employees work together, and a review of the reward and recognition scheme is another important factor to ensure and reinforce employee commitment and involvement.

At this stage, as senior managers become committed and involved in preparing the plan for TQM implementation, they start to:

(1) Point out the benefits of TQM for the organization in their meetings with middle managers and in their memos to them.

(2) Nominate key middle managers to attend seminars, conferences and workshops addressing quality issues.

(3) Keep employees informed and get their feedback. Establish top-down and bottom-up communication modes to keep employees informed (about the progress being made and successes of quality initiatives achieved by individuals and teams), and to get feedback (using employee survey, face-to-face meetings, workshops or suggestion schemes). This requires the use of a variety of communication modes emphasizing face-to-face communication.

- Briefings made by the general manager and senior managers.
- Face-to-face meetings.
- Question-answer sessions.
- Posters.
- In-house news bulletin.
- Training and workshops.
- Memos
- Employee surveys.
- Suggestion schemes.

This might require establishing a committee to review the communication modes and strategies and accordingly make recommendations for improvements.

(4) Ensure middle management buy-in. Ensure that supervisors, unit heads and divisional managers assume active roles as facilitators of continuous improvement, coaches of new methods, mentors and leaders of empowered employees. Middle managers may see TQM as another burden without any benefits, and may perceive a vested interest in the status quo. This requires:

- Increasing direct interaction between senior managers and middle managers to provide guidance and support, particularly in the early years of implementation,
- Organizing benchmarking visits to other organizations to feel the benefits that TQM can bring to the organization,
- Providing comprehensive training in the philosophy and concepts of teamwork and the techniques and applications of statistical process control in order to assume new roles as facilitators of continuous improvement, coaches of new methods and mentors and leaders of empowered employees.
- Participating, whenever possible, in the quality council as members,
- Reinforcing the behaviors of middle managers needed for their new roles by rewards and recognition.

Definition of 5S

5S is a participative programme. It is a effective approach of improving the work environment and total quality. It becomes a base for continuous improvement in the organization. It was only in the early 1980s that good housekeeping became an important issue in Japanese industries. The concept of good housekeeping has been with the Japanese for a very long time. At home and in school, children are disciplined to adhere to good housekeeping practices. Companies realized its powerful contribution towards productivity and quality improvement. Workplace become clean and better organized. Shop-floor and office operation become easier and safer. Results are visible to everyone—insiders and outsiders. Visible results enhance generation of more and new ideas.

Quality Circle

Every individual has lot of potential in his field of work – the potential, however, needs to be tapped. It was in the USA, sometime, in 40s that the idea was conceived and was effectively used by many companies in the form of workmen participation programmes. The concept, however, took practical shape in 50s. The Japanese in fact, understood the hidden charismatic value of the idea which had originally taken birth in USA and other Western countries. They developed it into a science and nurtured it with full devotion in the form of quality circle as shown in Figure 6.4.

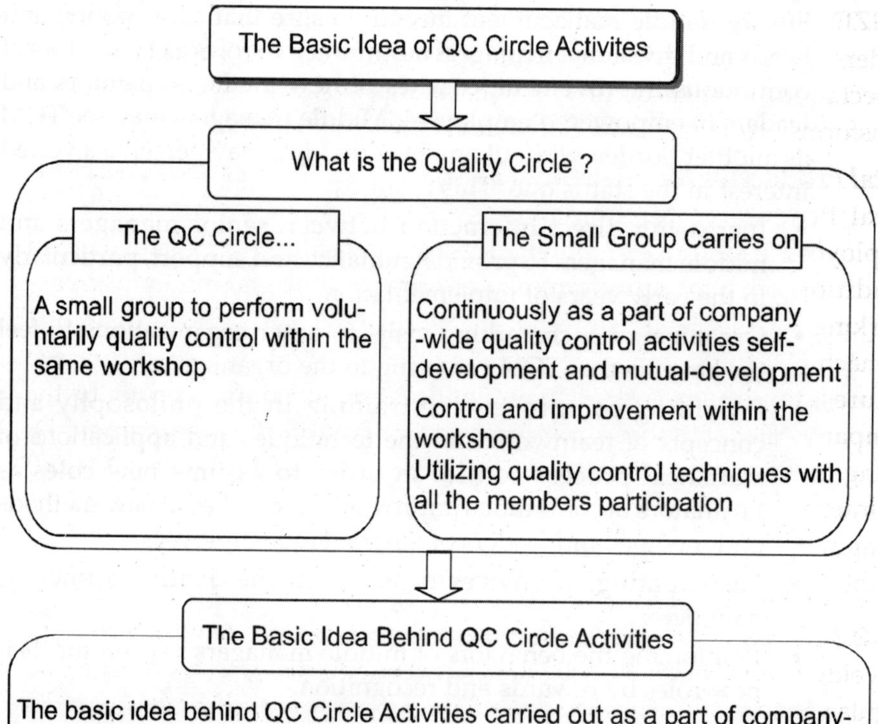

(QC Circle KORYO – General Principle of the QC Circle)

Fig. 6.4: Basic idea of QC circle

Kaizen

Kaizen as originally defined the book of "Kaizen, the Key to Japan's Competitive Success", by Mr. Masaaki Imai, is:

> *Kaizen means improvement. Moreover, KAIZEN means continuing improvement in personal life, home life, social life, and working life. When applied to the workplace KAIZEN means continuing improvement involving everyone – managers and workers alike.*

KAIZEN is a Japanese world meaning gradual and orderly, continuous improvement. The KAIZEN business strategy involves everyone in an organization working together to make improvements 'without large capital investments'.

KAIZEN is a culture of sustained continuous improvement focusing on eliminating waste in all systems and processes of an organization. The

KAIZEN strategy begins and ends with people. With KAIZEN, an involved leadership guides people to continuously improve their ability to meet expectations of high quality, low cost, and on-time delivery. KAIZEN transforms companies into 'Supplier Global Competitors'.

Total Productive Maintenance (TPM)

Total Productive Maintenance is to achieve maximum profit, all employees to minimize maintenance costs. A facility can be kept in good condition only by autonomous action and thought. All employees working for the well-keeping of machines with appropriate diagnosis of machines, good housekeeping, less breakdowns and less unforeseen failures, minimum cost of maintenance, and maximum profit to the company. The activities to improve productivity of the equipment by doing preventive maintenance (PM), corrective maintenance (CM) and maintenance preventive (MP) with regard to the overall life cycle of the equipment, are generically known as productive maintenance (PM). This further developed to TPM i.e. PM with total employee participation.

6.2.3.3 Develop Micro Level Monitoring and Evaluation System

Develop self-assessment as a periodic, comprehensive, systematic and regular review of organization systems, procedures and results against a recognized TQM model culminating in planned improvement actions. Large numbers of quality professionals are advocating the use of self-assessment with the ultimate objective of sustained quality improvement as its benefits (Zink and Schmidt, 1998; Kristensen and Juhl, 1999; Kristensen *et al.,* 2000; Jordan, 1994; Knutton, 1994; Zaremba and Crew, 1995; Brereton, 1996; Wu *et al.,* 1997; Fountain, 1998).

Van der Wiele *et al.* (1996b) defined QMSA as a management approach based on a mission to achieve business excellence. They concluded that QMSA should be done in stages. First, an organization has to be fairly advanced to be able to start self-assessment. Second, the assessment is to be done by quality specialists as assessors. The result of these two stages should be confidential to the unit concerned. In more advance stage, the organization can use line managers as assessors and share the results across units.

Self-assessment survey questionnaire should be administrated in a workshop environment to assess performance of the organization against each TQM variables. The average score based on the questionnaire should then be compared with the business excellence model and action plan should be made to bridge the gap. To get an indicative feel of the level of organizational maturity, the score can be compared with the levels given in Table 5.1. System dynamics model Table 5.4, 5.17 and 5.35 indicates the organizations regarding number of years required to achieve the world-class status at optimum effectiveness of enablers. These tables help the organization to decide about the time period required by the organizations to achieve the world-class status. The time period to achieve the TQM maturity level depends on the effectiveness of the strategic planning. Depending on the organization's strategic plan, the TQM maturity level can either be achieved faster or slower than what is stated in the tables.

6.2.4 Practice Phase

During this phase TQM programme should be launched. Strategy stage would have helped to identify the priorities and core competence areas. Various teams should use QC tools for bridging the gaps. Implementation of 5S should be done with everybody's participation. Quality circle should be encouraged to solve department-related problems. Model M/c should be selected in various departments for implementing TPM. After initial success, more M/c should be taken up for implementing TPM. Proper implementation of this phase will help the organization to reduce quality related problems and in turn will help to enhance customer and employees satisfaction.

6.2.4.1 Launching of First Phase of the TQM Program for Implementation Based on Action Plan

Based on the preparation done during earlier three phases, steering committee should launch TQM programme by involving each and every member of the organization. These activities should follow with commitment and oath-taking ceremony. Lot of encouraging talk should be there and workers and opinion leaders should also be encouraged to share their implementation plan.

6.2.4.2 Identify Critical Processes

Identify the core processes and the sub processes. Understand the core processes and break down the core processes into sub processes. This requires top management to:

- Define the most critical processes that impact the ability of the organization to meet customer requirements. This requires providing training in process managing for senior managers and middle managers, involvement of employees performing the process;

process documentation including internal customers and suppliers and their requirements.

- Assign a sponsor for each core process, preferably a member of the management team. The task of the process sponsor is to:
  (1) Ensure that appropriate resources are made available to map, investigate and improve the process.
  (2) Assist in selecting the process improvement team leader and members.
  (3) Create an appropriate work environment for the teams' progress.
  (4) Report progress to top management.
- Break down the core processes into sub processes, activities and tasks. Develop the skills of people so that they can understand how the new process structure will be analyzed and made to work.
- Establish performance measurement of the processes and sub processes.
- Establish performance measurement to monitor the performance of processes and to identify opportunities for continuous improvement. Ensure that measuring performance is meaningful in terms of inputs and outputs of the processes, and in terms of the customers and suppliers to the process. This should reflect the needs and wants of customers and the process capability.

Rely on reasonable suppliers. Evaluate and select suppliers on their ability to supply the product or service in accordance with the organization's requirements. Consider supplier audit records and evidence of previously demonstrated ability. Determine the type and extent of supervision applicable to the purchased materials/services.

6.2.4.3 Use QC Tools and Analysis for Quality Improvement

These tools are used for improvement and control of the quality. These tools are simple to learn, easy to apply, inexpensive and yet yield abundant results. Massive training was imparted on these tools in Japan to the people of various levels and discipline. Today Japan is the number one nation in quality, productivity and the resultant growth. In Japan 99.92% of middle school students know significantly well 7 QC tools. Application of these tools as shown in Figure 6.5 is universal in production, service and in fact in any activity.

The steps of problems solving

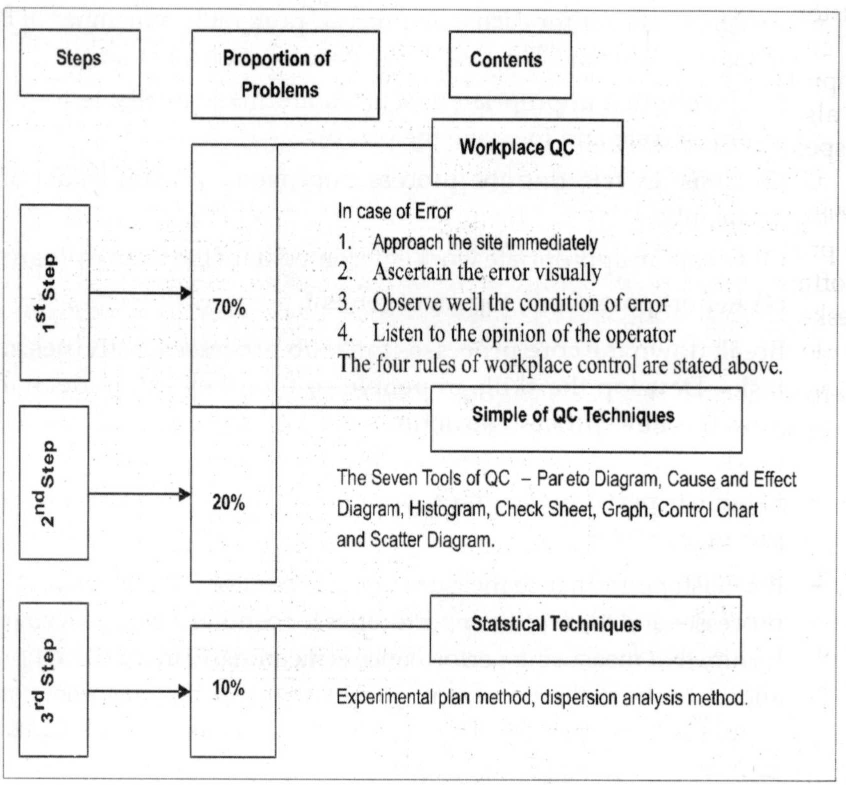

Fig. 6.5: Problem solving steps

6.2.4.4 Institutionalize Continuous Improvement Through PDCA Cycle

Continuous improvement, based on a Japanese concept called *kaizen,* is the philosophy of continually seeking ways to improve operations. In this regard, it is not unique to quality, but applies also to process improvement. Continuous improvement involves identifying benchmarks of excellent practice and instilling a sense of employee ownership in the process. The focus can be on reducing the length of time required to process requests for loans at a bank, the amount of scrap generated at a milling machine or the number of employee injuries at a construction site. Continuous improvement also can focus on problems with customers or suppliers, such as customers who request frequent changes in shipping quantities and suppliers who fail to maintain high quality. The bases of the continuous improvement philosophy are the beliefs that virtually any aspect of an operation can be improved and that the people most closely associated with an operation are in the best position to identify the changes that should be made. The idea is not to wait until a massive problem occurs before acting.

Continuous, or never-ending improvement is a powerful concept related to the pursuit of never-ending improvement in meeting external and internal customer needs. This concept must be firmly tied to a continuous assessment of customer needs and depends on a flow of ideas on how to make improvements, reduce variation and generate greater customer satisfaction. It also requires a high level of commitment and a sense of personal responsibility in those operating the processes (Oakland, 2000).

Continuous improvement requires management by facts (Kanji, 1995, 1998), and commitment to all employees with an emphasis on teamwork to promote a bottom-up thrust for quality improvement (Oakland, 2000; Hoffman & Mehra, 1999; Dale *et al.*, 2001; McAdam & Kelly, 2002; Cebeci & Beskese, 2002). Tools and techniques such as cost of quality should be used to identify continuous improvement opportunities (Hiezer &Render, 2001).

Getting Started with Continuous Improvement

Instilling a philosophy of continuous improvement in an organization may be a lengthy process, and several steps are essential to its eventual success.

1. Train employees in the methods of statistical process control (SPC) and other tools for improving quality and performance.
2. Make SPC methods a normal aspect of daily operations.
3. Build work teams and employee involvement.
4. Utilize problem-solving tools within the work teams.
5. Develop a sense of operator ownership in the process.

Problem Solving Process

Most firms actively engaged in continuous improvement train their work teams to use the plan-do-check-act cycle for problem solving. Another name for this approach is the Deming Wheel. Figure 6.6 shows this cycle, which lies at the heart of the continuous improvement philosophy.

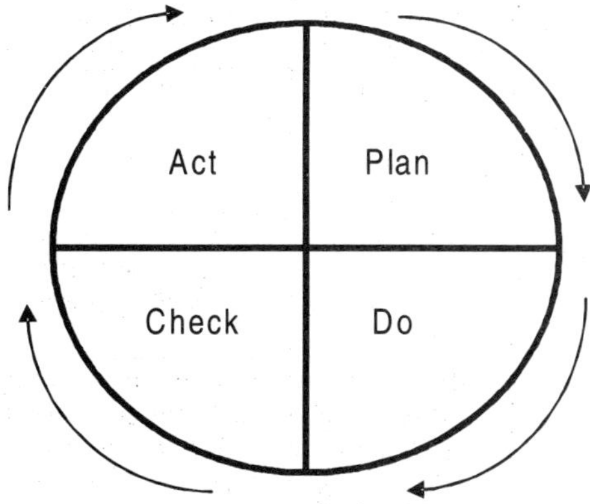

Fig. 6.6: Plan-Do-Check-Act cycle

Plan

The team selects a process (e.g., activity, method, machine, or policy) that needs improvement. The team then documents the selected process, usually by analyzing data (using the tools we shall discuss later in the chapter); sets qualitative goals for improvement; and discusses various ways to achieve the goals. After assessing the benefits and costs of the alternatives, the team develops a plan with quantifiable measures for improvement.

Do

The team implements the plan and monitors progress. Data are collected continuously to measure the improvements in the process. Any changes in the process are documented, and further revisions are made as needed.

Check

The team analyzes the data collected during the *do* steps to find out how closely the results correspond to the goals set in the *plan* step. If major shortcomings exist, the team may have to reevaluate the plan or stop the project.

Act

If the results are successful, the team documents the revised process so that it becomes the standard procedure for all who may use it. The team may then instruct other employees in the use of the revised process.

At Implementation Stage

(1) Ensure that continuous improvement and problem solving are based on facts and systematic review. Rely on facts in making decisions concerning continuous process improvement. Review documentation to identify improvement opportunities. Provide necessary training for problem identification and solving skills based on the use of facts.

(2) Promote teamwork as one of the organization's guiding values. Form various types of teams to work on continuous improvement projects. Reinforce teamwork by rewarding and recognizing successes.

(3) Measure customer satisfaction. Use various tools to get feedback from customers to measure their satisfaction. Collect data using customer surveys, and review internal data related to sales records, delivery time and customer complaints to measure customer satisfaction. Use these data sources to identify gaps for improvement.

(4) Use tools and techniques. Use tools and techniques to identify performance gaps for continuous improvement. Use the cost of quality and self-assessment tools developed in this study to identify opportunities for continuous improvement. Analyze the costs of quality and classify them using the PAF model. Conduct self-assessment exercise in the early years of implementation using the tool developed in this study.

At later stages, use National Quality Award Criteria to conduct self-assessment. Use benchmarking whenever possible. Provide training for key personnel on how to use the various tools and techniques. Continuous improvement is only possible when the quality objectives can be measured and quantified.

Marketing

1. Accuracy of forecast assumptions
2. Number of incorrect order entries
3. Overstocked field supplies
4. Contract errors
5. Late deliveries
6. Customer complaints

Purchase

1. Premium freight cost/demurrage charges.
2. Down-time because of parts shortages
3. Number of off specification parts used to keep line going
4. Cycle time from start of purchase request until items reach in house.
5. Excess inventory.
6. Percentage of purchased material rejected on receipt

Manufacturing

1. Yield per ton of raw materials.
2. Percentage of parts scrapped.
3. Percentage of parts reworked.
4. Percentage of parts accepted on concession.
5. Percentage of final product grades as seconds.
6. Production per man/machine

Product Engineering

1. Number of engineering changes per document.
2. Number of errors found during design review.
3. Number of errors found in design evaluation test.
4. Percentage of time over-run compared to planned time for development.
5. Percentage of cost over-run over estimated cost of deployment.
6. Number of tooling redesign after trial production.

Quality Assurance

1. Percentage of lots rejected due to errors.
2. Percentage of products having defects detected by customers.

3. Number of engineering changes that should have been detected in design review.
4. Errors in inspection/test reports.
5. Cycle time to get corrective actions.
6. Percentage of appraisal cost compared to production cost.

Accounting

1. Percentage of late payments.
2. Time to respond to customer request for information.
3. Billing errors.
4. Incorrect accounting entries.
5. Payroll errors.
6. Errors in cost estimates.

6.2.5 Monitoring Phase

One of the most important phases in sustaining the initiative taken during different points is effective monitoring against plan. Monitoring schedule should be made and followed. During presentation, decision should be taken regarding resource allocation for achieving the goal. Regular review should be conducted by steering committee.

Monitoring phase is very critical for the success of TQM journey. Every month presentations on achievements against targets should be organized. Presentation should be done by each team from various departments. Top management and steering committee should encourage such presentation and recognition should be done based on achievements. Support should be provided where teams are not able to achieve the plan. Quarterly presentation by different teams should be organized where the whole organization should participate. Quarterly convocation should be organized for the presentation of achievements by 5S, Quality circle and TPM teams. During these convocation, delegates should be invited from customer and suppliers. These convocations/quarterly meet should follow get-together lunch. During monitoring phase impact of successful activities on business be assessed and analysis should be done for the reasons of failures and corrective action should be discussed and finalized.

6.2.5.1 Monitor Plan v/s Actual Achievements

Top management and steering committee must monitor plan vs. actual achievement made by different teams. These presentations must be organized monthly and quarterly presentation should be shared by the whole organization. In no way these presentations should be missed. Top management must give top priority to this presentation. Steering committee should ensure that TQM action plan should get implemented through a team effort. The team should be headed by persons who are considered to contribute most to the task and should include 5 to 6 employees who are directly responsible for physical implementation.

6.2.5.2 Evaluate Impact of Successful Activities on Business and Analyze Failures

Once a project is completed, the leader of the team makes summary of the performance in terms of

a. Costs incurred
b. Benefits obtained

He also draws up a comparison of costs and benefits with original estimates as projected in the formulation of TQM improvement action plan. The results of implementation, once verified by the monitoring team, become a case for consideration under the reward scheme. Whereever achievements are not as per plans, reasons for such failures must be analyzed to take corrective actions in future.

6.2.5.3 Conduct Review by the Steering Committee and Endorse Corrective Measures

Each month self-assessment should be done by nominated teams against each enabler and result based on questionnaire (Appendix A1) and average TQM index should be computed to track the progress against goal. The steering committee must review the progress in TQM index over a period of time to track the progress of the organization. Review the strategy if progress is not going as per plan. Steering committee should suggest corrective measures/endorse corrective measures to enhance the progress. The ultimate aim for the steering committee review is to achieve the world-class status of the organization as per plan.

6.2.6 Growth Phase

Growth phase requires effort towards sustaining the achievement and moving towards horizons of attainments. For sustaining the achievement, quality control tools like control chart would be helpful. In the growth phase, once new areas are identified, all the steps explained earlier should be reused taking into account the successes and failures of earlier achievements.

6.2.6.1 Expand Areas of Success and Try Other Approaches

For identifying new vistas of attainment, continuous search for priority areas would be needed. Some of the QC tools that can support this activity would be Pareto chart, Ishikawa diagram etc. At the level of deployment of new techniques we recommend the organization to go for advanced tools such as failure mode and effect analysis, DOE, analysis of variance and monitoring of process capability.

6.2.6.2 Draw Up Plan for Next Phase of TQM Based on Learning from the Successes and Failures

TQM is not a one-time exercise. It is an ongoing exercise, and a continuous process. It is also dynamic in character and should take into consideration changes in the external environment (such as competition, demand and supply conditions, Government rules and regulations, statutory requirements, availability of resources, liberalization and globalization of economy). Similarly, the changes in the internal environment of the organization have to be considered on a continuous basis while drawing up the programme for TQM. It is a full time exercise and calls for a proper organizational structure. Corporate policy must declare that the organization is committed to the philosophy of achieving a continuous growth in TQM at all levels and at all times. Technology plays an important role in bringing down costs of production, upgrading quality and services and improving TQM. What is required is appropriate technology for the organization and not necessarily the 'latest' technology available. Human resource factor is equally important. A motivated, involved human resource is a prerequisite without which the gains of technology cannot be achieved. The foundations of a rational systematic approach to TQM improvement rests on organizational factors, the human factors and the technology factors. It is, therefore, imperative for the organization to draw up plan for next phase of TQM, based on learning from successes and failures. While drawing up this plan the help of benchmarking tool should be taken.

6.3 CONCLUSIONS

TQM is an imperative in the present-day business environment. In a globally competitive world of work, higher TQM is the only basis of survival and growth. Measurement is vital for managing. If we cannot measure, we cannot manage. Hence the issues of TQM measurement and management addressed to in this book can prove to be very useful.

Unfortunately, TQM is not perceived in totality in majority of situations. The main thrust of arguments in this book is the systems perspective in TQM so that a concerted effort can be planned to enhance TQM. This holistic concept developed is the unique feature that distinguishes it from other efforts. The aspects of external environment, goals and values, structure, technology, people-orientation are factors which have bearing on productivity and TQM. The approach proposed through this treatise is simple, yet comprehensive, is action-oriented and involves entire system in a dynamic sense. Many problems inherent in conventional approaches are circumvented in the process of measuring TQM Index.

TQM and productivity are seen here as interdependent concepts rather than two separate issues. High TQM should imply high productivity. That is why the philosophy proposed here is holistic and based on participative process of continuing nature to maximize customer satisfaction by eliminating waste and reducing variations in the quality of products and services.

A conducted and all-out effort is needed by captains of business and industry to do some serious soul searching and take concrete and effective steps to become world class. It is hoped that the methodology proposed in this book would prove to be an important instrument of change as it looks at the very concept of TQM from a different perspective.

The approach proposed is general purpose and is equally-applicable to small, medium and large systems in manufacturing as well as in service sectors. The quantitative as well as qualitative factors can be incorporated. The approach can be a very logical basis of evaluating organizations for the purpose of achieving world-class TQM Index.

It is hoped that modest contributions made through this volume will change current mindsets on TQM and provide a new fresh look at the concept, measurement approach and the action plans for TQM enhancement in all sphere of our corporate life. The concerned organizations should incorporate these into their efforts for gaining global competitive advantages.

ANNEXURE-1

Survey on TQM Practices in Automobile Industry

INSTRUCTIONS FOR FILLING THE QUESTIONNAIRE

- *This questionnaire comprises of two sections. Section-I deals with general background of the organization and also information on TQM, while Section-II seeks your opinion pertaining to various facets concerning TQM.*
- *There is no right or wrong answer. Please answer each question which suits your organization.*

SECTION-I

General

Name________________Designation________________

Name of the Organization________________________

Address________________________________

Telephone____________Fax____________E-mail____________

Please specify activity of your organization

☐ Automobile Manufacturer ☐ Supplier ☐ Sub-contractor ☐ Others, if any

Information about Total Quality Management (TQM)

a. Is TQM a guiding philosophy in your organization? Yes / No

b. When was it started (year) ? Yes / No

c. Is there any separate TQM cell in your organization?

d. What certification has your organization achieved?

☐ ISO 9000 ☐ QS 9000 ☐ ISO 14001 ☐ Others, if any

e. What is the percentage of on-time delivery?

☐ < 75% ☐ 75-85% ☐ 85-95% ☐ > 95%

f. What is the percentage of self-certified components?

☐ < 25% ☐ 25-50% ☐ 50-75% ☐ 75-100%

g. Do you have cost reduction programme in your organization? If yes, please indicate cost reduction as percentage of sales.

☐ <5% ☐ 5-10% ☐ 10-15% ☐ 15-20%

h. Performance Data

Financial year	1996-97	1997-98	1998-99
Rejection %			
Quality cost as % of sales			
Quality cost as % of total cost			
(i) Prevention cost			
(ii) Appraisal cost			
(iii) Internal failure cost			
(iv) External failure cost			

i. Please indicate quality model used in your organization

(i) CII-Business Excellence Award Model Yes / No
(ii) Crosby's approach to Quality Yes / No
(iii) Deming's approach to Quality Yes / No
(iv) Deming Prize Model Yes / No
(v) European Quality Award (EQA) Model Yes / No
(vi) Feiganbaum's TQC Model Yes / No
(vii) Ishikawa's Quality Model Yes / No
(viii) JRD Tata Quality Award Model Yes / No
(ix) Juran's Model for Quality Yes / No

(x) Malcolm Baldrige National Quality Award Model Yes / No

(xi) Rajeev Gandhi National Quality Award (RGNQA) Model Yes / No

(xii) Taguchi Model Yes / No

(xiii) Others, if any

j. Please indicate quality tools used in your organization.

□5S activities	□ Kaizen activities	□Suggestion scheme
□Pareto diagram	□Scatter plot	□Run chart
□Benchmarking	□SPC	□Brainstorming
□TPM	□PERT/CPM	□Fish bone diagram
□DOE	□PDCA Circle Development	□Quality function
□Why-Why analysis	□BPR	□Failure mode effect analysis A
□Control chart	□Six Sigma	□Histogram

k. Please indicate quality award, if any, has been given to your organization.

l. Please give weightage to the following TQM variables for effective implementation of TQM in your organization

TQM Variables	***Weightage***
Leadership	______
Strategic Planning	______
Information Management	______
Human Resource Focus	______
Customer and Market Focus	______
Suppliers Focus	______
Process Management	______
Impact on Society	______
Human Resource Satisfaction	______
Customer Satisfaction	______
Suppliers Satisfaction	______
Organization specific Business Results	______
Total	**1000**

SECTION-II

This section seeks your opinion pertaining to various facets concerning TQM. There are twelve sub-sections dealing with leadership, strategic planning, information management, human resource focus, customer and market focus, suppliers focus, process management, impact on society, human resource satisfaction, customer satisfaction, suppliers satisfaction & organization specific business results. Please answer the questions putting a tick mark in the appropriate box. 5 indicates excellent marks and '1' indicates poor marks.

1.0 LEADERSHIP

1.1 Top Management Leadership

a. The top management trains the members of the core team (constituted of senior level managers) on group jobs. Always active in providing and receiving training ① ② ③ ④ ⑤

b. The top management actively involve themselves in timely recognition and appreciation of Individual's / Team's contribution ① ② ③ ④ ⑤

c. The top management encourages the core team to set high performance goals and provide appropriate resources ① ② ③ ④ ⑤

d. The top management gives effective consideration to quality of work in appraisal system ① ② ③ ④ ⑤

e. The top management encourages core team to monitor and evaluate the level of performance and assess its effectiveness ① ② ③ ④ ⑤

f. The top management respect and value all employees and encourage open communication and exchange of information among different teams for enhancing innovativeness and creativeness in each individual ① ② ③ ④ ⑤

g. The top management show trust and confidence in their subordinates and empower them to take decision ① ② ③ ④ ⑤

h. The top management is supportive and pay sufficient attention to the needs of the people and maintain comparative status with other similar organizations ① ② ③ ④ ⑤

i. The top management is having personal visible involvement in all aspects of quality management. ① ② ③ ④ ⑤

1.2 Top Management Commitment

a. The top management commits itself to the organization's vision and mission and inform everyone down the line. ① ② ③ ④ ⑤

b. The top management views customers and suppliers as an integral part of value chain. ① ② ③ ④ ⑤

c. The top management gives importance to the suggestions made by the employees and encourages to take up incremental improvement efforts. ① ② ③ ④ ⑤

1.3 Change Management

The top management is committed to change management through

- Benchmarking the organization's performance against the 'best' performer, ① ② ③ ④ ⑤
- Challenges due to the changes in the environmental factors, ① ② ③ ④ ⑤
- Poor performance of the organization due to internal factors. ① ② ③ ④ ⑤
- Others, if any ① ② ③ ④ ⑤

2.0 STRATEGIC PLANNING

The top management gives importance to the following:

a. The top management is committed to spend enough time for understanding the changing business scenario and its implications. ① ② ③ ④ ⑤

b. The organization is ready to create a high level vision and mission of what it can be like in future in the changing business scenario. ① ② ③ ④ ⑤

c. The organization's strategic planning incorporates the needs of customers after a ① ② ③ ④ ⑤ thorough understanding of their needs, market trends & address realignment of work process to improve customer-focus and operational performance.

d. The profile of organization's strengths, weakness, opportunities and threats forms the basis of strategies. ① ② ③ ④ ⑤

e. Efforts are made to integrate Quality i.e., quality planning, quality control and quality improvement with business strategies. ① ② ③ ④ ⑤

f. The organization's strategies are targeted for quantified measurable improvement in quality, cycle/response time and waste reduction. ① ② ③ ④ ⑤

g. Long term perspective is more important than short term gains. ① ② ③ ④ ⑤

h. Commitment of resources for new facilities, process improvements, and training is done considering long term objectives. ① ② ③ ④ ⑤

3.0 INFORMATION MANAGEMENT

3.1 Information Technology (IT)

a. Information Technology (IT) is being used to improve the co-ordination and information access across various departments. ① ② ③ ④ ⑤

b. IT has transformed unstructured processes into routine transactions through shared databases. ① ② ③ ④ ⑤

c. IT is being used to transfer information rapidly and easily across large distances, making the process independent of geography. ① ② ③ ④ ⑤

d. IT is being used to connect two parties (internal or external) within a process that would otherwise communicate through intermediaries. ① ② ③ ④ ⑤

e. IT and communication technologies are used to spread information and to reduce time lag. ① ② ③ ④ ⑤

3.2 Shared Information

a. Organization's working system and procedures promotes easy upward flow of information. ① ② ③ ④ ⑤

b. Employees usually feel free to share information with their managers and/or colleagues. ① ② ③ ④ ⑤

c. Organization uses information on product performance, customer feedback/complaints etc. for quality improvement ① ② ③ ④ ⑤

d. Organization reviews and updates all data before integrating in process improvement plans. ① ② ③ ④ ⑤

e. Organization uses supplier performance related data for quality improvement efforts. ① ② ③ ④ ⑤

f. Organization's information management system is easily accessible throughout the organization. ① ② ③ ④ ⑤

g. Organization uses past performance data to improve understanding of processes ① ② ③ ④ ⑤

h. Organization periodically evaluates & improves its processes so as to further improve overall performance ① ② ③ ④ ⑤

i. Organization gives priority to product quality improvements decision vis-à-vis financial performance. ① ② ③ ④ ⑤

4.0 HUMAN RESOURCE FOCUS

4.1 Human Resource Development

a. Organization's business plan considers human resources capabilities for addressing quality leadership opportunities. ① ② ③ ④ ⑤

b. The investment in education and training is decided considering employee needs and future business needs. ① ② ③ ④ ⑤

c. Employees are encouraged to write, follow and improve upon the standard operating procedures. ① ② ③ ④ ⑤

d. Employees are empowered to reduce the non value adding activities. ① ② ③ ④ ⑤

e. Employees are encouraged to involve and participate in decision making of major policy changes, that enable to soften the resistance to change. ① ② ③ ④ ⑤

f. Employees are encouraged to develop multi skills and capabilities (through job rotation). ① ② ③ ④ ⑤

g. Organization evaluates and improves its human resource planning using employee's feedback ① ② ③ ④ ⑤

h. Organization encourages employees to bring their problems without any hesitation to the seniors for resolution ① ② ③ ④ ⑤

i. Organization makes effort to integrate employees job performance with key quality improvement targets and business results. ① ② ③ ④ ⑤

j. Organization offers stress control programmes for the employees, so as to improve quality of their work life. ① ② ③ ④ ⑤

k. Organization is concerned about employee well being (Health, safety, and ergonomics). ① ② ③ ④ ⑤

4.2 Employees Involvement

a. Employees are enthusiastic in supporting the vision and mission of the organization. ① ② ③ ④ ⑤

b. Each and every employee contributes significantly for the success of organization. ① ② ③ ④ ⑤

c. Employees are responsible in maintaining safe working environment. ① ② ③ ④ ⑤

4.3 Shared Information

a. Efforts are made to recognize and reward the accomplishments of the employees. ① ② ③ ④ ⑤

b. The recognition and rewards to the employees are timely and sincere. ① ② ③ ④ ⑤

c. Efforts are made to recognize and reward the team oriented behaviour. ① ② ③ ④ ⑤

d. Efforts are made to understand the family and home life of the employees. ① ② ③ ④ ⑤

5.0 CUSTOMER AND MARKET FOCUS

5.1 Customer Knowledge

a. Organization regularly determines customer's current requirements and expectations ① ② ③ ④ ⑤

b. Organization selects customer groups/ market segments with intention of adding quality-conscious customers ① ② ③ ④ ⑤

c. Organization determine specific product features and their relative importance using customer listening techniques like QFD etc. ① ② ③ ④ ⑤

d. Organization analyses and uses information on customer loss/gain and product performance to develop future strategies. ① ② ③ ④ ⑤

e. Organization addresses future needs taking into account competitor's customer, and changing market segments ① ② ③ ④ ⑤

f. Organization regularly evaluates and improves upon its processes based on changing customer expectations. ① ② ③ ④ ⑤

5.2 Customer Relationship

a. Commitment like guarantee/warranty etc. are simple and are effectively communicated to the customers. ① ② ③ ④ ⑤

b. Organization regularly evaluates and improves their commitments for service performance to match customer expectations. ① ② ③ ④ ⑤

c. Organization follow up with customers on product performance and builds long term relationship. ① ② ③ ④ ⑤

d. Organization has an effective system to reward and motivate customer-contact employees. ① ② ③ ④ ⑤

e. Organization regularly evaluates and uses the customer feedback to improve performance standards. ① ② ③ ④ ⑤

6.0 SUPPLIER FOCUS

a. Members of the major suppliers' work jointly in teams on issues like new product development, resource saving and energy conservation ① ② ③ ④ ⑤

b. The organization shares the following resources and system with major suppliers. ① ② ③ ④ ⑤

- Financial and accounting system, ① ② ③ ④ ⑤

- Financial resources, ① ② ③ ④ ⑤
- Information system, ① ② ③ ④ ⑤
- Quality system, ① ② ③ ④ ⑤
- Training facilities. ① ② ③ ④ ⑤
- Technical expertise, ① ② ③ ④ ⑤
- Others, if any ① ② ③ ④ ⑤

c. Material supplied by vendors is accepted:

- by thumb rule inspection, ① ② ③ ④ ⑤
- by sampling inspection, ① ② ③ ④ ⑤
- by certification of the vendor. ① ② ③ ④ ⑤
- by 100% inspection, ① ② ③ ④ ⑤
- Others, if any ① ② ③ ④ ⑤

d. The assessment of the strength of suppliers is based on:

- Vendor rating system (based on quality, price and delivery schedule) ① ② ③ ④ ⑤
- Technical competence, ① ② ③ ④ ⑤
- Others, if any ① ② ③ ④ ⑤
- Overall management competence. ① ② ③ ④ ⑤

e. The organization has a goal to develop the suppliers ① ② ③ ④ ⑤

7.0 PROCESS MANAGEMENT

7.1 Product Management

a. Organization's product design considers customer's implied and future likely needs also. ① ② ③ ④ ⑤

b. Organization validates its product designs taking into account performance, process, and supplier capabilities. ① ② ③ ④ ⑤

c. Company evaluates and improves design, and design processes so as to improve product quality and cycle/response time. ① ② ③ ④ ⑤

d. Organization determines the cause of variations, make corrections, and integrate them into the process using statistical techniques etc. ① ② ③ ④ ⑤

7.2 Process Management

a. Organization regularly evaluates and maintains ① ② ③ ④ ⑤

the key business process, their requirements, quality, and operational performance.

b. Organization makes use of benchmarking / customers information for business and support service process improvement. ① ② ③ ④ ⑤

c. Organization effectively uses alternative technology, process research and testing for business process improvement. ① ② ③ ④ ⑤

8.0 IMPACT ON SOCIETY

a. Organization is effectively satisfying the needs and expectations of the society at large. ① ② ③ ④ ⑤

b. Organization effectively evaluates possible impacts of its products and operations on society. ① ② ③ ④ ⑤

c. Adequate efforts are made in the alignment of work plans with the available resources. ① ② ③ ④ ⑤ ① ② ③ ④ ⑤

d. Organization effectively promotes ethical conduct in all activities that it does and organization's Ad-campaigns are truthful and reflects facts.

e. Organization effectively considers quality of work-life while deciding service conditions of employees. ① ② ③ ④ ⑤

f. Organization effectively considers energy conservation and preservation of global resources/ raw materials. ① ② ③ ④ ⑤

g. Organization consider utilization of the recycled materials and makes effective efforts to improve upon it. ① ② ③ ④ ⑤

h. Organization makes efforts to impart education and training to community at large/neighbourhood with respect to its products and services. ① ② ③ ④ ⑤

9.0 HUMAN RESOURCE SATISFACTION

a. Employees satisfaction level is regularly reviewed & corrective action taken. ① ② ③ ④ ⑤

b. Existing system of incentive and reward are adequate for maximum employee contribution. ① ② ③ ④ ⑤

c. Efforts are made by the organization to improve job skills of the employees and improvements are visible. ① ② ③ ④ ⑤

d. The employees' motivation level is very high and consistently high performance is effectively rewarded. ① ② ③ ④ ⑤

e. Organization's image as an employer is good and organization is able to attract best talent from market. ① ② ③ ④ ⑤

9.1 Team Work

a. The team members trust one another. ① ② ③ ④ ⑤

b. The team members appreciate constructive criticism. ① ② ③ ④ ⑤

c. There is intense communication within the teams to generate good and great ideas, about potential changes and solutions to problems. ① ② ③ ④ ⑤

d. Team members are exposed to training on benchmarking, project management and other tools and techniques to carry out the change effort successfully. ① ② ③ ④ ⑤

e. The team members create their performance measurement system. ① ② ③ ④ ⑤

9.2 Values

a. Employees in the organization understand that each and every job is essential and important, and every individual makes a difference. ① ② ③ ④ ⑤

b. Employees believe in accepting the ownership of problems and solve them. ① ② ③ ④ ⑤

c. Employees in the organization believe that "We succeed or fail together as a team not as individuals." ① ② ③ ④ ⑤

d. Employees believe in superior quality and service. ① ② ③ ④ ⑤

9.3 Industrial Relations

a. The organization has cordial and good industrial relations between the labour and management. ① ② ③ ④ ⑤

b. There is discussion across the table on the demands made by either side to sort out the issues, without keeping any issues pending. ① ② ③ ④ ⑤

10.0 CUSTOMER SATISFACTION

a. Organization effectively determines customer satisfaction and makes effective efforts to improve it further. ① ② ③ ④ ⑤

b. Customer satisfaction level is effectively compared with that of key competitors based on in-house scientific studies. ① ② ③ ④ ⑤

c. Customer satisfaction level is effectively compared with that of key competitors by using independent surveys. ① ② ③ ④ ⑤

d. Customers' feedback is collected and used to improve the products and customer service. ① ② ③ ④ ⑤

e. Efforts are made to anticipate the customers' needs, requests and probable complaints that will enable the company to respond in real time. ① ② ③ ④ ⑤

f. Management team and regular customers discuss on key policy issues. ① ② ③ ④ ⑤

g. Top management executives base their decisions on the customers data base analysis rather than their previous experience in business. ① ② ③ ④ ⑤

h. Customers have a 'single point of contact' in the organization. ① ② ③ ④ ⑤

i. Service to internal customers is improved by actively involving different functional departments and units. ① ② ③ ④ ⑤

j. The organization collects and analyses the data on customer dissatisfaction concerning ① ② ③ ④ ⑤
   - Organization's products, ① ② ③ ④ ⑤
   - Organization's service ① ② ③ ④ ⑤

11.0 SUPPLIER SATISFACTION

a. What is the level of the quality of your supplier performance as compared to suppliers of your key competitors? ① ② ③ ④ ⑤

b. Organization constantly endeavours for development of capabilities of its suppliers. ① ② ③ ④ ⑤

12.0 ORGANIZATION SPECIFIC BUSINESS RESULTS

a. Organization enjoys product quality leadership for the range of products it deals with. ① ② ③ ④ ⑤

b. Organization has significantly improved the product quality from last Financial Year. ① ② ③ ④ ⑤

c. Organization has significantly reduced the product cost from last Financial Year. ① ② ③ ④ ⑤

d. Organization has significantly improved the product from the view point of production cycle /response-time from last Financial Year. ① ② ③ ④ ⑤

ANNEXURE-2

SUB-MODEL 1: EXTERNAL ENABLER STRONG

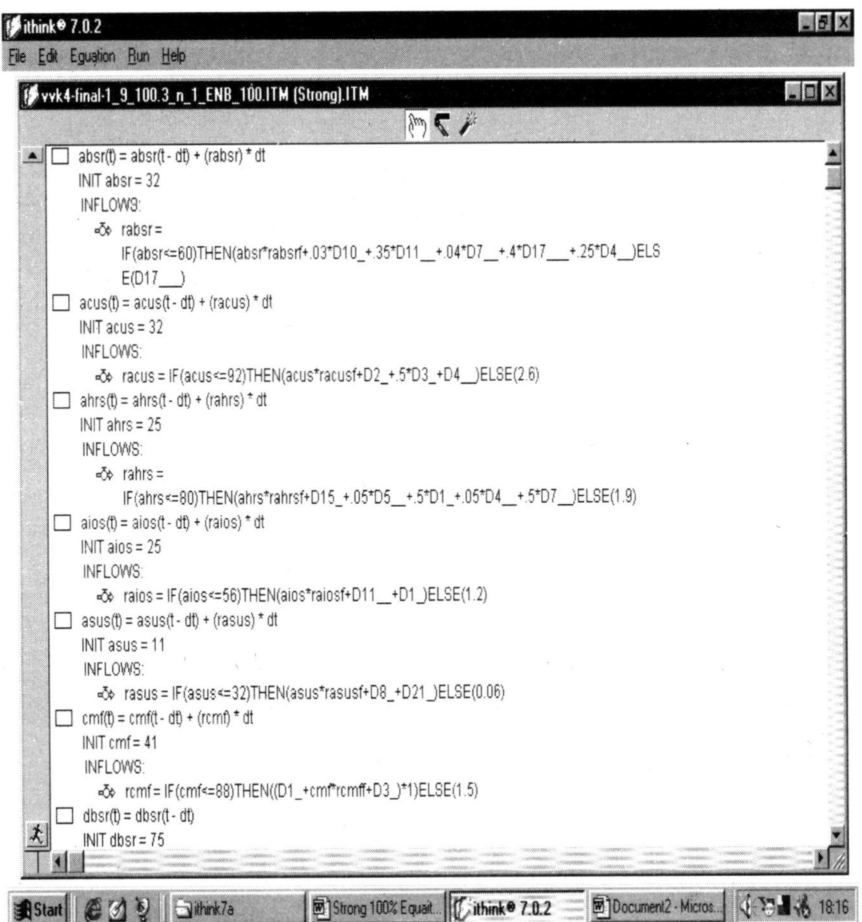

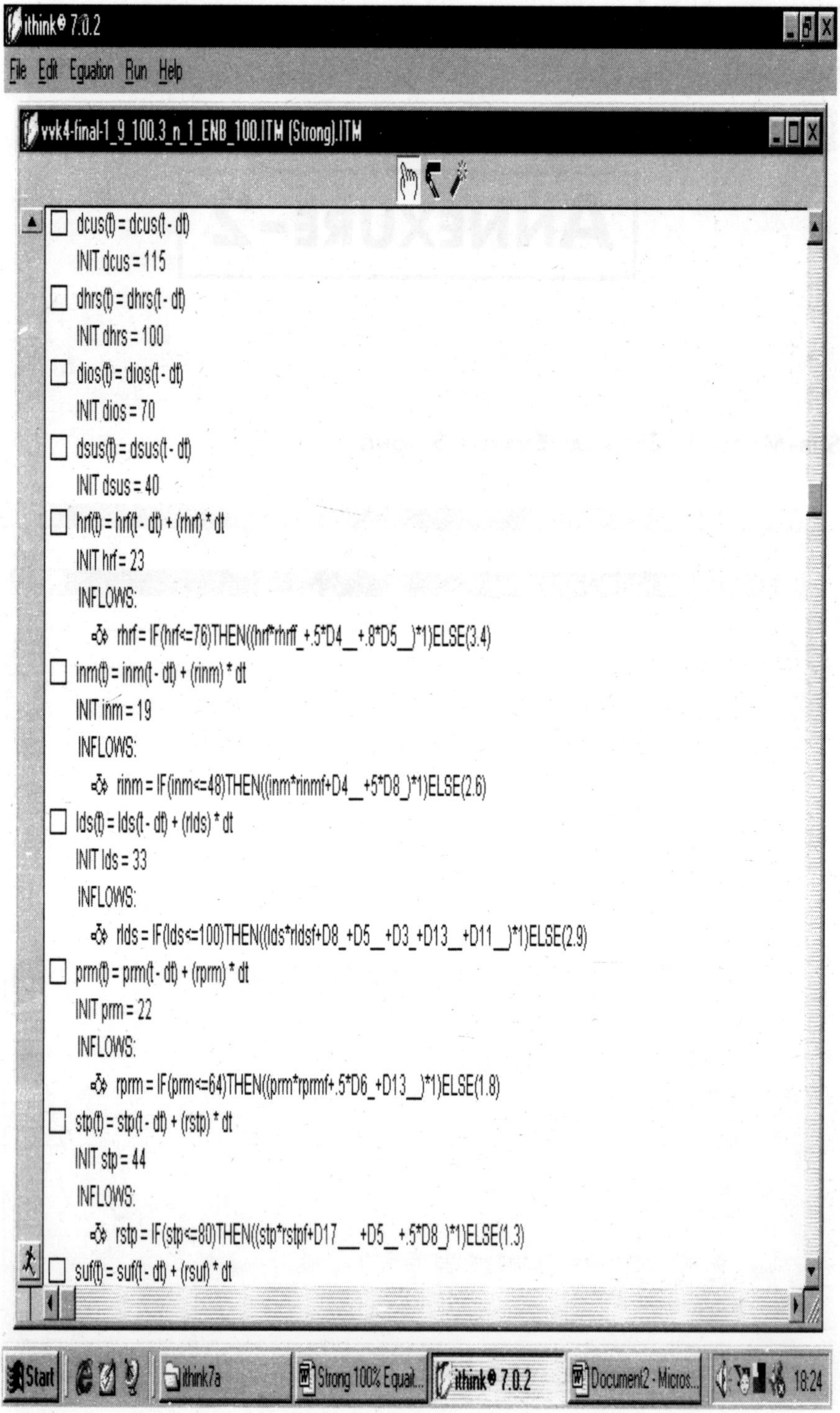

ithink® 7.0.2

File Edit Equation Run Help

vvk4-final-1_9_100.3_n_1_ENB_100.ITM (Strong).ITM

```
dcus(t) = dcus(t - dt)
  INIT dcus = 115
dhrs(t) = dhrs(t - dt)
  INIT dhrs = 100
dios(t) = dios(t - dt)
  INIT dios = 70
dsus(t) = dsus(t - dt)
  INIT dsus = 40
hrf(t) = hrf(t - dt) + (rhrf) * dt
  INIT hrf = 23
  INFLOWS:
    rhrf = IF(hrf<=76)THEN((hrf*rhrff_+.5*D4__+.8*D5__)*1)ELSE(3.4)
inm(t) = inm(t - dt) + (rinm) * dt
  INIT inm = 19
  INFLOWS:
    rinm = IF(inm<=48)THEN((inm*rinmf+D4__+5*D8_)*1)ELSE(2.6)
lds(t) = lds(t - dt) + (rlds) * dt
  INIT lds = 33
  INFLOWS:
    rlds = IF(lds<=100)THEN((lds*rldsf+D8_+D5__+D3_+D13__+D11__)*1)ELSE(2.9)
prm(t) = prm(t - dt) + (rprm) * dt
  INIT prm = 22
  INFLOWS:
    rprm = IF(prm<=64)THEN((prm*rprmf+.5*D6_+D13__)*1)ELSE(1.8)
stp(t) = stp(t - dt) + (rstp) * dt
  INIT stp = 44
  INFLOWS:
    rstp = IF(stp<=80)THEN((stp*rstpf+D17___+D5__+.5*D8_)*1)ELSE(1.3)
suf(t) = suf(t - dt) + (rsuf) * dt
```

Start | ithink7a | Strong 100% Equat... | ithink® 7.0.2 | Document2 - Micros... | 18:24

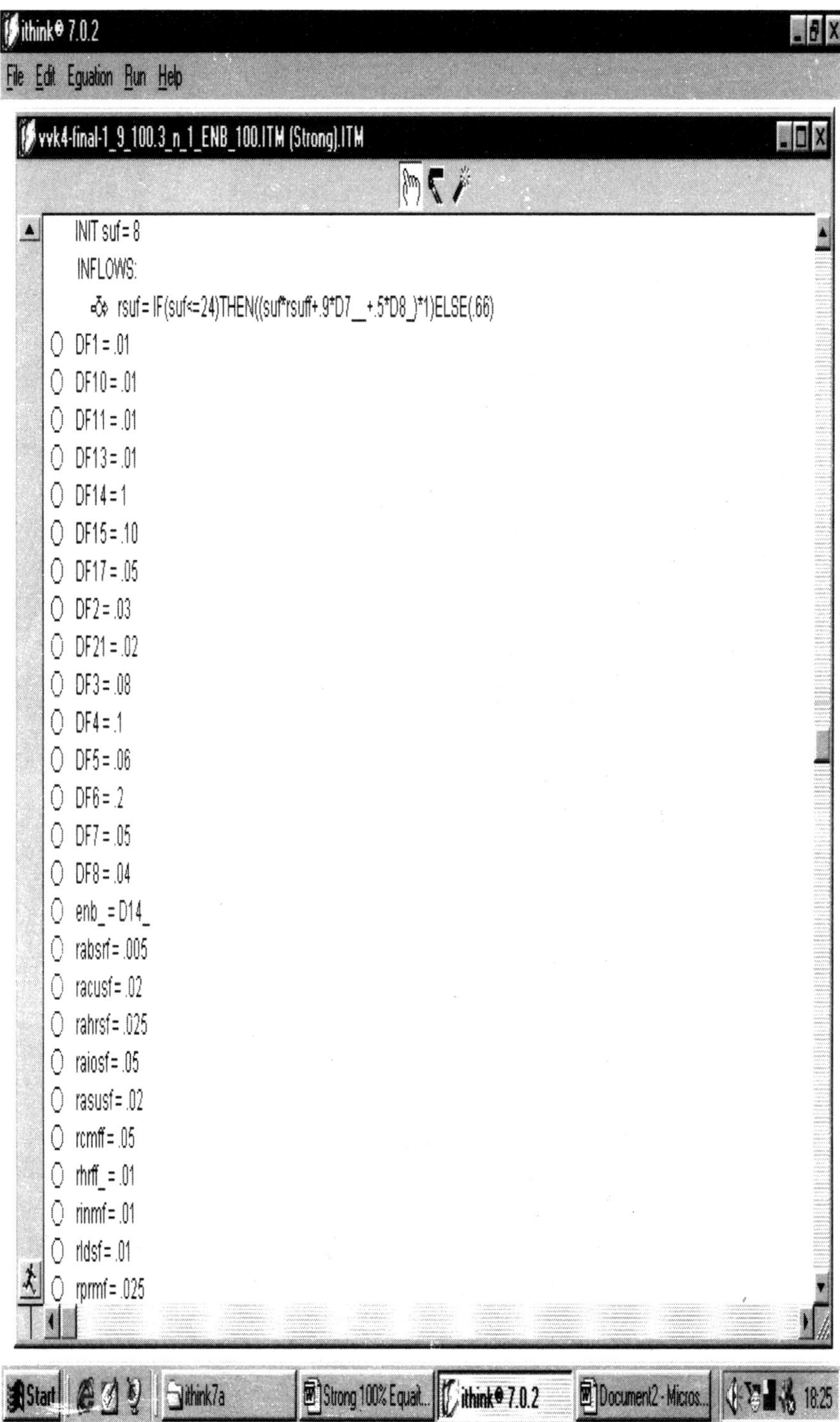
ithink® 7.0.2
File Edit Equation Run Help
vvk4-final-1_9_100.3_n_1_ENB_100.ITM (Strong).ITM
INIT suf = 8
INFLOWS:
rsuf = IF(suf<=24)THEN((suf*rsuff+.9*D7__+.5*D8_)*1)ELSE(.66)
DF1 = .01
DF10 = .01
DF11 = .01
DF13 = .01
DF14 = 1
DF15 = .10
DF17 = .05
DF2 = .03
DF21 = .02
DF3 = .08
DF4 = .1
DF5 = .06
DF6 = .2
DF7 = .05
DF8 = .04
enb_ = D14_
rabsrf = .005
racusf = .02
rahrsf = .025
raiosf = .05
rasusf = .02
rcmff = .05
rhrff_ = .01
rinmf = .01
rldsf = .01
rprmf = .025
Start
ithink7a
Strong 100% Equait...
ithink® 7.0.2
Document2 - Micros...
18:25

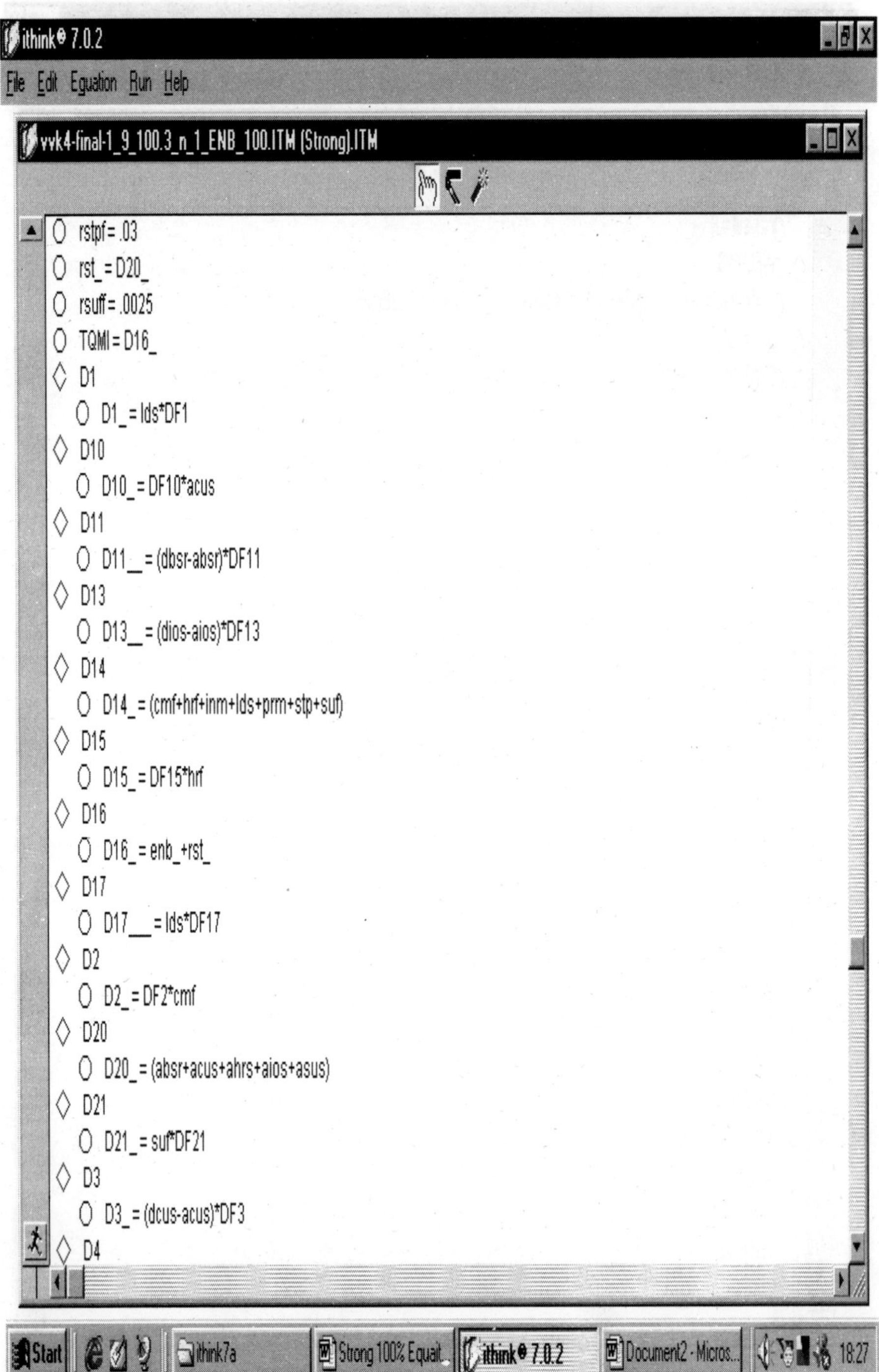
ithink® 7.0.2
File Edit Equation Run Help
vvk4-final-1_9_100.3_n_1_ENB_100.ITM (Strong).ITM
rstpf = .03
rst_ = D20_
rsuff = .0025
TQMI = D16_
D1
D1_ = lds*DF1
D10
D10_ = DF10*acus
D11
D11__ = (dbsr-absr)*DF11
D13
D13__ = (dios-aios)*DF13
D14
D14_ = (cmf+hrf+inm+lds+prm+stp+suf)
D15
D15_ = DF15*hrf
D16
D16_ = enb_+rst_
D17
D17___ = lds*DF17
D2
D2_ = DF2*cmf
D20
D20_ = (absr+acus+ahrs+aios+asus)
D21
D21_ = suf*DF21
D3
D3_ = (dcus-acus)*DF3
D4
Start
ithink7a
Strong 100% Equat...
ithink® 7.0.2
Document2 - Micros...
18:27

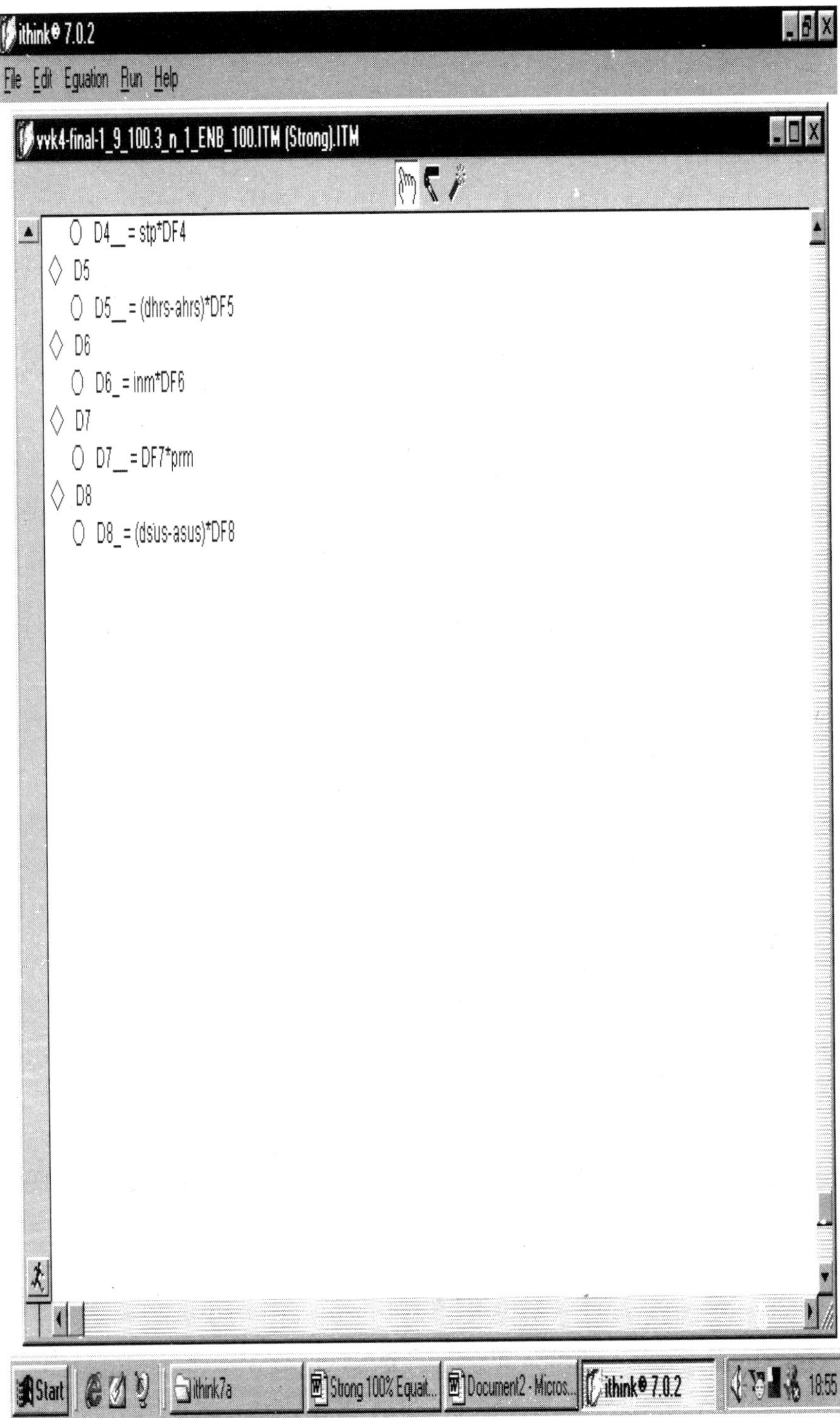
ithink® 7.0.2
File Edit Equation Run Help
vvk4-final-1_9_100.3_n_1_ENB_100.ITM (Strong).ITM
D4__ = stp*DF4
D5
D5__ = (dhrs-ahrs)*DF5
D6
D6_ = inm*DF6
D7
D7__ = DF7*prm
D8
D8_ = (dsius-asus)*DF8
Start
ithink7a
Strong 100% Equat...
Document2 - Micros...
ithink® 7.0.2
18:55

ANNEXURE-3

SUB-MODEL 2: EXTERNAL ENABLER MODERATE

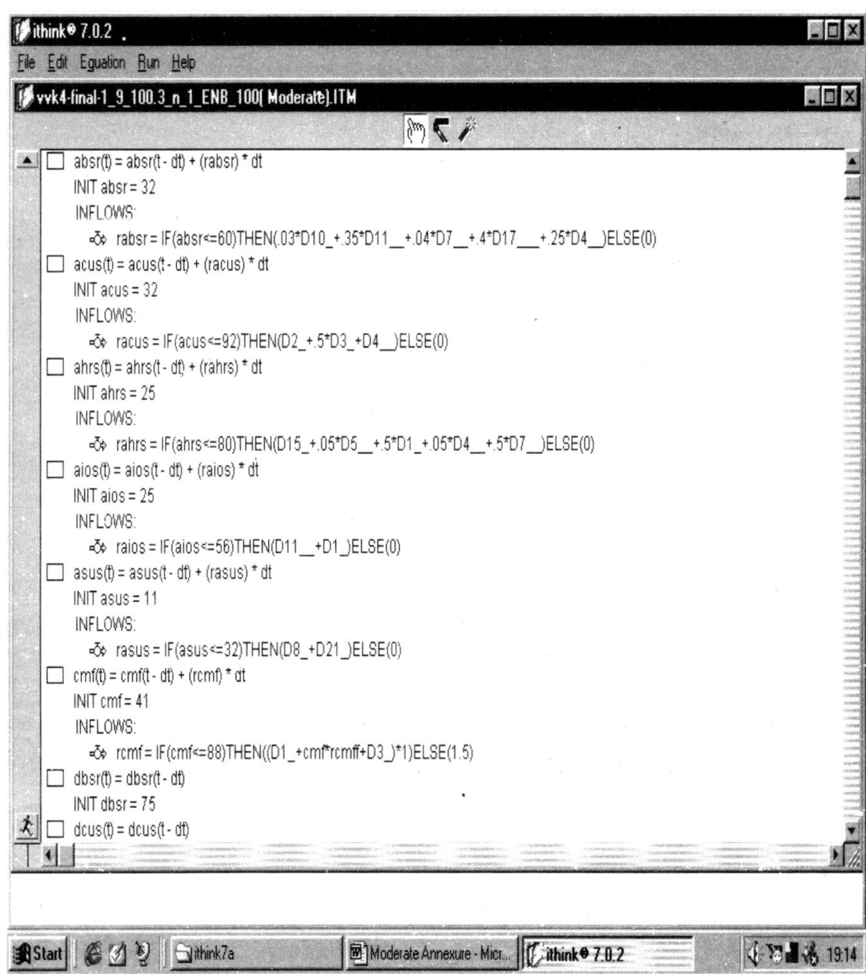

```
ithink® 7.0.2
File Edit Equation Run Help
vvk4-final-1_9_100.3_n_1_ENB_100( Moderate).ITM

absr(t) = absr(t - dt) + (rabsr) * dt
    INIT absr = 32
    INFLOWS:
        rabsr = IF(absr<=60)THEN(.03*D10_+.35*D11__+.04*D7__+.4*D17___+.25*D4__)ELSE(0)
acus(t) = acus(t - dt) + (racus) * dt
    INIT acus = 32
    INFLOWS:
        racus = IF(acus<=92)THEN(D2_+.5*D3_+D4__)ELSE(0)
ahrs(t) = ahrs(t - dt) + (rahrs) * dt
    INIT ahrs = 25
    INFLOWS:
        rahrs = IF(ahrs<=80)THEN(D15_+.05*D5__+.5*D1_+.05*D4__+.5*D7__)ELSE(0)
aios(t) = aios(t - dt) + (raios) * dt
    INIT aios = 25
    INFLOWS:
        raios = IF(aios<=56)THEN(D11__+D1_)ELSE(0)
asus(t) = asus(t - dt) + (rasus) * dt
    INIT asus = 11
    INFLOWS:
        rasus = IF(asus<=32)THEN(D8_+D21_)ELSE(0)
cmf(t) = cmf(t - dt) + (rcmf) * dt
    INIT cmf = 41
    INFLOWS:
        rcmf = IF(cmf<=88)THEN((D1_+cmf*rcmff+D3_)*1)ELSE(1.5)
dbsr(t) = dbsr(t - dt)
    INIT dbsr = 75
dcus(t) = dcus(t - dt)
```

Start | ithink7a | Moderate Annexure - Micr... | ithink® 7.0.2 | 19:14

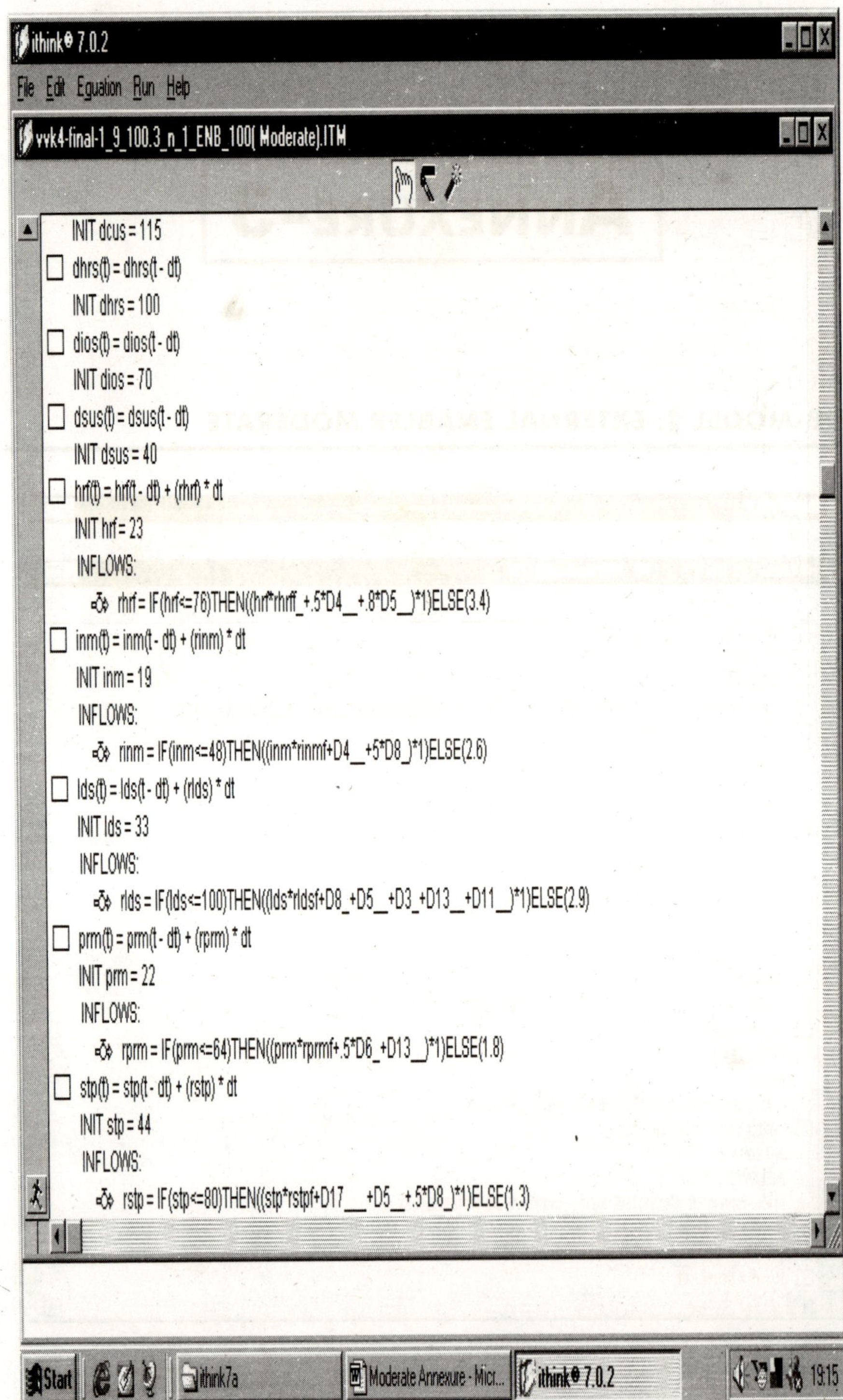
ithink® 7.0.2
File Edit Equation Run Help
vvk4-final-1_9_100.3_n_1_ENB_100(Moderate).ITM
INIT dcus = 115
dhrs(t) = dhrs(t - dt)
INIT dhrs = 100
dios(t) = dios(t - dt)
INIT dios = 70
dsus(t) = dsus(t - dt)
INIT dsus = 40
hrf(t) = hrf(t - dt) + (rhrf) * dt
INIT hrf = 23
INFLOWS:
rhrf = IF(hrf<=76)THEN((hrf*rhrff_+.5*D4__+.8*D5__)*1)ELSE(3.4)
inm(t) = inm(t - dt) + (rinm) * dt
INIT inm = 19
INFLOWS:
rinm = IF(inm<=48)THEN((inm*rinmf+D4__+5*D8_)*1)ELSE(2.6)
lds(t) = lds(t - dt) + (rlds) * dt
INIT lds = 33
INFLOWS:
rlds = IF(lds<=100)THEN((lds*rldsf+D8_+D5__+D3_+D13__+D11__)*1)ELSE(2.9)
prm(t) = prm(t - dt) + (rprm) * dt
INIT prm = 22
INFLOWS:
rprm = IF(prm<=64)THEN((prm*rprmf+.5*D6_+D13__)*1)ELSE(1.8)
stp(t) = stp(t - dt) + (rstp) * dt
INIT stp = 44
INFLOWS:
rstp = IF(stp<=80)THEN((stp*rstpf+D17___+D5__+.5*D8_)*1)ELSE(1.3)
Start
ithink7a
Moderate Annexure - Micr...
ithink® 7.0.2
19:15

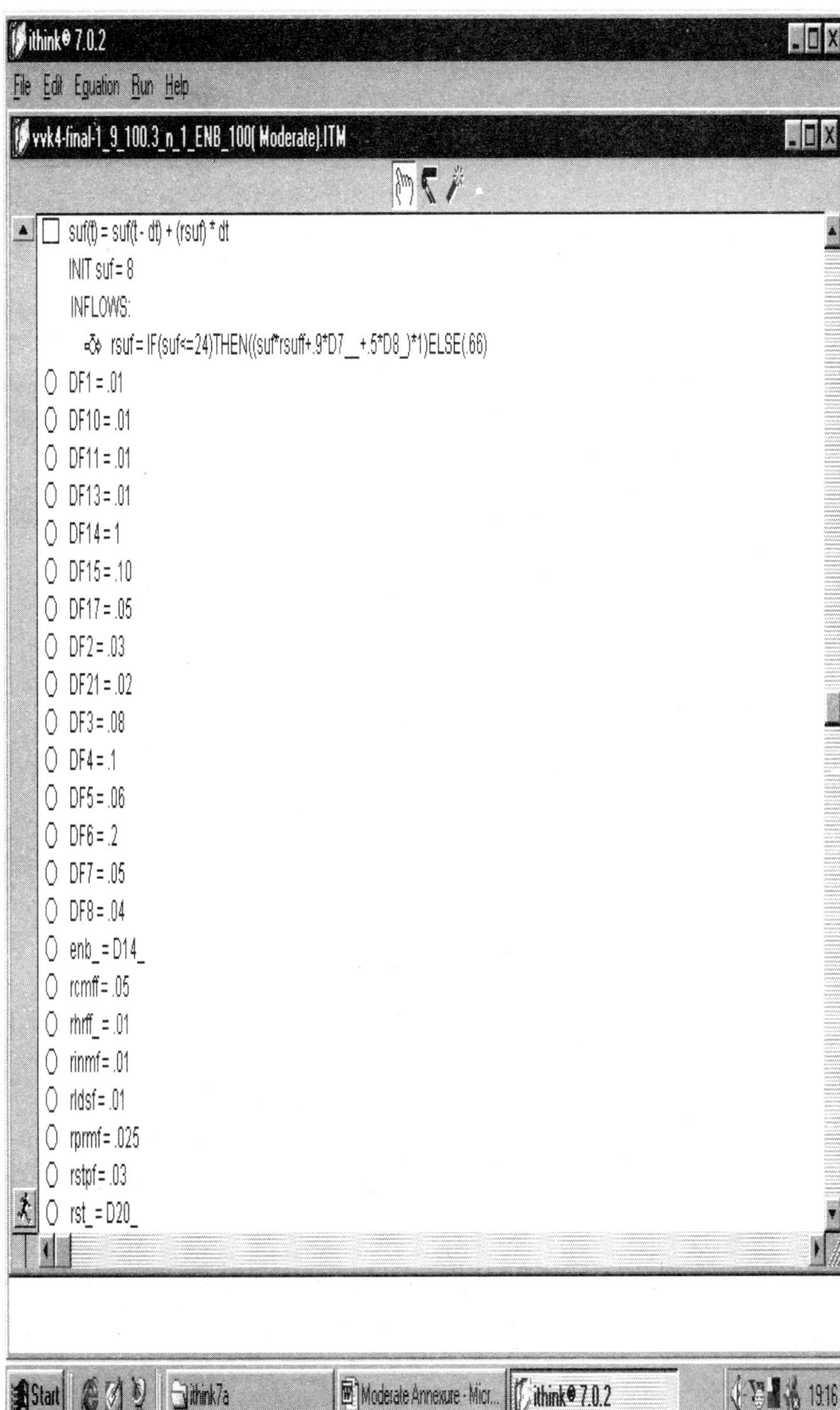
ithink® 7.0.2
File Edit Equation Run Help
vvk4-final-1_9_100.3_n_1_ENB_100(Moderate).ITM
suf(t) = suf(t - dt) + (rsuf) * dt
INIT suf = 8
INFLOWS:
rsuf = IF(suf<=24)THEN((suf*rsuff+.9*D7__+.5*D8_)*1)ELSE(.66)
DF1 = .01
DF10 = .01
DF11 = .01
DF13 = .01
DF14 = 1
DF15 = .10
DF17 = .05
DF2 = .03
DF21 = .02
DF3 = .08
DF4 = .1
DF5 = .06
DF6 = .2
DF7 = .05
DF8 = .04
enb_ = D14_
rcmff = .05
rhrff_ = .01
rinmf = .01
rldsf = .01
rprmf = .025
rstpf = .03
rst_ = D20_
Start
ithink7a
Moderate Annexure - Micr...
ithink® 7.0.2
19:16

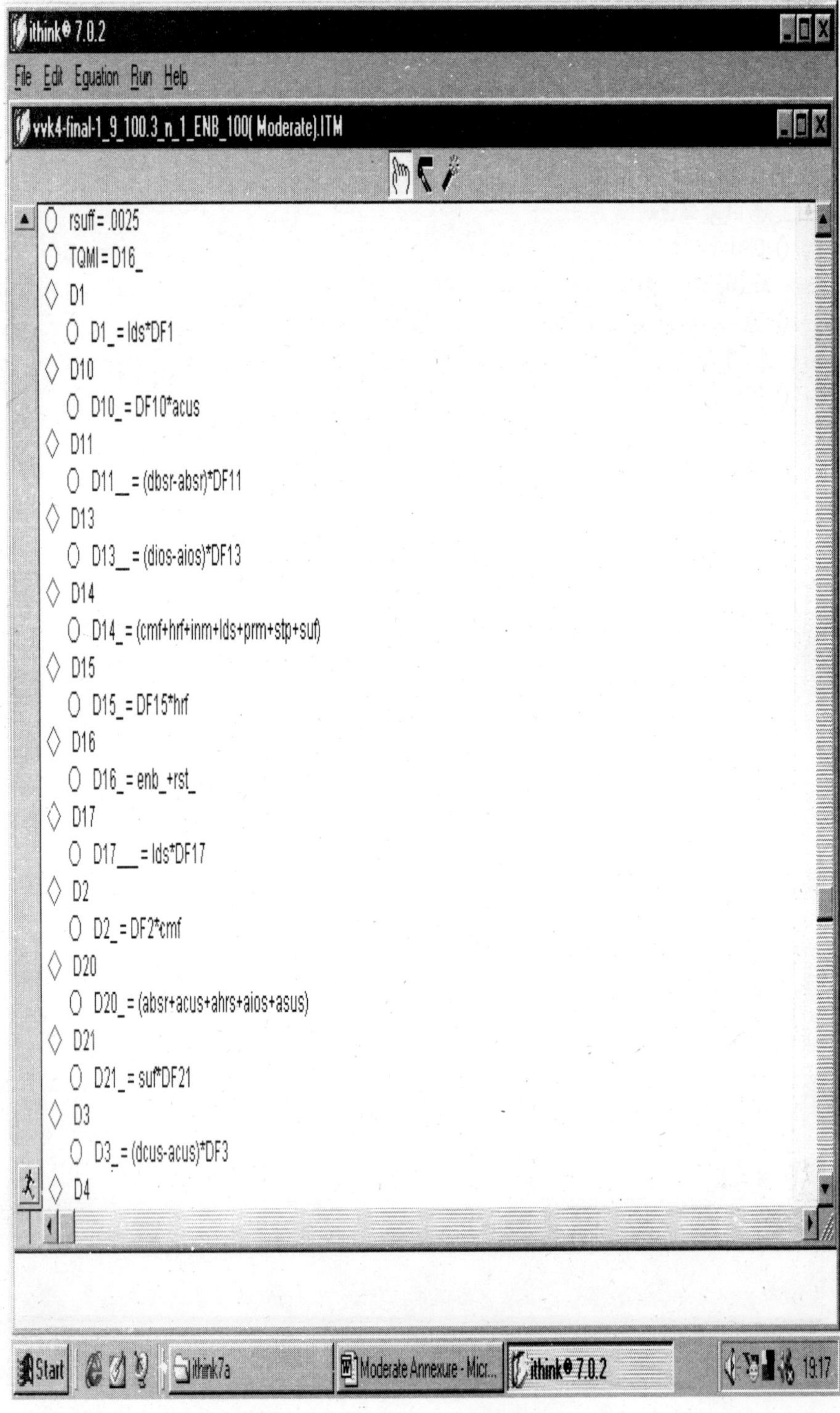
ithink® 7.0.2
File Edit Equation Run Help
vvk4-final-1_9_100.3_n_1_ENB_100(Moderate).ITM
rsuff = .0025
TQMI = D16_
D1
D1_ = lds*DF1
D10
D10_ = DF10*acus
D11
D11__ = (dbsr-absr)*DF11
D13
D13__ = (dios-aios)*DF13
D14
D14_ = (cmf+hrf+inm+lds+prm+stp+suf)
D15
D15_ = DF15*hrf
D16
D16_ = enb_+rst_
D17
D17__ = lds*DF17
D2
D2_ = DF2*cmf
D20
D20_ = (absr+acus+ahrs+aios+asus)
D21
D21_ = suf*DF21
D3
D3_ = (dcus-acus)*DF3
D4
Start
ithink7a
Moderate Annexure - Micr...
ithink® 7.0.2
19:17

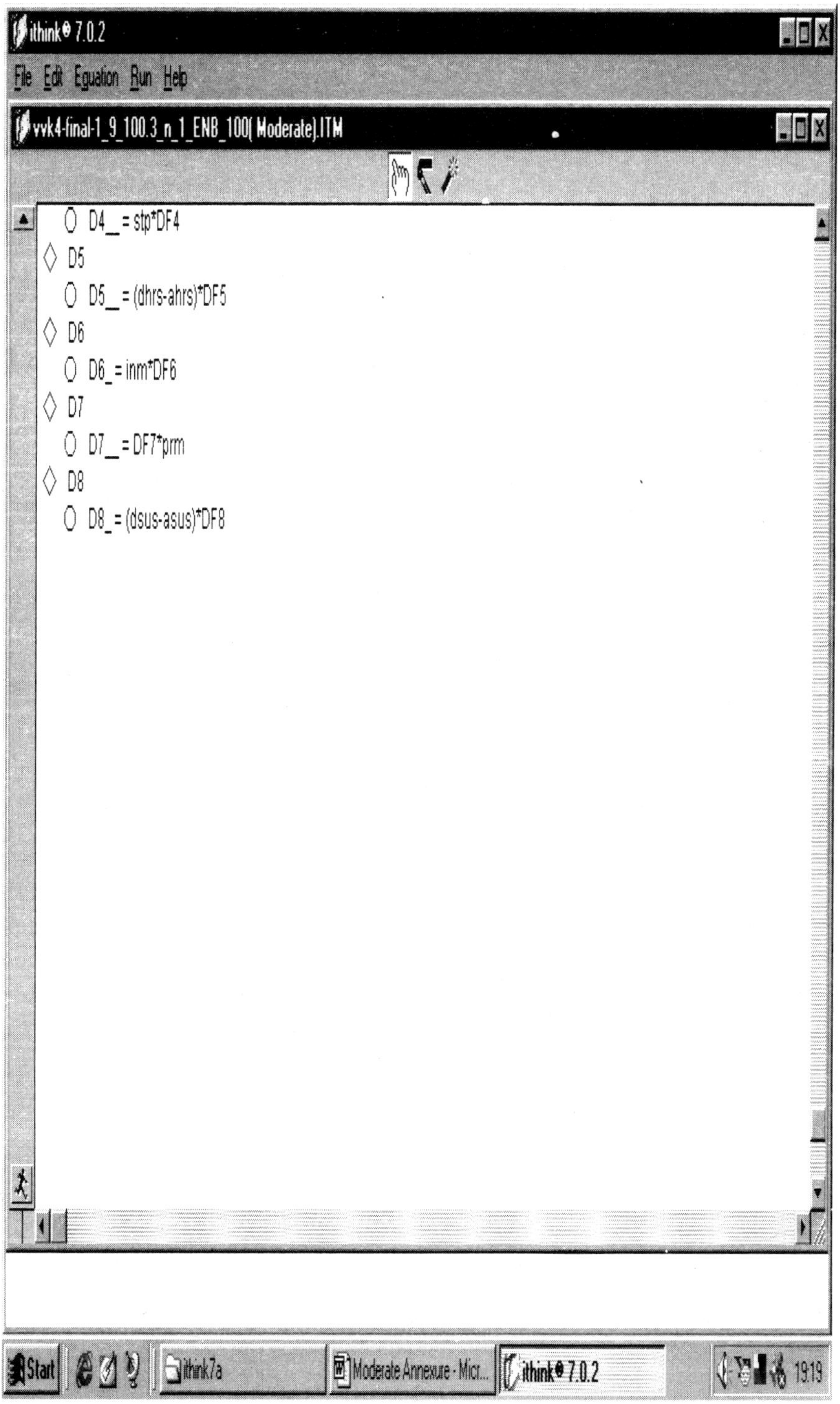

ithink® 7.0.2

File Edit Equation Run Help

vvk4-final-1_9_100.3_n_1_ENB_100(Moderate).ITM

D4__ = stp*DF4

D5

D5__ = (dhrs-ahrs)*DF5

D6

D6_ = inm*DF6

D7

D7__ = DF7*prm

D8

D8_ = (dsus-asus)*DF8

Start ithink7a Moderate Annexure - Micr... ithink® 7.0.2 19:19

ANNEXURE-4

SUB-MODEL 3: EXTERNAL ENABLER WEAK

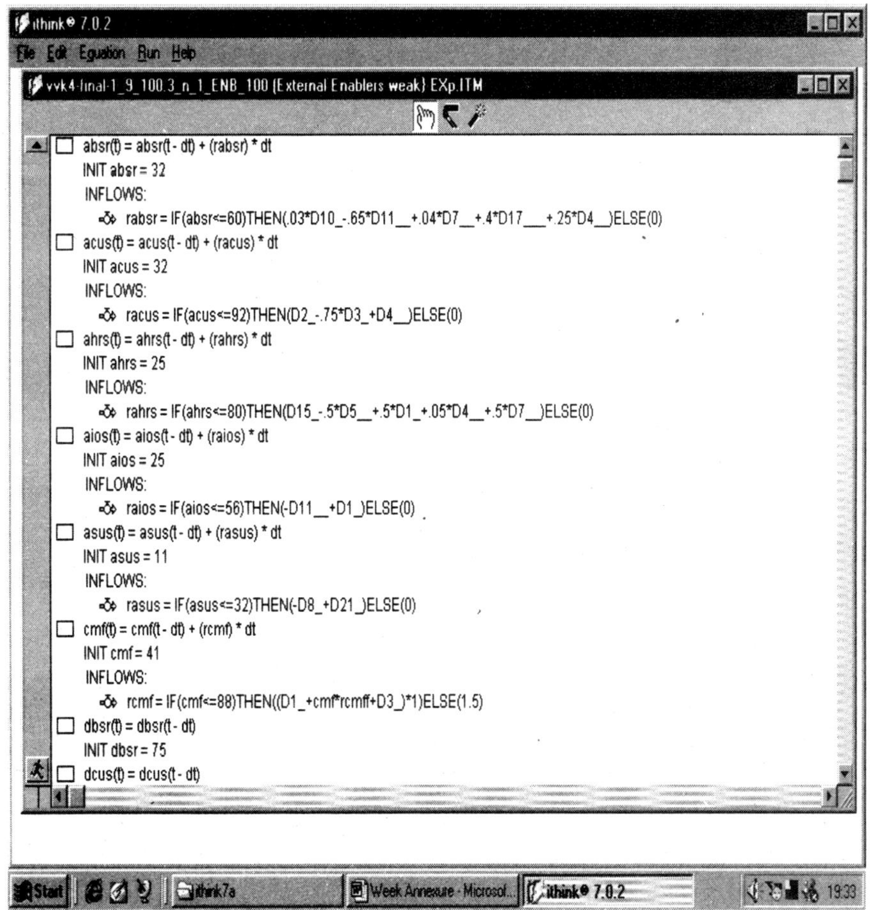

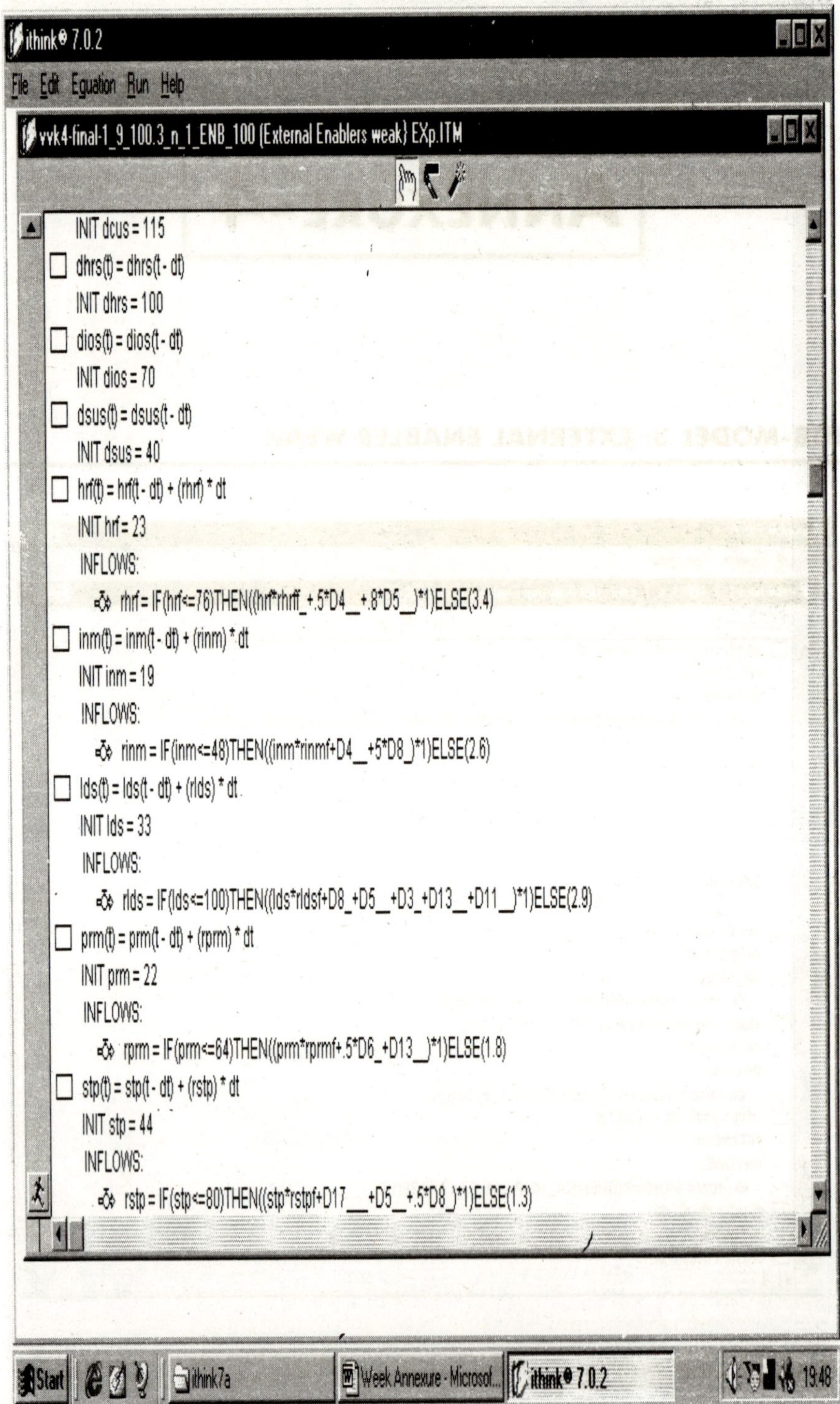
ithink® 7.0.2
File Edit Equation Run Help
vvk4-final-1_9_100.3_n_1_ENB_100 (External Enablers weak) EXp.ITM
INIT dcus = 115
dhrs(t) = dhrs(t - dt)
INIT dhrs = 100
dios(t) = dios(t - dt)
INIT dios = 70
dsus(t) = dsus(t - dt)
INIT dsus = 40
hrf(t) = hrf(t - dt) + (rhrf) * dt
INIT hrf = 23
INFLOWS:
rhrf = IF(hrf<=76)THEN((hrf*rhrff_+.5*D4__+.8*D5_)*1)ELSE(3.4)
inm(t) = inm(t - dt) + (rinm) * dt
INIT inm = 19
INFLOWS:
rinm = IF(inm<=48)THEN((inm*rinmf+D4__+5*D8_)*1)ELSE(2.6)
lds(t) = lds(t - dt) + (rlds) * dt
INIT lds = 33
INFLOWS:
rlds = IF(lds<=100)THEN((lds*rldsf+D8_+D5__+D3_+D13__+D11_)*1)ELSE(2.9)
prm(t) = prm(t - dt) + (rprm) * dt
INIT prm = 22
INFLOWS:
rprm = IF(prm<=64)THEN((prm*rprmf+.5*D6_+D13__)*1)ELSE(1.8)
stp(t) = stp(t - dt) + (rstp) * dt
INIT stp = 44
INFLOWS:
rstp = IF(stp<=80)THEN((stp*rstpf+D17___+D5__+.5*D8_)*1)ELSE(1.3)
Start
ithink7a
Week Annexure - Microsof...
ithink® 7.0.2
19:48

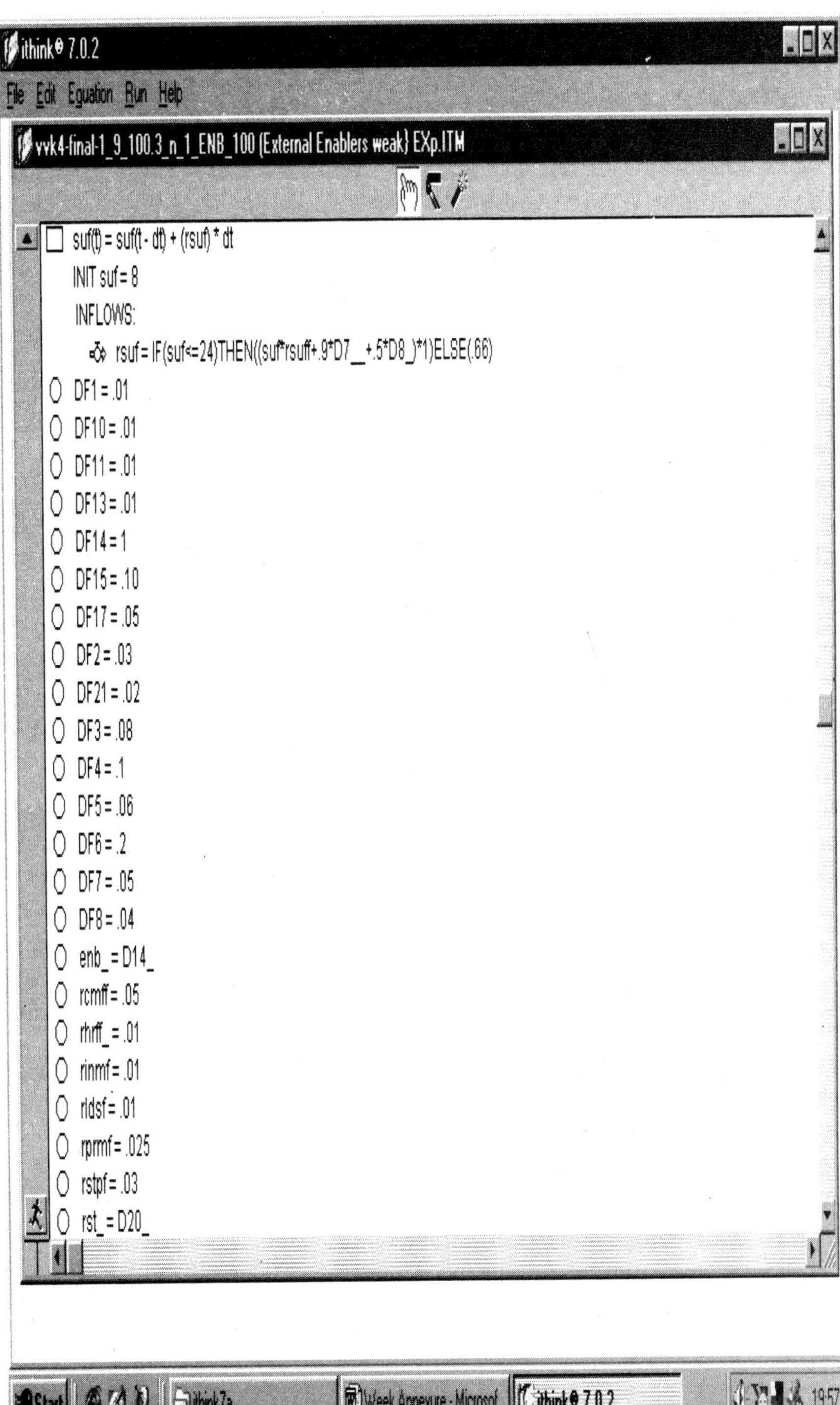
ithink® 7.0.2
File Edit Equation Run Help
vvk4-final-1_9_100.3_n_1_ENB_100 (External Enablers weak) EXp.ITM
suf(t) = suf(t - dt) + (rsuf) * dt
INIT suf = 8
INFLOWS:
rsuf = IF(suf<=24)THEN((suf*rsuff+.9*D7__+.5*D8_)*1)ELSE(.66)
DF1 = .01
DF10 = .01
DF11 = .01
DF13 = .01
DF14 = 1
DF15 = .10
DF17 = .05
DF2 = .03
DF21 = .02
DF3 = .08
DF4 = .1
DF5 = .06
DF6 = .2
DF7 = .05
DF8 = .04
enb_ = D14_
rcmff = .05
rhrff_ = .01
rinmf = .01
rldsf = .01
rprmf = .025
rstpf = .03
rst_ = D20_
Start
ithink7a
Week Annexure - Microsof...
ithink® 7.0.2
19:57

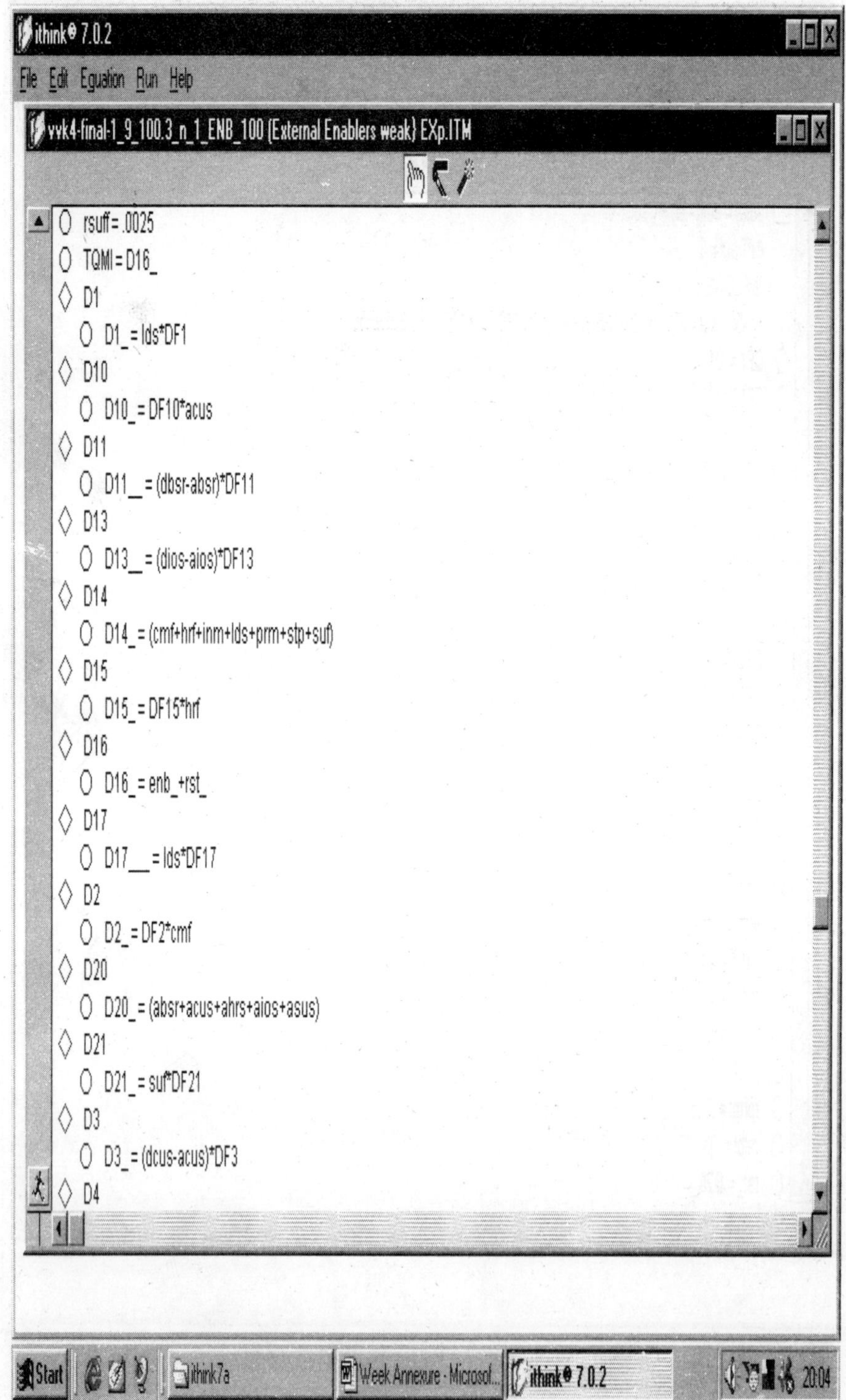
ithink® 7.0.2
File Edit Equation Run Help
vvk4-final-1_9_100.3_n_1_ENB_100 (External Enablers weak) EXp.ITM
rsuff = .0025
TQMI = D16_
D1
D1_ = lds*DF1
D10
D10_ = DF10*acus
D11
D11__ = (dbsr-absr)*DF11
D13
D13__ = (dios-aios)*DF13
D14
D14_ = (cmf+hrf+inm+lds+prm+stp+suf)
D15
D15_ = DF15*hrf
D16
D16_ = enb_+rst_
D17
D17__ = lds*DF17
D2
D2_ = DF2*cmf
D20
D20_ = (absr+acus+ahrs+aios+asus)
D21
D21_ = suf*DF21
D3
D3_ = (dcus-acus)*DF3
D4
Start
ithink7a
Week Annexure - Microsof...
ithink® 7.0.2
20:04

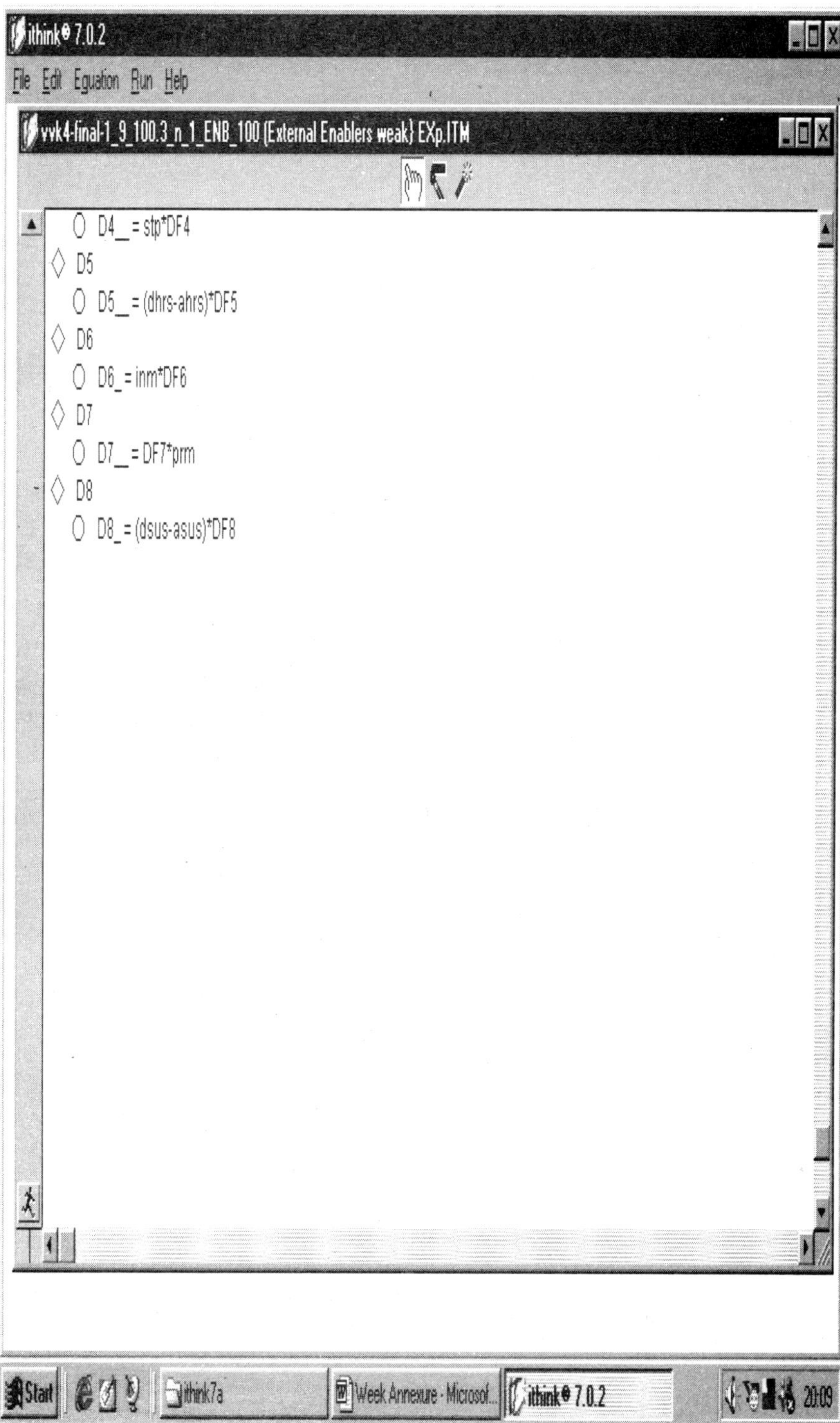
ithink® 7.0.2
File Edit Equation Run Help
vvk4-final-1_9_100.3_n_1_ENB_100 (External Enablers weak) EXp.ITM
D4__ = stp*DF4
D5
D5__ = (dhrs-ahrs)*DF5
D6
D6_ = inm*DF6
D7
D7__ = DF7*prm
D8
D8_ = (dsus-asus)*DF8
Start
ithink7a
Week Annexure - Microsof...
ithink® 7.0.2
20:09

References

1. Abby, G. and Hong, S. W., 1996, Characteristics, Benefits, and Shortcomings of Four Major Quality Awards, *International Journal of Quality & Reliability Management,* Vol. 13, No. 2, pp. 10-44.
2. Abdel-Hamid, T. K., 1984, The Dynamics of Software Development Project Management: An Integrative System Dynamics Perspective, *Unpublished Ph.D. Thesis, Sloan School of Management,* MIT, Cambridge, MA.
3. Adam, E. E., Corbett, L. M., Flores, B. E., Harrison, N. J., Lee, T. S., Rho, B., Ribera, J., Sampson, D. and Westbrook, R., 1997, An International Study of Quality Improvement Approach and Firm Performance, *International Journal of Operations and Production Management,* Vol. 17, No. 9, pp. 842-873.
4. Agrawal, S. K., 1993, ISO 9000 Implementation in Indian Industry, in: *Proceedings of the 8th ISME Conference on Mechanical Engineering,* Indian Institute of Technology Delhi, pp. 638-644.
5. Agrawal, S. K., 1999, Business Excellence Model in Indian Content: A Select Study, *Unpublished Ph.D. Thesis, Indian Institute of Technology (I.I.T.) Delhi,* New Delhi, India.
6. Agrawal, S. K. and Vrat, P., 1993, Issues in Effective Implementation of ISO 9000 in Indian Context, *in: Proceedings of the Seminar on TQM, Indian Institute of Plant Engineers (IIPE),* New Delhi, pp. XIII-1 to XIII-8.
7. Agrawal, S. K., Vrat, P. and Karunes, S., 1996, ISO 9000 Certification and TQM Movement: Some Thoughts on Indian Quality Initiative, *Productivity Promotion Journal,* Vol. 1, No. 2, pp. 78-90.
8. Agrawal, S. K., Vrat, P. and Karunes, S., 1998, Total Quality Management: Indian Experiences, *International Journal of Industrial Engineering,* Vol. 5, No. 3, pp. 214-224.
9. Agusdinata, B. and Klein, W. D., 2002, The Dynamics of Airline Alliances, *Journal of Air Transport Management,* Vol. 8, pp. 201-211, Available at: www.elsevier.com/locate/jairtraman.

10. Ahire, S. L. and Kiran, V., 1995, JIT and TQM: A Case for Joint Implementation, *International Journal of Operations and Production Management,* Vol. 15, No. 5, pp. 84-94.
11. Ahluwalia, J. S., 1993, Total Quality Management: Concepts and Practices, Vanity Books, New Delhi.
12. Ahluwalia, J. S., 1996, Total Quality, Creating Individual and Corporate Success, Institute of Directors Excel Books.
13. Ahmed, A. M., 2002, Virtual integrated performance measurement, *International Journal of Quality & Reliability Management,* Vol. 19, No. 4, pp. 414-441.
14. Ahmed, A. M., Abdalla, H. S. and Knight, J. A., 1998, A surpetitive Strategy for World-class Organizations, *in: Proceedings of the ECEC Conference on Concurrent Engineering: The Way Forward,* Erlangen-Nuremberg, Germany, pp. 37-42.
15. Ahmed, A. M., Yang, J. B. and Dale, B. G., 2003, Self-Assessment Methodology: The Route to Business Excellence, *Quality Management Journal,* Vol. 10, Issue 1, Available at: www.asq.org/pub/qmj/ahmed.html
16. Akao, Y., 1990, Quality Function Deployment, Productivity Press, Cambridge, MA.
17. Akao, Y., 2002, QFD and Knowledge Management, *in: Change Management: Proceedings of the 7th International Conference on ISO 9000 and TQM,* Eds. Samuel. K. M. H. and Dalrymple, J. F., RMIT University, Melbourne, Australia, pp. 83-84.
18. Akao, Y. and Glennh, M., 2003, The Leading Edge in QFD: Past, Present and Future, *International Journal of Quality & Reliability Management,* Vol. 20, No. 1, pp. 20-35.
19. Akkermans, H. A., Bogerd, P. and Vos, B., 1999, Virtuous and Vicious Cycles on the Road Towards International Supply Chain Management, *International Journal of Operations and Production Management,* Vol. 19, Nos. 5-6, pp. 565-581.
20. Anderson, E. G. Jr., 2001, Managing the Impact of High Market Growth and Learning on Knowledge Worker Productivity and Service Quality, *European Journal of Operational Research,* Vol. 134, pp. 508-524, Available at: www.elsevier.com/locate/dsw.
21. Anderson, G. E., 1993, Shouldn't You Own Your Future? Linking Education to Skills in Quality Organization, ASQC Quality Press, Milwaukee, WI.
22. Anderson, J., Rungtusanatham, M. and Schroeder, R., 1994, A theory of Quality Management Underlying the Deming Management Method: Preliminary Empirical Findings, *Academy of Management Review,* Vol. 19, No. 3, pp. 472-509.

23. Anderson, J. C., Rungtusanatham, M., Schroeder, R. G. and Devaraj, S., 1995, A path analytic model of a theory of quality management underlying the Deming management method: preliminary empirical findings, *Decision Sciences,* Vol. 26, No. 5, pp. 637-658.
24. Anderson, R., Sweeney, D. J. and Williams, T. A., 1994, An Introduction to Management Sciences, West New York.
25. Appleby, A. and Mitchell, E. D., 2000, Something for nothing, *in: Proceedings of the 3rd International (Euro) CINet Conference, CI 2000: from improvement to innovation,* Aalborg, 18-19 September, pp. 1-11.
26. Aravindan, P., Devadasan, S. R. and Selladurai, V., 1996, A focused system model for strategic quality management, *International Journal of Quality & Reliability Management,* Vol. 13, No. 8, pp. 79-96.
27. Arora, S. C., 1999, Quality Management – Inherent Link in Supply Chain Management, *in: Supply Chain Management-For Global Competitiveness,* Ed. Sahay, B. S., McMillan India Ltd., pp. 605-612.
28. Atkinson, H., Hamburg, J. and Christopher, I., 1994, Linking Quality to Profits: Quality-Based Cost Management, ASQC Quality Press, Milwaukee, WI.
29. Atkinson, R., 1992, Motivating People for Success, *The TQM Magazine,* Vol. 4, No. 4, pp. 251-253.
30. Aubrey, C. A. II and Felkins, P. K., 1988, Teamwork Involving People in Quality and Productivity Improvement, ASQC Quality Press, Milwaukee, WI.
31. Automeet, 2002, Auto Policy '98' A View from the Industry, Available at: www.automeet.com/ autopolicy1.html.
32. Automobileindia, 2002, Exports-An Overview Available at: www.automobileindia.com/timeline/time18.html.
33. Automotive Component Manufacturers Association of India (ACMA), 2001-02, Facts and Figures, Automotive Industry of India, Available at: www.acmainfo.com.
34. Baig, M. A., 2001, The Share of Cars to Come, THINK INC., New Delhi.
35. Band, W. A., 1991, Creating value for customers, Wiley, New York.
36. Banerjee, P. K. and Ramesh, N., 1993, TQM for Enhanced Plant Availability, Productivity and Profitability, *in: Proceedings of the National Seminar on TQM,* New Delhi, India, pp. 22-31.
37. Barclay, C. A., 1993, Quality strategy and TQM policies: empirical evidence, *Management International Review,* Vol. 33, pp. 87-98.
38. Barlas, Y. and Aksogan, A., 1999, Product Diversification and Quick Response Order Strategies in Supply Chain Management, Available at: http://ieiris.cc.boun.edu.tr/faculty/barlas.

39. Bauer, A., Reiner, G. and Schomschule, R., 2001, Organizational and quality systems development: an analysis via a dynamic simulation model, *Total Quality Management*, Vol. 11, No. 4, pp. 410-416.
40. Bell, J. A. and Senge, P. M., 1980, Methods for Enhancing Reputability in System Dynamics Modeling, *TIMS Studies in the Management Science*, Vol. 14, pp. 61-73.
41. Bemowski, K., 1991, Restoring the Pillars of Higher Education, *Quality Progress*, Vol. 24, No.10, pp. 37-42.
42. Bemowski, K., 1995, TQM: Flimsy Footing or Firm Foundation?, *Quality Progress*, Vol. 28, No. 7, pp. 27-28.
43. Bemowski, K. and Stratton, B., 1995, How do people use the Baldrige criteria?, *Quality Progress*, Vol. 28, No. 5, pp. 43-47.
44. Benson, P. G., Saraph, G. V. and Schroeder, R. G., 1991, The Effects of Organizational Context on Quality Management: An Empirical Investigation, *Management Sciences*, Vol. 37, No. 9, pp. 1107-1124.
45. Bertalanffy, L. V., 1969, General System Theory, Braziller, New York, NY.
46. Beskese, A. and Cebeci, U., 2001, Total Quality Management and ISO 9000 application in Turkey, *The TQM Magazine*, Vol. 13, No. 1, pp. 69-73.
47. Bester, Y., 2000, Analyzing the quality strategy for the 2000s, i*n: Proceedings of the ASQC Quality Congress*, Milwaukee, WI, pp. 359-370.
48. Besterfield, and Dale, H., 1990, Quality Control, Prentice Hall International Inc., New Jersey.
49. Black, S. and Porter, L. J., 1993, Measuring the Critical Factors of Total Quality Management, *Report of University of Bradford,* UK.
50. Black, S. and Porter, L. J., 1995, An Empirical Model for Total Quality Management, *Total Quality Management*, Vol. 6, No. 2, pp. 149-164.
51. Black, S. and Porter, L. J., 1996, Identification of the Critical Factors of TQM, *Decision Sciences*, Vol. 27, No. 1, pp. 1-21.
52. Blakeslee, J. A., 1999, Implementing the Six Sigma Solution, *Quality Progress*, July, pp. 77-85.
53. Boaden, R. J., 1997, What is Total Quality Management….And Does it Matter?, *Total Quality Management*, Vol. 8, No. 4.
54. Bohris, G. A., 1995, A comparative assessment of some major quality awards, *International Journal of Quality & Reliability Management,* Vol. 12, No. 9, pp. 30-43.
55. Boland, T. and Silbergh, D., 1996, Managing for Quality: The Impact of Quality Management Initiatives on Administrative Structure and Resource Management Process in Public Sector Organizations, *International Review of Administrative Science,* Vol. 62, No. 3, pp. 351-367.

56. Bora, M. C. and Mohapatra, P. K. J. 1985, DYNOSIM User's Manual, *Indian Institute of Technology Khargpur,* India.
57. Bossert, J. L., 1990, Quality Function Deployment: A Practitioner's Approach, ASQC Quality Press, Milwaukee.
58. Bounds, G., 1994, Assessing Progress in Total Quality Management, *Productivity,* Vol. 35, No. 3, pp. 405-417.
59. Bounds, G., Yorks, L., Adams, M. and Raney, G., 1994, Beyond Total Quality Management, McGraw-Hill Series Inc.
60. Boznak, R. G. and Decker, A. K., 1993, Competitive Product Development: A Quality Approach to Succeeding in the '90's and Beyond, ASQC Quality Press, Milwaukee, WI.
61. Braganza, A. and Mayers, A., 1997, Business Process Redesign: A View from the Inside, International Thomson Business Press, London.
62. Brans, J. P., Macharis, C., Kunsch, P. C., Chevalier, A. and Schwaninger, M., 1998, Combining multicriteria decision aid and system dynamics for the control of socio-economic processes, An iterative real-time procedure, *European Journal of Operational Research,* Vol. 199, pp. 428-441.
63. Brereton, M., 1996, Introducing self-assessment-One of the keys to business excellence, *Management Services,* Vol. 40, No. 2, pp. 22-23.
64. British Standard, BS 4778, 1991, Quality Vocabulary: Part 2, International Teams, British Standard Institute, London.
65. British Standard, BS 5750: Part 1: 1992, BSI, 1992, Guidance Notes for the Application of BS 5750 to Education and Training, British Standard Institute, London.
66. Broh, R. A., 1982, Managing Quality for Higher Profiles, McGraw-Hill, New York.
67. Brown, M. G., 1994, Baldridge Award Winning Quality: How to Interpret the Malcolm Baldridge Award Criteria, 4th Edition, ASQC Quality Press, Milwaukee, WI.
68. Brown, M. G., 1997, Measuring up against the 1997 Baldrige criteria, *The Journal for Quality and Participation,* Vol. 20, No. 4, pp. 22-28.
69. Brown, M. G., Hitchcock, D. and Willard, M., 1994, Why TQM Fails and What to Do about It, Irwin Professional Publishing, Burr Ridge, IL.
70. Buckley, P. J. and Chapman, M., 1997, The use of native categories in management research, *British Journal of Management,* Vol. 8, No. 4, pp. 283-299.
71. Burchill, G. and Shen, D., 1995, Concept Engineering, Document ML0080, Center for Quality of Management, Cambridge, MA.
72. Burt, D. N., 1989, Managing Product Quality Through Strategic Purchasing, *Sloan Management Review,* Vol. 30, No. 3, pp. 39-48.
73. Business Today, 1995, TQM Survey, January, 7-21, pp. 40-44.

74. Business Today, 1997, 7-21, August, pp. 20-31 and 104-109.
75. Business Today, 2000, The BT-IMC Quality Prescription Survey 2000, Living- Media Publishing, New Delhi, India.
76. Buzel, R. D. and Gale, B. T., 1987, The PIMS Principles: Linking Strategy to Performance, The Free Press, New York.
77. Capon, N., Kaye, M. M. and Wood, M., 1996, Measuring the Success of a TQM Programme, *International Journal of Quality & Reliability Management*, Vol. 12, No. 8, pp. 8-22.
78. Caravatta, M., 1997, Conducting an Organizational Self-Assessment using the 1997 Baldridge Award Criteria, *Quality Progress*, Vol. 30, No. 10, pp. 87-91.
79. Carr, D. K. and Littman, I. D., 1993, Excellence in Government: Total Quality Management in the 1990s, 2nd Edition, ASQC Quality Press, Milwaukee, WI.
80. Cary, M. S., 1995, How to Become a Quality Person, *Quality Progress*, Vol. 28, No. 6, pp. 75-78.
81. Chakarvarty, A., 1994, Total Quality Needs Quality Mindsets, *Hindustan Times*, 14th November.
82. Chase, R. B. and Aquilano, N. J., 1992, Production and operations management, 6th Edition, Homewood, IL: Irwin.
83. Chatterjee, P. K., 1993, Quality Excellence for Productivity Improvement, *Productivity*, Vol. 34, No. 2, pp. 288-291.
84. Checkland, P., 1981, Systems Thinking: Systems Practice, John Wiley and Sons, New York.
85. Chen, F. F. and Adam, E. E. Jr., 1991, The Impact of Flexible Manufacturing Systems on Productivity and Quality, *Transactions on Engineering Management*, Vol. 38, No. 1, pp. 33-45.
86. Cheng, H., 1996, Enterprise integration and modeling: the meta base approach, Kluwer Academic Publishers, Massachusetts.
87. Chin, K. S., Dale, B. G. and Pun, K. F., 2000, Implementing the UMIST Total Quality Management Framework in Hong Kong Manufacturing Industries, City University Press, Hong Kong.
88. Chin, K. S. and Pun, K. F., 2002, A proposed framework for implementing TQM in Chinese organizations, *International Journal of Quality & Reliability Management*, Vol. 19, No. 3, pp. 272-294.
89. Choi, T. and Behling, O., 1997, Top managers and TQM success: One more look after all these years, *Academy of Management Executive*, Vol. 11, No. 1, pp. 37-47.
90. Choong, Y. L., 1991, The Absorption of Japanese Manufacturing Technique in Korean Industries, *International Journal of Operational Production Management*, June, pp. 66-81.

91. Choppin, J., 1991, Quality through people – A blueprint for proactive total quality management, CA.: Pfeiffer & Company, San Diego.
92. Clinton, R. J., Williamson, S. and Bethke, A. L., 1994, Implementing total quality management: The role of human resource management, *SAM Advanced Management Journal*, Vol. 59, No. 2, pp. 10-16.
93. Cohen, L., 1995, Quality Function Deployment: How to Make QFD Work for You, Addison-Wesley, Reading, MA.
94. Cole, R. E., 1991, Comparing the Baldrige and Deming Awards, *Journal for Quality and Participation*, July-August, pp. 94-104.
95. Collins, F. C., Jr., 1994, Quality: The Ball in Your Court, 2nd Edition, ASQC Quality Press, Milwaukee, WI.
96. Conduit, J. and Mavondo, F. T., 2001, How critical is internal customer orientation to market orientation? *Journal of Business Research*, Vol. 51, pp. 11-24.
97. Connors, P. E., 1997, TQM: A selective commentary on its human dimensions, *Public Administration Review*, Vol. 57, No. 6, pp. 501-508.
98. Conti, T., 1993, Building Total Quality: A Guide to Management, Chapman and Hall, London.
99. Conti, T., 1994, Time of a critical review on quality self-assessment: The use of Quality Award Criteria and Models for Self-assessment Purposes, *in: Proceedings of the First European Forum on Quality Self-assessment*, European Organization for Quality, Torino, pp. 169-180.
100. Conti, T., 1997, Organizational Self-Assessment, Chapman and Hall, London.
101. Corrigan, J. P., 1995, Is ISO 9000 the Path to TQM?, *in: The Quality Yearbook*, Eds. Cortada, J. W. and Woods, J. A., McGraw-Hill, Inc., pp. 589-596.
102. Corsten, H. and Will, T., 1995, Integrated Production Concepts-Structural Reasons for Superior Competitive Performance, *MIR*, Vol. 35, No. 1, pp. 69-88.
103. Coulambidou, L. and Dale, B. G., 1995, The use of Quality Management in the UK: a state-of-the-art study, *Quality World*, September, pp. 110-118.
104. Coyle, R. G., 1972, The Dynamics of a Mining Enterprise, *in: Proceedings of the 10th International Conference on Decision Making in the Mineral Industry*, Johannesburg.
105. Coyle, R. G., 1979, Management System Dynamics, John Wiley and Sons, Great Britain.
106. Coyle, R. G., 1983, The Technical Elements of The System Dynamics Approach, *European Journal of Operational Research*, Vol. 14, pp. 359-370.

107. Coyle, R. G., 1996, System Dynamics Modeling, Chapman and Hall, London.
108. Crosby, P. B., 1979, Quality is Free: The Art of Making Quality Certain, Mc-Graw Hill, New York.
109. Crosby, P. B., 1981, Quality Without Tears: The Art of Hassle-Free Management, McGraw-Hill International Editions, N. J.
110. Crosby, P. B., 1984, Quality without Tears, Mc-Graw Hill, New York.
111. Crosby, P. B., 1991, Quality Management in Emerging Nations, *Productivity*, Vol. 32, No. 3, pp. 415-420.
112. Crosby, P. B., 1992, Completeness: Quality for 21st Century, Dutton Publisher, New York.
113. Curkovic, S. and Pagell, M., 1999, A Critical Examination of the Ability of ISO 9000 Certification to Lead to a Competitive Advantage, *Journal of Quality Management*, Vol. 4, No. 1, pp. 51-67.
114. Dahlgaard, J. J., Kanji, G. K. and Kristensen, K., 1990, A Comparative Study of Quality Control Methods and Principles in Japan, Korea and Denmark, *Total Quality Management*, Vol. 1, No. 1, pp. 115-132.
115. Dahlgaard, J. J., Kristensen, K., Kanji, G. K., Juhl, H. J. and Sohal, A. S., 1998, Quality management practices: a comparative study between East and West, *International Journal of Quality & Reliability Management*, Vol. 15, Nos. 8-9, pp. 812-826.
116. Dale, B. G., Lascelles, D. M. and Boaden, R. J., 1990, Managing Quality, Prentice Hall, U.K.
117. Dale, B. G. and Lascelles, D. M., 1997, Total Quality Management adoption: revisiting the levels, *The TQM Magazine*, Vol. 9, No. 6, pp. 418-428.
118. Dale, B. G. and Lightburn, K., 1992, Continuous quality improvement: why some organizations lack commitment, *International Journal of Production Economics*, Vol. 27, No. 1, pp. 57-67.
119. Dale, B. G. and Plunkett, J. J., 1990, Managing Quality, Philip Allan, New York.
120. Dale, B. G. and Plunkett, J. J., 1991, Quality Costing, Chapman and Hall, Quoted in Boaden, R. J., 1996, What is Total Quality Management....And Does it Matter?, *Total Quality Management*, August, Vol. 8, No. 4.
121. Dale, B. G., and Smith, M., 1997, Spectrum of Quality Management implementation grid: development and use, *Managing Services Quality*, Vol. 7, No. 6, pp. 307-311.
122. Dangerfield, B. C., 1979, Dynamics of Human Development: Achievement Crises, *MIT System Dynamics Group Memo*, Cambridge, pp. D-2850-2851.

123. Das, G., 1996, Indian Companies with a Global Mindset, *Times of India*, 9th December, New Delhi.

124. Davenport, H. and Short, J. E., 1990, The New Industrial Engineering Information Technology and Business Process Redesign.

125. Day, R. G., 1993, Quality Function Deployment: Linking a Company with its Customer, ASQC Quality Press, Milwaukee.

126. Dejonckheere, J., Disney, S. M., Lambrecht, M. R. and Towill, D. R., 2002, Measuring and avoiding the bullwhip effect: A control theoretic approach, Available at: www.elsevier.com/locate/dsw.

127. Delavigne, K. T. and Robertson, D. J., 1994, Deming's Profound Changes: When Will the Sleeping Giant Awake?, ASQC Quality Press, Milwaukee, WI.

128. Deming, W. E., 1982, Quality Productivity and Competitive Position, Massachusetts Institute of Technology, Centre of Advanced Engineering Study, Cambridge, MA.

129. Deming, W. E., 1986, Out of the Crisis, Institute for Advance Engineering Study, MIT, Cambridge, MA.

130. Deming, W. E., 1990, A System of Knowledge, Action Line, pp. 20-24.

131. Deming, W. E., 1993, Out of the Crisis – Quality, Productivity and Competitive Position, Cambridge University Press, Productivity and Quality Publishing Private Limited, Madras.

132. Dhawan, R., 1996, Benchmarking, *Business Today*, July, 7-21, pp. 92-103.

133. Dill, M., 1997, Capital Investment Cycles: A System Dynamics Modeling Approach to Social Theory Development, *in: Proceedings of the 15th International System Dynamics Conference: Systems Approach to Learning and Education into the 21st Century*, Istanbul, Turkey.

134. Dooley, K. and Mahmoodi, F., 1996, Regarding Quality, *Institute of Electronics and Electrical Engineers, Management Review*, Spring, pp. 4-5.

135. Dooley, K. J. and Flor, R. F., 1998, Perceptions of Success and Failure in TQM Initiatives, *Journal of Quality Management*, Vol. 3, No. 2, pp. 157-174.

136. Douglas, A., Kirk, D., Brennan, C. and Ingram, A., 1999, Maximizing the benefits of ISO 9000 implementation, *Total Quality Management*, Vol. 10, Nos. 4-5, pp. 507-513.

137. Doyle, K., 1992, Who's killing total quality?, *Incentive*, Vol. 116, No. 8, pp. 12-19.

138. Dow, D., Samson, D. and Ford, S., 1999, Exploding the myth: do all quality management practices contribute to superior quality performance?, *Production and Operations Management*, Vol. 8, No. 1, pp. 1-27.

139. Downey, C. J., Frase, L. E. and Peters, J. J., 1994, The Quality Education Challenge, Corwin Press Inc., A Sage Publication, Thousand Oaks, CA.

140. Dunham, J. R., Morrice, D. J., Scott, J. and Anderson, E. G., 2000, A Strategic Supply Chain Simulation Model, *in: Proceedings of the 2000 Winter Simulation Conference,* Eds. Joines, J. A., Barton, R. R., Kang, K. and Fishwick, P. A., pp. 1260-1264.

141. Dutta, R. K. and Mohapatra, P. K. J., 1968, Technological Upgrading and Energy Demand Scenarios For Indian Railways – A System Dynamics Study, *Technological Forecasting and Social Change,* Vol. 34, pp. 145-178.

142. Dyson, R. G., 1990, Strategic Planning, *in: Strategic Planning: Models and Analytical Techniques,* Ed. Dyson, R. G., John Wiley and Sons, Great Britain, pp. 3-14.

143. Easton, G. S. and Jarrel, S. L., 1998, The effect of total quality management on corporate performance: an empirical investigation, *Journal of Business,* Vol. 71, pp. 253-307, Available at: www.georgeeston.com/paper.html.

144. Easton, G. S., 1993, The 1993 state of U.S. total quality management: a Baldrige examiner's perspective, *California Management Review*, Vol. 35, No. 3, pp. 32-54.

145. Edgar, W. and Hodgson, P., 1991, Making Change Work, Viva Books, New Delhi.

146. Edosomwan, J. A., 1987, A Technology-oriented Total Productivity Measurement Model, *in: Productivity Management, (Ed.)* Sumanth, D. J., Frontiers-I, Elsevier, New York.

147. EFQM, 1995, European Quality Award Guidelines on Self-Assessment, European Foundation for Quality Management, Brussels.

148. EFQM, 1999a, The European Quality Award Application Handbook, European Foundation for Quality Management, Brussels.

149. EFQM, 1999b, Assessing for Excellence, European Foundation for Quality Management, Brussels.

150. Eisenhardt, K. M., 1989, Building theories from case study research, *Academy of Management Review*, Vol. 14, No. 4, pp. 532-550.

151. Ernst & Young and American Quality Foundation, 1991, International quality study: the definitive study of the best international quality management practices, Cleveland: Thought Leadership Series.

152. Eskildsen, J. K., Kristensen, K. and Juhl, H. J., 2001, The criterion weights of the EFQM excellence model, *International Journal of Quality & Reliability Management*, Vol. 18, No. 8, pp. 783-795.
153. Ettorre, B., 1996, Is the Baldrige still meaningful?, *Management Review*, Vol. 85, No. 3, pp. 28-31.
154. Eugene, L. G. and Richard, S. L., 1988, Statistical Quality Control, 6th Edition, ASQC Quality Press, Milwaukee, WI.
155. Evans, J. R. and Lindsay, W. M., 1999, The Management and Control of Quality, West Publishing Company, Minneapolis, MN.
156. Feigenbaum, A. V., 1951, Quality Control: Principles, Practice and Administration, McGraw-Hill, New York.
157. Feigenbaum, A. V., 1961, Total Quality Control: Engineering and Management, 2nd Edition, West Publishing Company, Minneapolis, MN.
158. Feigenbaum, A. V., 1982, Quality and Business Growth Today, *Quality Progress*, Vol. 15, No. 11.
159. Feigenbaum, A. V., 1983, Total Quality Control: Engineering and Management, 3rd Edition, McGraw-Hill, New York, NY.
160. Feigenbaum, A. V., 1990, Management of quality: the key to the nineties, *Journal for Quality and Participation*, Vol. 13, No. 2, pp. 14-19.
161. Feigenbaum, A. V., 1991, Total Quality Control, McGraw Hill, New York,
162. Feigenbaum, A. V., 1992, Quality: our new competitive edge, *Executive Excellence*, Vol. 9, No. 5, pp. 18-19.
163. Feigin, G. E., Connors, A. C. and Crawford, I., 1996, Shape up, ship out, *OR/MS Today*, Vol. 23, No. 2, pp. 24-30.
164. Fenghueih, H., 1998, Integrating ISO 9000 with TQM spirits: a survey, *Industrial Management and Data Systems*, Vol. 98, Nos. 7-8, pp. 373-379.
165. Fenwick, A. C., 1991, Five easy lessons: a primer for starting a total quality management program, *Quality Progress*, Vol. 24, No. 12, pp. 63-66.
166. Fey, W. R., 1962, An Industrial Dynamics Case Study, *Industrial Management Review*, Vol. 4, No. 1, pp. 79-99.
167. Firoozi, F. and Merrifield, J., 2002, An optimal timing model of water reallocation and reservoir construction, *European Journal of Operational Research*, Available at: www.elsevier.com/locate/dsw.
168. Flynn, B. B., Schroeder, R. G. and Sakakibara, S., 1994, A Framework for Quality Management Research and an Associated Measurement Instrument, *Journal of Operations Management*, Vol. 11, No. 4, pp. 339-366.
169. Flynn, B. B., Schroeder, R. G. and Sakakibara, S., 1995, The impact of quality management practices on performance and competitive advantage, *Decision Sciences*, Vol. 26, No. 5, pp. 659-692.

170. Forrest, W. B., III, 1992, Statistical Methods for Testing, Development and Manufacturing, ASQC Quality Press, Milwaukee, WI.
171. Forrester, J. W. and Senge, P. M., 1980, Tests for Building Confidence in System Dynamics Models, *TIMS Studies in the Management Science*, Vol. 14, pp. 209-228.
172. Forrester, J. W., 1958, Industrial Dynamics: A major breakthrough for decision makers, *Harvard Business Review*, Vol. 36, No. 4, pp. 37-66.
173. Forrester, J. W., 1961, Industrial Dynamics, MIT Press, Cambridge, Massachusetts.
174. Forrester, J. W., 1965, A new Corporate Design, *Sloan Management Review*, Vol. 7, No. 1, pp. 5-17.
175. Forrester, J. W., 1968, Principles of Systems, MIT Press, Cambridge, Massachusetts.
176. Forrester, J. W., 1969, Urban Dynamics, MIT Press, Cambridge, Massachusetts.
177. Forrester, J. W., 1971a, Counter-Intuitive Behaviour of Social System, *Technology Review*, Vol. 73, No. 3, pp. 53-68.
178. Forrester, J. W., 1971b, World Dynamics, MIT Press, Cambridge, Massachusetts.
179. Forrester, J. W., 1980, Computer Models and Public Policy, *System Dynamics Group School of Management*, MIT, p. D-3267.
180. Forrester, J. W., 1985, Industrial Dynamics, MIT Press, Cambridge, Massachusetts, USA.
181. Forridge, T. D. R., 1997, Principles of good practice in material flow, *Production, Planning and Control*, Vol. 8, No. 7, pp. 622-632.
182. Foster, S. T. Jr., 1993, Designing and initiating a Taguchi experiment in a services setting, *Operations Management Review*, Vol. 9, No. 3, pp. 37-50.
183. Fountain, M., 1998, The target assessment model as an international standard for self-assessment, *Total Quality Management*, Vol. 9, No. 4, pp. S95-S99.
184. Frank, C. K., Robet, D. D. and Richard, J. B., 1993, Statistics and Quality Control for the Workplace, ASQC Quality Press, Milwaukee, WI.
185. Froker, L. B., Mendez, D., and Hershauer, J.C., 1997, Total Quality Management in the Supply Chain: What is the impact on performance?, *International Journal of Productivity Research*, Vol. 35, No. 6, pp. 1681-1701.
186. Fuchs, E. and Stuntebeck, S. H., 1994, The use of Baldrige-based self-assessment in AT&T: The Use of Quality Award Criteria and Models for Self-assessment Purposes, *in: Proceedings of the First European Forum on Quality Self-assessment*, European Organization for Quality, Torino, pp. 15-26.

187. Galetto, F., 1999, The Golden Integrated Quality Approach: From Management of Quality to Quality of Management, *Total Quality Management*, Vol. 10, No. 1, pp. 17-35.

188. Ganapathy, K., Subramanian, and Narayana, V., 1994, Quality Circles Concept and Implementation, Quality Circle Forum of India, Secunderabad.

189. Garvare, R. and Wiklund, 1997, Facilitating the Use of Statistical Methods in Small and Medium Sized Enterprises, *in: Proceedings of the EOQ-97*, Vol. 3.

190. Garvin, D. A., 1983, Quality on the Line, *Harvard Business Review*, Vol. 61, No. 5, pp. 65-75.

191. Garvin, D. A., 1984, What Does Product Quality Really Mean?, *Sloan Management Review*, Vol. 26, No. 1, pp. 25-43.

192. Garvin, D. A., 1986, Quality Problems, Policies, and Attitudes in the United States and Japan: An Exploratory Study, *Academy of Management Journal*, Vol. 29, No. 4, pp. 653-673.

193. Garvin, D. A., 1987, Competing on the eight dimensions of quality, *Harvard Business Review*, Vol. 65, No. 6, pp. 101-109.

194. Garvin, D. A., 1988, Managing quality: The strategic competitive edge, Free Press, New York.

195. Garvin, D. A., 1991, How the Baldrige award really works, *Harvard Business Review*, Vol. 69, No. 6, pp. 80-93.

196. Gatewood, R. D. and Riordan, C. M., 1997, The Development and Test of a Model of Total Quality: Organizational Practices, TQ Principles, Employee Attitudes and Customer Satisfaction, *Journal of Quality Management*, Vol. 2, No. 1, pp. 41-65.

197. Gehani, R. R., 1993, Quality value chain: a meta synthesis of frontiers of quality movement, *Academy of Management Executive*, Vol. 7, No. 2, pp. 29-42.

198. Genna, A., 1997, Suppliers are key to giving customers what they want, *Purchasing*, Vol. 123, No. 8, pp. 33-34.

199. Ghahramani, H. and Bindra, S. P., 1999, An Integrated Urban Transportation – Land Use Dynamic Model, *International Journal of System Dynamics and Policy Planning*, Vol. XI, No. 2, pp. 1-18.

200. Ghobadian, A. and Woo, H. S., 1996, Characteristics, benefits and shortcomings of four major quality awards, *International Journal of Quality & Reliability Management*, Vol. 13, No. 2, pp. 10-14.

201. Gibson, T. C., 1990, Helping leaders accept leadership of total quality management, *Quality Progress*, November, pp. 45-47.

202. Gielen, D. J. and Yagita, H., 2002, The long-term impact of GHG reduction policies on global trade: A case study for the petrochemical industry, *European Journal of Operational Research*, Vol. 139, pp. 665-681, Available at: www.elsevier.com/locate/dsw

203. Gilbert, R. J., 1990, Are you committed or committed?, *Quality Progress*, May, pp. 45-48.
204. Gilligan, C., 1982, In a Different Voice, Harvard University Press, Cambridge, MA.
205. Gilmore, H. L., 1974, Product Conformance Cost, *Quality Progress*, Vol. 7, No. 5, pp. 16-19.
206. Gitlow, H. S. and Gitlow, S. J., 1987, The Deming guide to quality and competitive position, Englewood, Prentice-Hall, NJ.
207. Gitlow, H. S. and Hertz, P. T., 1983, Product Defects and Productivity, *Harvard Business Review*, Vol. 61, No. 5, pp.131-141.
208. Gitlow, H., 1989, Tools and methods for improvement of quality, Irwin Inc., Boston.
209. Gitlow, H., Gitlow, S., Oppenheim, H. and Oppenheim, R., 1989, Tools and Methods for the Improvement of Quality, Irwin, Homewood, IL.
210. Goldratt, E. M. and Cox, J., 1992, The Goal, ASQC Quality Press, Milwaukee, WI.
211. Golhar, D. Y., Ahire, S. L. and Waller, M. A., 1996, Quality Management in TQM versus non-TQM firms: An Empirical Investigation, *International Journal of Quality & Reliability Management*, Vol. 13, No. 8, pp. 8-27.
212. Gondhalekar, S., Babu, A. S. and Godrej, N. B., 1995, Towards TQM using Kaizen process dynamics: A Case Study, *International Journal of Quality & Reliability Management*, Vol. 12, No. 9, pp. 192-209.
213. Gondhalekar, S., Tripathi, A. and Hombali, S., 1991, The Godrej Kaizen System: Company Wide Productivity Improvement, *Productivity*, Vol. 32, No. 3, pp. 450-457.
214. Goodman, M. R., 1983, Study Notes in System Dynamics, MIT Press, Cambridge, Massachusetts.
215. Gradig, R. M. and Harris, J. K., 1994, The Baldrige award: a quest for excellence?, *Review of Business*, Vol. 15, No. 3, pp. 20-24.
216. Graham, A. K., 1980, Parameter Estimation in System Dynamics Modeling, *TIMS Studies in the Management Science*, Vol. 14, pp. 23-24.
217. Graham, A. K., 1989, Beyond Total Quality: Discussion with Professor Shoji Shiba, Personnel Communication, 22nd November, p. 13.
218. Graham, S., 1992, When Quality Control gets in the way of Quality, Section A, *Wall Street Journal*, p. 14.
219. Grant, R. M., Sahni, R. and Krishnan, R., 1995, TQM's Challenge to Management Theory and Practice, *in: The Quality Yearbook*, Eds. Cortada, J. W. and Woods, *J. A.*, McGraw-Hill, Inc., pp. 49-65.
220. Greene, R. T., 1993, Global Quality: A Synthesis of the World's Best Management Methods, ASQC Quality Press, Milwaukee, WI.

221. Greiner, A , Feichtinger, G., Haunschmied, J. L., Kort, P. M. and Hartl, R. F., 2001, Optimal periodic development of a pollution generating tourism industry, *European Journal of Operational Research*, Vol. 134, pp. 582-591, Available at: www.elsevier.com/locate/dsw.
222. Griffiths, D. N., 1990, Implementing Quality: With a Customer Focus, ASQC Quality Press, New York.
223. Groocock, J. M., 1986, The Chain of Quality, Chichester, John Willey.
224. Grossman, S., 1994, Why TQM doesn't work…and what you can do about it, *Industry week*, Vol. 243, No. 1, pp. 57-62.
225. Gryna, F. M., 1991, The quality director of the '90s, *Quality Progress*, May, pp. 51-54.
226. Gunasekaran, A., 1998, An integral product development – quality management system for manufacturing, *The TQM Magazine*, Vol. 10, No. 2, pp. 115-123.
227. Hammer, M., 1990, Reengineering Work: Do Not Automotive, Obliterate, *Harvard Business Review*, Vol. 68, No. 4, pp. 104-112.
228. Hammer, M., and Champy, J. A., 1993, Reengineering the Corporation: A Manifesto for Business Revolution, Harper Business, New York.
229. Hansen, J. E. and Bie, P., 1987, Distribution of body fluids, plasma protein, and sodium in dogs: a system dynamics model, *System Dynamic Review*, Vol. 3, No. 2, pp. 116-135.
230. Harber, D., Marriot, F. and Idrus, N., 1991, Employee participation TQC: An integrative review, *International Journal of Quality & Reliability Management*, Vol. 8, No. 5, pp. 24-34.
231. Hardie, N. and Walsh, P., 1994, Towards a Better Understanding of Quality, *International Journal of Quality & Reliability Management*, Vol. 11, No. 4, pp. 53-63.
232. Harrington, J. H., 1987, Poor Quality Cost, ASQC Quality Press, New York.
233. Harrington, J. H., 1991, Business Process Improvement, McGraw-Hill, New York.
234. Harrington, J. H., 1994, Total Improvement Management, ASQC Quality Press, Milwaukee, WI.
235. Harrington, J. H., 1997, The Facility of Universal Best Practices, *The TQM Magazine*, Vol. 9, No. 1, pp. 61-75.
236. Harry, M. J., 1988, The Nature of Six Sigma Quality, Discussion Document, Motorola.
237. Hart, C. W., 1993, What's wrong – and right – with the Baldrige awards?, Chief Executive, November-December, pp. 36-47.
238. Hauser, J. R. and Clausing, D. P., 1988, The House of Quality, *Harvard Business Review*, Vol. 88, No. 3, pp. 63-73.

239. Hendricks, K. B. and Singhal, V. R., 1997, The long-term stock price performance of quality award winners, *in: Advances in the management of organizational quality*, Eds. Fedor, D. B. and Ghos, S., CT: JAI Press, Greenwich, pp. 1-37.

240. Hermel, P. and Bartoli, A., 2001, Strategic and organizational innovations in the pharmaceutical industry – searching for total quality: the case of a large European pharmaceutical company, *The TQM Magazine*, Vol. 13, No. 3, pp. 169-174.

241. Hermel, P., 1997, The New Faces of Total Quality in Europe and the US, *Total Quality Management*, August, Vol. 8, No. 4.

242. Hewitt, S., 1994, Strategic Advantages emerge from tactical TQM tools, *Quality Progress*, Vol. 27, No. 10, pp. 57-59.

243. Higuchi, T. and Troutt, M. D., 2003, Dynamic simulation of the supply chain for a short life cycle product—lessons from the Tamagotchi case, *Computers and Operations Research*. Available at: www.elsevier.com/locate/dsw

244. Hill, R. C., 1993, When the going gets rough: a Baldrige award winner on the line, *Academy of Management Executive*, Vol. 7, No. 3, pp. 75-79.

245. Hillman, P. G., 1994, Making self-assessment successful, *The TQM Magazine*, Vol. 6, No. 3, pp. 29-31.

246. Hirano, H., 1995, 5 Pillars of The Visual Workplace, *Translated by Talbot, B.*, Productivity Press, Portland, Oregon.

247. Hirotaka, T. and Quelch, J. A., 1983, Quality is More Than Making a Good Product, *Harvard Business Review*, July-August, pp. 139-155.

248. Hitoshi, K., 1987, Statistical Methods for Quality Improvement, ASQC Quality Press, Milwaukee, WI.

249. Hoffman, J. M. and Mehra, S., 1999, Management Leadership and Productivity Improvement Programs, *International Journal of Applied Quality Management*, Vol. 2, No. 2, pp. 221-232.

250. Holloway, J., Jenny, L. and Geoft, M., 1995, Performance Measurement and Evaluation, The Open University, London.

251. Holmes, R. K. Wolstenholme, E. F. and King, P. D. A., 1983, Strategic Management the System Dynamics Way, System Dynamics Research Group Report, University of Bradform Management Centre, U.K.

252. Holweg, M. and Bicheno, J., 2002, Supply chain simulation – a tool for education, enhancement and endeavour, *International Journal of Production Economics*, Vol. 78, pp. 163-175, Available at: www.elsevier.com/locate/dsw.

253. Homer, J. B. and St. Clair, C. L., 1991, A Model of HIV Transmission through Needle Sharing, A model useful in analyzing public policies, such as a needle cleaning campaign, *Interfaces*, Vol. 21, No. 3, pp. 26-29.

254. Horowitz, 1990, Introduction, The Concern for Quality, *in: Developing Quality Systems in Education*, Ed. Doherty, *G. D.,* Routledge, London.
255. Hosotani, K., 1992, The QC Problem Solving Approach: Solving Workplace Problems the Japanese Way, 3A Corporation, Tokyo, Japan.
256. Hunt, V. D., 1990, Managing Quality: Integrating Quality and Business Strategy, Irwin, Homewood, IL.
257. Huntington, H. G., Weyant, J. P. and Sweeney, J. L., 1982, Modeling for Insights Not Numbers: The Experiences of the Energy Modeling Forum, *OMEGA*, Vol. 10, No. 5, pp. 132-137.
258. Hutchins, D., 1992, Standard Manual of Quality Auditing: A Step Workbook with Procedures and Checklists, Prentice Hall, Englewood.
259. Imai, M., 1986, Kaizen: The Key to Japan's Competitive Success, McGraw-Hill Publishing Company, N. J.
260. IMD, 2002, World Competitiveness Yearbook, Available at: www.imd.ch/wcy/ranking/pastresults.html.
261. Indiainfoline, 2001a, Indiainfoline sector reports, Available at: www.indiainfoline.com/sect/atca/ch07.html.
262. Indiainfoline, 2001b, Events and Milestones, Available at: www.indiainfoline.com/cars/events.html.
263. Indiainfoline, 2002, Indiainfoline sector reports, Available at: www.indianfoline.com/sect/atca/ch11.html.
264. Ingle, S. and Roe, W., 2001, Six Sigma Black Belt Implementation, *The TQM Magazine*, Vol. 13, No. 4, pp. 273-280.
265. Ishikawa, K., 1976, Guide to Quality Control, Asian Productivity Organization, Tokyo.
266. Ishikawa, K., 1984, A Guide to Quality Control, Asian Productivity Organization, Tokyo.
267. Ishikawa, K., 1985, What is Total Quality Control? The Japanese Way, *Translated by David, J. LU,* Prentice-Hall, Inc. Englewood Cliffs, N. J.
268. ISO 9000:2000, Quality Management Systems – Fundamentals and Vocabulary, International Standard, International Organization for Standardization, Geneva.
269. ISO 9004:1993, International Standard Organization, Vocabulary.
270. ISO 14001:1996, Environment Management System, Bureau of Indian Standard, New Delhi.
271. ISO 8402:1994, Quality Management and Quality Assurance Vocabulary, International Organization for Standardization, Bureau of Indian Standards, New Delhi.
272. ISO/TS 16949:2002, Technical Specification: Quality Management Systems- Particular requirements for the application of ISO 9001:2000 for automotive production and relevant service part organizations, Second Edition.

273. Itasaka, G., 1989, Gates to Japan—Its People and Society, *Translated by Loftus, J. H.,* Second Printing, 3A Corporation, Tokyo, Japan.
274. Jablonski, J. R., 1991, Implementing Total Quality Management, N. M., Technical Management Consortium, Albuquerque.
275. Jablonski, J. R., 1992, Implementing TQM: Competing in the Nineties through TQM, N. M., Technical Management Consortium, Albuquerque.
276. Jain, V. K. and Bagchi, T. P., 1998, Competitiveness and TQM: Synergy should be no surprise, *International Journal of Industrial Engineering,* Vol. 5, No. 3, pp. 182-187.
277. James, P., 1996, Total Quality Management: An Introductory Text, Prentice Hall, New Jersey.
278. Jarrer, Y. and Aspinall, E., 1999, TQM – is it enough? *Journal of Quality Management,* Vol. 10, No. 4, pp. 584-93.
279. Jernberg, B., Lindstrom, J. and Chocron, R., 1994, How smaller companies and smaller groups use and benefits from the criteria of an award: The Use of Quality Award Criteria and Models for Self-assessment Purposes, *in: Proceedings of the First European Forum on Quality Self-assessment,* Organizational for Quality, Torino, pp. 35-46.
280. John, T., 1995, Information Management, ELM: A Holistic Approach, *in: The Quality Yearbook,* Eds. Cortada, J. W. and Woods, J. A., McGraw-Hill, Inc., pp. 494-497.
281. Jordan, D. W., 1994, Using the Baldrige Award criteria for self-assessment, *Engineering Management Journal,* Vol. 6, No. 2, pp. 16-19.
282. Joseph, I. N., Rajendran, C. and Kamalanabham, T. J., 1999, An instrument for measuring total quality management implementation in manufacturing-based business units in India, *International Journals of Production Research,* Vol. 37, No. 10, pp. 2201-2215.
283. Juran, J. M. and Gryna, F. M. Jr., 1988, Juran's Quality Control Handbook, McGraw-Hill, New York, NY.
284. Juran, J. M. and Gryna, F. M., 1995, Quality Planning and Analysis, 3rd Edition, Tata McGraw-Hill Publishing Company Limited, New Delhi.
285. Juran, J. M., 1974, Quality Control Hand Book, 3rd Edition, McGraw-Hill, New York.
286. Juran, J. M., 1982, Management of Quality, The Free Press, New York.
287. Juran, J. M., 1985, Juran on Planning for Quality, The Free Press, New York, NY.
288. Juran, J. M., 1986, The Quality Trilogy, *Quality Progress,* Vol. 19, No. 8, pp. 81-85.
289. Juran, J. M., 1988a, Juran on Planning for Quality, Macmillan Publishers, London.

290. Juran, J. M., 1988b, Juran's new quality roadmap, The Free Press, New York.
291. Juran, J. M., 1989, Juran on Leadership for Quality, Macmillan, New York.
292. Juran, J. M., 1993, Made in USA: A Renaissance in Quality, *Harvard Business Review*, Vol. 71, No. 4, pp. 42-50.
293. Juran, J. M., 1995, A History of Managing for Quality, ASQC Quality Press, Milwaukee, WI.
294. Juran, J. M., 1992, Juran on Quality by Design: The New Steps for Planning Quality into Goods and Services, ASQC Quality Press, Milwaukee, WI.
295. Kahen, G., Lehman, M. M., Ramil, J. F. and Wernick, P., 2001, System dynamics modeling of software evolution processes for policy investigation: Approach and example, *The Journal of System and Software*, Vol. 59, pp. 271-281, Available at: www.elsevier.com/locate/jss.
296. Kalman, R. E., 1978, A System Theoratic Critique of Dynamic Economic Models, Global and Large Scale System Models, *in: Proceedings of the Centre of Advanced Studies (CAS), International Summer Seminar*, Dubrovnik.
297. Kamran, K., 1991, Making TQM Habitual, *Productivity*, Vol. 32, No. 3., pp. 435-441.
298. Kamran, K., 1993, Making TQM Benefits Reach the Bottom-Line Through Personal Change, *Productivity*, Vol. 34, No. 3, pp. 437-440.
299. Kanda, A., Deshmukh, S. G. and Shankar, R., 2002, Review of Quality Award Models, *Productivity*, Vol. 43, No. 2, pp. 225-236.
300. Kanji, G. K. and Asher, M., 1993, Total Quality Management Process: A Systematic Approach, Advances in Total Quality Management Series, Abingdon.
301. Kanji, G. K. and Asher, M., 1996, 100 Methods for Total Quality Management, Sage Publications, New Delhi.
302. Kanji, G. K. and Tambi, A. M. A., 1999, TQM in UK Higher Education Institutions, *Total Quality Management*, Vol. 10, No. 1, pp. 129-153.
303. Kanji, G. K., 1995, Quality and statistical concepts, *in: Total Quality Management: Proceedings of the First World Congress*, Ed. Kanji, G. K., Chapman and Hall, London.
304. Kano, N., 1993, A Perspective on Quality Activities in American Firms, *California Management Review*, Vol. 35, No. 3, pp. 12-31.
305. Karapetrovic, S. and Willborn, W., 2002, Self-audit of process performance, *International Journal of Quality & Reliability Management*, Vol. 19, No. 1, pp. 24-45.
306. Karl, A. S. and Motisaka, P. J., 1962, The Team Approach to Quality, ASQC Quality Press, Milwaukee, WI.

307. Kassiciech, S. K. and Yourstone, S. A., 1998, Training, Performance Evaluation, Rewards, and TQM Implementation Success, *Journal of Quality Management*, Vol. 3, No. 1, pp. 25-38.
308. Kasul, R. A. and Motwani, J. G., 1996, TQM in Manufacturing, *International Journal of Quality & Reliability Management*, Vol. 12, No. 13, pp. 57-76.
309. Katsuya, H., 1992, Japanese Quality Concepts: An Overview, Quality Press, New York.
310. Kehoe, D. F., 1996, The Fundamentals of Quality Management, Chapman and Hall, London.
311. Kekale, T. and Kekale, J., 1995, A mismatch of culture a pitfall of implementing a total quality approach, *International Journal of Quality & Reliability Management*, Vol. 12, No. 9, pp. 210-220.
312. Keloharju, R., 1983, Relativity Dynamics, ACTA Series, The Helsinki School of Economics, Helsinki.
313. Kenneth, N. W. and Gray, P. L., 1991, Developing and Training Human Resources in Organization, Harper Collins, USA.
314. Kepner, C. H. and Tregoe, B. B., 1981, The New Rational Manager, ASQC Quality Press, Milwaukee, WI.
315. Khanna, I. K., 1986, Transportation Planning and Policy Design for Delhi Urban Region: A System Dynamics Approach, *Unpublished Ph.D. Thesis, Indian Institute of Technology Delhi*, New Delhi, India.
316. Khanna, S. and Roy, A., 1995, Managing the Total Quality Revolution, *Business Today*, January 7-21, pp. 64-73.
317. Khanna, V. K., 1999, Mutual Prosperity Through Vendor Management, *in: Supply Chain Management: For Global Competitiveness*, Ed. Sahay, B. S., Macmillan India Ltd. New Delhi, pp. 432-451.
318. King, P. D. A., Coyle, R. G. and Wolstenholme, E. F., 1983, A General Dynamic Model of Business Performance, *in: Proceedings of the International System Dynamics Conference*, MIT, USA.
319. Kinlaw, D. C., 1992, Continuous Improvement and Measurement for Total Quality - A Team Based Approach, Pfieffer and Business One, ASQC Quality Press, Milwaukee, WI.
320. Kimmerling, G., 1993, Gathering best practices, *Training and Development*, Vol. 47, No. 9, pp. 38-47.
321. Knutton, P., 1994, A model approach to self-assessment, *Works Management*, Vol. 47, No. 12, pp. 12-16.
322. Kohlberg, L., 1981, The Philosophy of Moral Development, Harper and Row, San Francisco.
323. Kolka, J., 2002, ISO 9000 and 9004: a framework for disaster preparedness, *Quality progress*, Vol. 35, No. 2, pp. 57-62.

324. Koul, S., 1991, Corporate Policy Analysis of an Engineering Enterprise: A System Dynamic Study, *Unpublished Ph.D. Thesis, Indian Institute of Technology Delhi,* New Delhi, India.

325. Krajewski, L. J. and Ritzman, L. P., 2005, Operation Management – Strategy and Analysis, 6th Edition, Pearson Education (Singapore) Pte. Ltd., Indian Branch, 482, F.I.E. Patparganj, Delhi.

326. Kristensen, K., Juhl, H. J., and Eskildsen, J. K., 2000, The excellence index as a benchmarking tool, *in: Proceedings of the MAAOE Conference,* Estes Park, Colorado, USA.

327. Kristensen, K. and Juhl, H. J., 1999, Beyond the bottom line – measuring stakeholder value, *in: The Nordic School of Quality Management, Eds. Edvardsson, B. and Gustafsson, A.,* Studentlitterature, Lund.

328. Kuei, C. H., Madu, C. N. and Lin, C., 2001, The relationship between supply chain quality management practices and organizational performance, *International Journal of Quality & Reliability Management,* Vol. 18, No. 8, pp. 864-872.

329. Kumar, A., Ow, P. S. and Prietula, M. J., 1993, Organizational simulation and information systems design: An operations level example, *Management Sciences,* Vol. 39, No. 2, pp. 218-240.

330. Kumar, K. V., Umesh and Bhushi, M., 1999, Implementation of TQM in Indian Industries: A Review, *in: Operations Management for Global Economy—Challenges and Prospects,* Eds. Kanda et al., Phoenix Publisher, New Delhi, India, pp. 166-172.

331. Kumar, M. S., 1995, TQM Scenario in an Indian Industry: A System Dynamics Study, *Unpublished M. Tech. Thesis, Indian Institute of Technology Delhi,* New Delhi, India.

332. Kumar, M., 1997, A System Dynamic Study of Global Warming, *Unpublished M. Tech Thesis, Indian Institute of Technology Delhi,* New Delhi, India.

333. Kumar, R. and Garg, D., 2002, Quality Management Practices in Indian Industries, *Productivity,* Vol. 43, No. 3, pp. 426-433.

334. Kumar, R. and Kliene, O., 1983, System Dynamics Model of Material Flow—Case of a Steel Plant, *in: Proceedings of the International System Dynamics Conference,* MIT, USA.

335. Kunsch, P., Chevalier, A. and Brans, J. P., 2001, Comparing the adaptive control methodology (ACM) to the financial planning practice of a large international group, *European Journal of Operational Research,* Vol. 132, pp. 479-489, Available at: www.elsevier.com/locate/dsw.

336. Lai, C. L., Ip, W. H. and Lee, W. B., 2001, The system dynamics model for engineering services, *Managing Service Quality,* Vol. 11, No. 3, pp. 191-199.

337. Lakhe, R. R. and Mohanty, R. P., 1994, Total Quality Management Concepts Evaluation and Acceptability in Developing Economies, *International Journal of Quality & Reliability Management,* Vol. 11, No. 9, pp. 9-33.

338. Lakhe, R. R. and Tidke, D. J., 1991, A Study of Quality Assurance Practices in Small Scale Industries, *International Engineering Journal,* Vol. 22, No. 2, pp. 14-22.

339. Lam, S. S. K., 1996, The Process of Quality Planning: A Factor Analytic Investigation, *International Journal of Management,* Vol. 13, No. 4, pp. 440-445.

340. Lamprecht, J. L., 1992, ISO: 9000, Preparing for Registration, ASQC Quality Press, Milwaukee, WI.

341. Lane, D. C., 1997, Invited Review and Reappraisal: Industrial Dynamics, *Journal of the Operational Research Society,* Vol. 48, pp. 1037-1042.

342. Lascelles, D. M. and Dale, B. G., 1989, A review of the issues involved in quality improvement, *International Journal of Quality & Reliability Management,* Vol. 5, No. 5, pp. 76-94.

343. Lascelles, D. M. and Peacock, R., 1996, Self-Assessment for Business Excellence, Maidenhead, McGraw-Hill, UK.

344. Laszlo, G. P., 1999, Implementing a quality management program – three Cs of success: commitment, culture, cost, *The TQM Magazine,* Vol. 11, No. 4, pp. 231-237.

345. Lawler, E. E. and Mohraman, S. A., 1985, Quality Circles After the Fad, *Harvard Business Review,* January-February, Vol. 63, pp. 65-71.

346. Lawler, E. E. III, 1994, Total Quality Management and Employee Involvement: Are they Compatible?, *Academy of Management Executive,* Vol. 8, No. 1, pp. 68-76.

347. Lawler, E. E. III, Mohrman, S. A. and Ledford, G. E., Jr., 1992, Employee involvement and total quality management, Jossey-Bass, San Francisco.

348. Lee, P. M. and Quazi, H. A., 2001, A methodology for developing a self-assessment tool to measure quality performance in organizations, *International Journal of Quality & Reliability Management,* Vol. 18, No. 2, pp. 118-141.

349. Lee, S. Y., 1997, An integrated model of land use/transportation system performance: system dynamics modeling approach, *Transportation Research Part A: Policy and Practice,* Vol. 31, No. 1, p. 79.

350. Lee, H. L., Padmanabhan, V. and Whang, S., 1997, Information distortion in a supply chain: The bullwhip effect, *Management Sciences,* Vol. 43, No. 4, p. 551.

351. Legasto, A. A. and Maciariello, J., 1980, System Dynamics: A Critical Review, *TIMS Studies in the Management Science,* Vol. 14, pp. 23-24.

352. Lemak, D. J., Reed, R. and Satish, P. K., 1997, Commitment to Total Quality Management: is there a relationship with firm performance?, *Journal of Quality Management*, Vol. 2, No. 1, pp. 67-86.

353. Leonard, D. and McAdam, R, 2001, Grounded theory methodology and practitioner reflexivity in TQM research, *International Journal of Quality & Reliability Management*, Vol. 18, No. 2, pp. 180-194.

354. Leonard, D., 2000, The strategic dynamics of TQM, *Unpublished Ph.D. thesis*, University of Ulster.

355. Leonard, D., McAdam, R. and Reid, R., 2002, A grounded multi-model framework for TQM dynamics, *International Journal of Quality & Reliability Management*, Vol. 19, No. 6, pp. 710-736.

356. Leonard, F. and Sasser, W. E., 1982, The case of quality crusader, *Harvard Business Review*, Vol. 66, No. 3, pp. 12-20.

357. Lewis, R. G. and Smith, D. H., 1994, Total Quality in Higher Education, St. Lucie Press, Delray Beach, FL.

358. Liburd, I. M. and Zairi, M., 2001, TQM sustainability – a roadmap for creating competitive advantage, *in: Proceedings of the 6th International Conference on ISO 9000 and TQM*, 17-19 April, pp. 452-461.

359. Limburg, K. E., O'Neill, R. V., Costanza, R. and Farber, S., 2002, The Dynamics and Value of Ecosystem Services: Integrating Economic and Ecological Perspective, *Ecological Economics*, Vol. 41, pp. 409-420, Available at: www.elsevier.com/locate/ecolecon.

360. Lindsay, W. M. and Petrick, J. A., 1997, Total Quality and Organization Development, St. Lucie Press, Delray Beach, FL.

361. Little, D., Arthur and Kearney, A. T., 1992, Mc-kinsey Survey On Success of TQM Programmes in British and US Industries, *The Economist*, 18th April.

362. Lu, E. and Sohal, A., 1993, Success Factors, Weakness and Myths Concerning TQM Implementation in Australia, *Total Quality Management*, Vol. 4, No. 3, pp. 245-255.

363. Lyneis, J. M., 1980, Corporate Planning and Policy Design: A System Dynamics Approach, Pugh-Roberts Associates, Cambridge, MA.

364. Lyons, M. H., Burton, F., Egan, B., Lynch, T. and Skelton, S., 1996, Dynamic modeling of present and future service demand, *in: Proceedings of the Institute of Electronics and Electrical Engineers*, Vol. 85, No. 10, pp. 1544-1555.

365. Macdonald, J. and Piggot, J., 1992, Global Quality–The New Management Culture, Viva Book Ltd., New Delhi.

366. Maheswari, S. K. and Zhao, X., 1994, Benchmarking Quality Management Practice in India, *Benchmarking for Quality and Technology Management*, Vol. 1, No. 2, pp. 5-23.

367. Main, J., 1990, How to win the Baldrige award, *Fortune*, Vol. 121, No. 9, pp. 101-116.

368. Malliga, P. and Jayabalan, V., 1999, Implementation of ISO 9000 in Indian Industries, *in: Operations Management for Global Economy – Challenges and Prospects,* Eds. Kanda et al., Phoenix Publishers, New Delhi, India, pp. 173-179.

369. Malone, T., 1987, Modeling coordination in organizations and markets, *Management Sciences,* Vol. 33, No. 10, pp. 1317-1332.

370. Manufacturer's Association for Information Technology (MAIT), 1998, Quality Recognition Programme, Guideline and Information Brochure, MAIT, New Delhi.

371. Markels, A., 1999, The wisdom of Chairman Ko, *Fast Company Magazine,* November, pp. 259-276.

372. Marsh, B., 1994, Baldrige award gets fewer applicants from small business-costing tens of thousands, the price of pursuing Oscar for quality deters many, *Wall Street Journal,* October, Vol. 13, p. B2.

373. Martellani, L., 1994, Self-assessment as a way for the adaptive organization: The Use of Quality Award Criteria and Models for Self-assessment Purposes, *in: Proceedings of the First European Forum on Quality Self-assessment,* Organizational for Quality, Torino, pp. 109-116.

374. Martensen, A. and Dahlgaard, J., 1999, Strategy and planning for innovation – supported by creative and learning organizations, *International Journal of Quality & Reliability Management,* Vol. 16, No. 9, pp. 734-755.

375. Martin, K. and Florida, R., 1993, Beyond Mass Production: The Japanese System and Its Transfer to the United States, Oxford University Press, New York.

376. Maslen, R., 1996, Manufacturing vision in the strategy process, *Unpublished Ph.D. dissertation,* University of Cambridge, Cambridge.

377. Mathew, T. and Madrecha, K. M., 1994, Quality Management Strategy for Indian Industry, *Industrial Engineering Journal,* Vol. 23, No. 2, pp. 7-13.

378. McAdam, R. and McKeown, M., 1999, Life After ISO 9000: An Analysis of the Impact of ISO 9000 and TQM on Small Businesses in Northern Ireland, *Total Quality Management,* Vol. 10, No. 2, pp. 229-241.

379. McAdam, R. and O'Neill, E., 1999, Taking a Critical perspective to the European Business Excellence Model using a balanced scorecard approach: a case study in the service sector, *Managing Service Quality,* Vol. 20, No. 3, pp. 1-20.

380. McCabe, D., 2000, The swings and roundabouts of innovating for quality in UK financial services, *The Service Industries Journal,* Vol. 20, No. 4, pp. 1-20.

381. McLaurin, D. L. and Bell, S., 1991, Open Communication Lines before Attempting Total Quality, *Quality Progress*, Vol. 24, No. 6, pp. 25-28.
382. Melis, R. E., Yearout, R. D. and Yates, G. C., 1998, Total Quality Management (TQM) Motivational Techniques: An International Case Study, *International Journal of Industrial Engineering*, Vol. 5, No. 3, pp. 195-204.
383. Meyers, D. H. and Heller, J., 1995, The dual role of AT&T's self-assessment process, *Quality Progress*, Vol. 28, No. 1, pp. 79-83.
384. Michael, R. B., Raymond, J. M. and Olson, B. A., 1992, A Practical Guide to Statistical Quality Improvement, Van Nostrand, New York.
385. Miller, G. L. and Krumm, L. L., 1992, The What's, Why's, and How's of Improvement, ASQC Quality Press, Milwaukee, WI.
386. Miller, W. C., 1993, Quantum Quality, White Plains, NY, Quality Resources, *in: The Impact of TQM on Firms' Responsiveness: An Empirical Analysis, Eds. Youssef, M. A., Boyd, J. and Williams, E., Total Quality Management*, February, Vol. 7, No. 1.
387. Miller, W. J., 1996, A Working Definition for Total Quality Management (TQM) Researchers, *Journal of Quality Management*, Vol. 1, No. 2, pp. 149-159.
388. Milling, P. M., 1990, Time—A Key Issue in the Corporate Strategy, *in: Proceedings of the International Conference of System Dynamics*, Boston.
389. Mody, S. M., 1996, Self Assessment a Tool for Continuous Improvement, Published by D. L. Shah Trust, New Delhi.
390. Mody, S. M., 1995, World Class Competitiveness Through Total Quality Management, Published by D. L. Shah Trust, New Delhi.
391. Moffatt, I. and Hanley, N., 2001, Modeling sustainable development: system dynamic and input-output approaches, *Environmental Modeling and Software*, Vol. 16, pp. 545-557, Available at: www.elsevier.com/locate/envsoft.
392. Mohanty, R. P. and Lakhe, R. R., 1994, Total Quality Management, Concepts Evaluation and Acceptability in Developing Economies, *International Journal of Quality & Reliability Management*, Vol. 11, No. 9, pp. 8-33.
393. Mohanty, R. P. and Lakhe, R. R., 1998, Factors affecting TQM implementation: an empirical study in Indian Industry, *Production Planning and Control*, Vol. 9, No. 5, pp. 511-520.
394. Mohanty, R. P., 1992, Implementing Productivity Management: Why and How, *Work Study*, Vol. 41, No. 2, pp. 22-24.
395. Mohanty, R. P., 1995, Managing TQM Affairs: Some Lessons, *Work Study*, Vol. 44, No. 7, pp. 19-22.
396. Mohanty, R. P., 1996, TQM - a comparative approach, *Work Study*, Vol. 45, No. 1, pp. 13-19.

397. Mohapatra, P. K. J., Mandal, P. and Bora, M. C., 1994, Introduction to System Dynamics Modeling, Universities Press (India) Limited, Hyderabad.
398. Moore, M. T., 1995, Is TQM Dead?, Even quality leaders see gaps in ranks, *USA Today*, 17th October, p. 01B.
399. Morecroft, J. D. W., 1983, Rationality and Structure in Behavioural Models of Business Systems, *in: Proceedings of the System Dynamics Conference*, Plenary Session Papers, pp. 60-127.
400. Morecroft, J. D. W., 1986, System Dynamics for Reasoning About Business Policy and Strategy, MIT System Dynamics Group Memo, pp. D-3640-D-3643.
401. Morecroft, J. D. W., 1988, System Dynamics and Microworlds for Policy Makers, *European Journal of Operational Research*, Vol. 35, pp. 301-320.
402. Morecroft, J. D. W., 1992, Executive Knowledge, Models and Learning, *European Journal of Operations Research*, Vol. 59, No. 1, pp. 9-27.
403. Morecroft, J. D. W. and Sterman, J. D., 1994, Modeling for Learning Organizations, Productivity Press, Portland.
404. Morozowski, M. and Florentin, C. M. C., 1999, Hydrosystem Operation Planning in Competitive Market: Strategic Planning by System Dynamics Simulation, *International Journal of System Dynamics and Policy Planning*, Vol. XI, No. 2, pp. 19-37.
405. Mosekilde, E., Larsen, E. R. and Sterman, J. D., 1991, Coping with Complexity: Deterministic Chaos in Human Decision making Behaviour, *in: Beyond Belief: Randomness Prediction and Explanation in Science*, Eds. Casti, J. L and Karlqvist, A., CRC Press, Boston, MA.
406. Motorola, 2002, Six Sigma Program, Available at: www.mu.motorola.com/sigma.html
407. Motwani, J. G., Mohmoud, E. and Rice, G., 1994, Quality Practices of Indian Organizations: An Empirical Analysis, *International Journal of Quality & Reliability Management*, Vol. 11, No. 1, pp. 38-52
408. Murgatroyd, S. and Morgan, C., 1993, TQM and the School, Open University Press, Buckingham.
409. Nakamura, S., 1993, The New Standardization: Keystone of Continuous Improvement in Manufacturing, ASQC Quality Press, Milwaukee, WI.
410. Neves, J. S. and Nakhai, B., 1995, The Evolution of the Baldrige Award, *in: The Quality Yearbook*, Eds. Cortada, J. W. and Woods, J. A., McGraw-Hill, Inc., pp. 602-612.
411. NIST, 1995, Profiles of Malcolm Baldrige national quality award winners, National Institute for Standards and Technology, Gaithersburg, MD.

412. NIST, 1999, Overview of the criteria for performance excellence, National Institute for Science and Technology, Washington, DC, Available at: www.nist.gov
413. Nokhai, B. and Newes, J., 1994, The Deming, Baldrige and European Quality Awards, *Quality Progress,* April, pp. 33-37.
414. Noori, H., 1991, TQM and its building blocks learning from world-class organizations, Optimum, Vol. 22, No. 3, pp. 31-38.
415. Norothey, P. and Southway, N., 1993, Cycle Time Management: The Fast Track to Time-Based Productivity Improvement, ASQC Quality Press, Milwaukee, WI.
416. NPC, 1983, Productivity Award, Power Generation Transmission and Distribution Equipment Manufacturing Sector-Background Note, National Productivity Council, New Delhi.
417. Oakland, J. S. and Followell, R. F., 1990, Statistical Process Control, Butterworth/Heinemann, London.
418. Oakland, J. S., 1989, Total Quality Management–The Route to Improving Performance, 2nd Edition, Clays, St. Ives Plc., Great Britain.
419. Oakland, J. S., 1993, Total Quality Management, 2nd Edition, Butterworth-Heinemann, London.
420. Oakland, J. S., 2000, Total Quality Management-Text with cases, 2nd Edition, Butterworth-Heinemann.
421. OHSAS 18001, 1999, Occupational Health and Safety Management Systems–Specification, British Standards Institution, London.
422. O'Regan, B., and Moles, R., 2002, Modeling policies and decisions: A case study in mineral extraction, *Information and Management,* Vol. 1977, pp. 1-11, Available at: www.elsevier.com/locate/dsw.
423. Pande, P. S. Nueman, R. P. and Cavanagh, R. R., 1997, The Six Sigma Way, McGraw-Hill, New York, USA.
424. Pannirselvam, G. P. and Ferguson, L. A., 2001, A study of the relationships between the Baldrige categories, *International Journal of Quality & Reliability Management,* Vol. 18, No. 1, pp. 14-34.
425. Parasuraman, A., Zeithaml, V. A. and Berry, L. L., 1985, A Conceptual Model of Service Quality and its Implications for Future Research, *Journal of Marketing,* Vol. 4, No. 4, pp. 41-50.
426. Perelman, L. J., 1980, Time in System Dynamics, *TIMS Studies in Management Science,* pp. 75-89.
427. Peters, T. J. and Waterman, R. H., 1982, In Search of Excellence, Harper and Row, New York.
428. Peters, T. J. and Waterman, R. H., 1995, In Search of Excellence: Lessons From America's Best Run Companies, Collins, London.
429. Peters, T. J., 1987, Thriving on Chaos, Alfred A. Knopf, New York, NY.

430. Peters, T., 1988, Facing up to the need for a management revolution, *California Management Review*, Vol. 30, pp. 8-38.
431. Pfahl, D. and Lebsanft, K., 1999, Integration of system dynamics modeling with descriptive process modeling and goal-oriented measure, *The Journal of Systems and Software*, Vol. 45, Nos. 2-3, pp. 135-150.
432. Pfau, L. D., 1989, Total Quality Management Gives Company a Way to Enhance Position in Global Market Place, *Industrial Engineer*, Vol. 21, No. 4, pp. 77-87.
433. Philipose, S. and Venkateswarlu, P., 1980, Statistical Quality Control in Indian Industries, *Quality Progress*, Vol. 13, No. 4, pp. 34-37.
434. Pidd, M., 1988, Computer Simulation in Management Science, 2nd Edition, John Wiley and Sons, New York.
435. Pike, J. and Barnes, R., 1988, The Total Quality Management Research and Development Centre, Anglia Business School.
436. Polat, S. and Bozdag, C. E., 2002, Comparison of fuzzy and crisp systems via system dynamics simulation, *European Journal of Operational Research*, Vol. 138, pp. 178-190, Available at: www.elsevier.com/locate/dsw.
437. Port, O., Carey, J., Kelly, K. and Forrest, S., 1992, Quality: small and midsize companies seize the challenge—not a moment too soon, *Business Week*, 30th November, pp. 67-74.
438. Porter, J., Oakland, J. and Gadd, K., 1998, Unlocking business performance with self-assessment, *Management Accounting*, Vol. 76, No. 8, pp. 35-37.
439. Porter, L. J. and Parker, A. J., 1993, Total Quality Management: The Critical Success Factors, *Total Quality Management*, Vol. 4, No. 1, pp. 13-22.
440. Porter, L. and Tanner, S., 1998, Assessing Business Excellence, Butterworth-Heinemann, Oxford.
441. Povey, B., 1996, Continuous Business Improvement: Linking the Key Improvement Processes for Your Critical Long-term Success, McGraw-Hill, London.
442. Powell, T. C., 1995, Total quality management as competitive advantage: a review and empirical study, *Strategic Management Journal*, Vol. 13, No. 2, pp. 119-134.
443. Predpall, D. F., 1994, Developing Quality-Improvement Processes in Consulting Engineering Firms, *Journal of Management Engineering*, Vol. 10, No. 3, pp. 28-34.
444. Price, F., 1989, Out of Bedlam: Management by Quality Leadership, *Management Decision*, Vol. 27, pp. 15-26.

445. Prybutok, V. R. and Spink, A., 1999, Transformation of a health care information systems: A self-assessment survey, *Institute of Electronics and Electrical Engineers, Transactions of Engineering Management,* Vol. 46, No. 3, pp. 299-310.

446. Puffer, S. M. and McCarthy, D. J., 1996, A framework for leadership in a TQM context, *Journal of Quality Management,* Vol. 1, No. 1, pp. 109-130.

447. Pun, K. F., Chin, K.S., Gill, R. and Lau, H., 2000, The process of quality transformation in Hong Kong industries, *International Journal of Management,* Vol. 17, No. 2, pp. 175-183.

448. Pursglove, A. B. and Dale, B. G., 1995, Developing Quality Costing System: Key Features and Outcomes, *OMEGA,* Vol. 23, No. 5, pp. 567-575.

449. Quality System Requirements (QS 9000), 1998, Chrysler Corporation, Ford Motor Company and General Motors Corporation.

450. Rahman, S., 1990, Increasing Productivity: The Quality Circle Way, *Productivity,* Vol. 31, No. 2, pp. 205-211.

451. Ramamurthy, P. A., 1999, Quality Management for Sustainable Customer Goodwill, *in: Supply Chain Management—For Global Competitiveness,* Ed. Sahay, B. S., McMillan India Ltd., pp. 598-604.

452. Raman, M. V. V., 1985, Quality Productivity Interface, *Productivity,* Vol. 25, No. 4, pp. 475-479.

453. Rao, S. and Raghunathan, T. S., 1994, TQM and Work Culture: An Empirical Analysis, *Productivity,* Vol. 35, No. 3, pp. 443-446.

454. Rao, A., Carr, L. P., Dambolena, I., Kopp, R. J., Martin, J., Rafii, F. and Schlesinger, P. F., 1996, Total Quality Management: A Cross Functional Perspective, John Wiley and Sons, New York, NY.

455. Rao, S., Raghunathan, T. S. and Solis, L. E., 1997, A Comparative Study of Quality Practices and Results in India, China and Mexico, *Journal of Quality Management,* Vol. 2, No. 2, pp. 235-250.

456. Reddy, J., 1980, Incorporating Quality in Competitive Strategies, Quality in Competitive Strategies, Spring, Reddy and Berger Inc., pp. 53-60.

457. Reed, D. M. and Shergold, K., 1996, Striving for excellence: how self-assessment using the business excellence model can result in step improvements in all areas of business activities, *The TQM Magazine,* Vol. 8, No. 6, pp. 48-52.

458. Reed, R., Lemak, D. J. and Montgomery, J. C., 1996, Beyond process: TQM content and firm performance, *Academy of Management Review,* Vol. 21, No. 1, pp. 172-202.

459. Reeves, C. A. and Bednar, D. A., 1994, Defining quality: alternatives and implications, *Academy of Management Review,* Vol. 19, No. 3, pp. 419-445.

460. Reich, R., 1994, Leadership and the high performance organization, *Journal for Quality and Participation*, Vol. 17, No. pp. 2, 6-11.
461. Richardson, G. P. and Pugh III, A. L., 1981, Introduction to System Dynamics Modeling with Dynamics Modeling with Dynamo, MIT Press, Cambridge, Massachusetts.
462. Richmond, B. M., 1983, Enlarge the Paradigm but a substantive not a Methodological Extension is what we need, *in: Proceedings of the International System Dynamics Conference*, Plenary Session Papers, MIT.
463. Richmond, B., 2001, An Introduction to Systems Thinking, High Performance Systems, Inc., Hanover, NH.
464. Riddalls, C. E. and Bennett, S., 2002, Production-inventory system controller design and supply chain dynamics, *International Journal of Systems Science*, Vol. 33, No. 3, pp. 181-195.
465. Riordan, C. M. and Gatewood, R. D., 1996, Putting the (employee) into quality efforts: A process model of organizational practices, quality principles, and employee reactions, *in: Advances in the management of organizational quality*, Eds. Fedor, D. B. and Ghosh, S., Ct: JAI Press, Greenwich. pp. 299-335.
466. Ritchie, L. and Dale, B. G., 2000, An analysis of the self-assessment practices using the business excellence model, *in: Proceedings of the Institution of Mechanical Engineers*, Vol. 204, No. B4, pp. 593-602.
467. Roberts, E. B., 1976, Managerial Applications of System Dynamics, The Productivity Press, Cambridge, Massachusetts.
468. Roberts, E. B., 1978, Managerial Applications of System Dynamics, MIT Press, Cambridge, Massachusetts.
469. Roberts, E., 1997, Team training: when is enough....enough?, *The Journal of Quality and Participation*, Vol. 20, No. 3, pp. 16-20.
470. Roberts, E. B., Abrams, D. I. and Weil, H. B., 1968, A System Study of Policy Formulation in a Vertically-Integrated Firm, *Management Sciences*, Vol. 14, No. 12, pp. B 674-B 694.
471. Rodrigues, C. A., 1994, Employee participation and empowerment programs: problems of definition and implementation, *Empowerment in Organizations*, Vol. 2, No. 2, pp. 29-40.
472. Rodriguez, F. F., Artiles, M. D. G. and Guerra, J. H., 1999, Modeling Speculative Behaviour in Financial Market with System Dynamics, *International Journal of System Dynamics and Policy Planning*, Vol. XI, No. 1, pp. 25-48.
473. Roger, R. K., Gustafson, L. T., Memarie, S. M. and Mullane, J. V., 1994, Reframing the organization: why implementing total quality management is easier said then done, *Academy of Management Review*, Vol. 19, No. 3, pp. 565-584.

474. Ross, J. E., 1993, Total Quality Management: Text, Cases and Readings, St. Lucie Press, Delray Beach, FL.

475. Ross, J. E., 1995, Strategic Quality Planning: Total Quality Management – Text, Cases and Readings, McGraw-Hill Book Company, New York.

476. Roy, R., 1990, A primer on the Taguchi method, Van Nostrand-Reinhold, New York.

477. Ryan, K. D. and Oestreich, D. K., 1991, Driving Fear Out of the Workplace, ASQC Quality Press, Milwaukee, WI.

478. Ryzhenkov, A. V., 2000, An Environmental Extension of the System Dynamics Model of Long Waves, *International Journal of System Dynamics and Policy Planning,* Vol. XII, No. 1, pp. 1-16.

479. Saeed, K., 1986, The Practice of Policy Modeling, Including System Dynamics Modeling, *Industrial Engineering Journal,* Vol. 15, No. 10, India, pp. 133-143.

480. Saferpak, 2003, Deming Articles, Available at: www.saferpak.com/deming_ articles/application%20guide2003.pdf.

481. Sahay, B. S., 1994, Strategic Planning and Policy Modeling for Indian Fertilizer Industry—A System Dynamics Approach, *Unpublished Ph.D. Thesis, Indian Institute of Technology Delhi,* New Delhi, India.

482. Sahay, B. S., Vrat, P. and Jain, P. K., 1994, Dynamics of Prices and Subsidies in Fertilizer Industry in India—A System Dynamics Approach, *in: Proceedings of the Fifth National Conference on System Dynamics,* IIT Delhi, March, pp. 18-21.

483. Sahu, R., Mohapatra, P. K. J. and Srinivasan, S., 2000, A Comparative Study of Exchange Rate Forecasting Models Using System Dynamics with Traditional Times Series Models, *International Journal of System Dynamics and Policy Planning,* Vol. XII, No. 1, pp. 17-29.

484. Sakofsky, S., 1996, Solving the corporate action dilemma, *Journal for Quality and Participation,* October-November, pp. 56-58.

485. Sallis, E., 1996, TQM in Education, Kogan Page, London.

486. Samanta, B. and Araimi, A. S. A., 2001, An inventory control model using fuzzy logic, *International Journal of Production Economics,* Vol. 73, pp. 217-226, Available at: www.elsevier.com/locate/dsw.

487. Samson, D. and Terziovski, M., 1999, The relationship between total quality management practices and operational performance, *Journal of Operations Management,* Vol. 17, No. 4, pp. 393-409.

488. Samuels, A. F., 1994, Construction Facilities Audit: Quality System-Performance Control, *Journal of Management Engineering,* Vol. 10, pp. 60-65.

489. Samuelsson, P. and Nilsson, L. E., 2002, Self-assessment practices in large organizations: Experiences from using the EFQM excellence model, *International Journal of Quality & Reliability Management*, Vol. 19, No. 1, pp. 10-23.
490. Sanders, D. and Hild, C., 2000, A Discussion of Strategies for Six Sigma Implementation, *Quality Engineering*, Vol. 12, No. 3, pp. 303-309.
491. Saraph, G. V., Benson, G. and Schroeder, R. G., 1989, An Instrument for Measuring the Critical Factors of Total Quality Management, *Decision Sciences*, Vol. 20, No. 4, pp. 810-829.
492. Sashkin, M. and Kiser, K. J., 1993, Total quality management, Berett-Koehler, San Francisco.
493. Scherkenbach, W. W., 1986, Performance Appraisal and Quality Form's New Philosophy, *Quality Progress*, Vol. 18, No. 4, pp. 40-46.
494. Schmidt, A. and Zink, K. J., 1998, Practice and implementation of self-assessment, *International Journal of Quality Science*, Vol. 3, pp. 5-17.
495. Schnoberger, R. J., 1982, Japanese Manufacturing Techniques: Nine Hidden Lessons in Simplicity, The Free Press, New York.
496. Schnoberger, R. J., 1987, World Class Manufacturing Techniques, Collier Macmillan.
497. Schonberger, R. J., 1994, Human Resource Management Lessons from a decade or total quality management and reengineering, *California Management Review*, Vol. 36, No. 4, pp. 109-123.
498. Scholtes, P. R., and Hacquebord, H., 1988, Beginning the Quality Transformation, Parts 1 and 2, Quality Progress, Milwaukee, WI.
499. Seawright, K. W. and Young, S. T., 1996, A quality definition continuum, *Interfaces*, Vol. 26, No. 3, pp. 107-113.
500. Seng, C., 1989, An Integrative Model of Japanese Manufacturing Techniques, *International Journal of Operations and Production Management*, Revised September, pp. 37-50.
501. Senge, P. M., 1990, The Fifth Discipline, Century Business, London, UK.
502. Senge, P., 1991, The fifth discipline: The Art and Practice of the Learning Organization, Double Day, New York.
503. Shah, A. M., 1999, Total Quality Management: Critical Issues in Implementation, *in: Supply Chain Management-For Global Competitiveness*, Ed. Sahay, B. S., McMillan India Ltd., pp. 587-597.
504. Shankar, R., 2000, Industrial Engineering and Management, Galgotia Publication, New Delhi.
505. Sharma, S., 1997, TQM in Indian Engineering Industries, Business Publication Inc., New Delhi, India.
506. Sharma, S., 2000, Auto Industries seeks top gear incentives, *The Economic Times*, 7th August, p. 3.

507. Shetty, Y. K., 1993, The quest for quality excellence: lessons from the Malcolm Baldridge Quality Award, *SAM Advanced Management Journal*, Vol. 58, No. 2, pp. 34-40.

508. Shewhart, W. A., 1990, Economic Control of Quality of Manufactured Product, Van No Strand, New York.

509. Shiba, S., Graham, A. and Walden, D., 1993, A New American TQM, Productivity Press, Portland, OR.

510. Shores, A. R., 1990, A TQM Approach to Achieving Manufacturing Excellence, ASQC Quality Press, Milwaukee, WI.

511. Shortell, S. M., Levin, D. Z., O'Brien, J. L. and Hughes, E. F. X., 1995, Assessing the evidence on CQI: Is the glass half empty or half full? *Hospital and Health Services Administration*, Vol. 40, pp. 4-24.

512. Siamindia, 2002, Economic Affairs, Available at: www.siamindia.com/economic-affairs/economic.htm

513. Sila, I. and Ebrahimpour, M., 2002, An investigation of the total quality management survey based research published between 1989 and 2000: A literature review, *International Journal of Quality & Reliability Management*, Vol. 19, No. 7, pp. 902-970.

514. Sinclair, J. and Collins, D., 1994, Towards a quality culture? *International Journal of Quality & Reliability Management*, Vol. 11, No. 5, pp. 19-29.

515. Singh, A., 1991, Total Quality Management Concepts and Practices in India, *Productivity*, Vol. 32, No. 3, pp. 393-399.

516. Singh, A., 1993, Implementing of TQM, *Productivity*, Vol. 34, No. 1, pp. 167-168.

517. Singh, A., 1994, Work Culture and Quality: An Initiative to Corporate Transformation, *Productivity*, Vol. 35, No. 3, pp. 438-442.

518. Singh, J., 1997, Understanding and Managing Consumer Dissatisfaction for Global Competitiveness, February, p. 1.

519. Sink, D. S., 1991a, TQM: The Next Frontier of Just Another Bandwagon? *Productivity*, Vol. 32, No. 3. pp. 400-414.

520. Sink, D. S., 1991b, The Role of Measurement in Achieving World Class Quality and Productivity Management, *Industrial Engineering Journal*, June, pp. 23-28.

521. Siow, C. H. R., Yang, J. B. and Dale, B. G., 2001, A New Modeling Framework for Organizational Self-assessment: Development and Application, *Quality Management Journal*, October, Vol. 8, Issue 4, Available at: www.asq.org/pab/qmj/past/vol_8issue4/siow.html.

522. Sitkin, S. B., Sutcliffe, K. M. and Schroeder, R. G., 1994, Distinguishing control from learning in total quality management: a contingency perspective, *Academy of Management Review*, Vol. 19, No. 3, pp. 537-564.

523. Skaria, G., 1995, The Total Quality Imperative, *Business Today,* January 7-21, pp. 19-21.
524. Slater, R. H., 1991, Integrated Process Management: A Quality Model, Quality Progress, Milwaukee, WI.
525. Smith, G. F., 1993, The Meaning of Quality, *Total Quality Management,* Vol. 4, pp. 235-244.
526. Smith, P. C. and Ackere, A., 2002, A note on the integration of system dynamics and economic models, *Journal of Economic Dynamics and Control,* Vol. 26, pp. 1-10, Available at: www.elsevier.com/locate/econbase.
527. Smith, S., 1995, The Quality Revolution: Best Practice from the World's Leading Companies, Jaico Publishing House, Delhi.
528. Snowdon, M., 1986, The Japanese Approach to Productivity and Quality – A European's View, *International Journal Technology Management,* Vol. 1, Nos. 3-4, pp. 411-424.
529. Sohal, A. S., Tay, G. S. and Wirth, A., 1989, Total Quality Control in an asian division of a multinational corporation, *International Journal of Quality & Reliability Management,* Vol. 6, No. 6, pp. 60-74.
530. Soni, C., and Pandya, A., 2002, MUL performance: Challenging terrain ahead, *The Economic Times,* 3rd June, p. 13.
531. Spencer, B. A., 1994, Models of Organization and Total Quality Management—A comparison and Critical Evaluation, *Academy of Management Review,* Vol. 19, No. 3., pp. 446-471.
532. Spencer, R. S., 1966, Modeling Strategies for Corporate Growth, *in: Proceedings of the Conference of American Association for the Advancement of Science,* Washington, D. C.
533. Spenley, P., 1992, World Class Performance through Total Quality, Chapman and Hall, London.
534. Spitzer, R. D., 1995, TQM: The Only Source of Sustainable Competitive Advantage, *in: The Quality Yearbook,* Eds. Cortada, J. W. and Woods, J. A., McGraw-Hill, Inc., pp. 36-48.
535. Srikanth, M. L. and Cavallaro, H. E., Jr., 1993, Regaining Competitiveness: Putting the Goal to Work, ASQC Quality Press, Milwaukee, WI.
536. Stahan, J., 2002, Transition ISO 9000:2000, *Quality Progress,* Vol. 35 No. 3, pp. 27-30
537. Stallinger, F. and Griinbacher, P., 2001, System dynamics modeling and simulation of collaborative requirements engineering, *The Journal of Systems and Software,* Vol. 59, pp. 311-321, Available at: www.elsevier.com/locate/jss.
538. Stavros, D. A., 1997, The standard for the 21st century, *Industrial Distribution,* January, pp. 44-46.

539. Steeples, M. M., 1993, The Corporate Guide to the Malcolm Baldridge National Quality Award, Revised Edition, ASQC Quality Press, Milwaukee, WI.
540. Sterman, J. D., Forrester, J. W., Graham, A. K. and Senge, P. M., 1983, An Integrated Approach to the Economic Long Wave, *in: Proceedings of the Long Waves, Depression, Innovation,* Siena-Florence, Italy.
541. Sterman, J. D., 1987, Testing Behavioural Simulation Models by Direct Experiment, *Management Sciences,* Vol. 33, No. 12, pp. 1572-1592.
542. Sterman, J. D., 1989, Modeling Managerial Behaviour: Misperceptions of Feedback in Dynamic Decision Making Experiment, *Management Sciences,* Vol. 35, No. 3, pp. 321-339.
543. Sterman, J., 2000, Business Dynamics: Systems Thinking and Modeling for a Complex World, McGraw Hill, Tokyo.
544. Sterphen, G. and Arnold, W., 1994, Total Quality Management, John Wiley, New York.
545. Stone, D. L. and Eddy, E. R., 1996, A model of individual and organizational factors affecting quality related outcomes, *Journal of Quality Management,* Vol. 1, No. 1, pp. 21-48.
546. Stonebraker, P. W. and Leong, G. K., 1994, Operations Strategy, Focusing Competitive Excellence, Allyn and Bacon.
547. Stratton, A. D., 1991, An Approach to Quality Improvement That Works: Implementing Quality Improvement in the 90's, 2nd Edition, ASQC Quality Press, Milwaukee, WI.
548. Strolle, A., 1991, Creating a TQM Culture is Everyone's Business, *International Journal of Research Technology Management,* Vol. 34, No. 4, pp. 8-9.
549. Sumanth, D. J., 1984, Productivity Engineering and Management, McGraw Hill Book Company, New York.
550. Sun, H., 1999, Diffusion and contribution of total quality management: an empirical study in Norway, *Total Quality Management,* Vol. 10, No. 6, pp. 901-914.
551. Sun, H., 2000, Total quality management, ISO 9000 certification and performance improvement, *International Journal of Quality & Reliability Management,* Vol. 17, No. 2, pp. 168-179.
552. Sushil, 1993, System Dynamics A Practical Approach for Managerial Problems, Wiley Eastern Ltd., India.
553. Sushil, 2002, Physical system theory: fundamentals, recent developments and relationships with system dynamics, *Kybernetes,* Vol. 31, Nos. 3-4, pp. 496-528.
554. Suzuki, T., 1994, TPM in Process Industries, English Translation, *Translated by Loftus, J.,* Productivity Press, Originally Published by Japan Institute of Plant Maintenance.

555. Swain, J. J., 1995, Simulation survey: Tools for process understanding and improvement, *OR/MS Today*, Vol. 22, No. 4, pp. 64-75.

556. Swaminathan, J. M., Smith, S. F. and Sadeh, N. M., 1998, Modeling Supply Chain Dynamics: A Multiagent Approach, *Decision Sciences*, Vol. 29, No. 3, pp. 607-632.

557. Taguchi, G. and Wu, Y., 1985, Introduction to Off-Line Quality Control, Central Japan Quality Control Association, Nagoya.

558. Taguchi, G., 1986, Introduction to Quality Engineering, Asian Productivity Organization, Tokyo.

559. Takeuchi, H. and Quelch, J. A., 1983, Quality is More Than Making A Good Product, *Harvard Business Review*, July-August, Vol. 61, pp. 139-145.

560. Takeuchi, H., 1981, Productivity: Learning from the Japanese, *California Management Review*, Vol. 23, No. 4, pp. 5-19.

561. Tamimi, N., 1998, A second-order factor analysis of critical TQM factors, *International Journal of Quality Science*, Vol. 3, No. 1, pp. 71-79.

562. Tapiero, C. S., 1996, The Management of Quality and its Control, Chapman and Hall, London.

563. Tarafdar, M. and Roy, R., 1999, Business Process Reengineering – A System Dynamics Interpretation, *International Journal of System Dynamics and Policy Planning*, Vol. XI, No. 1, pp. 1-24.

564. Tedaldi, M., Fred, S. and Russotti, V., 1992, A Beginner's Guide to Quality in Manufacturing, ASQC Quality Press, Milwaukee, WI.

565. Teo, W. F. and Dale, B. G., 1997, Self-assessment in the methods, management and practice, *in: Proceedings of the Institution of Mechanical Engineers*, Vol. 211, No. B5, pp. 365-375.

566. Tersine, R. J. and Hummingbird, E. A., 1995, Lead-Time Reduction: The Search for Competitive Advantage, *International Journal of Operations and Production Management*, Vol. 15, No. 2, pp. 8-18.

567. Terziovski, M. and Samson, D., 1999, The link between total quality management practice and organizational performance, *International Journal of Quality & Reliability Management*, Vol. 16, No. 3, pp. 226-237.

568. The Economic Times, 2002, India up 8 notches in global ranking, 4th November, p. 6.

569. Thiagarajan, T. and Zairi, M., 1998, An empirical analysis of critical factor of TQM: a proposed tool for self-assessment and benchmarking purposes, *Benchmarking for Quality Management and Technology*, Vol. 5, No. 4, pp. 291-303.

570. Tillery, K. R. and Rutledge, A. L., 1991, Quality-strategy and quality-management connections, *International Journal of Quality & Reliability Management*, Vol. 8, No. 1, pp. 71-77.

571. Tobin, L. M., 1990, The new quality landscape: total quality management, *Journal of Systems Management*, Vol. 41, No. 11, pp. 10-14.

572. Towill, D. R., 1996, Industrial dynamics modeling of supply chains, *Logistics Information Management*, Vol. 9, No. 4, pp. 43-56.

573. Towill, D. R., Naim, M. M. and Wikner, J., 1992, Industrial dynamics simulation models in the design of supply chains, *International Journal of Physical Distribution and Logistics Management*, Vol. 22, No. 5, pp. 3-13.

574. Tracey, M. A. and Vonderembse, M. A., 1998, Building supply chains: a key to enhanced manufacturing performance, *in: Proceedings of the Decision Science Institute*, pp. 1184-1186

575. TS 16949:2002, 2002, Quality Management Systems–Particular, requirements for the application of ISO 9001:2000 for automotive production and relevant service part organizations, Second Edition, AIAG Edition.

576. Tuchman, B. W., 1980, The decline of quality, *New York Times Magazine*, 2nd November, pp. 38-47.

577. Tzafestas, S. and Kapsiotis, G., 1994, Coordinated control of manufacturing/supply chains using multi-level techniques, *Computer Integrated Manufacturing Systems*, Vol. 7, No. 3, pp. 206-212.

578. Ugboro, I. O. and Obeng, K., 2000, Top management leadership, employee empowerment, job satisfaction, and customer satisfaction in TQM organizations: an empirical study, *Journal of Quality Management*, Vol. 5, pp. 247-272, Available at: www.journalofqualitymanagement.com

579. Ulrich, K., Choudhry, R. S. and Rana, K. S., 2000, Managing Corporate Culture Leveraging Diversity to Give India a Global Competitive Edge, Macmillan, India.

580. Van Der Wiele, T. and Brown, A., 1999, Self-assessment practices in Europe and Australia, *International Journal of Quality & Reliability Management*, Vol. 16, No. 3, pp. 238-251.

581. Van Der Wiele, T., Brown, A., Millen, R. and Whelan, 2000, Improvement in organizational performance and self-assessment practices by selected American Firms, *Quality Management Journal*, Vol. 7, No. 4, pp. 8-22.

582. Van Der Wiele, T., Williams, A. R. T., Dale, B. G., Carter, G., Kolb, F., Luzon, D. M., Schmidt, A. and Wallace, M., 1996a, Self-Assessment – A Study of progress in Europe's leading organizations in Quality Management practices, *International Journal of Quality & Reliability Management*, Vol. 13, No. 1, pp. 84-104.

583. Van Der Wiele, T., Williams, A. R. T., Dale, B. G., Kolb, F., Luzon, D. M., Schmidt, A. and Wallace, M., 1996b, Quality Management Self-Assessment: An Examination in European Business, *Journal of General Management,* Vol. 22, No. 1, pp. 48-67.

584. Veit, K. P., 1969, System Dynamics and Corporate Long Range Strategic Planning, *in: Proceedings of the 20th International Congress of Actuaries,* Tokyo.

585. Vennix, J. A. M., 1996, Group Model Building: Facilitating Team Learning Using System Dynamics, John Wiley and Sons, Chichester.

586. Vij, A. K., Vrat, P. and Sushil, 1987, Application of System Dynamics to Energy Modeling in the National Economy – Conceptual Framework, *in: Proceedings of the Second National Conference on System Dynamics,* Varanasi, January 15-17.

587. Vij, A. K., 1990, Energy Policy Modeling and Analysis for the Indian Economy, *Unpublished Ph.D. Thesis, Indian Institute of Technology Delhi,* New Delhi, India.

588. Voss, C. A. and Johnson, R., 1995, Service in Britain: How do we measure up? A Study of Service Management and Performance in UK Organizations, Severn Trent, Birmingham.

589. Voss, C. A., Blackmon, K., Chase, R., Rose, B. and Roth, A. V., 1997, Achieving World Class Service: An Anglo-American Benchmark Comparison of Service Practice and Performance, Severn Trent, Birmingham.

590. Vrat, P., Sardana, G. D. and Sahay, B. S, 1998, Productivity Management – A Systems Dynamics Approach, Narosa Publishing House, New Delhi.

591. Waldman, D. A., 1994, The contributions of total quality management to a theory of work performance, *Academy of Management Review,* Vol. 19, No. 3, pp. 510-536.

592. Waldman, D. A. and Gopalakrishnan, M., 1996, Operational, organizational, and human resource factors predictive of customer perceptions of service quality, *Journal of Quality Management,* Vol. 1, No. 1, pp. 91-108.

593. Walton, M., 1986, The Deming Management Methods, ASQC Quality Press, Milwaukee, WI.

594. Weaver, C. N., 1995, How to Use Process Improvement Teams, *in: The Quality Yearbook,* Eds. Cortada, J. W. and Woods, J. A., McGraw-Hill Inc., pp. 398-405.

595. Westinghouse, 1999, Productivity Promotion, *Journal of Delhi University Council,* Vol. 4, No. 12.

596. Wickman, R. F. and Doyle, R. S., 1993, Breakthrough Quality Improvement for Leaders Who Wants Results, ASQC Quality Press, Milwaukee, WI.

597. Wiener, N., 1948, Cybernetics on Control and Communication in the Animal and Machine, Wiley, New York.

598. Wikner, J., Towill, D. R. and Naim, M., 1991, Smoothing supply chain dynamics, *International Journal of Production Economics*, Vol. 22, No. 3, pp. 231-248.

599. Wildemann, H., 1993, Productivity: A Key Factor for Market Success, *Productivity*, Vol. 34, No. 3, pp. 407-417.

600. Wilkinson, A. and Witcher, B., 1991, Fitness For Use? Barriers To Full TQM In The UK, *in: Proceedings of the British Academy of Management Conference*, Bath.

601. Wisner, J. and Eakins, S., 1994, A performance assessment of the U.S. Baldrige quality award winners, *International Journal of Quality & Reliability Management*, Vol. 11, No. 2, pp. 8-25.

602. Witcher, B. J., 1990, Total Marketing: Total Quality and the Marketing Concept, The Quarterly Review of Marketing, Winter.

603. Withers, B. and Ebrahinpour, M., 2000, Does ISO 9000 certification affect the dimensions of quality used for competitive advantage? *European Management Journal*, Vol. 18, No. 4, pp. 431-443.

604. Wolstenholme, E. F. and Coyle, R. G., 1983, The Development of System Dynamics as a Methodology for System Description and Quantitative analysis, *Journal of the Operations Research Society*, Vol. 34, No. 7, pp. 569-581.

605. Wolstenholme, E. F., 1982, Managing International Mining-A Case Study in the Application of System Dynamics to Complex, Multiple, Ownership Systems, *European Journal Operations Research Society*, Vol. 9, pp. 133-143.

606. Wong, A., Tjosvold, D. Wong, W. and Liu, C. K., 1999, Relationships for quality improvement in the Hong Kong-China supply chain, *International Journal of Quality & Reliability Management*, Vol. 16, No. 1, pp. 24-41.

607. Wright, R. D., 1971, Industrial Dynamics Implementation: Growth Strategies for a Trucking Firm, *Sloan Management Review*, Vol. 13, No. 1, pp. 71-86.

608. Wu, H., Wiebe, H. A. and Politi, J., 1997, Self-assessment of total quality management programs, *Engineering Management Journal*, Vol. 9, No. 1, pp. 25-31.

609. Xerox-Business Products and Systems, 1993, Malcolm Baldridge National Quality Award Submission Document 1989, ASQC Quality Press, Milwaukee, WI.
610. Yang, J. B., Dale, B. G. and Siow, C. H. R., 2001, Self-assessment of excellence: an application of the evidential reasoning approach, *International Journal of Production Research,* Vol. 39, No. 16, pp. 3789-3812.
611. Yang, J. B. and Xu, D. L., 1999, Intelligent Decision System via Evidential Reasoning, ver.1, Cheshire: IDSL, Northwich, UK.
612. Yong, J. and Wilkinson, A., 2001, In search for quality: the quality management experience in Singapore, *International Journal of Quality & Reliability Management,* Vol. 18, No. 8, pp. 813-835.
613. Youssef, M. A. and Zairi, M., 1995, Benchmarking critical factors for TQM: Part II – empirical results from different regions in the world, *Benchmarking for Quality Management and Technology,* Vol. 2, No. 2, pp. 3-19.
614. Youssef, M. A., Boyd, J. and Williams, E., 1996, The Impact of TQM on Firms' Responsiveness: An Empirical Analysis, *Total Quality Management,* Vol. 7, No. 1, pp. 127-144.
615. Yusof, S. M. and Aspinwal, E., 2001, Case studies on the implementation of TQM in the UK automotive SMEs, *International Journal of Quality & Reliability Management,* Vol. 18, No. 7, pp. 722-743.
616. Zairi, M. and Simintiaras, A. C., 1991, The Sales Link in the Customer-Supplier Chain, *Productivity,* Vol. 32, No. 3, pp. 427-434.
617. Zairi, M., 1991, TQM for Engineers, Woodhead Publishing, London.
618. Zairi, M., 1993, Competitive Manufacturing: Combining Total Quality with Advanced Technology, *Long Range Planning,* Vol. 26, No. 3. pp. 123-132.
619. Zairi, M., 1994, Measuring Performance for Business Results, Chapman and Hall, London.
620. Zairi, M., Letza, S. R. and Oakland, J. S., 1994, TQM: Its Impact On Bottom Line Results, Technical Communications (Publishing) Ltd., Letchworth.
621. Zairi, M. and Youssef, M. A., 1995, Benchmarking Critical Factors for TQM: Part I: Theory and Foundation, *Benchmarking for Quality Management and Technology,* Vol. 2, No. 1, pp. 5-20.
622. Zangwill, W. I., 1995, Ten Mistakes CEOs Make about Quality, *in: The Quality Yearbook,* Ed. Cortada, J. W. and Woods, J. A., McGraw-Hill, Inc., pp. 275-286.

623. Zaremba, D. and Crew, T., 1995, Increasing involvement in self-assessment: The Royal Mail Approach, *The TQM Magazine*, Vol. 7, No. 2, pp. 29-32.

624. Zha, X. F., Du, H. and Lim, Y. E., 2001, Knowledge intensive Petri net framework for concurrent intelligent design of automatic assembly system, *Robotics and Computer Integrated Manufacturing*, Vol. 17, pp. 379-398, Available at: www.elsevier.com/locate/rcim.

625. Zhu, Z. and Scheuermann, L., 1999, A Comparison of Quality Programmes: TQM and ISO 9000, *Total Quality Management*, Vol. 10, No. 2, pp. 291-297.

626. Zink, K. J. and Schmidt, A., 1998, Practice and implementation of self-assessment, *International Journal of Quality Science*, Vol. 3, No. 2, pp. 147-170.